W9-DHF-782

This book examines the longer-term aspects of the economic transformation currently taking place in Central and Eastern Europe. In particular, the vital issues of industrial structural change and trade performance are addressed first in their macroeconomic context, and then at the industrial and enterprise level. Information on recent East–West trade flows is used to analyse emerging patterns of industrial and trade specialisation. Other issues analysed include the impact of the withdrawal of export subsidies on Hungarian enterprises, the changing relationships between enterprises and banks in Poland, the evolution and reform of financial institutions and the vital issue of financial intermediation and industrial restructuring. The book ends with an examination of the case for using Western-style industrial policies in the transition.

University of Cambridge
Department of Applied Economics

Occasional paper 60

Industrial restructuring and trade reorientation in Eastern Europe

DAE Occasional papers

Earlier titles in this series and in the DAE Papers in Industrial Relations and Labour series may be obtained from:
The Publications Secretary, Department of Applied Economics, Sidgwick Avenue, Cambridge, CB3 9DE

Industrial restructuring and trade reorientation in Eastern Europe

EDITED BY

MICHAEL A. LANDESMANN
AND
ISTVÁN P. SZÉKELY

Published by the Press Syndicate of the University of Cambridge
The Pitt Building, Trumpington Street, Cambridge CB2 1RP
40 West 20th Street, New York, NY 10011-4211, USA
10 Stamford Road, Oakleigh, Melbourne 3166, Australia

First published 1995

Printed in Great Britain at the University Press, Cambridge

A catalogue record for this book is available from the British Library

Library of Congress cataloguing in publication data

Industrial restructuring and trade reorientation in Eastern Europe/
  edited by Michael A. Landesmann and István P. Székely.
    p. cm. – (Occasional paper/University of Cambridge,
Department of Applied Economics; 60)
    Includes index.
    ISBN 0 521 48085 X
    1. Industrial policy–Europe, Eastern. 2. Europe, Eastern–
–Commercial policy. 3. Europe, Eastern–Economic policy–1989–
I. Landesmann, Michael A. II. Székely, István P., 1959–.
III. Series: Occasional papers (University of Cambridge. Dept. of
Applied Economics); 60.
HC244.I493   1995
338.947–dc20   94–31517 CIP

ISBN 0 521 48085 X hardback

HC
244
I493
1995

VN

Contents

Contents ix

Figures

Tables

Contributors

I. Ábel   Professor, Department of Business Economics, Budapest University of Economics, and Deputy CEO, Budapest Bank, Hungary

M. Belka   Professor, Department of Economics, University of Lodz, Poland and Director, Institute of Economics, Polish Academy of Sciences

A. Blahó   Economic Affairs Officer, United Nations, Department of Economic and Social Information and Policy Analysis, New York, USA

A. Buchtíková   Research Fellow, Institute of Economics, Czech National Bank, Prague, Czech Republic

R. Dobrinsky   Deputy Director, XXI Century Foundation/Centre for Strategic Business and Political Studies, Sofia, Bulgaria

L. Halpern   Senior Research Fellow, Institute of Economics, Hungarian Academy of Sciences, Budapest, Hungary

S. Krajewski   Professor of Economics, Department of Economics, University of Lodz, Poland

J. Křovák   Section Director, Czech Statistical Office, Czech Republic

M. Landesmann   Professor of Economics, Johannes Kepler University, Linz, Austria and Research Associate, Department of Applied Economics, University of Cambridge, UK

E. Macourková   Former Research Fellow, Institute of Economics, Academy of Sciences, Czech Republic

N. Markov   Research Fellow, XXI Century Foundation/Centre for Strategic Business and Political Studies, Sofia, Bulgaria

P. Naujoks   Research Fellow, Kiel Institute of World Economics, Kiel, Germany

A. Nešporová   Senior Adviser, International Labour Office, Central and Eastern European Team, Budapest, Hungary

B. Nikolov   Research Fellow, XXI Century Foundation/Centre for Strategic Business and Political Studies, Sofia, Bulgaria

W. M. Orlowski   Department of Economics, University of Lodz, Poland

K-D. Schmidt   Senior Research Fellow, Kiel Institute of World Economics, Kiel, Germany

I. P. Székely   Economic Affairs Officer, United Nations, Department of Economic and Social Information and Policy Analysis, New York, USA and Budapest University of Economics, Hungary

L. Tomaszewicz   Professor of Economics, Department of Economics, University of Lodz, Poland

D. Yalnazov   Research Fellow, XXI Century Foundation/Centre for Strategic Business and Political Studies, Sofia, Bulgaria

Preface

This book emerged from the ACE project no. X/9109/000/085 financed by the Commission of the European Union under the PHARE programme which facilitates research collaboration between Eastern and Western European economists. The programme provided an unique historical opportunity to cross borders in two senses: to develop contacts with the 'other half of Europe', previously barred from the free flow of ideas and research collaboration, and to take up the intellectual opportunity to tackle an historically unprecedented process of systemic transformation.

Many of the academic economists who approached this problem in the first phase of economic transformation proceeded from the established framework of short-run macroeconomic stabilisation and spontaneous shift to a market order. While our group appreciated the importance of stabilisation as a prerequisite for successful transformation, we were from the very start of our project convinced that issues of longer-term structural change on the supply side of the Eastern European economies were crucial both to the success of the stabilisation policies themselves and to successful integration into the world economy.

Editing a volume dealing with contemporary historical change one always runs the risk of lagging behind: however, we were greatly helped by the up-to-date involvement and professionalism of our colleagues (the contributors to this book) who contributed a profound understanding of the complexity of developments not only in their own countries but also in the region as a whole. We should like to thank them for their intellectual engagement in this project and for a very stimulating series of workshops.

Our thanks go also to the Department of Applied Economics of the University of Cambridge for providing the research facilities for a large part of the project and to its Director, David Newbery, for continuous support; to Ann Newton, Publications Officer at the Department, for much editorial help and also to Beth Morgan and Barbara Docherty for very efficient copy-editing services. István Székely also received support from the United Nations Department of Economic and Social Information and Policy Analysis where some of the research was carried out. Finally, we should like to thank the hosts of our various workshops, Alena Nesporova from the former Institute for Forecasting of the (then) Czechoslovak Academy of Sciences, Peter Havlik from the Vienna Institute for Comparative Economic Studies (WIIW), István Ábel from the Budapest Bank and Rumen Dobrinsky from the XXI Century Foundation/Centre for Strategic Business and Political Studies in Sofia.

Our families had to give up of evenings, weekends and potential holidays to allow us to engage in this project. We dedicate this book to our wives, Ayesha and Eva, and our children, Andrea, Gábor and Raphael.

Michael A. Landesmann
István P. Székely

1 Introduction

Michael Landesmann and István Székely

This volume focuses on two of the most important longer-term aspects of economic transformation in Central and Eastern Europe (CEE), industrial restructuring and foreign trade reorientation. Institutional reforms and macroeconomic stabilisation have, so far, partly because of the intellectual challenge which institutional innovation represents and partly because of the urgency of the economic reforms and policies to be implemented, attracted much of the attention of policy makers and researchers. By now, economic transformation has been under way for some time in a number of the CEE economies and attention is shifting towards longer-term issues, particularly the ones under investigation in this volume. The long-term success of economic transformation in CEE depends to a large extent on how fast and how successful these economies are in restructuring their industries, sustaining their initial boost of exports to non-(ex-) Council for Mutual Economic Assistance (CMEA) markets by improving the quality and the composition of their exports, and generally building up the supply-side features which provide the basis for competitive corporate performance in domestic and world markets.

The three Parts of the volume approach these issues from different directions. Part One contains two comparative studies showing the similarities and differences between and among the CEE economies with respect both to features of their industrial structures and to trade structures and the potential evolution of comparative advantages. Part Two is devoted to the description of the macroeconomic environments within which industrial restructuring and foreign trade reorientation is taking place in the different CEE countries. As the authors frequently point out, there is a strong interaction between economic reforms, the macro-economic situation and economic policies, on the one hand, and industrial restructuring and foreign trade reorientation, on the other. Economic reform measures establish the institutions, mechanisms and forces which drive industrial restructuring and foreign trade reorientation, but their

1

success depends to a large degree on the extent to which, and the speed at which, industrial restructuring and improvement in trade performance take place.

The studies in Part Three concentrate on the enterprise, on changes in its behaviour and financial situation as well as on the role of industrial policy. A proper understanding of these issues is of the utmost importance. While institutional reforms, liberalisation, and economic policies are very important in creating the proper environment for industrial restructuring and foreign trade reorientation, without which the process is not likely to take place at all, or to take place only much more slowly, the process itself is actually carried out by individual firms. They have to change their production and product structures, internal organisation and management, improve their cost efficiency and competitiveness, find new markets for their products and secure the finance needed for restructuring and new investments. In many cases they have to find the partner for their privatisation as well. That is, economic transformation cannot be successful without achieving the necessary changes within the enterprise. On the other hand, we also look in Part Three at the changing relationship between banks and enterprises and at the constraints which the great problems of the rudimentary but evolving financial system impose upon corporate restructuring.

In the following sections of this Introduction we shall discuss a number of the general themes underlying the contributions in the volume, and also relate the issues raised in the individual chapters to each other.

The overall state of economic transformation, industrial restructuring and the macroeconomic environment

The transformation of the CEE economies from (different forms of) centrally planned economies (CPEs) into (possibly different forms of) market economies entails a series of reforms of the institutional and legal systems, changes in ownership structure away from state towards private ownership, substantial and fairly speedy deregulation and liberalisation, including the liberalisation of foreign trade and the introduction of some sort of convertibility of the national currencies. These reforms induce substantial changes in relative commodity and factor prices and in enterprise finance, and an increase in the degree of competition in the domestic markets of CEE economies.

As a natural consequence of these changes, the sustainable levels and structures of industrial production in the region changed dramatically. Industries built up to service almost exclusively the former CMEA markets and highly protected by either import (on the part of CEE governments, e.g. import licensing) or export restrictions (on the part of Western governments, e.g. COCOM) and/or by high production and export subsidies are bound to contract, or even disappear. The new commodity and factor prices, the new structure and level of market demand and the substantially changed domestic financial environment for enterprises, require marked changes in the organisation and composition of industrial production.

As a consequence, the level and structure of industrial employment changes as well. However, in the short run, the dynamics of employment and output adjustments may well be rather different, implying volatile changes in labour productivity; in the longer run, one would expect that changes in the level and structure of industrial employment will be even more radical than in those of output as productivity levels catch up with those prevalent in more efficiently organised economies.

The main impact of the economic transformation at the micro-level is that firms, even state-owned ones, suddenly find themselves in a much more competitive environment in which they have to compete with a substantially increased number of private and foreign firms for customers and also for production factors. Owing to the changing attitude of economic policy makers, production and export subsidies diminish and the central allocation of capital and foreign exchange is abolished. At the same time, foreign trade is liberalised, a certain degree of convertibility is introduced (although not always formally) and the exchange rate and fiscal and monetary policies become the main tools of economic policy. This is coupled with deregulation, enabling firms to choose production lines freely and, thus, enter markets from which they were previously barred.

As a result of these changes, even though tighter control over management and a strong residual claim on firms are hardly yet established, state-owned firms are becoming much more sensitive to market signals, that is to changes in (input, output and factor) prices and the level and structure of demand. The required changes in industrial production do have an enormous impact on the organisation and behaviour of firms. That change of behaviour is induced by the new competitive pressures firms face in both domestic and export markets, by their changing relationship to banks and other financial institutions and by the expectation of privatisation and the possibility of bankruptcy due to new regulations. The corporate sector thus segments into those firms which are expected to undergo restructuring, enabling them to introduce new products and production technologies and thus enter new markets, and those firms – a significant proportion – which will face liquidation, leading to the physical scrapping of their production capacities and to the laying-off of their employees. On the other hand, new firms will be created to produce products and services demanded by new markets and by the changed domestic and external environment.

There are thus both *'destructive'* and *'constructive'* aspects to the industrial restructuring process. As is well known, the industrial composition of an economy (overall industrial branch structure, but also firm composition within branches and product lines within enterprises) can change in two ways: through the *differential contraction* of different branches/firms/plants or through *differential* (positive) *growth*. As CEE economies underwent a period of dramatic overall contraction in the first phase of the post-1989 transformation, it is clear that the initial phase was dominated by the destructive aspect of structural change. Different industries and enterprises were differentially affected by the collapse of CMEA markets, by the contraction of the different components of aggregate demand (consumption, investment, government spending) and hence much of the structural change observed over this period (and reported in the chapters in Part Two) was of this type.

However, the contractionary components of the restructuring process also contributed to constructive processes: the collapse of the CMEA and of domestic markets exerted strong pressures upon enterprises to find alternative export opportunities; the expected crisis in large state-owned enterprises (SOEs) and public organisations created pressures to find employment opportunities elsewhere and this contributed to the fast development of small-scale (often self-employed) private sector activity.

There are also negative elements in the relationship between contraction and the viability of long-term growth: a very rapid process of destruction might lead to the irreversible scrapping of capacities, the dismissal of skilled labour, and the closing down of enterprises which could have become (economically) viable if the short-term macroeconomic conditions had not so drastically deteriorated; the particular circumstances of the transition might also draw resources into activities which do not reflect longer-run comparative advantages (e.g. if new forms of organisation or organisational changes could be achieved relatively rapidly in some types of activities, irrespective of the benefit of the reallocation of resources in the longer run). A too slow process of 'destruction', on the other hand, might also lock-in considerable resources in maintaining activities which should not be maintained in the longer run and thus delay the transfer of resources into promising new lines of production or enterprises (for example, the locking-in of financial resources in debt-ridden enterprises).

What one is likely to observe in the first phase of industrial restructuring is a degree of 'downgrading' of industrial capabilities. Given the 'dual structure' which had characterised productive activity and particularly export activity in the past (see pp. 15–16 and chapter 2), the parts of the industrial structure to suffer most in the immediate post-1989 period could be the ones which are potentially the industrially more advanced branches (such as engineering industries); in these industries CEE producers have larger competitive disadvantages against advanced Western producers than in branches which have a lower skill and technology content. This does, of course, reflect to some extent the current comparative advantage positions of CEE producers, but there are also reasons to believe that the immediate post-liberalisation phase undervalues the skill and technology potential of CEE producers in these branches. The reason for such an undervaluation is that although there are some strengths in certain factor endowments in these branches, the endowment structures are patchy (with regard to comparative input requirements in the West), and – most importantly – there are great inefficiencies in the utilisation of these endowments. In skill- and capital-intensive branches there are particularly strong impediments to organisational and technological restructuring. Potential competitive advantages in these areas will thus only become apparent once the existing 'gaps' in the skill and technology structure can be filled, and the organisational features of enterprise operations have been improved; it is only then that the skill and technology potential of CEE producers in these areas can emerge more strongly. One can thus expect a first phase of downgrading of industrial specialisation structures to be followed by a phase of upgrading.

'Destructive' and 'constructive' processes of industrial restructuring may take place in parallel, but the relative impact of these two types of processes shifts over time. The 'destructive' processes will be particularly dominant in the early phases of economic transformation and the reconstructive processes will gain in speed and weight as the transformation process proceeds. The impact of these two components of the transformation process also makes itself felt at different speeds and in different ways in different industries. There are, of course, dangers in this scenario: stocks of skills and technological capabilities need to be continuously maintained and modernised in order not to deteriorate in quality; long periods of underutilisation and underinvestment can have detrimental effects. There is also the danger that owing to the complicated dynamics of the restructuring process, CEE countries might lose irreversibly potential comparative advantage positions in certain sectors. The severe difficulty encountered in making the existing large SOEs located in a number of crucial manufacturing sectors viable and amenable to privatisation has emerged clearly in the experiences of all transition economies. On the other hand, private economic activity has emerged very unevenly in the different sectors of the economy.

Factors hindering industrial restructuring

The country studies in Part Two point to several common factors hindering industrial restructuring and a fast export expansion in world markets. It seems obvious that, in an unstable macroeconomic environment, the destructive aspect of industrial restructuring is dominant and the emergence of new activity is severely handicapped. In countries and in the periods where and when policy makers could not accomplish the goal of economic stabilisation, this was (and is) the major factor hindering any restructuring (see chapters 5, 7 and 8).

As we shall emphasise later in discussing the differences and similarities between and among CEE economies, the steep decline in investment is a general feature of the first phase of economic restructuring. The main contributory factors are the fall in domestic and external demand, high interest rates and the almost complete lack of long-term (investment) finance. On the one hand, households and financial investors are willing to hold only a small part of their portfolios in long-term financial assets (see, e.g., Ábel and Székely, 1993) owing to the uncertainties inherent in economic restructuring. On the other hand, the state is relying massively on domestic capital markets to finance the mounting budget deficits.

In some of the CEE countries, an important component of new investment is, and most probably will continue to be, foreign direct investment (FDI), either in existing or newly created firms. The degree to which foreign capital is prepared to move in depends to a great extent on the macroeconomic situation, on the state of institutional and legal reform and on the nature of foreign trade and foreign exchange regulation, that is, on the progress of the economic reform process. Countries which can maintain a relatively stable macroeconomic environment and proceed relatively fast with the reform of the institutional and legal systems appear to be relatively successful in attracting FDI (e.g. Hungary), while countries which are less successful in this respect attract hardly any.

On the other hand, the amount of FDI in CEE economies is also very much dependent on the overall state of the world economy. Economic transformation in CEE is, unfortunately, taking place in a period of deep and rather long recession in the world economy. The West European economies, and Germany in particular, have experienced a prolonged slowdown in economic growth. The impact of this recession was somewhat mitigated by extra demand created by German unification, but the German economy quickly headed towards a major slowdown, incurring severe budgetary problems. German unification made one of the largest capital exporting economies of the world into an importer of capital, leading to very high real interest rates on international and domestic credit markets. Since the climate for investment in the world economy is so discouraging, even countries in CEE which have so far been relatively successful in attracting FDI will face severe constraints in this respect in the future.[1]

Domestic saving will therefore be a key factor in financing investments in CEE countries during the economic transformation. Due to the pressures on both the income and the revenue sides of the budget mentioned above, the state can hardly be expected to be a net saver, and it would be rather odd if the corporate sector turned out to be a net saver either. Domestic private saving is therefore the key factor. Unfortunately, the inevitable decline in economic activity leads to a substantial decline in the real disposable income of households. Thus, even if the propensity to save is increasing, as one would expect in a period of high and increasing volatility and, in many countries, in the presence of positive real interest rates rarely experienced during the last decade or so, the real amount of finance available for borrowers is barely increasing, if not actually decreasing.

In addition, in almost all countries (with the possible exception of the Czech Republic), enterprises have to compete with the state which, in order to cover soaring budget deficits (5–10 % of GDP), has to borrow massively from domestic credit markets. As discussed earlier, the tendencies which led to these massive budget deficits are likely to accelerate further. Real interest rates for corporate borrowers, therefore, will remain very high in the foreseeable future. This crowds out a substantial part of private corporate investment and thereby hinders economic restructuring, particularly in manufacturing. The situation for small- and medium-sized firms will be even more disadvantageous, as they can hardly rely on direct finance and this segment of the banking market is notoriously uncompetitive. Enterprises, in particular small- and medium-sized enterprises, will have to capitalise on the savings of their owners and on their own profits, which is a rather slow process.

The underdeveloped state of the financial system in general and the delay in carrying out the necessary financial restructuring are also important factors hindering industrial restructuring. A number of authors point to the delay in the financial restructuring of large SOEs and the biased credit allocation mechanism favouring such enterprises is mentioned as the main reason for the lack of investment finance for viable firms. As we shall argue in more detail below, these are all parts of the same problem, the delay in reforming a financial system which is not able to collect and allocate savings efficiently.

This leads to a more general problem mentioned by many authors as a major obstacle to industrial restructuring. Institution building and implementation of a properly designed legal system are major components of the economic transformation, on which the success of many other elements of the transformation greatly depend. CEE countries had rather different starting positions in this regard. Hungary embarked upon the economic transformation with many of the market institutions and a considerable part of the legal system of a market economy already in place, while the other countries had to implement these changes alongside the other elements of economic transformation policies. It is thus not surprising that the country chapters on Bulgaria and Poland (7 and 8) mention the lack of a proper institutional framework as a major obstacle to industrial restructuring.

The slow (or at any rate slower than expected) pace of privatisation is also stressed by the authors as a factor explaining slow industrial restructuring. Though privatisation of existing (state-owned) enterprises is only one way of increasing the share of private activities in the economy, the slow pace of this process is partly explained by the same factors as the slow pace of growth of the newly emerging part of the private sector. Though Blahó and Halpern (chapter 5) document an enormous increase in the *number* of new private ventures, their overall share in employment, production, or exports is still rather limited. Ábel and Székely in chapter 12 argue that this is quite natural under the circumstances, and that it is very likely that the newly emerging private ventures will grow only slowly, mainly by capitalising on their profits. Again, one of the common causes of slow changes in this regard is enterprise finance, or finance for buying (into) a privatised firm. Besides other reasons mentioned above, this is partly the explanation why foreign investors have such an important role in the first phase of privatisation.

In order to understand the relatively slow pace of privatisation, one has to ask the question: what is the value of SOEs? Put differently, why would any investor opt for buying an existing enterprise as opposed to setting up a new firm? The former involves sometimes long and complicated negoti-ations with privatisation agencies, a long and painful process of restructur-ing the acquired firm, replacing management, changing corporate culture, laying-off a considerable part of the labour force, while the latter can be much faster and less painful.

Price is definitely a factor, though in many cases the value of the firm (that is, the difference between its market value and the sum of the market values of its assets sold separately) is so negative that the selling price should in fact be negative. While the Treuhandanstalt in Germany could afford such negative prices (that is, subsidies given to firms taking over SOEs), it remains to be seen even in the eastern German case how many of these firms sold at negative or very depressed prices will survive in the longer run. Privatisation will not necessarily save enterprises and industries. If the environment for an enterprise is very bad, private ventures as well as state-owned ones can get into desperate situations. The experience of privatisation shows that local market power (or, put differently, the ability to pose a potential threat to newly set up or foreign firms in the local market) is definitely valuable for investors, even though it contradicts the idea of market liberalisation. This is one factor which partly explains the uneven pace of privatisation across industries and sectors.

Many of the authors argue that a substantial part of restructuring will take place in the form of newly emerging enterprises whose production technology and product mix will reflect longer-term comparative advantage. This will change not only the branch structure of industry, but also the product structure and the size structure of enterprises (which has started to take place in a number of CEE economies as pointed out by Blahó and Halpern in chapter 5 for Hungary; see also Buchtíková and Flek, 1993, and Charap and Zemplinerova, 1993), which will move towards smaller units and less capital- and R&D-intensive products and production technologies.

Finally, the degree of social tolerance regarding the social costs and consequences of industrial restructuring, most importantly unemployment, is a major factor policy makers have to take into account. In a socially unstable environment, it is very difficult to make the necessary adjustments within firms and industries. The geographic concentration of industries, as is pointed out in many chapters, further aggravates the problematic features of this process. Notwithstanding the major differences, the east German experience provides useful lessons for other CEE countries.

The accumulated external debts and their domestic counterparts in the form of public debts form another, in most of the countries rather severe, constraint on keeping up subsidies to industrial production. Institutional reforms, increasing the level of private ownership, reforms of the tax systems and financial reforms, bring about an unprecedented pressure on the revenue side of the central budget. In general, a decline in the overall level of economic activity leads to a decline in revenues (from personal income and corporate taxes), and at the same time an increase in social security (unemployment and welfare) payments. In any modern economy, there is a built-in instability of the budget in a period of economic contraction; in CEE economies this pressure is further amplified by accumulated external and internal debts and by the changes mentioned above which tend to decrease the capacity of the state to collect tax revenues and which force the central (and local) authorities to borrow and refinance previous debts under market conditions. Though inflationary finance appears to be a way out in the very short run, there is a threshold above which this tool becomes a boomerang, further accelerating economic decline by deterring domestic saving and foreign investment.

Naturally, privatisation will increase the share of the private sector which, hopefully, will improve the efficiency of production and, consequently, the income-generating capacity of the economy, creating additional sources for business investment. The question is whether this process can offset the inevitable contraction of economic activity and income which takes place in the early phases of the economic transformation.

To sum up, the analysis of the macroeconomic situation of the CEE economies in general suggests that the destructive aspect of economic restructuring, that is, the closing down of obsolete capacities, will proceed rather rapidly (in many countries it is already partly completed), while the constructive part of restructuring, that is, the creation of new capacities reflecting longer-run comparative advantages, will for many reasons be rather slow. During this process, due to the enormous pressure on the budget, some of the relative advantages of CEE economies (particularly, the high quality of education) will inevitably erode. The level and structure of production finally achieved will, at least in the medium run, probably be inferior to what the initial conditions could have permitted.

Similarities and differences in the nature of industrial restructuring among CEE countries

The volume concentrates on four CEE countries: Bulgaria, the former Czechoslovakia, Hungary, and Poland. However, it also contains a further contribution on the former GDR in order to broaden the scope and give a better understanding of the process of industrial restructuring and foreign trade reorientation in general. Notwithstanding its special characteristics, an understanding of the eastern German case is important for a number of reasons. It can provide an extreme benchmark case against which we can compare developments in other countries and it may also foreshadow several developments not yet experienced in other CEE economies. The eastern German experience is also important because the ex-GDR is so far the only country where the 'constructive' phase of industrial restructuring is, though to a much lesser extent than originally hoped for or still desired, considerably advanced. Privatisation is far ahead of that in CEE countries; private investment in manufacturing has picked up considerably more than in other CEE economies, including those which were relatively successful in attracting FDI. Towards the end of chapter 4, Schmidt and Naujoks ask the challenging question whether eastern Germany is a special case, or just the forerunner of the CEE economies, where for some special reasons, such as, for example, rapid monetary union and the consequent extremely rapid appreciation of the national currency, everything was taking place at a more rapid pace. Will CEE economies also lose an overwhelming part of their industrial base? Will they have to go through a process of dramatic deindustrialisation and then one of reindustrialisation?

Schmidt and Naujoks point out that the eastern German transformation process is driven by often contradictory factors in the short and long run. The analyses presented in Part Two show that this is also true for the other countries. Since the process of privatisation is slow and FDI is available only to a rather limited extent even for the most successful countries, the much-needed transfer of technology and knowledge is rather limited. Without this transfer and new investments, however, the ability of CEE producers to adjust to a dramatically changed environment and to change their product structure is severely impaired. Thus, industries which can produce marketable products more easily in the short run, irrespective of their longer-term perspectives, will gain higher shares in the short to medium run, thus creating another form of structural distortion. What is perhaps different is that CEE countries, unlike Germany, have very limited resources to massively subsidise internationally uncompetitive industries for any longer period, which might, on the one hand, create much stronger pressures to rationalise but, on the other, might lead to the irreversible losses of capacities and skills discussed earlier. CEE economies might thus avoid the sort of distortion that was created in eastern Germany by the 'deep pockets' of the Treuhandanstalt, and, in fact, by many governments in the West, but also lose the opportunity of maintaining some of the capital- and skill-intensive activities which might in other circumstances have had a future.

The authors uniformly agree that the major structural changes are still lying ahead. The 'constructive' phase of industrial restructuring evolves very slowly even in the most advanced of the CEE economies. This, in turn, means that the 'destructive' phase itself is also somewhat handicapped, as the lack of efficient industries able to generate sufficient foreign currency earnings and to create new jobs pushes policy makers to keep alive whatever is possible by any available means. This is done particularly through exchange rate policy, but increasingly also by direct regional or enterprise level intervention.

The analysis of the macroeconomic environment of economic restructuring given above is of course very general. As the chapters in Part Two point out, the situation in individual CEE economies varies to a great extent, as did their initial conditions. Poland and Hungary embarked upon several reform packages well before the beginning of the dramatic transformation post-1989 (see, e.g., Berend, 1990; Boote and Somogyi, 1991), while the political leaders in Bulgaria, Czechoslovakia and the former GDR resisted changes up to the very end. As we shall point out at several places, one of the major characteristics of traditional CPEs is the delayed and muted response to the changing external (and internal) economic environment, which was intimately related to the nature of CMEA trade relations (see Köves, 1985; van Brabant, 1987).

Consequently, as shown by the analyses of the chapters in Parts One and Two, Hungarian and Polish producers had a relatively long experience with Western markets and were more responsive to market signals coming from them. These economies thus experienced more structural change in the pre-1989 period than the other economies of the region and the quality gap between their products and Western products was somewhat smaller than for the other CEE economies. The economies of Bulgaria, Czechoslovakia, and the GDR, on the other hand, were very strongly embedded in CMEA markets, shielding them from the major structural changes that have taken place in the world economy since the first oil crises.

Another very important element in the different starting positions of CEE economies was the difference in the level of foreign indebtedness. Bulgaria, Hungary, Poland and the former USSR inherited rather high levels (as compared with their hard-currency exports and, with the exception of the former USSR, even in relation to their GDPs) of external indebtedness not backed up with proper quality assets (either financial or real). Czechoslovakia, on the other hand, had a relatively low level of foreign indebtedness, mainly reflecting the policy of central planners in maintaining a balanced state budget.

Hungary has managed so far to service her debts without any disruption and has clearly committed herself to doing so in the future. However, the other countries, at different points in time, had to suspend regular payment. The suspension of debt servicing had devastating repercussions on the macroeconomic situation in these countries, leading to abrupt and substantial declines in economic activity and in exports. In Poland, all this happened more than a decade ago, but the repercussions are still tangible and the recently granted politically motivated debt reduction has had hardly any positive impact on the macroeconomic situation. In Hungary, the financing of these debts uses up most of the available financial and economic resources, putting an enormous pressure on the economy, and sooner or later this will be the case in the other countries as well. Bulgaria still has to come up with a solution to this problem. Whatever the solution chosen, this will put a heavy burden on the economy.

A further aspect of differences was the degree of internal imbalance in the countries. While Hungary – partly due to previous reforms, but also as a result of the policy of easing internal imbalances by imports and thus piling up foreign debts – managed to escape major internal imbalances, the other economies were basically shortage economies, though not to the same extent. Czechoslovakia had a relatively moderate extent of shortage (see Charemza, 1991); Bulgaria, Poland, and the former USSR, on the other hand, suffered from much higher degrees of shortage. In Poland, internal and external imbalances, coupled with wage pressures and budget deficits, led to relatively high inflation even during central planning, and eventually to hyperinflation before the beginning of the economic transformation. The fight against hyperinflation and the stabilisation of the economy in the shortest possible time became thus the key priority for policy makers at the beginning of economic transformation. Most of the former republics of the ex-USSR are also experiencing hyperinflation, a phenomenon which will dominate economic policies for some time to come.

In a highly inflationary environment all possible macroeconomic policy tools have to be used in order to bring down inflation. The price for this is, however, rather high. Very high interest rates immediately lead to a sharp decline in investment, the credit crunch on firms leads to serious liquidity problems in the system, pushing even healthy firms into desperate situations. Stabilisation policies tend to make industrial structural change and foreign trade reorientation more difficult in the short run while, of course, in the medium to long run, a stable macroeconomic environment facilitates these processes.

The level of private activities under central planning was also rather diverse in CEE economies. Poland had the strongest private sector, partly due to the fact that agriculture was not collectivised in the 1950s and 1960s, as it was in the other countries, followed by Hungary, where, mainly during the 1980s, different forms of private and semi-private activities gradually developed in certain sectors in the economy.

The political conditions in which economic restructuring in the CEE countries has to take place are also differentiated. Some countries disintegrated, leading to situations ranging from (civil) war to a 'velvet' divorce. Economic spaces with new, for the foreseeable future, non-convertible currencies, are created with previous ties cut off and with rather obsolete production capacities. Tensions with minorities emerge (in practically all countries except Poland, Hungary and the Czech Republic) and political (election) systems turn out to produce rather fragile situations.

The different starting positions and political and economic situations of CEE countries have a strong bearing on the process of economic transformation. However, there are a number of common features highlighted by the country studies in Part Two. As a result of stabilisation programmes, import liberalisation and the loss of CMEA markets, production and investment declined rapidly and sharply, the decline being much deeper in investment. With the exception of the Czech part of the former Czechoslovakia, unemployment in a short period of time reached, and in some countries exceeded, West European levels. Even so, lay-offs did not in general keep pace with the decline in production and thus labour productivity, which was very low already at the beginning of the process, further declined. The authors in Part Two attribute the slower adjustment of employment to different factors ranging from strong trade unions to the lack of industrial policy. Regarding structural change, it is a generally observed characteristic of industrial restructuring and foreign trade reorientation that the major losers are those industries which were developed within the framework of CMEA specialisation and which, therefore, relied most on CMEA markets. The more R&D- and skill-intensive the industry, the deeper the decline.

Finance, institutional change and industrial restructuring

An important element of the environment within which economic re-structuring takes place is the financial system. As pointed out above, financial resources for restructuring and investment are, and will be, scarce. It is thus of paramount importance that the available finance is allocated properly and at the lowest possible cost and that the proper financial instruments are made available for financial investors to meet their preferences on time and risk. The role of the financial system in both collecting and allocating savings is essential. This can, however, be achieved only by a competitive financial system replacing the old finan-cial system which was designed to accommodate central planning and by the proper design and actual implementation of the necessary legal, institutional and regulatory framework. The starting positions of the different CEE countries were rather different in this respect as well. Hungary, on the one hand, started to implement the necessary reforms in 1987, while in the other countries these were started only in 1990/1. The reforms in banking are by now relatively well advanced in many countries, but the remaining parts of a developed financial system are still practically non-existent in countries other than Hungary. This means that, on the one hand, enterprises will have to rely solely on bank finance and, on the other hand, banks will have to assume all the risks involved in financing economic restructuring. This may exceed their capacity to incur risk. In general, countries which will be able to advance reforms in the financial system may expect much smoother economic restructuring and more foreign (direct and portfolio) investment.

The financial system can also play an important role in enterprise restructuring. Due to the dominance of bank finance and the vast amount of inherited and accumulated bad and dubious corporate loans, banks are major players in bankruptcy procedures and have the necessary means for financing restructuring plans emerging from bankruptcy procedures. Through this, they can exercise the rather tight control over management necessary to force firms to improve their performances by carrying out successful restructuring. Belka and Krajewski in chapter 10 analyse the evidence for changes in the bank–enterprise relationship during the most recent phase of the transition.

The legal and institutional structure is also an important element of any successful economic restructuring. Bankruptcy regulations are important in making it possible to distinguish insolvent firms from illiquid ones, that is, short-run problems from long-run ones. However, the timing of the introduction of bankruptcy regulations has proved to be decisive in speeding up the contractionary nature of the transformation. Consequently, a more gradualist position is currently being adopted in a number of countries to allow banks and enterprises time to restructure both real and financial assets before bankruptcy regulations are introduced and enforced. It is also clear that – given the highly concentrated structure of many CEE industries – competition policy and the corresponding institutions are also vital elements of a proper environment, and a process of learning about adequate regulatory bodies (especially in natural monopoly areas) is underway. In general, the conclusion drawn above can be generalised: countries which proceed faster with certain components of legal and institutional reform may expect a smoother process of restructuring.

Reorientation of trade and trade performance

The changes in the level and structure of industrial production are intimately related to those in the geographical and commodity structure of sales. With the exception of the former USSR, the CEE economies were and are very open economies in the sense that a major part of their industrial capacities was built up to produce for foreign markets. Given the experience of other industrialised countries of comparable size and location, this will remain true in the future. The big change for CEE economies is, of course, that the positions of their export markets have changed dramatically. Not only is the structure of demand in the new markets quite different from that prevalent in CMEA markets but domestic markets are also gradually becoming as competitive as foreign markets. Since this is true for all the ex-CMEA markets the required adjustment encompasses all the markets to which CEE countries sell.

The starting point for all the CEE countries in 1989 was the 'dual' structure of their exports, the composition of commodities which were (and still are) sold to Western export markets being quite different from that which characterised sales to CMEA markets. It is well known that many CEE economies had the characteristics of industrially developed economies in their export sales to other CMEA markets (and the Soviet market in particular) but were low value added exporters (largely of products with high raw material content) to the West. Recent developments have accentuated this export profile to the West (while exports to ex-CMEA markets virtually collapsed). However, there are intercountry variations in this respect, which are discussed in chapter 2. The interesting question is which direction the (inescapable) tendency of 'unification' of this previously dual structure will take in the different CEE economies in the medium and long run. One type of scenario is outlined in chapter 3 where, in the short run, the structure of export growth will be predominantly characterised by the legacy of inherited (and presently vastly underutilised) capacities in branches which were most heavily dependent upon selling to CMEA markets in the past. However, over the longer run, a catching-up process is outlined which directs export developments towards a trade structure more typical for the more advanced Western European economies. This only becomes an overly optimistic scenario if the date of such convergence is set too early; otherwise it only sets a target 'reference' export structure which could – depending upon the success of an eventual catching-up process – be reached earlier or later. Since trade amongst advanced industrial economies is also characterised by a range of possible specialisation patterns, the long-run projections discussed in chapter 3 allow for a range of comparative advantage positions of CEE economies in their future trade with other European economies. The scenario of catching-up, its timing and overall success, is, of course, intricately linked to the question of whether, when and in which industrial sectors the structural adjustment process takes place with which the other chapters in this volume are concerned. The move from an interindustry specialisation pattern which currently characterises a major part of East–West trade towards an intra-industry trade pattern is a crucial component of such structural adjustment. Of course, a substantial increase in international direct investment and corporate East–West integration is a vital part of a shift towards more intra-industry trade.

Enterprise behaviour during the transition

Following foreign trade liberalisation, the dismantling of price control and convertibility, relative prices changed substantially and foreign producers gained an almost free access to the domestic markets of CEE economies. The excess demand previously characterising many of the CEE economies rapidly disappeared. This made the production technology and corporate structure of many firms suddenly uncompetitive. The market shares of a great number of firms formerly dominating the domestic market shrank dramatically, mainly in consumer goods markets (e.g. household electronics, electrical goods, cosmetics, etc.). This process, though to different extents, took place in all the former CMEA countries; the same happened in the major part of the foreign markets which, in the past, were predominantly other CMEA markets. The loss of former CMEA markets was a more important factor in industries producing production goods, but it had a tangible effect also in consumer goods industries (e.g. the Czech footwear industry).

The contraction of foreign and domestic markets went along with a drying up of bank finance. As pointed out previously, the major part of domestic saving was mopped up by the budget, pushing up real interest rates. As convertibility on the capital account was still not implemented, firms could not resort to foreign capital markets and had to accept very high capital costs (much higher than their foreign competitors). Though, in principle, a certain level of exchange rate could still make them competitive, for different reasons, policy makers in CEE countries were not prepared to maintain such levels. In fact, in many industries, production costs implied an exchange rate which would have been unsustainable for these economies.

There were also other developments brought about by these changes. First, excess demand on labour markets all but disappeared, eroding the bargaining power of unions and individual workers and softening the pressure on wage costs. Unemployment increased rapidly, reaching, and in many countries far exceeding, the typical European levels in less than two years. Unemployment in each CEE economy tends to be concentrated in certain regions, either those dominated by heavy industry, and/or in backward regions, where the infrastructure was underdeveloped, the labour force was undertrained but in which industry was previously developed through heavy state support. Due to the generally low level of labour mobility in CEE economies, the laid-off labour force in these regions imposes no serious pressure on other more prosperous regions, while in these regions the fall in labour costs does not compensate for the effects of cumulative overall decline. Regional disparities in unemployment levels are already great and will widen further though, as economic contraction continues, there remain very few regions (mainly the regions around the capitals and border regions with Western Europe) where the labour market situation is not severe. Naturally, this enables firms to curb wage costs and tighten work discipline, though laying-off labour is far from costless for firms. Another aspect which is of great significance for the success of corporate restructuring is whether the existing structures of skills can be maintained and further adapted to the new conditions. Much of the training of the manufacturing labour force was previously carried out in the large state-owned combines; these have now been or are in the process of being dismantled and thus there is a danger that training and retraining is seriously being disrupted; some countries have started to put in place active training and retraining programmes but these are mostly on a small scale and the future supply and the continued maintenance and adaptation of the skill structure of the labour supply is far from being put on solid new foundations. Given the great need for technological and quality catching-up this aspect is of utmost importance for the success of corporate restructuring. We shall come back to this point later.

A positive change for firms was the easier access to production inputs. Liberalisation of foreign trade and the increased competition on domestic markets made it possible for firms in CEE economies to have access to better quality production inputs under improved conditions (e.g. delivery). This made the previously very high level of input inventories due to delivery uncertainties obsolete, allowing firms to eliminate this source of cost inefficiency. On the other hand, the same changes made it necessary for firms to have somewhat higher levels of output inventories.

A role for industrial policy in the transition?

The severity of industrial restructuring currently taking place in Central and Eastern Europe makes industrial policy unavoidable; 'no policy' is not an option, but there is a choice between reactive and active industrial policies. We call those policies *reactive* which will be set in motion in response to the social and political pressures which will inescapably emerge as the painful process of structural adjustment affects social groups, regions and branches in different ways. As the restructuring process proceeds, the heavy burden imposed on the budget by such reactive policies could historically be observed in the drawn-out process of running down the ship-building, steel and mining industries in Western Europe (Carlsson, 1983; Strath, 1988). The reactive use of industrial policy funds is largely inefficient. If one defines restructuring as running down the old and building up the new, an *active* industrial policy emphasises the second component, which may greatly facilitate and ease the political and social pressures resulting from the first component as well.

Given the past orientation of industrial development patterns in Eastern Europe, there are strong reasons to believe that there will be strong linkage effects from public infrastructural investment and training policies. Past industrial development has led to a dramatic underdevelopment of certain skills and activities (particularly managerial skills, marketing, and product design). In such conditions, where the general level of skill of production workers is high but important complementary skills and activities are missing or in very short supply, one can expect strong effects from industrial policies if one is able to stimulate the supply of those complementary inputs.

Geroski and Jacquemin (1985, p. 177) distinguish between two alternative kinds of industrial policies: one is the 'picking winners' approach, when governments try to anticipate changes and make decisions about the allocation of resources to be invested for future growth. The alternative is to provide an institutional framework in which private sector adjustment is facilitated. In the context of Eastern Europe, it is not important at this stage to create 'national champions' but to lift the general level of performance and provide a basic (human and material) infrastructure; thus the 'picking winners' strategy is not favoured. Public policy in this case should be to *lower the barriers to entry* for participation in market processes, and it has a major role to play in restructuring the existing state sector. Retraining programmes, support for modernising existing capacities through investment support and help in sales networks in Western markets, re-equipping domestic products with imported machinery better suited to world market production, as well as access to scarce managerial, marketing and advertising capacities are among the numerous possibilities for lowering both exit and entry barriers.

An important target for industrial policy in the process of transition to a market economy is – apart from the potential benefit to the private sector itself – to orientate the state-administrative machinery towards the goals of competing in national and international markets. Industrial policies can assist the infiltration of managerial objectives of an internationally open economy into the thinking of administrators and bureaucrats.

To sum up: first, the economic transformation currently taking place in Eastern Europe involves a major conversion of existing capacities, capabilities and organisational structures as well as the building up of new ones; such a process is, by definition, time-consuming. It will, on current estimates, take anything up to 20 or 30 years.

Secondly, given that the existence of markets and of market-conforming behaviour is a necessary prerequisite for the effective functioning of a market economy, and that these conditions are only gradually emerging in CEE economies, the transition process cannot, in our view, occur without a relatively *high degree of state involvement*. We believe that the current experience of economic reform in Eastern Europe provides much evidence for such a view.

Thirdly, it is in the nature of the evolution of market behaviour that in periods in which environmental parameters are constantly and dramatically changing, resources are less likely to be committed for the long term than the short term. Under such conditions, there is an important role for industrial policy to bring public resources to bear in areas which would be neglected by private agents, even in normal circumstances, let alone in the current circumstances of Eastern Europe. Infrastructural investment and training are two such areas which have been shown to be crucial for a catching-up process (see, e.g., Cohen, 1991).

Fourthly, training structures have to be devised to adapt to new conditions. Formerly, training was carried out in large SOEs. With the disappearance of these large combines, there is a danger that training facilities will disappear altogether. There are lessons to be learned from Western European experience in retraining workers in declining industries, counteracting the danger of erosion of skill through long periods of unemployment, and launching schemes to avoid large-scale youth unemployment.

Fifthly, the main impact of the state on the evolution of market structure will lie in the policies pursued with respect to the reorganisation of 'strategic' SOEs, on the one hand, and small- and medium-sized enterprises, on the other. In both these areas, policy makers in Eastern Europe should take a pragmatic look at the experience of Western Europe over the past two decades in which policies of restructuring of state enterprises and support of the small- and medium-sized enterprise sector have evolved. In the current context of Eastern Europe, the latter is intricately linked to the evolution of financial markets and financial organisations.

Sixthly, a strong emphasis on export orientation has been the hallmark of successful catching-up of a great number of economies. Eastern Europe has some extraordinary potential comparative advantages (particularly in its human infrastructure) which could allow it to embark upon a successful upward movement in the international division of labour. Evidence from other successful economies indicates that industrial policy can be an important ingredient in tapping that potential.

Notes

1 The truth is that international capital (syndicated loans and bond) markets are at the moment practically inaccessible to governments, financial institutions, or firms of CEE countries. The shares of CEE economies in total borrowing on international capital markets between 1988 and 1992 were 1.0, 1.1, 1.3, 0.4 (!) and 0.3 (!)% respectively. Although in 1993 Hungary managed to increase substantially its borrowing from international bond markets, the overall share of the region remained below 1.0% and Hungary's share of this was 83.0%. As the

inevitable consequences of economic transformation emerged, private capital turned away from the region. By 1991, there remained in practice only two countries which could borrow on this market, Hungary (borrowing US$ 1.3 bn almost exclusively in the form of bonds) and Czechoslovakia (borrowing US$ 0.3 bn, also in bonds). Given the present state and future growth prospects of the world economy, and in particular those of the major capital exporting economies, this tendency will hardly change.

Most of the foreign finance made available to CEE countries in 1990 and 1991 came from non-private sources, mainly from the World Bank, the International Monetary Fund, EC funds and from funds set up by central and local governments in the industrialised countries. Although the total amount pledged to the region is rather substantial, the actual disbursement is disappointingly small. This is mainly due to the fact that the major part of these loans has to be disbursed through proper commercial channels, that is, by commercial banks.

References

Ábel, I. and Székely, I. P., 1993. 'Changing structure of household portfolios in emerging market economies: the case of Hungary, 1970–1989', in I. P. Székely and D. G. M. Newbery (eds.), *Hungary: An Economy in Transition*, Cambridge: Cambridge University Press, 163–80

Berend, I. T., 1990. *The Hungarian Economic Reforms 1953–1988*, Cambridge: Cambridge University Press

Boote, A. R. and Somogyi, J., 1991. 'Economic reform in Hungary since 1968', *Occasional Paper* 83, IMF, Washington, DC

Brabant, J. M. van, 1987. *Adjustment, Structural Change, and Economic Efficiency*, Cambridge: Cambridge University Press

Buchtíková, A. and Flek, V., 1993. 'The impact of deconcentration and indirect industrial policy on structural development and export performance in the Czech Republic, 1989–1992', paper presented at the ACE Workshop on 'Industrial Restructuring, Trade Reorientation and East West European Integration', WIIW, Vienna (March), 27–29

Carlsson, B., 1983. 'Industrial subsidies in Sweden: macro-economic effects and an international comparison', *Journal of Industrial Economics*, 32, 1–29

Charap, J. and Zemplinerova, A., 1993. 'Restructuring the Czech economy', *Working Paper* 2, European Bank of Reconstruction and Development, London

Charemza, W, 1991. 'Alternative paths to macroeconomic stability in Czechoslovakia', *European Economy*, Special edition, 2

Cohen, D., 1991. 'The solvency of Eastern Europe', *European Economy*, Special edition, 2

Geroski, P. and Jacquemin, A., 1985. 'Corporate competitiveness in Europe', *Economic Policy*, 1 (November), 170–218

Köves, A., 1985. *The CMEA Countries in the World Economy*, Budapest: Akadémia Kiadó

Pinto, B., Belka, M. and Krajewski, S., 1993. 'Transforming state enterprises in Poland: evidence on adjustment by manufacturing firms', *Brookings Papers on Economic Activity*, 1, 213–70

Stråth, B., 1988. *The Politics of Deindustrialization*, London: Croom Helm

Svejnar, J., 1991. 'Microeconomic issues in the transition to a market economy', *Journal of Economic Perspectives*, 5(4), 123–38

Part One

Industrial structural change and East–West trade integration

2 Industrial structural change in Central and Eastern European economies

Michael Landesmann and István Székely

Introduction

This chapter presents a comparative analysis of the process of industrial restructuring (first–fourth sections) and trade reorientation (fifth section) in the three leading transition countries, the former Czechoslovakia, Hungary, and Poland. These economies were the first to embark on major social and economic reforms and also the ones which are at the forefront of developments in this respect (see, e.g., Székely and Newbery, 1993; Portes, 1993). Data availability also determined this choice.[1]

The characteristics of this process in the three countries are to a considerable extent determined by the starting positions of the countries at the beginning of economic transformation. Their ability to adjust to the dramatically changed external environment and the eventual industrial structure they reach upon accomplishing economic transformation, though perhaps to a somewhat lesser extent, depends on the industrial structures they inherited from central planning and also on the extent to which they had experience of carrying out structural adjustment beforehand. Economies with very little experience of structural change and with industrial structures and relative prices very dissimilar to what they are likely to head for, thought to be similar to those of open market economies with similar size and location, have furthest to go when embarking upon a major restructuring programme. On the other hand, economies which have already undergone significant structural change in the past and whose industrial structures are closer to those of market economies are in a better position in this respect. That is why a considerable part of the analysis is devoted to the investigation of industrial structural change in the three countries before the beginning of the recent wave of economic transformation.

As pointed out in the Introduction to the volume, economic transformation induces structural changes in industrial production in many different ways. Producers in the former CMEA economies face a dramatically

25

changed situation. As a result of the collapse of the CMEA markets, a large decline in domestic demand – partly due to the loss of the CMEA markets, and particularly strong in the demand for investment goods – and import liberalisation, coupled with real appreciation of the domestic currencies for certain countries and certain periods, they lost a substantial part of their traditional markets.

The only way for CEE producers to survive was (and is) to increase exports to the markets of developed market economies, in particular to EC and some of the EFTA markets. This, however, requires rather fast and deep adjustment on the part of CEE producers regarding production and product structures, production technologies, management, and marketing. On the other hand, financing production and investment became much tighter for CEE producers. State subsidies are practically eliminated, cheap bank finance is no longer available and liquidity has become a serious concern for enterprises. The daunting task CEE producers faced in the short run was thus to find new markets for products that could be produced basically with the existing production capacities and to achieve prices that, at least, covered variable costs. As we shall see in the analysis below, some producers in certain industries managed to achieve this goal, while many more found this equation unsolvable.

Import liberalisation and a higher degree of reliance on Western markets also brought about sizeable changes in relative prices. Sudden relative price changes of this order would induce large changes in production structure even in a well established market economy, leading to a temporary decline in the overall level of economic activity. In the analysis below, to the extent that available data allow it, we shall try to show the extent of relative price changes that have taken place in the countries under investigation.

As the chapters in Part Two describe, the level of industrial production, in particular that of manufacturing, declined rapidly after the beginning of economic transformation in all ex-CMEA economies, in spite of the relatively substantial increase in exports to European markets (see, e.g., Blejer et al., 1993). Moreover, the level of investment activity, in particular that in manufacturing, declined substantially. The period we can observe is thus dominated by the 'destructive' phase of industrial restructuring. There were very few manufacturing industries which could increase the level of production or employment. The decline was however not evenly distributed among industries: a sizeable change in the structure of industrial production took place during the first three years of economic transformation.

However, it remains to be seen whether these changes reflect the long-run viability of manufacturing industries – or, put differently, the long-run comparative advantages of these economies – or only the short-term market conditions and the sometimes rather arbitrary initial financial and other conditions of enterprises and industries. In analysing the eastern German situation in this regard, Schmidt poses a similar question in chapter 4, in spite of the fact that privatisation there is much more advanced, the macroeconomic environment is stable and there is a strong willingness on the part of the state to help firms through their adjustment processes.

Experience with structural change and starting positions

The appendix (pp. 68–9) gives a detailed description of the data used in the empirical analysis presented here and the coefficient of structural change we apply to measure the degree of structural change over time (year-to-year and over a longer period). The coefficient we use basically measures the distance between two structures by using a standard distance measure. The same type of coefficient is used to measure structural similarity between different countries. We selected three indicators of the level of economic activity in a manufacturing industry: employment, value added, and gross output. Due to the well known fact that relative prices (as compared to prevailing relative prices in international trade) were highly distorted in CEE economies, one has to measure different aspects of industrial structure. Employment structure is different from output structure to the extent of differences in labour productivity across manufacturing sectors that are substantial in market economies as well. Regarding comparison over time, this measure is biased to the extent of changes that have occurred in relative labour productivity in different industries. Value added, on the other hand, is clearly subject to price distortion, and in the case of comparison over time, to changes in relative factor and output prices. The same applies to gross output.

Table 2.1 presents the values of the structural change coefficient measuring structural changes over the periods 1966–88, 1966–89 and 1966–90 applied to employment, value added and real output figures for 3-digit ISIC industries. The most important conclusion we can draw in this regard is that Czechoslovakia clearly lags behind the other two countries so far as the extent of structural change over the period 1966–88 (that is, for the period until the beginning of economic transformation) is concerned.

Figure 2.1, plotting the year-to-year values of the same coefficient for the three countries for the same period, reveals the reason for the differences regarding the output structure. In Poland and Hungary, there were two waves of major structural adjustments, the first around 1968–69 and the second around 1975–77. Czechoslovakia seems to have gone through these periods without any major adjustment in her industrial structure.

The other important finding in this regard, which is uniformly true for all

Table 2.1. *Structural change coefficients, 1966–90*

	1966–88	1966–89	1966–90
Czechoslovakia			
Employment	1.19[c]	1.20	1.18
Value added	1.48	1.43	1.11
Gross output[a]	1.43	1.41	1.21
Hungary			
Employment	2.85	2.99	3.19
Value added	2.89	2.61	2.55
Gross output	1.98	1.87	2.20
Poland			
Employment	2.03	1.95	1.95
Value added	3.73	2.06	3.41
Gross output[b]	n.a.	n.a.	n.a.

Notes:
[a] Gross output stands for the value of gross output at current prices.
[b] For Poland, nominal gross output figures are not available.
[c] The indicators above measure the weighted average difference in the shares of respective (ISIC) 3-digit manufacturing industries expressed in percentage points. The smaller the value of this indicator the more similar the two structures compared. For a description of the indicator and data used, see the appendix, pp. 68–9.

three countries, is that adjustments in the employment structures were considerably less than in production over the same period. Figures 2.3–2.5, plotting for each country the time series of structural change coefficients for employment and gross output together, further corroborate this finding.

Figure 2.2 however shows that – as far as employment is concerned – the lower value for Czechoslovakia in this case is not due to her distinctly smaller degrees of adjustment in the two major adjustment periods, but rather to her systematically lower degrees of changes throughout the 1970s and 1980s (with the exception of 1976–77).

The differences among countries regarding industrial structural change is intimately linked to their foreign trade orientation during this period. Among the three countries under investigation, Czechoslovakia was by far the most oriented towards CMEA markets, highly specialised in certain manufacturing sectors.

The lack of sufficient structural adjustment in the Czechoslovak economy under central planning is widely recognised in the literature (see, e.g., Dyba, 1989; Charap and Dyba, 1991; Landesmann, 1991) and

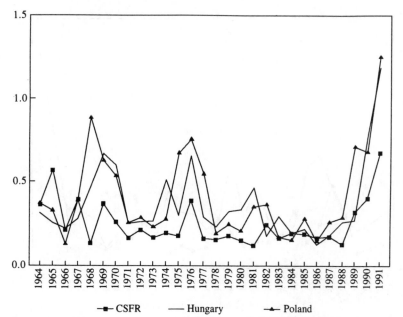

Figure 2.1 Year-to-year structural change coefficients for real gross output, 1964–91

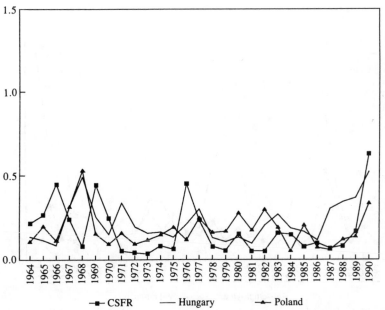

Figure 2.2 Year-to-year structural change coefficients for employment, 1964–90

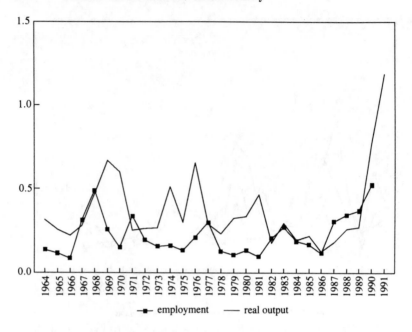

Figure 2.3   Hungary, year-to-year structural change coefficients, 1964–91

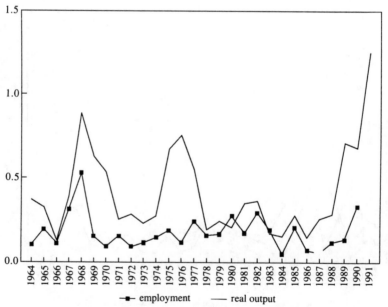

Figure 2.4   Poland, year-to-year structural change coefficients, 1964–91

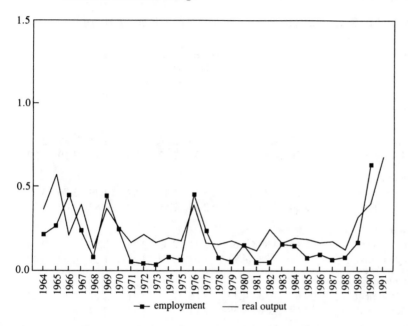

Figure 2.5 Czechoslovakia, year-to-year structural change coefficients, 1964–91

emphasised in chapter 6 by Nesporova.[2] What we can add to this is a comparison of the values of the structural change coefficient indicating the extent to which Czechoslovakia was lagging behind the other countries (see table 2.1 and figures 2.1 and 2.2).

Another way of trying to judge the relative position of the three countries at the time of embarking upon economic transformation is to compare them to some of the market economies. For this purpose we chose two individual countries, Austria and western Germany, and two groups of European countries, the first which, for the sake of simplicity, we shall call Northern Europe, consisting of small industrialised countries (Austria, Belgium, Denmark, Finland, the Netherlands, Norway, and Sweden) and the second referred to as Southern Europe, of the less developed market economies (Greece, Ireland, Portugal, and Spain).

The choice of Austria is self-evident, because of the similarity in size, factor endowment, traditions, location, etc. Germany is chosen in order to show the extent of differences among market economies. The group called Northern Europe is the group of countries with similar size, openness (in terms of foreign trade), and factor endowment. The countries in the group called Southern Europe are the ones which are the nearest to CEE countries

Table 2.2. *Structural similarities among Western and Eastern European economies, 1966–90*

	Czechoslovakia			Hungary			Poland		
	1966	1988	1990	1966	1988	1990	1966	1988	1990
Austria									
Employment	4.15^c	4.74	4.16	2.06	2.86	2.93	2.51	2.89	2.81
Value added	4.70	4.59	4.22	2.30	2.57	2.06	2.71	3.10	2.90
Western Germany									
Employment	3.69	4.26	3.96	3.29	4.46	4.57	3.79	3.76	3.92
Value added	3.24	4.30	4.33	2.59	2.81	3.70	3.62	3.02	4.33
Southern Europe^a									
Employment	5.44	4.89	4.67	3.81	2.53	2.75	2.53	2.53	2.34
Value added	4.51	4.98	4.91	2.37	3.58	3.28	1.51	4.69	2.47
Northern Europe^b									
Employment	4.03	4.53	4.17	1.86	2.72	2.81	2.27	2.52	2.44
Value added	4.64	4.76	4.39	2.17	3.18	2.49	2.94	3.51	2.66

Notes:
^{a} Southern Europe: Greece, Ireland, Portugal, Spain.
^{b} Northern Europe: Austria, Belgium, Denmark, Finland, the Netherlands, Norway, Sweden.
^{c} The indicators above measure the weighted average difference in the shares of respective (ISIC) 3-digit manufacturing industries expressed in percentage points. The smaller the value of this indicator the more similar the two structures compared. For a description of the indicator and data used, see the appendix, pp. 68–9.

as far as income levels and overall levels of development are concerned. As we shall see, Austria is in fact a very good representative of the Northern European group, the distance between this group and Austria in terms of employment and output structures being by far the smallest among the countries and groups investigated.

The analysis is based on the structural similarity coefficient defined in the appendix, which is very similar in nature to the structural change coefficient we used in table 2.1 to measure structural change over time, but now it measures the distance between two countries (or groups of countries) at a given point in time. Table 2.2 gives the value of this coefficient for each of the possible pairs.

Comparing the three countries in this respect, Czechoslovakia stands out again, as the country which, at the beginning of economic transformation, was the least similar to any of the individual market economies or groups of market economies considered here. This difference between Czechoslovakia and the other two countries is least pronounced in comparison with western Germany, reflecting the fact that within the CMEA Czechoslovakia specialised mostly in the engineering industries.

Industrial structural change during economic transformation

As we discussed in detail in the Introduction, theoretical considerations[3] suggested that economic transformation would induce substantial changes in the structure of production and employment, in particular in manufacturing.[4] Theory could however say relatively little about the dynamics of this process, and the exact degree of change in different countries and industries. The dynamics of the process, as was also pointed out, depends to a great extent on many factors including, among others, the overall macroeconomic situation, the state of institutional and financial reforms, and the prevailing political constellation which may be rather volatile.

Figures 2.1 and 2.2 and table 2.1 revealed the extent of industrial structural change in the first three years of economic transformation, as measured by our structural change coefficient. In Poland in 1989 and in Hungary in 1990, the extent of changes in the structure of manufacturing real output had reached the peak levels observed during the previous major adjustment periods (around 1968–69 and 1975–77) and had substantially exceeded them in 1991. In Czechoslovakia, the development was similar in nature, but the extent of changes lagged behind the other two countries at least until 1991. As Nesporova points out in chapter 6, the changes experienced until 1991 were mainly due to the accelerating decline in trade with the former CMEA countries and also to some extent to the decline in investments. She also points out that most of the changes that have already taken place in the other two countries were expected to happen in the course of 1993 (e.g., the impact of new bankruptcy regulations which, however, were further delayed). The division of the country into the Czech Republic and the Slovak Republic only aggravates the situation.

So even the three leading reforming countries under investigation had different dynamics. The structural similarity coefficients for 1988 and 1990 presented in table 2.2, comparing the three countries to some of the European market economies, further corroborate this conclusion.

Figure 2.6 shows the direction of industrial structural changes in the three countries under investigation. Here again, forecasts based on theoretical considerations turned out to be on the whole correct. As imports were liberalised and the previously highly protected domestic and

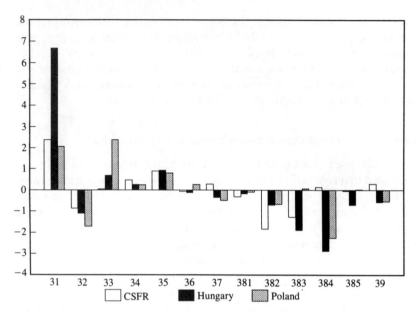

Figure 2.6 Changes in the structure of manufacturing real gross output, 1988–91

Notes: Absolute changes in the shares of (ISIC 2- and 3-digit) industries in manufacturing total real gross output (= 100), expressed in percentage points. For a description of the ISIC codes used to identify industries, see the appendix, pp. 68–9.

CMEA markets thus became much more competitive and demand on both markets started to shrink rapidly, industries that relied on autarky and the artificially created and highly protected specialisation within the CMEA had to downsize their production. Food and beverages, wood and furniture, paper and printing and chemical industries increased their shares, while the major losers were the engineering industries, in both relative and absolute terms. A closer look at figure 2.7 (p. 35) reveals that, after a jump in 1989, even the Czechoslovak transport equipment industry has been gradually losing its share, though changes are indeed incremental. The Czechoslovak iron and steel industry is thus the only real outlier in this regard, though changes in all countries are very small in this industry's share.

Comparing the three countries in this respect, the numbers in figure 2.6 clearly indicate that the country which was most specialised in an industry within the CMEA always suffered most in that industry. The only notable exception is the Czechoslovak transport equipment industry which, due to massive FDI, could maintain its relative position. It is worth pointing out that this industry was relatively successful in penetrating Western markets

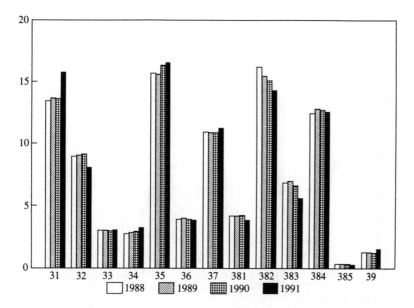

Figure 2.7 Structure of real output in Czechoslovakia, 1988–91

Notes: Shares of (ISIC 2- and 3-digit) industries in total manufacturing real gross output (= 100), expressed in percentages. For a description of the ISIC codes used to identify industries, see the appendix, pp. 68–9.

in the past, as well. With the exception of the textile industry, light industries suffered less from the overall decline in manufacturing and could thus improve their relative positions. Given the factor endowments, labour costs and production technologies of these countries, this picture is not at all surprising. Without EC protection, these changes would probably have been much more pronounced. Among the relative 'winners', the Hungarian food processing and the Polish wood and furniture industries' gains are outstanding. It is again worth noting that these industries were quite successful in the past in penetrating Western European markets.

The yearly changes for the individual countries are shown in figures 2.7–2.9. These figures shed some more light on the differences in the dynamics of industrial restructuring among the three countries under investigation. For Poland two sub-periods can clearly be distinguished. Until 1990, as is discussed in some detail in chapter 8 by Tomaszewicz and Orlowski, the government made several efforts to keep up the level of exports, in particular that of manufactured goods to the former USSR and other CMEA countries. CMEA exporting industries, engineering industries in particular, could therefore somewhat improve their relative positions. By 1991, however, this policy had to be abandoned and

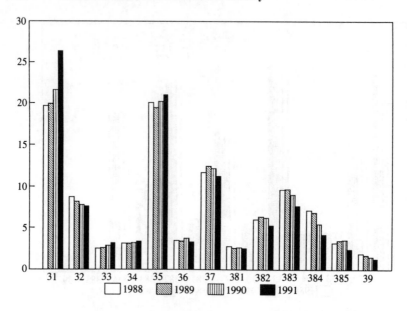

Figure 2.8 Structure of real output in Hungary, 1988–91

Notes: Shares of (ISIC 2- and 3-digit) industries in total manufacturing real gross output (= 100), expressed in percentages. For a description of the ISIC codes used to identify industries, see the appendix, pp. 68–9.

industries benefiting from the previous regime started to decline rapidly, while those which were relatively successful in penetrating Western European markets at once substantially improved their relative positions.

In Hungary, and surprisingly enough in Czechoslovakia as well, on the other hand, existing tendencies were unchanged and well pronounced, though in Czechoslovakia, due to the reasons mentioned above, change took place mainly in 1991.

A further very interesting aspect of industrial restructuring is the short-term changes in labour productivity – or put differently, the differences in the dynamics of output and employment – and relative price changes. As we discussed in the Introduction, the country studies in Part Two uniformly found that, with very few exceptions, during the first phase of industrial restructuring dominated by the overall decline of economic activities, that is during the period one could observe so far, adjustment in the employment structure took place with considerable delays and to a much lesser extent. Figures 2.10–2.12 corroborate this finding in general, though they do show some exceptions. Unfortunately, these graphs could be compiled only until 1990, so that the major changes that took place in 1991 are not reflected by them.

Figures 2.10–2.12 show that relative price changes, and thus also relative

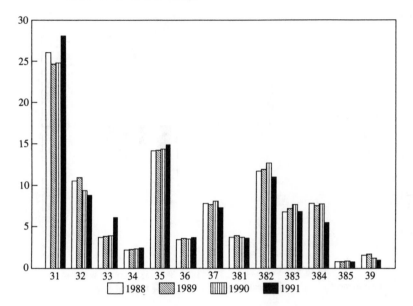

Figure 2.9 Structure of real output in Poland, 1988–91
Notes: Shares of (ISIC 2- and 3-digit) industries in total manufacturing real gross output
(= 100), expressed in percentages. For a description of the ISIC codes used to identify
industries, see the appendix, pp. 68–9.

income positions, were much more substantial than changes in the real
structure. Import liberalisation and (*de facto* or *de jure*) convertibility and
increased competition, partly as a consequence of the former, had a tangible
impact on relative prices and thus dominated the changes in nominal
structures. In Czechoslovakia, these changes mainly took place in 1991, thus
figure 2.10 does not reveal a clear-cut tendency; in Hungary, relative prices
moved clearly in favour of those industries which could increase their exports
to Western European markets. These changes, as shown by the analysis in
chapter 9 by Halpern, show up at the enterprise level, providing exporting
firms with higher than average levels of liquidity and profitability.

Conclusions on structural change

In investigating the structure of manufacturing and its changes for the three
leading reforming countries, Czechoslovakia, Hungary and Poland, this
part of the chapter had two main goals. First, we wanted to show the
differences in the starting positions of these countries in this regard.
Secondly, we aimed at investigating the characteristics and directions of the
structural changes that took place from the beginning of economic
transformation until the end of 1991.

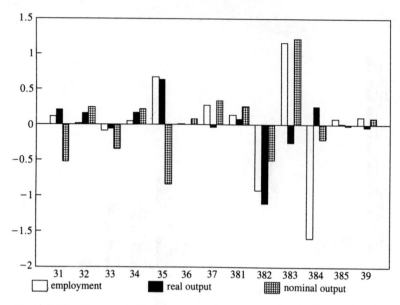

Figure 2.10   Changes in the structure of manufacturing in Czechoslovakia, 1988–90

Notes: Absolute changes in the shares of (ISIC 2- and 3-digit) industries in total manufacturing employment, real and nominal gross output (= 100), respectively, expressed in percentage points. For a description of the ISIC codes used to identify industries, see the appendix, pp. 68–9.

The major finding regarding the starting positions of the three countries is the almost complete lack of structural adjustment in Czechoslovakia during the two decades preceding economic transformation. As a result, her industrial structure became very dissimilar to those of market economies of similar size, openness and factor endowments.

Structural changes in the period 1988–91 were dominated by an unprecedented overall decline in economic activity in the region. For several reasons, this was more pronounced in manufacturing industries than in the rest of the economy. Therefore, what we observe in terms of structural change is the outcome of a rather uneven distribution of decline.

The financial situations of individual firms in an economy undergoing economic transformation is determined not only by the changes resulting from economic transformation, but also by their starting positions. Large SOEs in these countries were typically operating with high gearing ratios. A high gearing ratio makes an enterprise very vulnerable in a period of declining demand even in a well established open market economy. In CEE

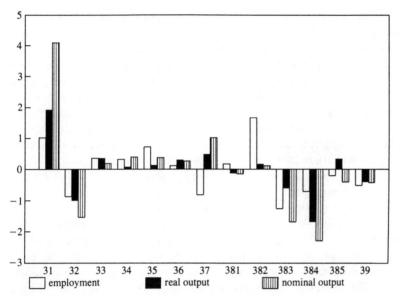

Figure 2.11 Changes in the structure of manufacturing in Hungary, 1988–90

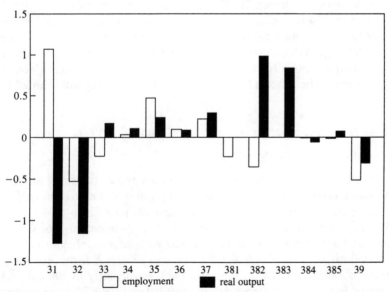

Figure 2.12 Changes in the structure of manufacturing in Poland, 1988–90

Notes: Absolute changes in the shares of (ISIC 2- and 3-digit) industries in total manufacturing employment, real and nominal gross output (= 100), respectively, expressed in percentage points. For a description of the ISIC codes used to identify industries, see the appendix, pp. 68–9.

economies, the situation is further complicated by the fact that the financial system is underdeveloped (see, e.g., Calvo and Frankel, 1991), thus it provides very few instruments for risk sharing. Though in the absence of industrial policy, these decisions are asked and answered for the individual enterprises *separately*, as the outcome of this process, the system, in one way or the other, decides the fate of entire industries (and with it, entire regions). The decisions are further delayed and complicated because of the obvious social consequences of closing down firms and industries. In Poland, Hungary, and Slovakia (but not in the Czech part of the former Czechoslovakia), in three years, unemployment, starting, at least officially, from a zero level, has exceeded the European average, which itself is currently rather high.

One also has to point out the fact that privatisation was rather slow during the period under investigation (see, e.g., Gajdka and Hamilton, 1992; Gatsios, 1992; Grosfeld and Hare, 1991; Járai, 1993) and many of the adjustments necessary in the medium to long run were not yet made: we do not know whether what has survived until now will be viable even in the near future. The enterprise-level analyses presented in Halpern's chapter 9 hint at the fact that firms partly used up their capital to cover costs. In investigating enterprise finance in chapter 12, Ábel and Székely argue that for a number of reasons enterprise finance, in particular investment finance, will be a difficult matter for quite some time to come. Thus, though the importance of the 'constructive' part of industrial restructuring, that is, the emergence of new firms and capacities, will certainly gradually increase, the 'destructive' forces will also shape the process for much longer than we originally thought.

Foreign trade specialisation and trade reorientation, 1989–92

Introduction: trade reorientation, 1989–92

In this section we want to analyse the foreign trade structures of CEE economies, both as they were at the starting point of the wave of radical economic transformation and how they have changed since 1989.

We start with an overview of the geographical orientation of CEE's export and import patterns (table 2.3). The reorientation of exports from Eastern Europe to the West had started in most Eastern Europe economies (an exception was Bulgaria) prior to 1989, particularly in Poland and Hungary; however, it accelerated dramatically from 1989. This process has been discussed extensively in the literature (see UN-ECE, 1992, 1993; Rodrik, 1992; Landesmann, 1993a) and we will not reiterate the analysis here; our focus will be on the structural features of this reorientation.

The process of trade reorientation can be decomposed into two

Table 2.3. *Geographical distribution of exports and imports, %, 1980–91*

EXPORTS

	1980	1985	1989	1990	1991
Bulgaria					
ECE–East[a]	54.05[d]	56.16	62.26	53.35	54.94
ECE–West[b]	25.70	17.86	20.45	23.71	26.16
Other[c]	20.11	25.98	17.44	22.94	18.90
Czechoslovakia					
ECE–East	51.62	53.08	46.62	37.00	32.83
ECE–West	34.16	31.66	40.95	51.54	56.93
Other	14.12	15.26	12.43	11.46	10.24
ex-GDR					
ECE–East	53.12	38.15	37.69	35.31	
ECE–West	35.30	51.36	53.94	57.38	
Other	11.58	10.43	8.38	7.32	
Hungary					
ECE–East	50.29	52.30	40.95	31.20	19.16
ECE–West	37.98	34.24	47.98	58.32	70.38
Other	11.73	13.34	11.07	10.47	10.46
Poland					
ECE–East	39.86	46.67	40.83	33.35	16.83
ECE–West	46.60	40.36	47.31	52.21	75.12
Other	13.54	12.97	11.86	14.43	8.05
Romania					
ECE–East	26.36	27.09	24.63	23.85	28.24
ECE–West	46.85	45.23	52.48	56.89	48.94
Other	26.79	27.68	22.90	19.47	22.82
Eastern Europe					
ECE–East	45.69	44.62	41.31	36.69	25.54
ECE–West	38.55	39.19	45.81	52.21	63.02
Other	15.77	16.17	12.88	12.68	11.44
Soviet Union					
ECE–East	30.74	31.56	24.35	18.79	19.78
ECE–West	46.08	41.54	44.05	52.57	59.62
Other	23.18	26.90	31.58	28.63	20.60

Table 2.3. (*cont.*)

IMPORTS

	1980	1985	1989	1990	1991
Bulgaria					
ECE–East[a]	64.72[d]	56.01	45.98	46.24	49.08
ECE–West[b]	27.53	27.87	36.15	35.30	33.95
Other[c]	7.75	16.12	17.87	18.46	16.97
Czechoslovakia					
ECE–East	52.92	49.61	47.83	38.27	37.50
ECE–West	37.66	31.12	40.19	50.47	53.38
Other	9.51	10.47	11.98	11.26	9.12
ex-GDR					
ECE–East	47.65	46.50	34.26	19.94	
ECE–West	42.81	43.67	58.66	74.72	
Other	9.61	9.83	7.02	5.34	
Hungary					
ECE–East	46.90	49.39	39.16	33.76	22.27
ECE–West	42.22	41.69	52.93	54.99	69.08
Other	10.99	8.92	7.79	11.25	8.65
Poland					
ECE–East	40.11	52.83	38.02	33.76	19.00
ECE–West	46.36	36.43	50.77	49.05	70.19
Other	13.53	10.74	11.13	17.12	10.82
Romania					
ECE–East	20.98	32.54	37.39	27.87	23.99
ECE–West	38.52	23.13	17.67	32.51	43.21
Other	40.51	44.33	44.94	39.62	32.80
Eastern Europe					
ECE–East	43.86	49.74	39.91	32.70	26.55
ECE–West	40.50	35.48	46.43	55.02	60.51
Other	15.63	14.78	13.66	14.11	12.93
Soviet Union					
ECE–East	31.14	32.12	26.35	23.15	19.31
ECE–West	46.86	44.34	51.31	54.46	60.82
Other	22.00	23.56	22.35	22.38	19.86

Notes:
[a] ECE-East: Soviet Union and former European members of CMEA.
[b] ECE-West: ECE market economies plus Japan.
[c] Other: all remaining countries.
[d] Values of intra-Eastern trade were adjusted by using a common rouble-dollar cross rate.
Source: UN–ECE, *Economic Survey of Europe in 1992–1993*, (1993), appendix tables C.4 and C.5; own calculations.

components: (1) the sharp *contraction of trade links between CMEA countries*; and, (2) the *growth of trade with the West*. As regards the sharp contraction of trade flows between the ex-CMEA economies, the shift from 'transferable rouble' trade to trade contracted in convertible currencies has been cited as one important factor. This, together with the dissolution of 'planned trade' links and the general liberalisation of trade with the West (from the Western as well as the Eastern side) allowed a reallocation of exports and of imports according to the wishes of producers and consumers who became largely independent from the direct control by central authorities. Additionally, of course, the contraction of domestic demand in the East reinforced by strong intercountry multiplier effects contributed substantially to the decline of trade links between the ex-CMEA trading partners. The sharp fall in export demand from other ex-CMEA countries was experienced rather uniformly by all the CEE economies, with its impact upon the different national economies becoming a function of their initial geographical trade dependence. The second factor, the growth of exports to the West, took place with significant differentiation across the different CEE economies. As we will see, Poland and Hungary reacted most quickly to the export opportunities opening up in the West (and to the pressures from falling demand from the East), being the first to liberalise their relationship (trade and currency) with the West. Czechoslovakia followed with roughly a year's lag but experienced, over the three-year period 1989–92, similar overall growth in exports to the West as did Hungary and Poland. Bulgaria, most deeply affected by the fall in demand from the USSR, also increased its exports to the West substantially. The precise structural features of this export growth to the West, and to the EC in particular, which quickly became the dominant group of trading partners for the newly emerging market economies of eastern Europe, will be discussed below.

An important aspect of CEE economies' trade relationships in the past was the *'dual structure'* of their trade links with other CMEA countries on the one hand (and the USSR in particular) and with Western (mostly advanced) market economies on the other. This 'dual structure' of trade relationships results from the well known feature that most CEE economies (with the exception of the USSR) had the characteristics of advanced economies in their relations with each other (i.e. selling and buying industrially advanced products to/from each other involving a considerable amount of intra-industry trade) but not in relation to the USSR while trade relations with the West were (and still are) of a type more typical for developing economies (i.e. exporting relatively raw-material-intensive products and importing industrially more processed, higher value added products). The 'dual' structure is clearly visible from table 2.4 which (in

Table 2.4. *Structure of exports and imports, and export growth to EC, 1989–92*

Czechoslovakia

NACE		Exp Composition 1987			Exp Growth to EC 1989–92[b]	Struct of Exp to EC		Tot EC Exp[c] 1990	Struct of Imps from EC		Tot EC Imps[d] 1990
		Exp West	Exp EE6[a]	Exp USSR		1989	1991		1989	1991	
21	Metals Ex.	16.08	7.29	4.46	−0.28	0.36	0.12	0.14	0.44	0.10	0.03
(21+)22	Metals (Ex.)&Pr.	1.05	0.49	0	0.25	14.82	13.06	6.64	3.57	3.66	2.84
23	Minerals Extr.	5.13	4.4	2.42	0.18	1.62	1.23	0.30	0.29	0.53	0.11
24	Minerals Manuf.				0.33	6.81	7.70	2.30	1.71	1.51	1.75
25	Chemicals	13.75	8.98	4.88	0.17	13.37	12.60	12.28	20.45	12.16	12.61
26	Man-made Fibres	0.44	0.87	0.26	0.28	1.00	0.99	0.47	0.76	0.44	0.23
31	Metal Products	1.22	2.71	1.08	0.63	2.41	5.15	3.61	2.44	3.10	3.15
32	Mech. Eng.	13.95	29.35	34.61	0.28	7.83	8.99	13.36	32.20	27.96	17.48
33	Office Mach.	0.3	2.02	2.75	0.70	0.11	0.15	3.44	3.51	4.73	2.51
34	Elect. Eng.	3.42	10.76	6.11	0.45	3.50	4.74	10.11	9.72	12.01	9.46
35	Motor Veh.	3.04	15.08	10.03	0.43	4.70	6.75	11.83	1.99	5.23	7.88
36	Other Transp. Equ.	1.78	4.42	11.64	0.48	0.63	2.07	4.59	0.34	3.96	5.01
37	Instru. Eng.	0.15	2.64	1.45	0.38	0.37	0.45	1.78	2.28	2.26	1.84
41(+42)	Food, Drink & Tob.	6.85	1.06	1.04	−0.08	6.17	3.00	6.78	7.19	4.44	8.77
42	Dr. & Tobacco				0.23	0.72	0.91	1.50	0.34	0.81	2.59
43	Textiles	8.27	2.42	2.41	0.28	5.62	5.84	2.45	4.10	5.48	9.55
44	Leather	0.11	0.04	0	0.38	0.82	1.00	0.64	0.26	0.73	0.73
45	Footwear & Clothing	5.38	1.95	11.18	0.39	6.76	8.78	3.26	0.95	1.80	2.70
46	Timber & Wooden Fu.	7.68	0.79	2.84	0.16	9.41	6.50	1.75	0.62	1.02	0.92
47	Paper	5.5	1.16	0.36	0.12	6.41	4.19	3.10	1.50	2.22	2.96
48	Rubber & Plas.	1.21	1.42	0.54	0.28	3.06	2.89	3.55	2.37	2.83	3.53
49	Other Manuf.	4.63	2.19	1.96	0.26	3.48	2.91	6.13	2.96	3.02	3.37
	Manuf.	100	100	100	0.28	100	100	100	100.00	100.00	100.00

Poland

NACE		Exp Composition 1987			Exp Growth to EC 1989–92[b]	Struct of Exp to EC		Tot EC Exp[c] 1990	Struct of Imps from EC		Tot EC Imps[d] 1990
		Exp West	Exp EE6[a]	Exp USSR		1989	1991		1989	1991	
21	Metals Ex.				0.60	0.13	0.25	0.14	0.14	0.03	0.03
(21+)22	Metals (Ex.)&Pr.	18.05	7.13	5.4	0.21	17.89	15.99	6.64	6.23	2.84	2.84
23	Minerals Extr.	3.42	3.96	2.15	0.88	0.13	0.53	0.30	0.19	0.11	0.11
24	Minerals Manuf.	2.59	1.63	0.3	0.33	2.74	3.76	2.30	1.53	1.75	1.75
25	Chemicals	10.93	4.6	13.21	0.19	10.15	11.62	12.28	17.53	12.61	12.61
26	Man-made Fibres	0.08	0.32	0.02	0.34	0.31	0.32	0.47	0.54	0.23	0.23
31	Metal Products	3.77	5.19	3.8	0.41	4.09	5.96	3.61	2.50	3.15	3.15
32	Mech. Eng.	5.94	33.35	19.63	0.21	5.17	5.34	13.36	25.09	17.48	17.48
33	Office Mach.	0.27	4.82	5.81	0.39	0.04	0.06	3.44	1.39	2.51	2.51
34	Elect. Eng.	5.06	12.73	12.26	0.16	5.27	3.93	10.11	7.25	9.46	9.46
35	Motor Veh.	4.21	8.07	5.69	0.24	4.54	1.58	11.83	3.34	7.88	7.88
36	Other Transp. Equ.	6.75	6.96	13.81	0.28	1.31	1.36	4.59	0.19	5.01	5.01
37	Instru. Eng.	0.52	3.73	2.08	0.20	0.36	0.37	1.78	1.91	1.84	1.84
41(+42)	Food, Drink & Tob.	14.68	1.78	3.13	0.08	17.32	12.89	6.78	10.38	8.77	8.77
42	Drink & Tobacco	6.85	1.06	1.04	0.05	0.15	0.10	1.50	2.06	2.59	2.59
43	Textiles	4.69	1.8	1.4	0.31	2.98	3.36	2.45	9.23	9.55	9.55
44	Leather	0.15	0	0	0.39	0.63	0.92	0.64	0.48	0.73	0.73
45	Footwear & Clothing	8.86	1.39	8.01	0.33	13.08	16.23	3.26	1.79	2.70	2.70
46	Timber & Wooden Fu.	6.47	0.4	1.73	0.33	8.96	10.68	1.75	0.29	0.92	0.92
47	Paper	1.5	0.34	0.27	0.30	1.38	1.36	3.10	1.63	2.96	2.96
48	Rubber & Plastic	0.67	0.65	0.51	0.32	1.26	1.31	3.55	3.18	3.53	3.53
49	Other Manuf.	1.4	1.15	0.8	0.29	2.09	2.11	6.13	3.13	3.37	3.37
	Manuf.	100	100	100	0.25	100	100	100	100	100.00	100.00

Table 2.4 (*cont.*)

Hungary

NACE		Exp Composition 1987			Exp Growth to EC 1989–92[b]	Struct of Exp to EC		Tot EC Exp[c] 1990	Struct of Imps from EC		Tot EC Imps[d] 1990
		Exp West	Exp EE6[a]	Exp USSR		1989	1991		1989	1991	
21	Metals Ex.				0.04	0.13	0.02	0.14	0.17	0.08	0.03
(21+)22	Metals (Ex.)&Pr.	11.72	9.21	6.29	−0.01	10.82	7.06	6.64	5.48	3.46	2.84
23	Minerals Extr.	0.22	0.21	0.01	0.05	0.09	0.08	0.30	0.14	0.14	0.11
24	Minerals Manuf.	3.13	1.98	0.89	0.22	2.24	2.76	2.30	2.14	2.05	1.75
25	Chemicals	20.89	17.28	15.97	0.13	11.88	11.46	12.28	18.87	15.25	12.61
26	Man-made Fibres	0	0	0	0.13	0.46	0.47	0.47	1.24	0.65	0.23
31	Metal Products	2.73	3.5	2.85	0.32	3.13	4.70	3.61	2.85	3.99	3.15
32	Mech. Eng.	4.19	28.64	22.11	0.21	6.35	8.55	13.36	22.78	20.68	17.48
33	Office Mach.	0	0	0	0.59	0.17	0.22	3.44	1.68	2.63	2.51
34	Elect. Eng.	0.85	3.15	0.67	0.29	7.64	9.32	10.11	11.38	10.11	9.46
35	Motor Veh.	0.14	0.67	0.42	0.57	0.98	1.63	11.83	5.17	8.28	7.88
36	Other Transp. Equ.	0.14	0.67	0.42	0.25	0.18	0.50	4.59	0.63	0.42	5.01
37	Instru. Eng.	0	0	0	0.38	0.38	0.56	1.78	2.18	2.25	1.84
41(+42)	Food, Drink & Tob.	25.01	18.16	27.92	0.04	22.52	18.92	6.78	2.99	2.56	8.77
42	Drink & Tobacco	6.85	1.06	1.04	−0.18	0.16	0.05	1.50	0.46	0.55	2.59
43	Textiles	7.06	3.44	3.81	0.19	5.31	5.74	2.45	10.02	11.79	9.55
44	Leather	1.74	0.99	0.41	0.12	1.50	1.44	0.64	2.39	2.86	0.73
45	Footwear & Clothing	11.79	4.47	12.91	0.20	15.70	16.36	3.26	2.42	4.14	2.70
46	Timber & Wooden Fu.	4.84	1.45	0.91	0.22	3.94	4.46	1.75	0.50	1.17	0.92
47	Paper	1.31	0.98	0.75	0.20	1.11	1.11	3.10	2.78	3.08	2.96
48	Rubber & Plastic	2.12	2.32	1.3	0.16	2.77	2.74	3.55	3.35	3.37	3.53
49	Other Manuf.	2.13	2.87	2.36	0.10	2.54	1.87	6.13	0.38	0.49	3.37
	Manuf.	100	100	100	0.16	100	100	100	100	100	100

[a] Composition of exports to the European CMEA excluding USSR.
[b] Annual growth rates.

columns (1)–(3)) gives an industrial breakdown of exports to Western market economies, the EE-6 and the USSR in 1987. Here we can see that the three CEE economies (CSFR, Hungary, and Poland) were involved in a fair amount of *interindustry specialisation* in their export links with both the West and the CMEA. However, export specialisation patterns (as shown by the commodity breakdown of exports) was distinctly different in trade with CMEA trading partners than with Western trading partners (there are some exceptions to this such as the prominence of food exports in Hungary's exports to both groups of countries).[5]

An important question in the light of developments since 1989 is whether there is a tendency of this 'dual' structure to merge, i.e. whether, in due course, a CEE economy will occupy a unified position in the international division of labour in both trade with Western and with other ex-CMEA countries. If the answer is 'yes', what will this more unified trade position look like? Will it take on the features of trade relations typical for industrially advanced economies (as used to be the case in intra-CMEA trade before 1989) or will it have the features of a less developed economy (as was traditionally the case for CEE's trade relations with the West)? An answer to this question would require a careful analysis both of recent trade flows amongst ex-CMEA countries and of the trade links with Western trading partners. We will not attempt this here since the database concerning intra-(ex-) CMEA trade flows after 1989 is extremely unreliable (often non-existent and fraught with valuation problems). Instead, we will examine rather carefully the recent pattern of growth of exports to and imports from the West or, more particularly, to/from the European Community. For these trade flows we have rather detailed information which, being collected by the EC as reporting trading area, is – in the current circumstances – rather more reliable than the information on trade supplied by the CEE countries themselves (see, however, the country studies in Part Two which mostly use CEE-supplied information on trade). Apart from the data problem there is of course the problem that longer-run tendencies might not be deducible from the short span of data available for developments since 1989.

Quality indicators of CEE countries' exports to the EC

Before analysing export and import growth patterns since 1989 we want to show some additional features of CEE's export performance to the West prior to 1989 (we focus on exports to the EC). Table 2.5 presents a number of *quality indicators* for two broad industry groups, Mechanical Engineering (NACE 32) and Electrical Engineering (NACE 34). These quality indicators were calculated from detailed trade statistics so that information about 480 commodities (in the case of Mechanical Engineering) and 254

Table 2.5 *Quality indicators of East European exports to EC markets, 1977 and 1987*

Mechanical Engineering (NACE 32) – 480 products

		Germany	Hungary	Poland	Czecho-slovakia	Italy	Austria	EFTA
Sh(%)[a]	1977	35.5	0.1	0.4	0.4	10.3	2.2	16.1
	1987	34.3	0.2	0.1	0.2	12.4	3.8	19.7
QP	1977	1.000	0.528	0.612	0.587	0.793	0.928	1.112
	1987	1.000	0.421	0.353	0.417	0.829	0.933	1.109
QV	1987	1.000	0.877	0.802	0.612	0.940	0.952	0.775
QS	1987	1.000	0.799	0.713	0.584	1.027	0.965	0.961
dQP	77–87	0.987	0.738	0.569	0.701	1.032	0.993	0.985
dQV	77–87	1.852	1.875	1.499	1.392	1.895	1.845	2.059
dQS	77–87	1.394	1.291	1.062	1.098	1.445	1.338	1.557

Electrical Engineering (NACE 34) – 254 products

		Germany	Hungary	Poland	Czecho-slovakia	Italy	Austria	EFTA
Sh(%)	1977	30.7	0.4	0.3	0.3	10.5	3.5	12.2
	1987	29.7	0.2	0.2	0.2	10.7	3.6	18.0
QP	1977	1.000	0.319	0.422	0.327	0.794	0.925	1.076
	1987	1.000	0.591	0.480	0.497	0.825	1.050	1.103
QV	1987	1.000	0.609	1.010	1.123	2.010	0.737	0.544
QS	1987	1.000	0.444	0.531	0.601	0.952	0.874	1.261
dQP	77–87	0.924	1.711	1.053	1.404	0.961	1.049	0.947
dQV	77–87	2.276	1.509	1.511	1.528	1.858	3.264	2.123
dQS	77–87	1.633	1.062	0.982	1.190	1.312	1.512	1.851

Note:

[a] Sh(%) refers to the country's market share (in percent) in total EC imports inclusive of intra-EC trade in that industry category.

Source: Eurostat, Detailed Trade Data; see text for method of calculation.

commodities (in the case of Electrical Engineering) were used. The exact definitions of the various quality indicators are given in the appendix, pp. 69–70, but here is a short description of their meaning:

QP_j^c reveals the relative *price gap* of the different commodity items in a country's commodity basket relative to the respective price leader in each commodity market;

these price gaps are weighted by the respective shares of the different commodities in a country C's exports of industry j.

QV_j^c shows the relative composition of a country C industry j's exports towards high or low *volume growth* items in the EC's traded goods markets, and

QS_j^c does the same as QV_j^c but with respect to high or low *value growth* items.

All the above 'quality' indicators have been normalised in relation to Germany (= 100). The additional variables dQP, dQV and dQS represent, respectively, changes of the above indicators over the period 1977–87. They thus reflect whether compositional changes between 1977 and 1987 were in the direction of fast/slow growing traded product markets (in volume, dQV, and value, dQS, terms) or whether the weighted price gap to the price leader (in each traded product market) has been closed or has grown (dQP).

The results presented in table 2.5 are quite revealing. They show:

(i) That there was, according to most indicators, a considerable gap between Germany and the Eastern European countries. That gap was considerable with respect to each of the indicators examined except (in some instances) with respect to QV which is the indicator for the orientation towards high volume growth areas in traded products; however, the gap was large with respect to QS which indicates the orientation towards high growth areas in value terms. The price gap (indicator QP) also remained high over the period 1977–87 although it has closed somewhat for electrical engineering products where it had started from an even lower level than in mechanical engineering. For comparative purposes, we also include information about Italy, Austria and the group of EFTA countries in these tables, which shows that, concerning most indicators, these countries have closed their gap with Germany and, where no gap existed in the first place, have maintained pace with Germany.

(ii) There are considerable differences between the different Eastern/Central European economies: in many ways Hungary was by 1987 more favourably placed than the other two Eastern/Central European economies. In some cases, Hungary started from a lower base in 1977 than the other two economies, but improved more rapidly. This is particularly the case when one considers the value growth (QS) or the price gap (QP) indicators.

(iii) As an aside, we can also see the tiny market share positions (Sh% in table 2.5) CEE economies occupied in EC markets (say, in comparison to Austria) and even these were declining in most cases over the decade 1977–87.

Table 2.6 returns to the calculations of quality indicators for a wider range of engineering industries (NACE 31–37) over the years 1988–91. It is

Table 2.6. *Quality (price) gaps and market shares for engineering industries, 1988–91*

	Quality Indicators				Market shares in EC markets[a]			
	EC-6	Poland	Czecho-slovakia	Hungary	EC-6	Poland	Czecho-slovakia	Hungary
NACE 31 (Metal Products)								
1988	1	0.49	0.639	0.598	88	69.75	0.4	0.23	0.3
1989	1	0.506	0.561	0.566	89	69.76	0.43	0.24	0.27
1990	1	0.464	0.547	0.589	90	69.99	0.67	0.29	0.39
1991	1	0.492	0.512	0.546	91	68.49	0.91	0.64	0.45
NACE 32 (Mechanical Engineering)								
1988	1	0.385	0.489	0.564	88	64.42	0.13	0.18	0.11
1989	1	0.515	0.478	0.566	89	63.65	0.14	0.17	0.13
1990	1	0.366	0.477	0.497	90	63.81	0.21	0.19	0.18
1991	1	0.384	0.447	0.533	91	63.3	0.25	0.26	0.26
NACE 33 (Office Machinery)								
1988	1	0.263		0.193	88	46.23	0	0	0.01
1989	1	0.596	0.274	0.435	89	47.3	0	0.01	0.01
1990	1	0.54	0.375	0.326	90	48.81	0	0	0.01
1991	1	0.616	0.306	0.207	91	48.27	0	0.01	0.01
NACE 34 (Electrical Engineering)								
1988	1	0.382	0.442	0.514	88	51.43	0.15	0.09	0.13
1989	1	0.431	0.473	0.517	89	51.07	0.17	0.08	0.14
1990	1	0.458	0.399	0.607	90	52.71	0.26	0.09	0.19
1991	1	0.565	0.587	0.653	91	50.91	0.19	0.14	0.24
NACE 35 (Motor Vehicles)								
1988	1	0.495	0.413	0.445	88	73.45	0.18	0.1	0.01
1989	1	0.513	0.468	0.522	89	72.15	0.14	0.11	0.01
1990	1	0.512	0.477	0.461	90	72.17	0.09	0.11	0.02
1991	1	0.47	0.523	0.524	91	69.74	0.07	0.25	0.03
NACE 36 (Other Transp. Equ.)								
1988	1	1.019	0.282	1.408	88	44.38	0.59	0.06	0.02
1989	1	1.049	0.468	0.082	89	43.38	0.16	0.05	0.02
1990	1	1.3	0.329	0.141	90	44.66	0.17	0.04	0.03
1991	1	0.513	0.616	0.804	91	45.82	0.21	0.21	0.06
NACE 37 (Instru. Eng.)								
1988	1	0.451	0.427	0.433	88	46.03	0.05	0.05	0.04
1989	1	0.355	0.527	0.354	89	45.8	0.05	0.05	0.03
1990	1	0.35	0.334	0.462	90	46.79	0.07	0.04	0.03
1991	1	0.484	0.397	0.62	91	46.33	0.08	0.07	0.06

Note:
[a] Market shares refer to percentage shares in total EC imports (including extra-EC trade).

Table 2.7. *Factor intensity analysis of Czechoslovakia's trading structure with the EC – Regressions of Czechoslovakia's trade specialisation factor intensities*[a]

Dep. Variable Regressors	Sp_m^c		Sp_x^c		X/M^d	
	1991	1990	1991	1990	1991	1990
K/L	−0.234	−0.109	−0.351	−.0205	−0.193	0.065
	(0.103)[b]	(0.08)	(0.512)	(0.546)	(0.272)	(0.713)
L/Q	0.134	0.077	0.338	0.292	0.171	0.021
	(0.055)	(0.041)	(0.270)	(0.289)	(0.199)	(0.379)
R&D	−0.163	−0.154	−0.520	−0.559	−0.441	−0.779
	(0.08)	(0.059)	(0.392)	(0.417)	(0.205)	(0.544)
Skill	−0.062	−0.066	−0.278	−0.304	−0.233	−0.425
	(0.023)	(0.017)	(0.113)	(0.121)	(0.057)	(0.157)
Energy	0.125	0.191	0.027	0.027	0.354	0.567
	(0.101)	(0.075)	(0.490)	(0.521)	(0.257)	(0.677)

Number of cross-section observations: 85
Degrees of freedom: 83

Notes:
[a] The table reports coefficient estimates of regressions with each of the factor intensity measures introduced individually as regressors (plus an intercept term).
[b] Standard errors.
[c] Sp_m and Sp_x refer to specialisation indices of Czechoslovakia's exports to the EC relative to the EC's import and export structure respectively.
[d] X/M refer to trade coverage ratios.
Source: The factor intensity measures were supplied by Eurostat and refer to relative factor intensities in EC industries; see appendix, pp. 70–1 for precise definition.

interesting to see that while market shares in EC markets of CEE producers have substantially increased in a number of important engineering industries, quality indicator QP which measures the weighted 'price gap' relative to EC producers has not improved.[6] We will come back to this feature of recent developments later on.

Factor intensity analysis of Czechoslovak exports

In the following we complement the quality analysis with another exercise which shows that CEE's current export structure (and the specialisation structure in general in relation to the EC) is heavily biased against skill- and R&D-intensive industries. This conforms to the view stated above concerning the 'dual' structure of trade relations which characterised CEE economies.

Table 2.7 gives the results of a simple regression analysis (reproduced

Table 2.8. *Czechoslovakia's export structure and the EC's export and import structures in terms of R&D and skill intensity of different industrial branches*

	Coefficient estimates[a]	
Shares of industries in Czech exports to the EC		
f(R&D intensity of industries)	−0.056	(0.051)[b]
f(Skill intensity of industries)	−0.035	(0.015)
Shares of industries in total EC exports		
f(R&D intensity of industries)	0.161	(0.048)
f(Skill intensity of industries)	0.024	(0.015)
Shares of industries in total EC imports		
f(R&D intensity of industries)	0.160	(0.048)
f(Skill intensity of industries)	0.030	(0.015)

Notes: [a] Regressions have been estimated on the sample of 85 3-digit NACE industries with 83 degrees of freedom.
[b] Standard errors.

from Landesmann, 1993b) carried out for Czechoslovakia relating various trade specialisation indices to factor intensity measures. The most consistent results are the significant *negative relationships* obtained for Czechoslovakia's trade structure in relation to the EC (measured by two specialisation indices and the trade coverage ratios) and the R&D and skill intensity of these industries. Similar results were obtained by Rosati (1993a) for Poland, Dobrinsky (1993) for Bulgaria and Gacs (1993) for Hungary.

The results in table 2.8 concerning the low skill and R&D intensity of Czechoslovakia's exports and trade specialisation in general *vis-à-vis* the EC is reinforced by a comparison of Czechoslovakia's export and the EC's export and import structure in terms of their bias towards or against R&D- and skill-intensive branches. From table 2.8 we can see that while EC export and import structures are (significantly) biased towards a high representation of R&D- and skill-intensive branches, Czechoslovakia's composition of exports to the EC is negatively related to R&D and skill intensity (only the latter is significant here).

Tables 2.9 and 2.10 present comparative estimates of the factor intensity model as an explanation of export specialisation (defined, as before, as the structure of a CEE country's exports to the EC compared to that of overall EC imports) in order to analyse factor-intensity biases. The estimates (only the significant estimates are presented in table 2.9) – this time undertaken in

Table 2.9. *Export specialisation analysed by factor intensities: summary of significant coefficients in cross-section regressions*[a]

	K/L	L/Q	R&D	Skill	Energy	R^2
1992	-1.090			-2.532	1.061	0.412
1991	-1.43			-2.0333	1.080	0.332
1990	-0.767^b			-1.607	0.853	0.297
1989	-0.614^b			-1.712	0.764	0.274
1992 wo. sk.[c]	-1.557				1.323	0.331
1991 wo. sk.	-1.518				1.291	0.290
1990 wo. sk.	-1.063		-0.273		1.019	0.269
1989 wo. sk.	-0.930^b		-0.240		.941	0.238

Hungary

	K/L	L/Q	R&D	Skill	energy	R^2
1992	-1.787^b	-0.572^b		-2.244	0.397^b	0.174
1991	-1.480	-1.030		-1.608	0.780	0.217
1990	-1.257	-1.010		-1.935	0.740	0.252
1989	-1.282	-1.483		-2.404	0.676	0.250
1992 wo. sk.	-1.201		-0.144^b		0.629	0.112
1991 wo. sk.	-1.777		-0.179^b		0.946	0.189
1990 wo. sk.	-1.614		-0.256		0.940	0.211
1989 wo. sk.	-1.725		-0.216		0.924	0.189

the context of a full multivariate regression model – confirm the results previously obtained for Czechoslovakia: they show clearly the positive bias in export specialisation in the direction of energy-intensive exports, and negative biases away from capital-, skill-, R&D- intensive exports; in the case of Hungary and Poland there was also a negative bias against labour-intensive exports, although that bias significantly weakened in 1992. In order to overcome the potential multicollinearity problem of strong correlation between the R&D and skill intensities, the model was estimated twice, once with and once without the skill-intensity variable (wo. sk.); in the latter case the negative bias against R&D- intensive exports emerged clearly.

While the model has rather strong explanatory power in explaining export specialisation between CEE economies and the EC, an attempt to estimate the same type of model to explain export specialisation between a number of EFTA economies (Austria, Switzerland and Sweden) was rather

Table 2.9. (*cont.*)

Poland

	K/L	L/Q	R&D	Skill	Energy	R^2
1992	−1.692	−0.689[b]		−2.448	1.047	0.444
1991	−1.792	−1.226		−2.338	1.094	0.530
1990	−1.688	−1.084		−2.408	1.089	0.495
1989	−1.428	−0.755[b]		−2.114	0.935	0.419
1992 wo. sk.	−2.144		−0.242		1.300	0.378
1991 wo. sk.	−2.223	−1.095	−0.289		1.335	0.457
1990 wo. sk.	−2.132		−0.278		1.338	0.422
1989 wo. sk.	−1.822		−0.324		1.516	0.365

Notes:
Estimates of this type for Austria, Switzerland and Sweden give the following results:
Austria: no significant coefficients.
Switzerland: weakly significant positive coefficients for specialisation in R&D- and energy-intensive exports.
Sweden: significant positive coefficients for specialisation in R&D- and energy-intensive exports
CSFR
[a] Degrees of freedom in these regressions: 79 (specification in logarithms).
[b] These coefficients were insignificant but were left in table 2.9 so that these values could be compared with other years.
[c] Estimates without skill-intensity variable, to avoid multicollinearity (see text).

unsuccessful with very few coefficients turning out to be significant. This confirms the idea that the factor-intensity model can have rather strong explanatory power to explain interindustry trade specialisation between economies which have fundamentally different production structures, factor endowments and different technological capabilities, but has rather little to offer towards the analysis of trade patterns between countries which have reached a rather similar developmental state. Hence one can expect that the factor-intensity model will remain powerful for some time to come to explain trade patterns between CEE economies and their Western European counterparts as long as their developmental state, technological capabilities and factor endowments differ in a significant way, but that the explanatory power of this type of framework will decline if and as a successful catching-up process takes place.

Adjustment of import and export structures, 1989–92

We now turn to developments in 1989–92. The first interesting fact was a dramatic *asymmetry in the adjustment processes of import and export structures* of CEE economies from and to the EC.

Figure 2.13 shows the developments of each CEE's export and import structure relative to the EC's import and export structure respectively over the period 1989–92. The charts thus show whether an industry in a CEE economy's export (import) structure to/from the EC is overrepresented (> 0.0) or underrepresented (< 0.0) when compared to overall EC imports (exports).

A number of interesting features emerge from these graphs:

(i) The initial deviation of *import* structures from the EC relative to the structure of overall EC exports is much greater than the initial deviation of CEE's export structure to the EC from the general structure of EC imports (notice the difference in the overall dimensions of the bars). We can see that CEE imports from the EC in 1989 were highly biased in the direction of imports of chemicals (25), mechanical engineering (32) and textiles (43). There was a gross underrepresentation of cars (35) and other transport equipment (36) and, to a lesser degree, of computing equipment (33) and a variety of light industrial and consumer goods (45–49) as compared to what the world would generally import from the EC. This confirms the view that, prior to liberalisation in Eastern Europe, imports from the West were largely meant to supply production inputs (machinery, chemicals) while imports of consumer goods (particularly durable consumer goods) were neglected.

On the *export* side, what is particularly remarkable is the strong underrepresentation of engineering products in CEE exports to the EC compared to what the EC would generally import from the RoW. Overrepresented were metals (22), minerals (24) and metal products (31); food (41,42a) in the case of Hungary and Poland and drinks (42b, largely accounted for by beer, 427) in the case of Czechoslovakia, as well as footwear and clothing (45) and timber and timber products (46). This picture agrees with the previously stated view that CEE countries largely exported raw-material-intensive products and – to some extent – traditional labour-intensive products or products which require inherited craft skills (such as in brewing).

(ii) The *adjustment of the structure of imports* from the EC after 1989 was much more dramatic than the adjustment of the structure of exports to the EC The 'overrepresentation' of chemical and engineering products in CEE imports from the EC shrank dramatically in all the three

Figure 2.13 Export and import structure to/from the EC compared with the EC's total export and import structure, 1989–92

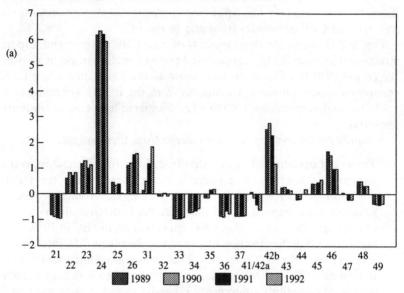

(a)

| | 21 | 23 | 25 | 31 | 33 | 35 | 37 | 42b | 44 | 46 | 48 |
| | 22 | 24 | 26 | 32 | 34 | 36 | 41/42a | 43 | 45 | 47 | 49 |

■ 1989   ▨ 1990   ■ 1991   ▨ 1992

Czechoslovakia, export structure to the EC compared with total import structure of the EC

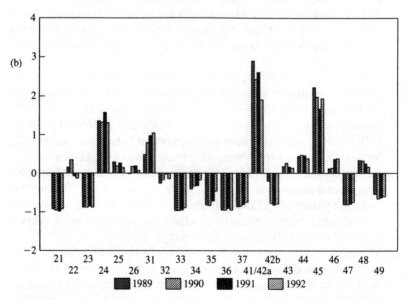

(b)

| | 21 | 23 | 25 | 31 | 33 | 35 | 37 | 42b | 44 | 46 | 48 |
| | 22 | 24 | 26 | 32 | 34 | 36 | 41/42a | 43 | 45 | 47 | 49 |

■ 1989   ▨ 1990   ■ 1991   ▨ 1992

Czechoslovakia, import structure from the EC compared to total EC export structure

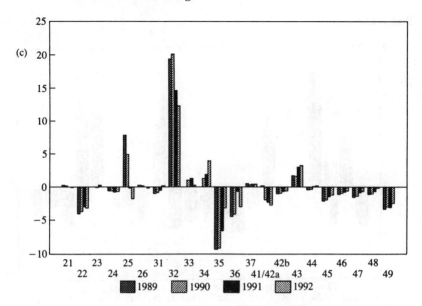

Hungary, export structure to the EC compared with total EC import structure

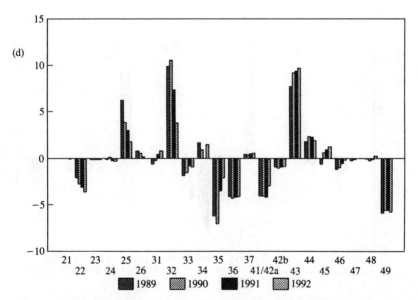

Hungary, import structure from the EC compared with total EC export structure

Figure 2.13 (*cont.*)

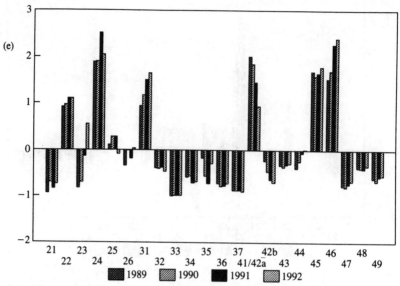

Poland, export structure to the EC compared with total EC import structure

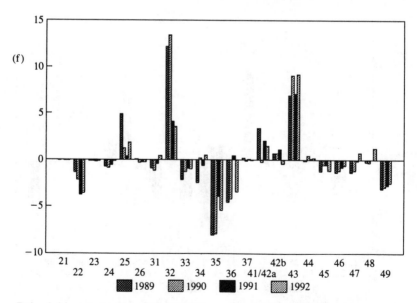

Poland, import structure from the EC compared with total EC export structure

Table 2.10. *Distance measures of CEE countries' export (import) structures to/from the EC relative to overall EC import (export) structures*

	CEE exports rel. to overall EC imports				CEE imports rel. to overall EC exports			
	1989	1990	1991	1992	1989	1990	1991	1992
Poland	4.705[a]	4.692	4.936	4.757	3.973	4.073	2.271	2.763
Hungary	5.101	4.601	4.528	4.063	3.817	3.969	3.353	3.000
Czechoslovakia	3.623	3.709	3.492	3.487	5.154	5.092	3.700	3.214

Note:
The distance measure used is the same as that used in the industry production structure comparisons on p. 28 and p. 32 of this chapter; see the appendix, pp. 68–9 for precise definition.

CEE economies while the 'underrepresentation' of cars (35) and other transport equipment (36) similarly declined dramatically and various light industrial and consumer goods also increased their shares. The overall measures of similarity between CEE import structures from the EC and overall EC export structures show a dramatic process of convergence particularly for Czechoslovakia and Poland (table 2.10).

On the *export* side, there is much less dramatic adjustment (remember again the difference in the dimensions of the import and export boxes), but there is evidence of some loss of traditional specialisation patterns which characterised CEE-EC trade links: examples are the decline to a certain extent of the strong specialisation of Hungary and Poland on food exports to the EC (EC protection might have played an important role here) and of beer from Czechoslovakia; the representation of chemical exports to the EC is also declining following the loss of cheap oil supplies from the ex-USSR. However, there is also evidence that CEE countries' specialisation in the exports of metals (22) from Czechoslovakia and Poland and of minerals (24) from all three CEE countries is being maintained or even further strengthened; footwear and clothing (45) are also in this position. In the engineering branches the picture is somewhat differentiated, with Czechoslovakia and Hungary partly closing the specialisation gap relative to overall EC engineering imports while the gap for Poland is increasing. We return to these intercountry differences below.

Recent export growth and short-, medium- and longer-run trade specialisation

In an attempt to analyse the structure of recent export growth performance we want to distinguish the following three factors:

(i) The potential beginning of a convergence towards an export structure to the EC more similar to that of other Western European economies which would imply higher/lower growth rates of those exports which were in the past underrepresented or overrepresented in CEE countries' export structure relative to those in comparative Western European economies.

(ii) The impact of high/low relative 'quality/price gaps' of different CEE industries relative to EC standards. The conjecture could be that industries which have a lower 'quality gap' initially could expand more easily their exports to the West in the short run; in the longer run, however, a higher technology/quality gap could lead to higher catching-up growth rates as (and if) such gaps are being closed.

(iii) The historical heritage of large excess capacities (often also of high levels of inventories) in those industries which, in the past, exported predominantly to the ex-CMEA markets (and the USSR in particular) and thus experienced a particularly severe contraction of export sales; the pressure to expand export sales to the West was consequently greater.

Table 2.11 reports the results of a simple cross-section regression analysis which attempts to analyse the impact of these three factors upon the recent export growth performance of Czechoslovak industries to the EC.[7]

The results reported in table 2.11 suggest that the recent pattern of export growth is most strongly explained by the availability of large excess capacities (and unsold inventories) in industries which were most strongly oriented towards selling in CMEA markets (see regressions (i) and (v)). There is no evidence that the recent export growth pattern can be explained by the long-run convergence with Western European export patterns to the EC (regression (iv)); the strong export performance of industries in EC markets which were pre-1989 most strongly dependent upon export sales to other CMEA markets was not deterred by the relatively high 'quality gap' which exists in these industries relative to EC competitors. The situation has changed more recently: the same type of cross-section analysis for the year 1991–2 shows a strong weakening of the relationship between relative export growth rates and previous dependence on sales to CMEA markets.

This analysis of export and import specialisation of CEE economies and

Table 2.11. *Regression results: growth of Czechoslovak exports to the EC, 1989–91, and previous export orientation towards the CMEA and the USSR and price (quality) gap*

	Coefficient estimates	
Export growth 1989–91 f(exports to CMEA/total exports in 1987)	1.28^a $(0.51)^b$	(i)
Export growth 1989–91 f(exports to USSR/exports to CMEA in 1987)	1.15 (0.78)	(ii)
Export growth 1989–91 f(relative quality of Czecho. to EC exports)	−172.5 (55.7)	(iii)
Export growth 1989–91 f(long-run target growth rate^c)	−1.76 (2.35)	(iv)
Export growth 1989–91 f(short-run conversion growth rate^c)	−8.80 (4.01)	(v)

Note: ^{a} Regressions have been estimated on the sample of 20 2-digit NACE industries with 18 degrees of freedom. These were single variable regressions with an intercept term.
^{b} Standard errors in brackets next to coefficient estimates.
^{c} For the definition of the long-run target growth rates and the short-run conversion rates see p. 71, n. 7.

of its evolution since 1989 points to a structure of comparative advantage which did characterise CEE exports to the West in the pre-1989 period and which, in spite of the impact of a complicated system of export subsidies and other governmental interference with exporting activities from CEE countries, will continue to have an impact on CEE-Western trade even after 1989 at least over the short and medium run. However, as we have seen, another factor has had a rather strong impact on the export developments which we observe since 1989 and that is the legacy of rather huge export capacities which were formerly oriented towards exporting to other CEE economies (and the USSR in particular) and which became seriously underemployed as a result of the trade collapse in the ex-CMEA and also the dramatic contraction of domestic demand. Since exports to other ex-CMEA countries were in their composition very different from those exported to the West (the 'dual' structure discussed on p. 43 above) the availability of such large excess capacities (and, in many instances, also of unsold inventories) in industrial branches which, in the past, exported very little to the West, had a dramatic impact upon the pattern of export growth to the West.

How does EC protection affect the structure of CEE exports?

In this section we will use the results of the detailed study by Schumacher and Möbius (1993) to discuss the impact of EC protection on CEE producers. Schumacher and Möbius analysed a variety of tariff and non-tariff barriers (NTBs) which the EC imposed on CEE producers and which are undergoing rather dramatic changes in the wake of the so-called 'Europe Agreements' (for a detailed discussion of the contents of the Europe Agreements see Winters, 1992; Messerlin, 1992; Rollo, 1992; Rollo and Smith, 1993). However, the reduction of trade barriers is being phased in gradually and hence, although barriers will be rather dramatically reduced over the 1990s, the shorter-term dynamic of export growth to the EC will still be affected by the existing protectionist barriers. Furthermore, as barriers are lifted, the impact will be differentiated across the different industries since they initially face different levels of protection.

The data upon which Schumacher and Möbius' analysis of EC trade barriers *vis-à-vis* CEE economies are based are the detailed trade statistics for 8-digit product lines of the Combined Nomenclature of the EC. NTBs comprise quantitative restrictions (QR) such as the MFA and other restraint agreements and 'voluntary' export restraints, as well as other non-tariff barriers (ONTB) such as anti-dumping duties, variable components of duties, etc. QRs are highly concentrated in about 9–11 sectors including steel sectors, artificial fibres, textiles and clothing sectors. Other NTBs affect 22–27 sectors including steel, chemicals, electrical motors, optical instruments, leather products, footwear, fur goods and musical instruments.

Schumacher and Möbius started off by analysing the incidence of different protectionist measures at the 8-digit CN level but then proceeded to calculate discrete measures of protection (0 no impact, 1 weak, 2 average, 3 strong) at the 3-digit NACE level. Table 2.12 extracts the NACE industries which have a share of 1% or more in total Czechoslovak industrial exports to the EC and shows the relevance of the various types of protectionist measures to these. We concentrate in the following upon Czechoslovakia but similar analyses have been made by Dobrinski (1993), Gacs (1993) and Rosati (1993b) for Bulgaria, Hungary and Poland respectively.

We can see that – with few exceptions – protectionist barriers are rather high in those branches which feature prominently in Czechoslovak exports to the EC. QRs are high in iron and steel and non-ferrous metals, as well as in woven fabrics, knitting, clothing and household textiles; other NTBs are also high in iron and steel, metal processing, glassware, basic chemicals, electrical motors, footwear and rubber products; tariff protection is again

Table 2.12. *EC protection against Czechoslovak exports, 1991*

NACE		Exports in mn ECU	% of industrial exports	Duties	QR	ONTB	Public procure- ment	Total
221	Iron and steel	268 255	7.3	2	3	3	0	8
222	Steel tubes	55 998	1.5	3	0	3	0	6
223	Steel drawing	56 746	1.5	2	0	3	0	5
229	Non-ferrous manuf.	99 104	2.7	1	3	3	0	7
231	Building mat.	40 995	1.1	1	0	0	0	1
242	Cement, lime	64 738	1.7	1	0	0	0	1
247	Glassware	160 974	4.4	3	0	3	2	8
248	Ceramics	35 402	1.0	3	0	0	2	5
252	Petrochemic.	319 886	8.6	3	0	1	0	4
253	Other basic chemic.	92 142	2.5	3	0	3	0	6
260	Met. structures	40 559	1.1	2	0	0	0	2
316	Tools, met. pr.	92 169	2.5	2	0	1	0	3
321	Agric. mach.	53 387	1.4	3	0	0	2	5
322	Mach. tools	85 619	2.3	2	0	0	2	4
325	Plant for mines	67 014	1.8	2	0	0	2	4
328	Other mach.	63 490	1.7	2	0	1	0	3
342	El. motors	74 977	2.0	2	0	3	3	8
351	Motor vehicles	214 163	5.8	3	0	0	2	5
362	Railway eq.	60 479	1.6	2	0	0	3	5
43B	Woven fabrics	87 389	2.6	3	3	0	2	8
436	Knitting	79 912	2.2	3	3	0	0	6
451	Footwear	71 700	1.9	3	0	3	2	8
453	Clothing	204 373	5.5	3	3	1	2	9
455	Household text.	42 829	1.2	3	3	0	2	8
461	Sawing of wood	79 364	2.1	1	0	0	0	1
465	Other wood pr.	43 603	1.2	1	0	1	0	2
467	Wood furniture	78 477	2.1	2	0	1	0	3
471	Pulp, paper	109 074	2.9	2	0	0	0	2
481	Rubber pr.	57 538	1.6	3	2	3	2	10
483	Plastics	42 969	1.3	3	0	1	0	4

Note: Table 2.12 gives information about the strength of various protectionist measures on those 3-digit NACE industries which have a greater than 1% representation in total Czechoslovak exports to the EC.
Source: Schumacher and Möbius, 1993.

high in iron and steel, steel products and metal structures, basic chemicals, rubber products and plastics, as well as in glassware, ceramics, fabrics, knitting, footwear, clothing and motor vehicles.

Table 2.13 meshes the information concerning the structure of EC protection vis-à-vis Czechoslovakia with the information on factor intensities of different industrial branches. It extracts the 30 most capital-, labour-, R&D-, skill-, and energy-intensive sectors and analyses Czechoslovakia's export patterns with the EC in terms of factor content.[8] Furthermore, table 2.13 groups these industries in terms high-, medium- and low levels of protection by the EC (using the Schumacher–Möbius index). For example, the group of industries falling into the top left section of table 2.13 show which of the 30 most capital-intensive branches in the EC are also amongst the most highly (trade) protected branches. Next to the NACE codes are the shares of these industries in Czechoslovakia's manufacturing exports to the EC in 1991. We can see:

(i) That capital-, energy- and labour-intensive industries have the largest number of industries in the 'high-protected' segment of trade with the EC, while R&D- and skill-intensive industries are the least represented in that group; R&D- and skill-intensive industries are, on the other hand, most represented in the 'low protected' group of industries.

(ii) As regards Czechoslovakia's export structure to the EC, the 30 most energy-intensive industries account for the largest shares of total Czechoslovak exports (33.6% and 34.9% respectively) followed by the 30 most labour-intensive (25.2%) and R&D-intensive ones (24.3%). The 30 most skill-intensive industries are the least represented in the current structure of Czechoslovak exports to the EC (19.0%).

(iii) About half of the export shares of the 30 most capital-, energy- and labour-intensive types of industries are also amongst the most 'high protected' types of industries. Only the smallest share of Czechoslovakia's exports in the 30 most capital-, energy- and labour-intensive group of industries fall into the 'low protected' range of industries. In the R&D- and skill-intensive group, Czechoslovakia has the highest share in the 'medium protected' range.

The above analysis suggests that the more Czechoslovak (and other Eastern European) exporters to the EC move into R&D- and skill-intensive branches the less will they be affected by EC trade barriers.[9] As the previous analysis has shown, this is presently not the case for Czechoslovakia which has specialised in labour- and energy-intensive exports to the European Community.

We have seen earlier that recent export growth to EC markets correlates positively and significantly with the degree to which industries

Table 2.13. *EC protection and factor intensities, by branch*

		Capital-intensive sectors		Labour-intensive sectors		R&D-intensive sectors		Skill-intensive sectors		Energy-intensive sectors	
		Code	Export (%)[a]	Code	Export (%)	Code	Export (%)	Code	Export (%)	Code	Export (%)
	High	221	7.51	453	5.72	342	2.10	342	2.10	221	7.51
		224	2.77	451	2.01					247	4.51
		414	0.67	455	1.20					224	2.77
		247	4.51	342	2.10					481	1.61
		421	0.11	481	1.61					438	0.26
										414	0.67
			15.57		12.64		2.10		2.10		17.33
EC trade protection	Medium	418	0.01	493	0.01	257	0.25	330	0.16	260	1.02
		330	0.16	442	0.77	345	0.51	256	0.71	248	0.99
		260	1.02	466	0.12	346	0.91	257	0.25	222	1.57
		416	0.00	492	0.52	347	0.30	344	0.33	418	0.01
		422	0.10	372	0.05	344	0.33	345	0.51	256	0.71
		256	0.71	495	1.24	341	0.56	341	0.56	223	1.59
		351	5.99	248	0.99	330	0.16	347	0.30	439	0.59
		462	0.65	361	0.02	256	0.71	346	0.91	462	0.65
		423	0.10	494	0.59	372	0.05	372	0.05	483	1.34
		257	0.25	362	1.69	351	5.99	361	0.02	341	0.56
		413	0.29	436	2.24	362	1.69	362	1.69	362	1.69
		345	0.51	326	0.44	323	0.62	260	1.02	326	0.44
		483	1.34	439	0.59	321	1.49	323	0.62	361	0.02
		223	1.59	347	0.30	322	2.40	322	2.40		
				344	0.33	325	1.88	321	1.49		
			12.72		9.89		17.84		11.01		11.18

Table 2.13. (cont.)

	Capital-intensive sectors		Labour-intensive sectors		R&D-intensive sectors		Skill-intensive sectors		Energy-intensive sectors	
	Code	Export (%)[a]	Code	Export (%)	Code	Export (%)	Code	Export (%)	Code	Export (%)
Low	471	3.05	365	0.07	364	0.04	255	0.12	241	0.07
	411	0.28	464	0.05	343	0.17	259	0.12	471	3.05
	245	0.26	373	0.13	258	0.06	258	0.06	245	0.26
	241	0.07	313	0.37	259	0.12	471	3.05	311	0.31
	424	0.02	374	0.11	255	0.12	472	0.36	482	0.02
	259	0.12	465	1.22	374	0.11	473	0.90	312	0.29
	258	0.06	371	0.17	373	0.13	343	0.17	243	0.26
	243	0.26	311	0.31	371	0.17	373	0.13	313	0.37
	472	0.36	482	0.02	352	0.26	371	0.17	465	1.22
	353	0.69	343	0.17	353	0.69	374	0.11	472	0.36
	373	0.13			365	0.07	364	0.04	343	0.17
					363	0.31	365	0.07		
					328	1.78	363	0.31		
					324	0.29	324	0.29		
		5.30		2.64		4.33		5.92		6.39
Share of total exports		33.60		25.16		24.27		19.03		34.90

Note:
[a] Export (%) refers to an industry's share in total industrial exports to the EC.
Source: Factor intensity measures are the same as those used in the regressions in tables 2.7–2.9.

exported in the past to CMEA rather than to Western markets. The trade patterns which emerged immediately after liberalisation might or might not be indicative of the trade patterns in the future; but these tendencies nonetheless raise the question whether the degree of past distortions will be an advantage or a disadvantage for prospective export growth once a country moves towards liberalisation which, in due course, removes these distortions. Particularly interesting, and for the ex-CSFR particularly important, are the engineering industries which exported mostly to CMEA markets; most of these have at the moment very low export–import coverage ratios with the EC. The scope for increased export growth to EC markets of these industries is a matter of debate. In the short run, it is a matter of redirecting their existing capacities to selling on Western markets, competing mainly on price rather than quality; in the longer run, the more advanced of the CEE economies and those endowed with a skilled labour force will probably be able to modernise production techniques and product programmes, acquire essential complementary skills in marketing, advertising, etc. and thus attempt to move upstream in this area of industrial production. Long-run comparative advantages are a function of whether a catching-up process will take place in the different CEE economies and this in turn depends upon those factors which facilitate (and hinder) industrial restructuring processes (capital shortage, building up complementary skills, FDI, exchange rate policies, labour unit costs, etc.) We expect much differentiation across CEE economies in the future in this respect.

Chapter 3 will discuss quantitatively the features of, and the various stages through which, East-West European trade integration may proceed, based on a scenario of a successful catching-up process of CEE economies with the West.

Conclusions on export and import structures

The picture which emerges from the analysis conducted on pp. 40–67 is as follows:

(i) The historical legacy of large export capacities oriented towards Eastern European markets had a very strong impact upon the pattern of recent export growth to the West.

(ii) High export growth to the West (predominantly the EC) was driven by the strong pressure exerted by collapsing ex-CMEA markets; Eastern European producers increased the volume of their sales to the West without any closure of the 'quality' (price) gap relative to EC competitors.

(iii) There was a sharp adjustment of import structures which became much more similar to those which characterise other Western countries' imports from the EC.

(iv) Export structures adjusted much more slowly and there are both significant similarities as well as differences across CEE economies in their respective pattern of export growth to the West.

(v) Both the continued (and sometimes strengthened) reliance upon branches which were traditionally 'overrepresented' in CEE countries' exports to the West (e.g. metals) as well as some reduction of their share in exports to the EC (e.g. food) could be detected; on the other hand, some branches which were traditionally 'underrepresented' in CEE countries' exports to the EC experienced above-average export growth (such as engineering exports from Czechoslovakia and Hungary). This means that the question whether the traditional pattern of CEE countries' export specialisation to the EC will become more or less pronounced in the future remains open.

(vi) The factors which will decide about CEE countries' trade specialisation in the longer run include, first of all, the speed and success of the processes of industrial restructuring but also trade policies from the side of Western trading partners. A move away from the traditional structure of export specialisation which characterised CEE–EC trade will diminish the incidence of strong protectionist barriers of the EC towards the CEE countries (at least given the current structure of EC protection).

Technical appendix

Structural change and similarity measures

The following general measure was used both to analyse structural shifts in manufacturing industry and to compare industrial structures across economies:

$$S = \left[\sum (sh_k^i - sh_k^j) \cdot (sh_k^i / 100) \right]^{\frac{1}{2}}$$

where sh_k^i and sh_k^j are either the (employment or value added) shares of industry k in years i and j when the extent of structural change in a country over a given period is investigated, or the shares of industry k in countries i and j when the structures of two countries are compared at a given point in time: year i provides the weights in the first case, and country i in the second. When i and j refer to years, i always stands for the more recent year.

The shares sh_k^i, sh_k^j are in percentages. The time series shown in the graphs in figures 2.1–2.5 are the series of $S_{i,j}$ measuring the degree of structural shift from one year to the next (that is, $i = j + 1$).

Both indicators above measure the weighted average difference in the shares of respective (ISIC) 3-digit manufacturing industries. The smaller the value of this indicator, the more similar the two structures compared. For identical structures its value is 0 and in the extreme case of perfectly complementary structures (that is, when there is one industry (k) for which $sh_k^j = 100$ and $sh_k^i = 0$) it is 100.

Data used in the analysis of industrial structural change

The data used to analyse structural change in manufacturing industries are from the UNIDO Industrial Statistics Data Base, which provide the following time series for 28 3-digit ISIC industries (ISIC codes 311, ..., 390)

Employment   average number of employees (code 4)
Output   gross output in current prices (code 14)
Value added   value added in current prices (code 20)
Output index index number of industrial production (1980 = 100)

Real output series were calculated from nominal output and output index series. The shares used in the structural change and similarity coefficients were calculated by the authors, taking total manufacturing (ISIC 300) as 100%. Time series cover the period 1963–91 (for 1991 only output indexes are available for most countries). For groups, nominal values are in US$.

Quality indicators of East European export performance in EC markets

$$Q_j^c = \sum_{i \varepsilon J} p_i^{EC} x_i^c$$

Q_j^c, QP_j^c, QV_j^c, QS_j^c are all various 'quality' indicators of country c's exports in a particular industry j. Within that industry j a (large) number of products $i \varepsilon J$ are traded.

$$QP_j^c = \sum_{i \varepsilon J} rp_i^c x_i^c$$

x_i^c represents the share of product i in country c's exports to EC markets.

$$QV_j^c = \sum_{i \varepsilon J} g_i^{EC} x_i^c$$

p_i^{EC} is the average price per kg of product i traded in EC markets; rp_i^c is the relative price of c's exports of commodity i relative to the 'price leader' (i.e. the producer charging the highest price per kg) in EC markets.

$$QS_j^c = \sum_{i\varepsilon J} \tilde{g}_i^{EC} x_i^c$$

($rp_i^c = \dfrac{p_i^c}{p_i^L}$ where p_i^L is the price per kg which the 'price leader' in EC markets charges for commodity i).

g_i^{EC} and $\tilde{g}_i^{EC}$ are respectively the volume and value growth rates of commodity i in EC markets for traded products.

In words, Q, QV and QS are all *compositional indicators* showing respectively whether CEE countries' exports in a particular industry j are biased in their commodity composition towards products which are (in the EC spectrum of intra-industry trade) high or low value per kg items (Q) or towards high or low growth items (QV and QS depending on whether volume or value growth is considered). QP is a (weighted) *price gap* variable between the CEE producer and the price leader in each EC product market.

Selected ISIC industries

Table 2.A1. *List of selected ISIC industries*

31	Food, beverages and tobacco
32	Textiles
33	Wood products and furniture
34	Paper, printing and publishing
35	Chemical, petroleum, plastic products
36	Non-metallic mineral products
37	Basic metal industries
381	Metal products
382	Machinery n.e.c.
383	Electrical machinery
384	Transport equipment
385	Professional goods
39	Other industries

Factor intensity measures used

The factor intensity measures used in the regressions reported in tables 2.7–2.9 and table 2.13 were derived from EC industrial statistics for the four largest EU member states (Germany, France, Italy and the UK) with the intention of examining the current structure of Eastern European export specialisation in relation to the relative factor content characteristic of the different industries as defined by EU (rather than EE) technology; for a rationale of this procedure, see e.g. Landesmann (1993b). The definition of the factor intensity measure is as follows:

capital intensity	cumulative investment (3 years)/number of employees
labour intensity	number of employees/output
R&D intensity	R&D expenditure/output
skill intensity	non-manual labour/total employment
energy intensity	energy costs/output

The factor intensity measures were provided by Mr P. Buigues and his team from DGII of the European Commission in the context of work done for the EU project 'The Economic Interpenetration of the EC and Eastern Europe'. For the results of this project see Buigues (1994).

Notes

1 The data used in the empirical analysis presented in this chapter are described in the appendix. We are grateful to the Industrial Statistics and Sectoral Survey Branch of UNIDO for kindly providing us with the UNIDO Industrial Statistics Database on diskette.
2 Van Brabant (1987, p. 96) also points out that one of the main characteristics of traditional CPEs, a system which was largely preserved in Czechoslovakia, but not in Hungary, is the delayed and muted response to the changing external (and internal) economic environment. He also rightly points out that this characteristic is intimately related to the nature of CMEA trade relations to which, as mentioned above, Czechoslovakia (and other CPEs also preserving the traditional system of central planning, for example, Bulgaria, as discussed in chapter 7) was much more exposed than Poland or Hungary.
3 For a comprehensive discussion of the theoretical issues of economic transformation see, e.g., Blanchard *et al.* (1991); McKinnon (1991).
4 See also the discussion of this issue in chapter 4.
5 For a more detailed analysis of the structure of trade specialisation of CEE economies in their trade with the EC see pp.51–60 below.
6 The normalisation of the quality indicators in table 2.6 is with respect to the EC-6 (Germany, France, Italy, United Kingdom, the Netherlands, Belgium) = 100.
7 In a separate analysis (see Landesmann, Hont and Székely, 1992; Landesmann and Shields, 1992), we constructed a 'target structure' for Czechoslovak exports to the EC for the very long run, say the year 2010, when we assumed that Czechoslovakia's export structure and market shares in EC markets would have become more similar to other West European countries. The implied annual growth rates of exports to obtain such a market share position are the 'target growth' rates which were used in the regressions reported in table 2.11. The

forecasts on *short-run export growth* made in the Landesmann-Shields study were based on assumptions about the conversion possibilities of export capacities from East to West. The resulting 'conversion growth' rates are those used in the regressions reported in table 2.11; for details see Landesmann and Shields (1992).

8 Of course, Czechoslovakia's industries almost certainly employ different technologies than do EC industries. Analysing Czechoslovakia's export structures in terms of EC factor intensities might nonetheless be of interest if some convergence in Czechoslovak–EC technological practices over the coming years is to be expected.

9 This conclusion is confirmed by further regression analysis (not fully reported here) which shows a (weak) negative relationship between EC trade protection (using the Schumacher–Möbius index) and the relative R&D and skill intensity of different branches.

References

Baldwin, R., 1992. 'An eastern enlargement of EFTA: why the East Europeans should join and the EFTAns should want them', *CEPR Occasional Paper*, 10, London: CEPR

Bekker, Zs., 1988. *Growth Patterns, Dynamic Branches*, Budapest: Akadémia Kiadó

Blanchard, O., Dornbusch, R., Krugman, P., Layard, R. and Summers, L., 1991. *Reform in Eastern Europe*, Cambridge, MA: MIT Press

Blejer, M. I., Calvo, G. A., Coricelli, F. and Gelb, A. H. (eds.), 1993. 'Eastern Europe in transition: from recession to growth', *Discussion Paper* 196 (May), Washington, DC: World Bank

Blommestein, H. and Marrese, M. (eds.), 1991. *Transformation of Planned Economies: Property Rights Reform and Macroeconomic Stability*, Paris: OECD

Brabant, J. M. van, 1987. *Adjustment, Structural Change, and Economic Efficiency*, Cambridge: Cambridge University Press

Buigues, P. (ed.), 1994. 'The economic interpenetration of the EC and Eastern Europe', *European Economy*, Special Issue

Calvo, G. A. and Frakel, J. A., 1991. 'Obstacles to transforming centrally-planned economies: the role of the capital markets', *Working Papers Series*, 3776, Cambridge, MA: NBER

CEPR, 1990. 'Monitoring European integration, the impact of Eastern Europe', *CEPR Annual Report*, London: CEPR

Charap, J. and Dyba, K., 1991. 'Economic transformation in Czechoslovakia', *European Economic Review*, 35

Collins, S. M. and Rodrik D., 1991. *Eastern Europe and the Soviet Union in the World Economy*, Washington, DC: Institute for International Economics

Dobrinsky, R., 1993. 'The Economic interpenetration between the EC and Eastern Europe: Bulgaria', IV Workshop on the Economic Interpenetration between the EC and Eastern Europe, Brussels (13–14 December)

Dyba, K., 1989. 'Understanding Czechoslovak economic development: 1968–1988; growth, adjustment, and reform', *Jahrbuch der Wirtschafts Osteuropas*, 13(2), 141–65

Gacs, J., 1993. 'The economic interpenetration between the EC and Eastern Europe: Hungary', IV Workshop on the Economic Interpenetration between the EC and Eastern Europe, Brussels (13–14 December)

Gajdka, J. and Hamilton, A., 1992. 'Privatization in Poland', CIBER, University of Maryland, Occasional Paper no. 19

Gatsios, K., 1992. 'Privatization in Hungary: past, present, and future', *CEPR Discussion Paper* 640, London: CEPR

Grosfeld, I. and Hare, P. G., 1991. 'Privatisation in Hungary, Poland and Czechoslovakia', *European Economy*, special edition, no. 2, 129–56

Hamilton, C. and Winters, A., 1992. 'Opening up international trade in Eastern Europe', *Economic Policy*, 14, 77–116

Havrylyshyn, O. and Pritchett, L., 1991. *European Trade Patterns after Transition*, Working Paper 748, Washington, DC: The World Bank

Hindley, B., 1993. *Helping Transition through Trade? EC and US Policy towards Exports from Eastern and Central Europe*, EBRD Working Paper, 3, London: EBRD

Hughes, G. and Hare, P. G., 1991. 'Competitiveness and industrial restructuring in Czechoslovakia, Hungary and Poland', *European Economy*, special edition, 2, 83–110

Járai, Zs., 1993. 'Ten per cent already sold, privatization in Hungary', in I. P. Székely and D. M. G. Newbery (eds.), *Hungary: An Economy in Transition*, Cambridge: Cambridge University Press, 77–83

Kolanda, M. and Kubista, V., 1991. 'Costs, performances and behaviour of Czechoslovak manufacturing enterprises on world markets in the 1980s', Institute for Forecasting of the Czechoslovak Academy of Sciences, internal document

Kolanda, M. and Tous, O., 1986. 'Average prices per unit of weight of engineering products in Czechoslovak exports to the EEC in 1960–1983', *Research Memorandum*, 46, Prague: VUVEV

Landesmann, M. A., 1991. 'Industrial restructuring and the reorientation of trade in Czechoslovakia', *European Economy*, special edition, 2, 57–82

1993a. 'Monitoring and projecting the evolution of competitiveness of CEE industries', paper prepared for the EC Working Group on the Interpenetration of the EC and Central and Eastern Europe, Brussels: European Commission, mimeo

1993b. 'Czechoslovakia – trade structure and EC protection', paper prepared for the EC Working Group on the Interpenetration of the EC and Central and Eastern Europe, Brussels: European Commission (forthcoming in *European Economy*)

Landesmann, M. and Shields, J., 1992. *Projections of East-West Trade Integration in Manufactured Goods*, London: NERA

Landesmann, M. and Székely, I., 1991. *Industrial Restructuring and the Reorientation of Trade in Czechoslovakia, Hungary and Poland*, CEPR Discussion Paper no. 546, London: CEPR

Landesmann, M. with Hont, A. and Székely I., 1992. 'Industrial Restructuring in Eastern Europe and East–West trade integration', Department of Applied Economics *Working Paper*, 9213, Cambridge: University of Cambridge

Marrese, M., 1992. 'Solving the bad-debt problem of Central and Eastern European banks: an overview', Evaston, IL: Northwestern University, mimeo

McKinnon, R., 1991. *The Order of Economic Liberalization*, Baltimore: Johns Hopkins University Press

Messerlin, P. A., 1992. 'The Association Agreements between the EC and Central Europe: trade liberalisation vs constitutional failure', in J. Flemming and J.. Rollo (eds.), *Trade, Payments and Adjustment in Central and Eastern Europe*, London: Royal Institute of International Affairs, 111–43

1993. 'The EC and Central Europe: the mixed rendez-vous of 1992?', *Economics of Transition*, I(1), 89–109

Michael, T., Revesz, T., Hare, P. and Hughes, G., 1992. *The Competitiveness of Hungarian Industry*, CEPR Discussion Paper, no. 736, London: CEPR

Munnell, A. H., 1992. 'Infrastructure investment and economic growth', *Journal of Economic Perspectives*, 6(4), 189–98

Nesporova, A., 1993. 'Preconditions of the industrial restructuring in the skill, professional and age structure of the labour force in the Czech Republic', paper presented at the ACE Workshop on 'Industrial Restructuring, Trade Reorientation and East-West European Integration; WIIW, Vienna (27–29 March)

Ostry, S., 1993. 'The threat of managed trade to transforming economies', EBRD Working Paper no. 3, London: EBRD

Portes, R. (ed.) 1993. *Economic Transformation in Central Europe: A Progress Report*, Luxembourg: Commission of the European Communities and CEPR

Rodrik, D., 1992. *Foreign Trade in Eastern Europe's Transition: Early Results*, CEPR Discussion Paper, no. 676, London: CEPR

Rollo, J., 1992. *The Association Agreements between the EC and the CSFR, Hungary and Poland: A Half-Empty Glass*, London: The Royal Institute of International Affairs

Rollo, J. and Smith, A., 1993. 'The political economy of Central European trade with the European Community: why so sensitive?; *Economic Policy*, 16, 140–81

Rosati, D. K., 1993a. 'Problems of post-CMEA trade and payments', in J. Flemming and J. Rollo (eds.), *Trade, Payments and Adjustment in Central and Eastern Europe*, London, Royal Institute of International Affairs, 75–108

Schumacher, D. and Möbius, U., 1993. 'Community trade barriers facing Central and East European Countries. Impact of the European Agreements: supplementary and updated results', IV Workshop on the Economic Interpenetration between the EC and Eastern Europe, Brussels (13–14 December)

Smith. A., 1992. '"Comment" on C. Senik-Leygonie and G. Hughes: *Industrial profitability and trade among the former Soviet Republics*', *Economic Policy*, 15,

378–81

Svejnar, J., 1991. 'Microeconomic issues in the transition to a market economy', *Journal of Economic Perspectives*, 5(4), 123–138

Székely, I. P., 1992. 'Industrial restructuring and financial reforms in Central and Eastern Europe', paper presented at the ACE Workshop on 'Industrial Restructuring, Trade Reorientation and East-West Integration', WIIW, Vienna (26–28 November)

1993. 'Economic transformation and the reform of the financial system in Central and Eastern Europe', Proceedings of the Tenth World Congress of the International Economic Association, Moscow (24–28 August 1992), London: Macmillan, forthcoming

Székely, I. P. and Newbery, D. M. G. (eds.), 1993. *Hungary: An Economy in Transition*, Cambridge: Cambridge University Press

UN-ECE, 1992, 1993. *Economic Bulletin for Europe*, Geneva: United Nations

UN-ECE, 1993. *Economic Survey of Europe in 1992–1993*, Geneva: United Nations

Wang, Z. K. and Winters, L. A., 1991. *The Trading Potential of Eastern Europe*, CEPR Discussion Paper no. 610, London: CEPR

Winters, L. A., 1992. 'The Europe Agreements: with a little help from our friends', in *The Association Process: Making it Work*, CEPR Occasional Paper, no. 11, London: CEPR

3 Projecting East-West trade integration

Michael Landesmann

Introduction

In chapter 2 we reviewed some of the recent developments of East–West European integration. In this chapter we project an optimistic scenario of East-West trade integration for the long run (which, for purposes of this chapter, we define as up to the year 2010). The main assumption behind this scenario is that the 'frontier' countries (Poland, Hungary and Czechoslovakia) will occupy market shares in EC markets which are roughly in line with those of other Western European countries which either are not yet members of the EC or have only recently joined. We shall use measures of the current 'quality gap' and 'distance measures' of industrial structure comparisons (see the analysis in chapter 2) to allow for the fact that the 'historical legacy' will still play a role in the longer run and affect the different Eastern European economies' positions in inter-industry and intra-industry specialisation in European trade. We also make short-run projections of trade integration (for the period up to 1995) using a very different methodology. Here trade reorientation from East-East to East-West trade and the conversion of old capacities and investment into new export capacities play the major role. The use of different methodologies for short-, medium-, and long-run projections reveals, first, the great difficulty of achieving growth rates which allow Eastern European countries to reach market share positions similar to those of Western European economies and, secondly, significant differences in shorter- and longer-term specialisation patterns of Eastern European economies in international trade. The chapter ends by confronting the methodology employed in this exercise with the factual information we now have about tendencies in the East-West integration process and maps out a number of possible scenarios for future specialisation patterns between Eastern and Western Europe.

76

Long-term projections

The objective is to forecast the long-run level of exports from Eastern Europe by country and commodity into the European Community as well as imports from the European Community into Eastern Europe. A country's export success will depend on a range of factors – its level of development, size, comparative advantage (which will depend on factor endowments, skill, managerial and technological competence, infrastructure and distance from the market). Many of these are unobservable, and others will evolve in response to the market forces and institutional reforms currently developing in Eastern Europe. The forecasting approach taken here is pragmatic, as it must use observable data, but it is defensible. It proceeds in a series of steps, each of which takes account of one factor. This has the advantage that the relative importance of different factors can be examined and adjusted if other evidence suggests the need for such adjustment. The long-run equilibrium is assumed to be reached in the year 2010, by which time a large part of the technological catching-up will be assumed to have taken place in the Eastern European countries.

'Naive' long-term projections (step 1)

The first step is to attempt to identify the equilibrium level of exports (in the year 2010) to the EC which might be expected from countries at the level of development observed in the East. Ideally, one would estimate a model in which exports to the EC were a function of GDP per capita, size, industrial structure (as a proxy for comparative advantage), distance, contiguity, tariff levels and non-tariff barriers, etc. In practice, this is an overambitious task and we adopt the following short cut. The idea is to select a group of roughly similar countries (in terms of size, proximity to EC markets and average GDP/head in 2010), and then work out the extent to which any given Eastern European country approximates this group. Its trade share in the EC in 2010 will then be taken as equally similar. The reference group of countries is Austria, Switzerland, Finland, Sweden, Denmark, Spain, Portugal, Greece and Turkey, and the reference year is 1986/7. These are comparable in population to the core group of Eastern European countries (CSFR, Poland and Hungary, but we shall take Czechoslovakia (CSFR) as our benchmark country). They are on average richer and so might be expected to enjoy larger trade shares in the EC, but we are looking considerably ahead and taking an optimistic view.

Before taking any other factors into account we will assume that the trade shares (in the year 2010) of any given Eastern European country in the EC are weighted averages of the trade shares of these reference countries.[1] The weights measure the degree of similarity of the given Eastern European country to each reference country, which is in turn defined as proportional to the inverse of the 'distance' of its employment pattern to that in the reference country.[2] In turn, the distance of country c from reference country D' is given by the distance coefficient $D_{cc'}$, defined as

$$D_{cc'} = \sqrt{\frac{1}{n} \sum_{j=1}^{n} (\omega_j^c - \omega_j^{c'})^2}, \tag{1}$$

where ω_j^c is the share of industry j in country c in total manufacturing employment (and similarly for the reference country c'), and n is the number of manufacturing industries in the UNIDO database (already used in chapter 2). The employment shares are for 1987 and are based on UNIDO industrial statistics. If these shares are expressed in percentage terms, we have $0 < D_{cc'} < 100$, though there is no special merit in this particular scaling (table 3.1a presents these distance measures comparing employment structures in 1987).

The actual similarity weight by which the trade share of country c' is multiplied is

$$\alpha_{cc'} = \frac{D_{cc'}^{-1}}{\sum_{k=1}^{K} D_{ck}^{-1}} \tag{2}$$

where K is the number of reference group countries (9 in this case). Table 3.1b gives these weights, and in the final column, the *distance* of each country from its own 'employment target structure' which is the weighted average of the employment structures of the reference countries with the $S_{cc'} = 1/D_{cc'}$ used as weights.

These weights are then used to calculate the long-term *target market shares* for each Eastern European country as the weighted average of the market shares of the reference group of countries. (For the market shares in EC markets of these reference countries see table 3.1c.) These unadjusted 'target market shares' are presented in table 3.2 and are compared with the original market shares of each Eastern European country in the EC markets in 1986/7. At the bottom of each country's projection are the average EC market shares for total manufacturing under the hypothetical and the original scenario. We call these 'naive' (or step 1) projections since no other factor is taken into account besides the market share structure of the group of reference countries. At this stage what we have attempted to determine are the predicted market shares at the product level taking account of the proxied level of development of the Eastern European countries.

Table 3.1. *Distance coefficients and market share*

a Distance coefficient (differences in employment structure)

	Austria	Switz.	Finland	Sweden	Denmark	Spain	Portugal	Greece	Turkey	Own target
Hungary	1.98	2.95	2.89	3.22	2.55	2.00	3.79	3.01	3.16	1.74
Poland	1.91	2.84	2.55	2.70	2.35	1.81	3.53	3.05	2.98	1.39
Czechoslovakia	2.91	2.98	3.14	2.88	3.09	3.11	4.75	4.58	4.13	2.63
Bulgaria	3.16	3.89	3.63	4.00	3.64	3.22	4.29	3.96	3.90	2.89
Romania	4.34	3.67	4.37	4.79	4.24	4.81	5.34	5.57	4.95	4.05
USSR	5.18	4.29	5.40	5.33	4.50	5.54	6.84	6.58	6.27	4.97
Yugoslavia	1.74	3.21	2.55	3.09	2.92	1.63	2.72	2.42	2.75	1.22

Source: (1987) industrial statistics made available to author: own calculations

b Similarity coefficients (used as weights for target export share structure)

	Austria	Switz.	Finland	Sweden	Denmark	Spain	Portugal	Greece	Turkey
Hungary	0.15	0.10	0.10	0.09	0.12	0.15	0.08	0.10	0.10
Poland	0.15	0.10	0.11	0.10	0.12	0.16	0.08	0.09	0.09
Czechoslovakia	0.13	0.13	0.12	0.13	0.12	0.12	0.08	0.08	0.09
Bulgaria	0.13	0.11	0.11	0.10	0.11	0.13	0.10	0.10	0.11
Romania	0.12	0.14	0.12	0.11	0.12	0.11	0.10	0.09	0.10
USSR	0.12	0.14	0.11	0.11	0.13	0.11	0.09	0.09	0.10
Yugoslavia	0.15	0.08	0.11	0.09	0.09	0.17	0.10	0.11	0.10

Source: UNIDO (1987) industrial statistics: own calculations.

Table 3.1. (*cont.*)

c Market shares in EC markets, 1987, %

	EEC-6	Austria	Switz.	Finland	Sweden	Denmark	Spain	Portugal	Greece	Turkey
Met. Ex. 21	8.61	0.01	0.01	0.04	5.30	0.01	0.86	0.09	0.48	0.34
Met. Pr. 22	55.59	2.97	5.64	1.27	3.44	0.54	2.25	0.19	0.71	0.10
Min. Ex. 23	37.90	1.89	0.41	1.09	1.22	0.60	3.44	0.71	1.82	3.74
Min. Pr. 24	72.31	3.46	1.33	0.69	1.38	0.90	3.58	1.74	0.35	0.24
Chemic. 25	66.65	1.23	5.46	0.37	1.41	0.96	1.39	0.37	0.07	0.16
Fibres 26	67.83	3.62	5.00	0.67	0.48	1.55	1.48	0.20	0.85	2.03
Met. Pd. 31	66.68	3.37	4.79	0.50	3.63	1.80	2.22	0.60	0.08	0.14
Mech. En. 32	61.32	2.53	6.93	0.74	3.70	1.92	1.50	0.20	0.04	0.04
Off. Eq. 33	44.58	0.21	0.75	0.31	1.87	0.38	1.58	0.09	0.01	0.00
El. Eng. 34	49.55	2.77	3.88	0.56	2.17	1.25	0.66	0.10	0.03	
Motor 35	73.07	1.92	0.46	0.18	3.62	0.21	5.82	0.55	0.00	0.01
Transp. 36	42.38	0.74	1.42	0.24	0.99	0.49	0.69	0.13	0.15	0.00
Instr. 37	44.79	1.49	10.02	0.27	1.30	1.40	0.65	0.29	0.01	0.00
Food 41	57.98	0.66	1.12	0.13	0.37	5.24	1.16	0.23	0.85	1.38
Drink 42	74.71	0.41	0.63	0.05	0.12	2.34	3.84	3.00	0.47	0.06
Text. 43	55.36	2.67	3.27	0.26	0.59	0.83	1.38	2.76	2.61	3.11
Leath. 44	42.29	2.12	0.87	0.28	1.00	0.48	2.51	0.37	0.11	0.30
Ft./Cl. 45	42.65	2.14	1.06	0.46	0.38	0.55	3.41	4.62	2.55	4.27
Timber 46	37.08	5.03	1.32	6.10	8.68	2.66	1.77	2.72	0.03	0.03
Paper 47	44.71	4.01	2.40	10.66	13.52	0.80	1.85	1.56	0.06	0.01
Rubber 48	71.14	2.76	2.87	0.50	2.06	1.79	2.17	0.31	0.17	0.11
Other 49	29.39	2.04	4.14	0.32	1.06	0.90	1.13	0.22	0.13	0.03
Tot. Manuf.		2.14	3.40	1.07	2.73	1.33	2.10	0.82	0.45	0.55

Source: Eurostat, Detailed Trade Statistics.

Table 3.2. *Market shares projections: steps 1 and 2*

NACE	Hungary				Poland			
	1987	diff. step 1–87	diff. step 2–1	step 2	1987	diff. step 1–87	diff. step 2–1	step 2
Met. Ex. 21	0.00	0.72	0.59	1.31	0.19	0.59	−0.04	0.73
Met. Pr. 22	0.33	1.66	0.13	2.12	0.60	1.39	0.64	2.64
Min. Ex. 23	0.04	1.70	0.00	1.75	0.07	1.68	0.00	1.75
Min. Pr. 24	0.33	1.39	−0.06	1.65	0.45	1.26	0.08	1.80
Chemic. 25	0.25	1.05	0.28	1.58	0.29	1.00	0.62	1.91
Fibres 26	0.14	1.74	−0.39	1.49	0.07	1.77	−0.62	1.23
Met. Prod. 31	0.30	1.72	−0.41	1.61	0.35	1.68	−0.63	1.40
Mech. Eng. 32	0.15	1.85	−0.45	1.55	0.14	1.87	−0.80	1.21
Office Eq. 33	0.01	0.60	−0.40	0.21	0.00	0.63	−0.12	0.51
Elec. Eng. 34	0.16	1.31	−0.10	1.38	0.12	1.36	−0.25	1.22
Motor 35	0.02	1.64	−0.32	1.33	0.14	1.56	−0.71	0.99
Transp. 36	0.01	0.56	−0.01	0.56	0.27	0.30	−0.18	0.39
Instrum. 37	0.06	1.63	−0.98	0.71	0.06	1.60	−0.90	0.77
Food/Dri. 41	0.63	0.67	0.12	1.42	0.66	0.64	0.20	1.49
Food/Dri. 42	0.02	1.28	0.17	1.47	0.06	1.24	0.31	1.62
Textiles 43	0.30	1.62	−0.38	1.53	0.24	1.63	−0.63	1.24
Leather 44	0.46	0.58	0.09	1.14	0.23	0.81	−0.17	0.88
Foot./Clo. 45	0.99	1.15	0.23	2.36	1.07	1.04	−0.74	1.36
Timber 46	0.49	2.67	−0.84	2.33	1.15	2.10	−0.52	2.73
Paper 47	0.05	1.31	−0.62	0.74	0.10	1.61	0.59	2.29
Rubber 48	0.17	1.38	−0.20	1.36	0.11	1.45	−0.25	1.31
Other 49	0.16	1.02	−0.26	0.92	0.14	1.03	0.73	1.89
Tot. Manuf.	0.24	1.23	−0.22	1.26	0.30	1.19	−0.16	1.33

Modified long-term projections (step 2)

Two sets of further factors have been taken into account to modify the 'naive' projections:

(i) Differences across industries in the degree to which they will reach the target market shares in EC markets.

(ii) Global adjustment factors such as size of the country, distance from EC markets, differences across the Eastern European economies of how much of the final target they will reach by the year 2010, and some (subjective) adjustment for the expected degree of political instability impinging upon economic (export) performance.

Table 3.2. (cont.)

NACE	Czechoslovakia				Bulgaria			
	1987	diff. step 1–87	diff. step 2–1	step 2	1987	diff. step 1–87	diff. step 2–1	step 2
Met. Ex. 21	0.05	0.84	−0.10	0.78	0.00	0.76	−0.24	0.52
Met. Pr. 22	0.46	1.66	0.44	2.55	0.15	1.79	0.80	2.74
Min. Ex. 23	0.74	0.88	0.00	1.62	0.02	1.68	0.00	1.70
Min. Pr. 24	1.04	0.57	−0.24	1.37	0.05	1.56	0.15	1.75
Chemic. 25	0.27	1.14	0.37	1.78	0.07	1.20	0.39	1.66
Fibres 26	0.36	1.52	−0.15	1.72	0.07	1.74	0.12	1.93
Met. Prod. 31	0.23	1.90	−0.59	1.54	0.02	1.92	−0.53	1.41
Mech. Eng. 32	0.21	2.00	−0.43	1.78	0.04	1.93	−0.64	1.33
Office Eq. 33	0.01	0.64	−0.37	0.28	0.01	0.58	0.07	0.66
Elec. Eng. 34	0.09	1.46	−0.14	1.41	0.02	1.41	−0.44	0.99
Motor 35	0.10	1.48	−0.67	0.91	0.00	1.51	−0.64	0.88
Transp. 36	0.07	0.53	−0.33	0.27	0.00	0.55	−0.43	0.12
Instrum. 37	0.06	1.87	−0.72	1.21	0.01	1.69	−0.50	1.19
Food/Dri. 41	0.15	1.13	0.81	2.09	0.08	1.18	0.00	1.26
Food/Dri. 42	0.22	0.97	0.01	1.19	0.01	1.23	0.28	0.96
Textiles 43	0.37	1.47	−0.48	1.37	0.08	1.84	−0.27	1.65
Leather 44	0.42	0.56	−0.19	0.79	0.06	0.90	−0.61	0.35
Foot./Clo. 45	0.50	1.46	−0.49	1.47	0.12	2.02	−0.84	1.31
Timber 46	1.10	2.33	−0.44	2.99	0.08	3.10	−1.15	2.03
Paper 47	0.37	3.95	0.89	5.21	0.02	1.60	0.48	2.10
Rubber 48	0.25	1.33	−0.22	1.36	0.02	1.45	−0.38	1.10
Other 49	0.25	0.98	0.50	1.74	0.09	1.04	−0.45	0.68
Tot. Manuf.	0.26	1.38	−0.12	1.53	0.05	1.39	−0.19	1.25

Accounting for the industry-specific quality gap

Each EE country will have a different pattern of comparative advantage in products compared to other countries, and we should take account of this in forecasting product level export shares. In the following the assumption will be made that comparative advantage is measured by *relative* product quality. The methodology at this point should be seen as a framework into which other indicators on comparative advantage could be inserted as further research into evolving specialisation patterns reveal deeper insights into relative strengths and weaknesses of different areas of (actual and potential) industrial activity.[3] If Poland is relatively better at chemical production than manufacturing as a whole, then we should expect a larger share of Polish exports to be chemicals. For the purposes of this study,

Table 3.2. (*cont.*)

NACE	Romania				USSR			
	1987	diff. step 1–87	diff. step 2–1	step 2	1987	diff. step 1–87	diff. step 2–1	step 2
Met. Ex. 21	0.00	0.75	0.00	0.75	0.11	0.67	0.07	0.85
Met. Pr. 22	0.28	1.77	1.30	3.35	1.15	0.93	0.56	2.64
Min. Ex. 23	0.00	1.60	0.00	1.60	0.54	1.04	0.00	1.58
Min. Pr. 24	0.34	1.19	−0.11	1.42	0.06	1.48	−0.01	1.54
Chemic. 25	0.14	1.28	0.95	2.38	0.55	0.90	0.44	1.89
Fibres 26	0.51	1.40	0.23	2.13	0.16	1.75	−0.28	1.63
Met. Prod. 31	0.23	1.82	−0.13	1.91	0.07	2.02	−1.16	0.93
Mech. Eng. 32	0.07	2.10	−0.24	1.93	0.10	2.12	−0.39	1.82
Office Eq. 33	0.00	0.59	−0.40	0.19	0.00	0.60	−0.11	0.50
Elec. Eng. 34	0.06	1.46	−0.63	0.88	0.06	1.48	−0.72	0.82
Motor 35	0.07	1.33	−0.02	1.38	0.41	1.02	−0.66	0.77
Transp. 36	0.16	0.42	−0.32	0.26	0.05	0.54	−0.07	0.52
Instrum. 37	0.02	1.99	−1.23	0.79	0.10	1.95	−1.26	0.78
Food/Dri. 41	0.12	1.17	0.25	1.54	0.26	1.09	0.23	1.58
Food/Dri. 42	0.00	1.18	0.33	1.51	0.30	0.89	−0.06	1.14
Textile 43	0.38	1.56	0.07	2.01	0.22	1.69	−0.41	1.50
Leather 44	0.20	0.71	0.09	1.01	0.04	0.88	−0.44	0.48
Foot./Clo. 45	1.12	0.92	−0.50	1.55	0.05	1.94	0.00	1.99
Timber 46	2.00	1.20	−0.61	2.59	3.81	−0.59	0.56	3.78
Paper 47	0.06	3.90	1.24	5.19	0.61	0.65	0.33	1.58
Rubber 48	0.11	1.40	−0.24	1.27	0.02	1.52	−0.49	1.05
Other 49	0.04	1.20	−0.15	1.08	1.95	−0.70	−0.61	0.64
Tot. Manuf.	0.22	1.27	0.09	1.57	0.47	0.93	−0.14	1.26

longer-term comparative advantages/disadvantages will be measured by the relative 'quality' of the different commodities CEE producers sell in EC markets. The 'quality' measure adopted here will be the QP described in chapter 2 of this book. To remind the reader, 'quality gap' QP was measured by the value per kg of the product relative to the highest value per kg observed in EC imports of that product (the market leader). The calculation of these 'quality' (or 'price gap') indicators is derived from detailed trade statistics supplied by Eurostat at the 6-digit NIMEXE level.[4] For an industry such as mechanical engineering (NACE 32) this allows 480 commodities to be distinguished, so the hope is that products are sufficiently narrowly defined to be comparable on the basis of weight. For each of these commodities i belonging to an industry j the price per kg (p_i)

has been calculated for each of the competitor countries trading in EC markets (i.e. EC, Eastern Europe and other non-EC economies). The price per kg of competitor c, p_i^c, has then been divided by the price per kg of the price leader, p_i^l, that is by the price of the competitor with the highest price per kg for this commodity item.

The ratios p_i^c/p_i^l have then been weighted by the share which commodity i has in industry j's total exports to EC markets, and the 'quality indicator' Q_j^c is the sum of the weighted price per kg ratios across commodities $i\varepsilon J$ (where J is the set of all commodities traded by industry j in EC markets):

$$Q_j^c = \sum_{i \in J} \left(\frac{p_i^c}{p_i^l} \right) \chi_i^c, \tag{3}$$

where χ_i^c is the share of exports of commodity i in c's total exports in industry j to EC markets. The Q_j^c are then scaled by dividing by the Q_j^{EC} achieved by the EC-6 (Germany, France, Italy, United Kingdom, the Netherlands, Belgium) to give the ratios $Q'_j = Q_j^c/Q_j^{EC}$, shown in table 3.3a.

The first modification to the 'naive' projections is to correct for these proxies for industry-level comparative advantage, in turn measured for industry j as $Q'_j/\bar{Q}$ where $\bar{Q}$ is the average value of the Q'_j. The values of $\bar{Q}$ for the different countries are reported in the last row of table 3.3a. The matrix in table 3.3b reports the ratios $Q'_j/\bar{Q}$, that is, the range of quality by industry around the country mean, $\bar{Q}$. These ratios have been used as simple multiplicative factors to adjust the 'naive' projections of industrial-level export shares in order to account for the differential qualities of the different industries, though they will not affect the country's overall share of manufactured exports in the EC.

Thus, if in the 'naive' projections the market shares were χ_j^c, we now obtain the modified shares as

$$\bar{\chi}_j^c = \chi_j^c \cdot \left(\frac{Q_j^c}{\bar{Q}^c} \right). \tag{4}$$

This adjustment means that if industry j had a quality gap of, say, 40% below the average quality gap for country c's total manufacturing exports in EC markets, it will also obtain 40% less of its long-run target market share calculated under the 'naive' projections. If the quality gap is lower than the average for total manufacturing it will overachieve the target market shares.

Accounting for size, distance, overall catching-up and political instability (steps 3–5)

The next correction recognises the importance of the countries' relative size and of their relative distance from EC markets.

Table 3.3. *Quality measures*
a Compared to EC-6: QP

NACE	EC-6	Poland	Czecho.	Hungary	Romania	Bulgaria	Yugo.	USSR
Met. Ex. 21	1	0.68	0. 593	1.461	0.545	0.439	0.984	0.799
Met. Pr. 22	1	0.951	0.809	0.859	0.89	0.914	0.836	0.934
Min. Ex. 23	1	0.720	0.671	0.807	0.545	0.646	0.775	0.735
Min. Pr. 24	1	0.754	0.57	0.778	0.505	0.706	0.619	0.732
Chemic. 25	1	1.066	0.848	0.981	0.91	0.842	1.043	0.96
Fibres 26	1	0.478	0.616	0.64	0.61	0.689	0.681	0.625
Met. Pd. 31	1	0.496	0.486	0.643	0.51	0.469	0.622	0.326
Mech. Eng. 32	1	0.434	0.539	0.624	0.486	0.437	0.661	0.604
Off. Eq. 33	1	0.585	0.289	0.278	0.176	0.72	0.682	0.604
El. Eng. 34	1	0.596	0.611	0.754	0.317	0.446	0.62	0.39
Motor 35	1	0.421	0.387	0.651	0.539	0.374	0.964	0.396
Transp. 36	1	0.488	0.305	0.795	0.247	0.136	0.463	0.647
Instr. 37	1	0.332	0.419	0.338	0.213	0.454	0.542	0.281
Food 41	1	0.832	1.092	0.881	0.651	0.646	0.821	0.862
Drink 42	1	0.893	0.676	0.916	0.697	0.500	0.814	0.700
Text. 43	1	0.477	0.496	0.646	0.565	0.556	0.752	0.578
Leath. 44	1	0.602	0.542	0.88	0.6	0.234	0.711	0.385
Ft./Cl. 45	1	0.466	0.503	0.894	0.413	0.394	0.78	0.735
Timber 46	1	0.604	0.584	0.594	0.442	0.413	0.616	0.861
Paper 47	1	0.967	0.809	0.438	0.716	0.84	0.63	0.925
Rubber 48	1	0.606	0.579	0.703	0.459	0.481	0.641	0.5
Other 49	1	1.167	0.943	0.632	0.479	0.389	1.243	0.377
Average ($\bar{Q}$)		0.720	0.671	0.807	0.545	0.646	0.775	0.735

Distance from EC markets: Adjustments for relative distance from EC markets will be derived from gravity model estimates which the Kiel group of regional economists obtained by NACE industries. Two effects have been found to be important in regional models:

- Distance (in '000km) from the market in question: it is obvious that such distance matters more for some commodities (such as heavy pipes) than for others.
- Neighbourhood effects: if countries share a common border the trade intensity is increased in addition to the distance effect. We will introduce both these two factors into our final estimates.

Table 3.3. (*cont.*)

b Compared to country's total manufacturing: $QP_j/\bar{Q}$

NACE	EC-6	Poland	Czecho.	Hungary	Romania	Bulgaria	Yugo.	USSR
Met. Ex. 21	1	0.944	0. 884	1.810	1.000	0.679	1.270	1.088
Met. Pr. 22	1	1.321	1.206	1.064	1.632	1.414	1.079	1.272
Min. Ex. 23	1	1.000	1.000	1.000	1.000	1.000	1.000	1.000
Min. Pr. 24	1	1.047	0.850	0.964	0.926	1.092	0.799	0.997
Chemic. 25	1	1.480	1.265	1.215	1.669	1.303	1.346	1.307
Fibres 26	1	0.664	0.919	0.793	1.119	1.066	0.879	0.851
Met. Pd. 31	1	0.689	0.725	0.797	0.935	0.726	0.803	0.444
Mech. Eng. 32	1	0.603	0.804	0.773	0.891	0.676	0.853	0.822
Off. Eq. 33	1	0.812	0.431	0.344	0.323	1.114	0.880	0.822
El. Eng. 34	1	0.828	0.911	0.934	0.581	0.690	0.800	0.531
Motor 35	1	0.585	0.577	0.806	0.988	0.579	1.244	0.539
Transp. 36	1	0.678	0.455	0.985	0.453	0.210	0.597	0.881
Instr. 37	1	0.461	0.625	0.419	0.391	0.703	0.699	0.383
Food 41	1	1.156	1.628	1.091	1.194	1.000	1.059	1.174
Drink 42	1	1.240	1.008	1.135	1.278	0.774	1.050	0.953
Text. 43	1	0.662	0.740	0.800	1.036	0.860	0.970	0.787
Leath. 44	1	0.836	0.808	1.090	1.100	0.362	0.917	0.524
Ft./Cl. 45	1	0.647	0.750	1.108	0.757	0.610	1.006	1.000
Timber 46	1	0.839	0.871	0.736	0.811	0.639	0.795	1.172
Paper 47	1	1.343	1.206	0.543	1.313	1.300	0.813	1.259
Rubber 48	1	0.482	0.863	0.871	0.842	0.744	0.827	0.681
Other 49	1	1.621	1.406	0.783	0.878	0.602	1.604	0.513

Size: As proxy for size we use total export capacity of the different Eastern European economies as revealed by their total exports in 1987 (we could have taken an average over a number of years). In order to obtain data for total exports (rather than just exports to the EC) we had to have recourse to another dataset provided by the United Nations Economic Commission for Europe (UN-ECE): these provide trade flows (in US$) divided into rouble (USSR and EE-6) and non-rouble (EC, other developed, developing) areas. Since the rouble–dollar rates applied by the different Eastern European economies to measure their tradable flows into rouble areas are widely different, they have been recalculated applying the 1987 Hungarian rouble-dollar rates to all the other Eastern European economies' trade flows.

The resulting trade flows (and trade shares of export markets) as well as the total (non-fuel) export capacity (in US$) are given in table 3.4. From these figures our size adjustment coefficients have been derived with

Table 3.4. *Calculation of export capacity, 1987, at official and adjusted $ exchange rates*

	World	Socialist	Non-soc.	Exch. adj.	World adj.	Soc. adj.	%fuel soc.	%fuel non-soc.	Non-fuel exports	Index
Hungary	9584	5259	4324	1.000	9584	5259	0.5	7.4	9237	0.79
Czechoslovakia	13 632	8871	4761	0.8561	12 355	7595	2.0	9.4	11 756	1.0
Poland	12 210	5921	6288	1.3183	14 095	7806	7.8	14.5	12 574	1.07
Bulgaria	15 855	13 090	2766	0.3877	7840	5075	0.2	22.2	3352	0.29
Romania	10 491	4748	5743	0.7540	9323	3580	1.8	22.4	5516	0.47
Yugoslavia	12 549	3711	8838	0.8561	12 015	3177	2.0	9.4	11 121	0.95
USSR	107 623	69 808	37 814	0.3666	63 408	25 594	47.9	43.9	34 548	2.94

Czechoslovakia's (non-fuel) export capacity used as numeraire. Alternative scaling factors might be constructed by attempting to predict total exports as a function of level of development and population, using the methodology of Chenery and Syrquin (1975), but this has not been attempted.

Accounting for global differences in overall catching-up: So far we have assumed that on average (for total manufacturing) the countries will reach their target market share, although the different industries will underperform or overperform relative to this target. This effectively assumes that the Eastern European countries will achieve the same average quality level as the reference countries by 2010, but while this may be reasonable for the more advanced of the East European countries, i.e. Czechoslovakia, Poland and Hungary, it is less plausible for the remainder.[5] For the remaining countries, that is, Romania, Bulgaria, Yugoslavia and Russia, we assume that they will only achieve a fraction of the equilibrium market share by 2010, where the fraction is equal to their current ratio of average quality to that of the 'frontier countries'. Thus we multiply their target market share by the ratio $\bar{Q}^c/Q^{HU}$, where HU is the abbreviation for Hungary, as a proxy for their difference in technological ability to export to EC markets. Since Hungary has the highest measured $\bar{Q}$ in 1987, the market shares of the 'lagging' Eastern European countries (i.e. Romania, Bulgaria, Yugoslavia, USSR) are adjusted downwards by that ratio.[6]

   Table 3.5 summarises all the global adjustment factors, and shows that the size variable is the most important in this set of global adjustment factors. Since these different adjustment factors are used as simple multiplicative terms (to adjust the market shares for all industries of each country) the total impact of these combined global adjustment factors can be easily calculated (see last row of table 3.5). The additional impact of these global adjustments (steps 3–5) is summarised in table 3.6 which shows the original market shares in 1986/7, the market shares arrived at in the 'naive' (step 1) projections, and the two additional sets of modifications for total manufacturing. Using the final long-term projections (step 5) we can calculate the total increase in market shares of the whole group of Eastern European economies (for total manufacturing see table 3.6) and we can come to our last question linked to the market shares projections for the year 2010.

At whose cost will increases in market shares by Eastern European economies in EC markets occur? (step 6)

We used a very simple method to calculate the future market shares (by the years 2000/2010) of the other trading groups in EC markets. We assumed

Table 3.5. *Global adjustment factors*

	Poland	Czecho.	Hungary	Romania	Bulgaria	Yugo.	USSR
Qav/QHungary	1	1	1	0.676	0.801	0.960	0.910
Distance from EC	1	1	1	0.9	0.9	0.95	0.8
Political instabil.	1	1	1	0.9	0.9	0.85	0.85
Export capacity	1.07	1.00	0.79	0.47	0.29	0.95	2.94
Tot. adj.	1.070	1.000	0.786	0.257	0.185	0.733	1.818

Table 3.6. *Shares in EC markets, total manufacturing, 1987, and projections for the year 2010*

	Poland	Czecho.	Hungary	Romania	Bulgaria	Yugo.	USSR	East Eur.
Actual 1987	0.30	0.26	0.24	0.22	0.05	0.70	0.47	2.25
Step 1	1.49	1.65	1.47	1.49	1.44	1.33	1.40	10.26
Step 2	1.33	1.53	1.26	1.57	1.25	1.41	1.26	9.61
Step 5	1.42	1.53	0.99	0.40	0.23	1.03	2.30	7.90
Step 6	1.32	1.42	0.91	0.37	0.21	0.96	2.13	7.33

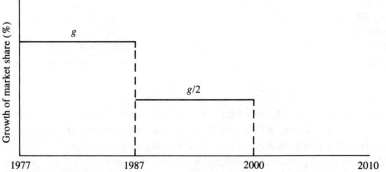

Figure 3.1 Market share increases of other (non-Eastern European) trading groups, 1977–2010

that their market shares would continue to expand or contract relatively at half the annual rates they experienced over the period 1977/8–1986/7 from 1987 to 2000, and thereafter remain constant (see figure 3.1).

From these projections for the non-EE trading groups plus the East European projections derived above we obtained initial market shares for the year 2010 which add up to more than 100%. The market shares of East

Table 3.7. *Market shares in EC markets*
a Actual in 1987

NACE	EEC-6	Rest EC	Rest WEur.	EEur.	Japan	Rest OECD	NICs	RoW
Met. Ex. 21	8.61	2.83	7.60	0.35	0.01	32.57	0.03	48.01
Met. Pr. 22	55.59	3.94	16.59	4.11	0.69	10.78	0.42	7.89
Min. Ex. 23	37.90	7.51	8.40	1.62	0.09	15.55	0.03	28.90
Min. Pr. 24	72.31	7.48	7.14	3.12	1.98	4.54	1.84	1.60
Chemic. 25	66.65	4.16	9.15	1.95	3.22	9.10	0.54	5.23
Fibres 26	67.83	6.90	9.82	2.31	1.34	8.00	0.97	2.82
Met. Pd. 31	66.68	5.89	12.90	1.73	2.21	5.04	3.73	1.81
Mech. Eng. 32	61.32	4.33	14.43	0.99	5.53	10.44	0.80	2.16
Off. Eq. 33	44.58	8.63	3.52	0.09	11.60	23.57	7.35	0.65
El. Eng. 34	49.55	4.42	9.74	1.05	12.79	12.31	6.17	3.96
Motor 35	7307	6.67	6.31	1.34	10.25	1.79	0.14	0.43
Transp. 36	42.38	1.65	4.19	0.95	6.37	25.99	1.86	16.61
Instr. 37	44.79	3.48	13.30	0.51	18.50	11.36	5.43	2.64
Food 41	57.98	11.41	2.88	2.41	0.21	9.80	0.30	15.01
Drink 42	74.71	13.01	1.24	0.65	0.10	1.59	0.05	8.65
Text. 43	55.36	8.63	6.93	2.71	1.82	6.79	5.57	12.19
Leath. 44	42.29	3.79	4.45	2.29	1.00	6.52	13.25	26.40
Ft./Cl. 45	42.65	11.75	4.13	7.53	0.34	8.45	13.71	11.43
Timber 46	37.08	7.81	21.77	10.67	0.15	10.01	2.32	10.19
Paper 47	44.71	4.85	32.57	1.65	0.72	10.82	0.59	4.10
Rubber 48	71.14	6.00	8.65	1.29	2.68	5.64	2.63	1.97
Other 49	29.39	3.47	8.18	2.88	3.13	10.02	6.01	36.93

European and non-EE economies were then scaled down to add up to exactly 100%. Table 3.7 shows the results and derives the increases/ decreases in market shares of the different trading countries by the year 2010 as well as percentage differences from the original 1986/7 market shares and table 3.8 presents the same information for each of the Eastern and Central European countries. This completes our long-term projections apart from some modifications, made to highly natural resource-based industries (minerals and furs) which are treated differently.

Short-term projections

The projections of exports up to 1995 are done separately from the long-term projections using a different methodology. (At one point,

Table 3.7. (*cont.*)

b Projections for 2010

Market shares in EC markets: projections for 2000/2010

NACE	EEC-6	Rest EC	Rest WEur.	EEur.	Japan	Rest OECD	NICs	RoW
21	9.68	2.69	6.33	4.81	0.01	31.32	0.01	45.15
22	50.83	4.22	16.75	13.23	0.44	7.61	0.50	6.41
23	36.50	8.63	7.85	8.93	0.05	10.96	0.02	27.07
24	66.33	8.58	6.71	8.56	1.81	4.28	2.00	1.72
25	60.34	4.47	8.64	9.68	3.63	7.38	0.74	5.13
26	61.19	8.02	9.23	8.55	1.28	6.57	1.76	3.41
31	62.22	5.97	12.62	7.40	1.89	4.13	4.12	1.64
32	55.27	4.18	13.71	8.67	6.52	8.45	1.06	2.14
33	42.47	7.16	3.41	2.46	12.37	22.71	8.47	0.96
34	44.51	4.73	9.17	6.04	13.54	11.25	6.49	4.26
35	66.10	7.08	6.93	6.09	11.61	1.19	0.33	0.67
36	37.89	1.42	2.51	1.93	5.03	28.14	2.43	20.65
37	42.22	3.55	11.33	4.93	18.78	10.99	5.61	2.59
41	56.66	10.75	2.52	8.53	0.15	8.36	0.20	12.83
42	71.70	11.81	0.89	7.04	0.10	1.45	0.04	6.98
43	50.72	10.06	6.83	8.39	2.22	4.75	5.59	11.43
44	40.76	3.83	4.85	4.42	0.79	5.89	14.00	25.47
45	38.70	15.27	3.86	10.37	0.33	6.68	13.07	11.74
46	34.34	8.49	19.88	16.20	0.08	9.17	1.76	10.09
47	41.23	4.94	26.98	12.28	0.75	8.89	0.59	4.35
48	65.56	5.83	8.36	6.74	3.18	4.99	3.10	2.25
49	28.79	3.52	6.69	7.07	3.28	8.97	7.52	34.16
Total Manuf.	51.44	6.25	8.92	7.33	6.93	9.84	3.75	5.55

however, the long-term projections do play a role, and this will be pointed out below.) We take two factors as determining the growth in export volumes from Eastern Europe to EC markets:

(i) The conversion of export capacities which were – in the past (i.e. in 1987) – oriented towards Eastern European markets (including the USSR).
(ii) The building up of new export capacities designed to capture an increasing share of EC markets.

Table 3.7. (*cont.*)

c Changes in market shares, 1987 to 2010

NACE	EEC-6	RestEC	Rest WEur.	EEur.	Japan	Rest OECD	NICs	RoW
21	1.07	−0.14	−1.27	4.45	−0.00	−1.24	−0.02	−2.86
22	−4.76	0.28	0.15	9.13	−0.25	−3.16	0.09	−1.48
23	−1.40	1.12	−0.55	7.31	−0.04	−4.59	−0.01	−1.83
24	−5.98	1.10	−0.43	5.45	−0.16	−0.26	0.16	0.13
25	−6.31	0.31	−0.51	7.73	0.41	−1.72	0.20	−0.10
26	−6.64	1.12	−0.59	−0.59	6.24	−0.06	−1.43	0.78
31	−4.46	0.08	−0.28	5.67	−0.32	−0.91	0.39	−0.17
32	−6.06	−0.15	−0.72	7.69	0.99	−1.99	0.26	−0.01
33	−2.11	−1.47	−0.11	2.36	0.77	−0.86	1.12	0.31
34	−5.04	0.31	−0.57	4.99	0.75	−1.06	0.32	0.30
35	−6.97	0.41	0.62	4.75	1.37	−0.60	0.19	0.24
36	−4.49	−0.23	−1.67	0.98	−1.35	2.15	0.57	4.04
37	−2.57	0.07	−1.97	4.43	0.28	−0.37	0.17	−0.04
41	−1.32	−0.66	−0.36	6.12	−0.06	−1.44	−0.10	−2.18
42	−3.01	−1.21	−0.35	6.39	−0.00	−0.14	−0.01	−1.68
43	−4.64	1.43	−0.10	5.68	0.40	−2.05	0.03	−0.75
44	−1.53	0.04	0.40	2.13	−0.21	−0.63	0.74	−0.93
45	−3.95	3.52	−0.27	2.84	−0.02	−1.77	−0.65	0.31
46	−2.74	0.68	−1.89	5.53	−0.07	−0.83	−0.56	−0.11
47	−3.48	0.09	−5.59	10.63	0.03	−1.93	−0.00	0.25
48	−5.58	−0.17	−0.30	5.45	0.51	−0.65	0.47	0.28
49	−0.60	0.05	−1.49	4.19	0.15	−1.05	1.52	−2.76
Total *Manuf.*	−4.37	0.02	−0.60	5.58	0.50	−1.27	0.35	−0.20

To analyse these two factors we had to take recourse to a database supplied by UNCTAD in Geneva which was on an SITC (revision 2) classification basis – and not on a NIMEXE basis as the Eurostat trade statistics used so far. The data for Eastern European countries as reporting countries included only Czechoslovakia, Hungary and Poland. The figures for the remaining countries (Bulgaria, Romania, Yugoslavia and the USSR) were calculated from global trade figures supplied by the UN-ECE (see table 3.4) supplemented by the industrial structural information contained in the statistics for Czechoslovakia, Hungary and Poland.

Table 3.8. *Market shares projections, 2010 compared to 1987*

NACE	Hungary			Poland			Czechoslovakia		
	1987	step 6	diff.	1987	step 6	diff.	1987	step 6	diff.
21	0.00	0.98	0.98	0.19	0.75	0.56	0.05	0.75	0.70
22	0.33	1.50	1.18	0.60	2.55	1.95	0.46	2.31	1.85
23	0.04	1.27	1.23	0.07	1.73	1.66	0.74	1.50	0.76
24	0.33	1.22	0.90	0.45	1.82	1.36	1.04	1.29	0.25
25	0.25	1.14	0.89	0.29	1.88	1.59	0.27	1.64	1.37
26	0.14	1.10	0.96	0.07	1.23	1.15	0.36	1.61	1.25
31	0.30	1.19	0.89	0.35	1.41	1.06	0.23	1.45	1.22
32	0.15	1.12	0.97	0.14	1.19	1.06	0.21	1.64	1.43
33	0.01	0.16	0.15	0.00	0.54	0.53	0.01	0.27	0.27
34	0.16	1.03	0.87	0.12	1.24	1.12	0.09	1.34	1.25
35	0.02	1.00	0.98	0.14	1.01	0.87	0.10	0.86	0.77
36	0.01	0.43	0.42	0.27	0.41	0.14	0.07	0.27	0.20
37	0.06	0.53	0.47	0.06	0.78	0.72	0.06	1.15	1.09
41	0.63	1.04	0.41	0.66	1.50	0.84	0.15	1.95	1.81
42	0.02	1.08	1.06	0.06	1.61	1.55	0.22	1.11	0.90
43	0.30	1.13	0.84	0.24	1.25	1.00	0.37	1.29	0.91
44	0.46	0.87	0.42	0.23	0.92	0.68	0.42	0.77	0.36
45	0.99	1.80	0.81	1.07	1.41	0.35	0.50	1.42	0.92
46	0.49	1.71	1.22	1.15	2.74	1.58	1.10	2.80	1.70
47	0.05	0.52	0.47	0.10	2.18	2.09	0.37	4.64	4.28
48	0.17	1.01	0.83	0.11	1.33	1.22	0.25	1.29	1.04
49	0.16	0.69	0.54	0.14	1.94	1.80	0.25	1.67	1.41
Tot. Manuf.	0.24	0.91	0.67	0.30	1.32	1.02	0.26	1.42	1.15

Since we are interested in conversion of capacities previously oriented towards Eastern European markets we had to obtain information on past export flows to rouble and non-rouble areas, and thus it was essential to complement our Eurostat statistics by the UN statistics. This implied that we also had to put considerable effort into mapping the SITC-based data into a NIMEXE/NACE classification.[7] This was done at a 3-digit SITC and 2-digit NACE level.[8] The result of this conversion of SITC trade flows into NACE industry exports is reported in table 3.9 (columns (1)-(4)).[9] We

Table 3.8. (*cont.*)

NACE	Bulgaria			Romania			USSR		
	1987	step 6	diff.	1987	step 6	diff.	1987	step 6	diff.
21	0.00	0.09	0.09	0.00	0.18	0.18	0.11	1.48	1.37
22	0.15	0.46	0.31	0.28	0.78	0.50	1.15	4.34	3.20
23	0.02	0.29	0.27	0.00	0.38	0.38	0.54	2.66	2.12
24	0.05	0.31	0.26	0.34	0.34	0.00	0.06	2.64	2.57
25	0.07	0.28	0.21	0.14	0.56	0.42	0.55	3.16	2.61
26	0.07	0.33	0.26	0.51	0.51	0.00	0.16	2.76	2.61
31	0.02	0.25	0.22	0.23	0.46	0.23	0.07	1.59	1.52
32	0.04	0.23	0.19	0.07	0.46	0.39	0.10	3.05	2.96
33	0.01	0.12	0.11	0.00	0.05	0.04	0.00	0.89	0.88
34	0.02	0.17	0.15	0.06	0.21	0.16	0.06	1.41	1.35
35	0.00	0.15	0.15	0.07	0.34	0.26	0.41	1.33	0.92
36	0.00	0.02	0.02	0.16	0.07	−0.09	0.05	0.93	0.89
37	0.01	0.21	0.20	0.02	0.19	0.17	0.10	1.36	1.26
41	0.08	0.22	0.14	0.12	0.37	0.25	0.26	2.70	2.43
42	0.01	0.17	0.16	0.00	0.36	0.36	0.30	1.94	1.64
43	0.08	0.29	0.21	0.38	0.49	0.11	0.22	2.57	2.35
44	0.06	0.06	0.00	0.20	0.25	0.05	0.04	0.86	0.82
45	0.12	0.23	0.11	1.12	0.38	−0.73	0.05	3.50	3.46
46	0.08	0.35	0.27	2.00	0.62	−1.38	3.81	6.44	2.63
47	0.02	0.35	0.33	0.06	1.19	1.13	0.61	2.57	1.96
48	0.02	0.19	0.17	0.11	0.31	0.20	0.02	1.80	1.78
49	0.09	0.12	0.03	0.04	0.27	0.23	1.95	1.12	−0.83
Tot. Manuf.	0.05	0.21	0.16	0.22	0.37	0.16	0.47	2.13	1.66

again recalculated rouble trade flows of each country using the Hungarian rouble/dollar exchange rate in 1987.

The methodology applied to calculate conversion rates (i.e. which proportions of export capacity previously oriented towards Eastern European markets will be converted into trade with the West) was the following.

First we calculated the shares of exports of each of the Eastern European

Table 3.8. (*cont.*)

NACE	Yugoslavia			EEFSU		
	1987	step 6	diff.	1987	step 6	diff.
21	0.01	0.63	0.62	0.35	4.87	4.52
22	1.15	1.36	0.21	4.11	13.30	9.19
23	0.21	1.23	1.02	1.62	9.06	7.43
24	0.84	0.97	0.13	3.12	8.59	5.47
25	0.38	1.08	0.71	1.95	9.75	7.80
26	1.00	1.08	0.09	2.31	8.63	6.32
31	0.53	1.06	0.53	1.73	7.41	5.67
32	0.29	1.06	0.76	0.99	8.75	7.76
33	0.06	0.38	0.32	0.09	2.41	2.31
34	0.55	0.78	0.23	1.05	6.18	5.13
35	0.61	1.49	0.88	1.34	6.18	4.84
36	0.41	0.23	−0.17	0.95	2.36	1.41
37	0.20	0.73	0.53	0.51	4.95	4.45
41	0.52	0.85	0.34	2.41	8.63	6.23
42	0.04	0.96	0.92	0.65	7.24	6.59
43	1.12	1.30	0.18	2.71	8.32	5.61
44	0.88	0.70	−0.18	2.29	4.43	2.15
45	3.69	1.63	−2.06	7.53	10.39	2.86
46	2.03	1.70	−0.33	10.67	16.36	5.69
47	0.45	0.90	0.45	1.65	12.34	10.69
48	0.60	0.85	0.25	1.29	6.77	5.49
49	0.25	1.24	0.99	2.88	7.04	4.16
Tot. Manuf.	0.70	0.96	0.25	2.25	7.33	5.08

countries to Eastern Europe (including the USSR) in total exports (column (6)). We made the following assumption: if an industry's exports went entirely to Eastern European markets (i.e. none to the Western markets) in 1987 only 25% of those exports could be converted into trade to Western markets, but if a fraction t went to the West, the fraction reallocated to Western markets would be $0.25 + 0.75t$, as shown in figure 3.2.

These calculated conversion rates for the different industries were further

Table 3.9. *Short-run projections: capacity conversion and export growth, 1987–95*

| | | | CZECHOSLOVAKIA | | | | |
NACE	(1) EE-6	(2) USSR	(3) Other Eur.	(4) Other devpd	(5)[a] EC share	(6)[b] EEFSU share	(7) EE) factor
Total	5 055 609	7 079 981	1 431 826	404 074	53.32	75.53	0.59
22	351 376	314 059	271 235	14 385	48.86	54.37	0.71
23	23 514	0	15 251	0	58.24	39.17	0.49
24	211 838	170 147	27 984	24 237	70.70	68.19	0.54
25	432 587	343 218	185 348	13 727	58.33	61.89	0.40
26	41 839	18 068	3 804	0	74.97	79.77	0.38
31	130 572	76 153	10 214	557	74.64	82.96	0.33
32	1 413 959	2 434 944	144 719	200 620	28.77	88.81	0.28
33	97 209	193 286	10 496	0	0.00	96.51	0.33
34	518 143	430 132	49 305	5 858	53.64	88.85	0.30
35	726 326	705 599	22 683	2 412	76.23	93.13	0.29
36	212 792	818 665	42 536	10 998	13.35	94.35	0.27
37	127 088	102 183	2 903	152	41.17	97.79	0.74
41/42	50 996	72 841	84 174	19 377	56.51	34.22	0.63
43	116 348	169 287	111 365	35 302	48.94	49,86	0.75
44	1 833	0	2 208	564	24.59	33.27	0.38
45	93 783	786 674	47 327	26 878	60.29	82.49	0.65
46	37 919	200 074	87 873	3 648	65.68	47.16	0.78
47	55 716	25 079	64 204	807	65.98	29.71	0.46
48	68 209	37 673	7 275	4 861	71.08	71.61	0.55
49	105 610	137 959	23 528	21 651	71.92	60.22	

NACE	(8) USSR share[c]	(9) USSR factor	(10) Convers. rate	(11) EC 1987	(12) EC 1995	(13) Average growth rate	(14) QP	(15) Growth rate new inv.	(16) Overall growth rate
22	47.20	0.92	0.54	272 901	449 447	2.71	0.809	5.70	8.41
23	44.54	0.93	0.66	21 272	30 294	1.92	0.671	4.76	6.68
24	44.54	0.93	0.46	126 005	249 084	3.70	0.57	4.08	7.78
25	44.24	0.93	0.50	278 656	505 262	3.23	0.848	5.97	9.20
26	30.16	1.02	0.41	11 393	29 780	5.22	0.616	4.39	9.60
31	36.84	0.98	0.37	31 703	88 777	5.59	0.486	3.50	9.09
32	63.26	0.82	0.27	139 458	442 759	6.27	0.539	3.87	10.14
33	66.54	0.80	0.22	0	0	6.75	0.289	2.17	8.91
34	45.36	0.93	0.31	63 814	221 249	6.75	0.611	4.36	11.10
35	49.28	0.90	0.27	80 464	378 066	8.40	0.387	2.83	11.23
36	79.37	0.72	0.21	8 251	37 401	8.20	0.305	2.27	10.48
37	44.57	0.93	0.25	2 138	25 608	13.48	0.419	3.05	16.53
41/42	58.82	0.85	0.63	134 544	178 610	1.54	1.092	7.63	9.16
42						1.54	0.676	4.80	6.34
43	59.27	0.84	0.53	140 589	214 491	2.29	0.496	3.57	5.87
44	59.27	0.84	0.63	904	1 190	0.542	3.89	5.38	
45	89.35	0.66	0.25	112 648	247 020	4.26	0.503	3.62	7.88
46	84.07	0.70	0.45	175 166	245 444	1.83	0.584	4.17	6.00
47	31.04	1.01	0.79	126 112	168 114	1.56	0.809	5.70	7.26
48	35.58	0.99	0.46	29 834	64 204	4.16	0.579	4.14	8.30
49	56.64	0.86	0.47	115 716	198 340	2.93	0.943	6.61	9.54

Notes: [a] Column (5) $= 11/(3 + 4 + 11)$ [b] Column(6) $= (1 + 2)/(1 + 2 + 3 + 4 + 11)$ [c] Column(8) $= 2/(1 + 2)$

Table 3.9. (cont.)

	(1) EE-6	(2) USSR	(3) Other Eur.	(4) Other devpd	(5)[a] EC share	(6)[b] EEFSU share	(7) EE factor
			HUNGARY				
Total	930 735	1 853 484	988 503.8	318 187	56.38	48.17	0.70
22	78 409	102 004	92 283	48 618	47.68	40.12	0.79
23	1 802	234	3 759		25.87	28.65	0.77
24	16 878	14 380	20 928	9 902	57.18	30.27	0.66
25	147 059	258 936	157 025	54 298	55.98	45.82	0.73
26					41.12	35.93	0.59
31	29 776	46 236	14 095.8	2 868.997	72.93	54.81	0.35
32	243 756	358 362	18 885.65	3 875.999	76.36	86.22	0.28
33					16.64	96.34	0.50
34	26 818	10 904	8 512.795	78.9972	55.77	66.01	0.40
35	5 738	6 843	951.7953	69.9972	68.72	79.39	0.40
36	5 738	6 843	951.7953	69.9972	68.72	79.39	0.35
37					76.36	86.22	0.61
41/42	154 541	452 616	154 642.5	60 385.5	62.59	51.61	0.73
43	29 293	61 711	65 023	30 521	41.12	35.93	0.79
44	8 433	6 610	9 424	4 135	66.03	27.37	0.64
45	38 032	209 233	35 499	58 888	65.16	47.72	0.85
46	12 314	14 764	29 053	8 676	66.09	19.57	0.70
47	8 349	12 113	15 816.88	1 015.75	44.28	40.38	0.66
48	19 754	21 072	13 572.88	9 342.75	53.07	45.54	0.58
49	24 396	38 245	12 282.25	6 629.5	61.28	56.19	

NACE	(8) USSR share[c]	(9) USSR factor	(10) Convers. rate	(11) EC 1987	(12) EC 1995	(13) Average growth rate	(14) QP	(15) Growth rate new inv.	(16) Overall growth rate
22	56.54	0.86	0.60	128 399	180 163	1.84	0.859	6.04	7.88
23	11.49	1.13	0.89	1 312	1 780	1.66	0.807	5.69	7.34
24	46.00	0.92	0.71	41 169	53 934	1.47	0.778	5.49	6.96
25	63.78	0.82	0.54	268 694	390 605	2.03	0.981	6.87	8.90
26	67.81	0.79	0.58			2.16	0.64	4.55	6.71
31	60.83	0.84	0.49	45 703	72 964	2.54	0.643	4.57	7.11
32	59.52	0.84	0.30	73 504	210 447	5.71	0.624	4.44	10.15
33	66.48	0.80	0.22			3.78	0.278	2.09	5.87
34	28.91	1.03	0.52	10 832	21 736	3.78	0.754	5.33	9.11
35	54.39	0.87	0.35	2 244	5 300	4.66	0.651	4.63	9.29
36	54.39	0.87	0.35	2 244	5 300	4.66	0.795	5.61	10.27
37	59.52	0.84	0.30			5.71	0.338	2.50	8.21
41/42	74.55	0.75	0.46	359 686	535 507	2.16	0.881	6.19	8.35
42						2.16	0.916	6.43	8.59
43	67.81	0.79	0.58	66 727	88 409	1.53	0.646	4.59	6.12
44	43.94	0.94	0.74	26 360	33 752	1.34	0.88	7.53	
45	84.62	0.69	0.44	176 492	248 105	1.85	0.894	6.28	8.13
46	54.52	0.87	0.74	73 547	86 875	0.90	0.594	4.24	5.14
47	59.20	0.84	0.59	13 378	18 715	1.82	0.438	3.18	5.00
48	51.61	0.89	0.59	25 909	38 609	2.17	0.703	4.98	7.15
49	61.05	0.83	0.48	29 929	48 444	2.61	0.632	4.50	7.11

Notes: [a] Column (5) $=11/(3+4+11)$ [b] Column(6) $=(1+2)/(1+2+3+4+11)$ [c] Column(8) $=2/(1+2)$

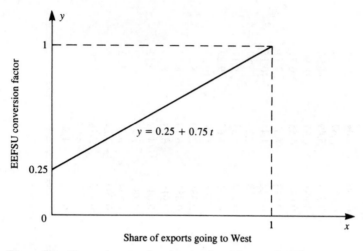

Figure 3.2   Determinants of export reorientation to the West

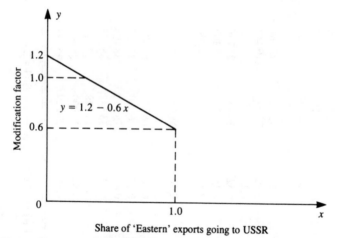

Figure 3.3   Further modification of calculated conversion rates

modified to account for the proportion of exports to the USSR in total exports to Eastern Europe (column (8)). That is, if a high proportion of total exports to Eastern Europe went to the USSR, then the previously calculated conversion rates would be further modified by multiplication with the ratios derived from the following linear relationship: $y = 1.2 - 0.6x$, where x is the ratio of exports to the USSR divided by total exports to EE, and y is the multiplicative factor (figure 3.3).

The derived conversion rates (to Western markets) of capacities

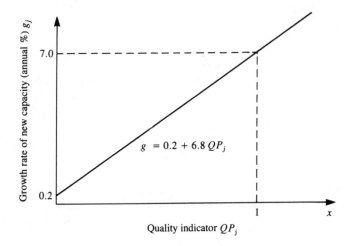

Figure 3.4 Quality gap and new export capacities

previously oriented towards exports to Eastern Europe are given in table 3.9 (column (10)). The shares of these converted capacities (by 1995) going to the EC as compared to other Western markets has been assumed to remain a fixed ratio (the same as in 1987). The implied annual growth rates of exports to the EC (at 1987 prices) until 1995 which result from this conversion of capacities are given in column ((13)) of table 3.9.

In addition to this conversion of capacities previously oriented towards Eastern European markets we have to take account of the *building up of new export capacities* to the West. Here we assume the following: if there were no *quality gap* (i.e. $QP_j = 1.0$) the growth rate of new export capacity to the EC would be equal to 7% p.a. (This translates into an average growth rate for the core Eastern European countries of about 5% p.a., which could be scaled up if thought appropriate.) Different industries which had a different starting position in terms of the quality gap in their exports to EC markets would – in the period up to 1995 – then build up their *new* export capacities at differential rates given by the relationship: $g_j = 0.2 + 6.8 QP_j$, shown in figure 3.4.

The resulting annual growth rates of new export capacity to EC markets (starting with their levels in 1987) are in columns (15) of table 3.9. The overall growth rates – i.e. the combined growth rates derived from the conversion of capacities previously oriented towards Eastern European markets and from the assumption about the building up of new export capacities oriented towards EC markets – are in column (16) of table 3.9.

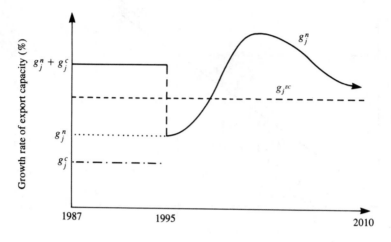

Figure 3.5   Time profile of the catching-up process

Medium-term projections and the pattern of catching-up

The assumption underlying the medium-term projections – i.e. from 1995 to 2000 – is that no more conversion of Eastern European capacities previously oriented towards Eastern Europe will take place after 1995. Whatever has not been converted up to 1995 will play no further role in the growth of exports to the West. The growth rates of exports of the different industries to EC markets will be entirely driven by its target share for 2010 derived from the long-term projections, and the positions achieved by 1995 determined by the short-term projections. On the basis of these assumptions, the time profile of the catching-up process is going to look like that in figure 3.5.[10] g_j^c refers to the industry j's growth rate of exports to EC markets derived from conversion of existing capacities, g_j^n refers to growth in exports to EC markets from new capacities, and g_j is simply $g_j = g_j^c + g_j^n$. We can see that, by assumption, $g_j = g_j^n$ for the period after 1995.

For comparative purposes we have also drawn the average annual growth of the expansion of the EC traded goods market for industry j, denoted by g_j^{EC}. The overall catching-up process implied by our analysis, which requires a substantial increase in the market shares of Eastern European countries in EC markets, implies that g_j^{EE} (where Eastern Europe stands for an Eastern European country) is substantially above g_j^{EC} over much of the period 1987–2010. Whenever there is a shortfall in one sub-period there must be a compensating speeding-up of growth in subsequent periods. The main reason for the catching-up process as postulated in our model was that there is a quality gap, expressed by our indicator $QP_j(t)$, which closes over time. Literature (see e.g. Verspagen, 1991) suggests that when a quality gap is very high, it is difficult to start a catching-up process; when the quality gap is less than this threshold level but still large, a country can achieve the highest differential growth rates between the advanced competitors and themselves, and as the quality gap closes (i.e. $QP_j \to 1$) the growth rates also asymptotically approach the rate of overall market growth (in our case $g_j^{EE} \to g_j^{EC}$). In algebraic terms, the differential in export growth rates can thus be made a function of a closing quality gap, such as:

$$g_j^{EE}(t) - g_j^{EC}(t) = \lambda_j \ (1.0 - QP_j(t)) \text{ where } QP_j(t) \leq 1.0$$

The above discussion is quite consistent with the assumption made in the short-run projections where we assumed that investment into new capacities is inversely related to the quality gap, i.e. the higher the quality gap the lower the rate of initial export expansion. This is what characterises the short-run differential expansion of new export capacity over the period 1987-95. Over the medium to long term, however, the relationship reverses and we assume that the higher the initial quality gap the greater the scope for catching-up and differential growth rates of exports, as described by the equation above. The switch from a negative short-run relationship between the size of the quality gap and differential export growth in the short run to a positive relationship over the medium to long term is compatible with the threshold phenomenon mentioned above.[11]

The quantitative estimates of the respective average annual growth rates over the periods 1987–95, 1995–2000 and 2000–10 as well as the levels of exports achieved at each target date are summarised in table 3.10:

In the last column of table 3.10 we present for comparative purposes a long-run steady-state growth rate of exports (g_i^{8710}) of an industry if it were to attain the 'target' market share in EC markets at a continuous steady-state rate of expansion starting in 1987. If the short-run growth rate (g_i^{8795}) is below that steady-state rate, the medium- to long-run growth rate would obviously have to exceed that steady-state rate to achieve the final 'target'. The information on total manufacturing gives a clear picture of the implied short-run and medium-run growth rates of exports to EC markets which is compatible with our analysis of catching-up processes discussed above and summarised in figure 3.5.

Import projections

The projections of imports proceeded in the following way.

First, we limited ourselves to projecting the composition of imports, i.e. the shares of different commodities in total imports. We denote these shares

Table 3.10. *Projections for exports and export growth, 1987–95, 1995–2010*

CZECHOSLOVAKIA NACE	1987[a]	g_i^{8795b}	1995[a]	2000[a]	g_i^{9510b}	2010[a]	g_i^{8710b}
21 Metal Ex.	2 465	6.94	4 296	17 255	17.38	58 251	13.75
22 Metal Pr.	228 991	8.41	448 744	1 010 176	10.14	2 054 686	9.54
23 Miner Ex.	28 706	6.68	48 993	59 557	2.44	70 652	3.92
24 Miner Pr.	125 026	7.78	232 888	348 095	5.02	494 800	5.98
25 Chemicals	223 339	9.20	466 124	1 400 994	13.76	3 669 691	12.17
26 Fibres	17 332	9.60	37 373	99 923	12.29	236 255	11.36
31 Metal Pds	42 441	9.09	87 856	328 968	16.50	1 044 389	13.93
32 Mech. Eng.	130 395	10.14	293 391	1 069 340	16.17	3 315 706	14.07
33 Office Eq.	1 822	8.91	3 718	67 916	36.31	862 897	26.78
34 Electr. En.	65 668	11.10	159 646	767 167	19.62	3 029 735	16.66
35 Motor Veh.	68 944	11.23	169 320	586 495	15.53	1 739 309	14.03
36 Other Tra.	12 071	10.48	27 913	29 402	0.65	30 770	4.07
37 Instr. Eng.	8 320	16.53	31 217	187 811	22.43	902 892	20.38
41 Food	79 279	9.16	165 019	685 864	17.81	2 385 630	14.80
42 Drink	13 397	6.34	22 242	61 745	12.76	150 873	10.53
43 Textiles	133 864	5.87	214 028	450 176	9.29	862 839	8.10
44 Leather	20 667	5.38	31 774	45 926	4.61	63 395	4.87
45 Footwear	142 848	7.88	268 385	476 271	7.17	786 707	7.42
46 Timber, F.	187 855	6.00	303 648	472 522	5.53	695 772	5.69
47 Paper	111 824	7.26	199 910	949 898	19.48	3 714 607	15.23
48 Rubber	53 397	8.30	103 708	371 287	15.94	1 133 360	13.28
49 Other Man.	74 163	9.54	159 059	443 239	12.81	1 086 633	11.67
Tot. Manuf.	1 772 814	8.43	3 479 252	9 930 026	13.99	28 389 849	12.6

Notes: [a] In ECUs at 1987 prices. [b] Volume growth rates.

as $\mu_j = m_j/M$ where m_j are imports of commodity j and M total imports. The import structure is then defined by the vector μ. Furthermore, we will henceforth confine ourselves to imports from EC producers (where the elements of vector μ refer to the shares of commodities i in imports from EC producers).

For projecting the *long-term* structure of imports, we make use of a relationship between the composition of imports and GNP per head. Support for this relationship is presented in tables 3.11 and 3.12. There we can see that the distance (using the same distance measures as described on p. 78 above) between a country's composition of imports from the EC and total EC exports correlates with GNP per head. That is, countries with a high GNP per head are closer to the typical composition of EC exports.

Table 3.10. (*cont.*)

HUNGARY NACE	1987	g_i^{8795}	1995	2000	g_i^{9510}	2010	g_i^{8710}
21 Metal Ex.	66	11.97	172	4458	40.69	76921	30.70
22 Metal Pr.	162437	7.88	305116	671095	9.85	337560	9.17
23 Miner Ex.	1748	7.34	3145	15122	19.63	59749	15.36
24 Miner Pr.	39365	6.96	68676	191451	12.82	469518	10.78
25 Chemicals	204555	8.90	416956	1096761	12.09	2556414	10.98
26 Fibres	6701	6.71	11465	46873	17.60	160708	13.81
31 Metal Pds	55656	7.11	98312	311503	14.42	854500	11.88
32 Mech. En.	92774	10.15	209025	746278	15.91	2272562	13.91
33 Office Eq.	3675	5.87	5878	64454	29.93	523902	21.56
34 Electr. En.	115629	9.11	293613	804322	15.14	2320648	13.04
35 Motor Veh.	12042	9.29	25323	260808	29.15	2006895	22.24
36 Other Tra.	1544	10.27	3511	14499	17.73	50144	15.13
37 Instr. Eng.	8811	8.21	16991	93755	21.35	417867	16.78
41 Food	338586	8.35	660426	934832	4.34	1267009	5.74
42 Drink	989	8.59	1966	19544	28.71	145801	21.71
43 Textiles	107791	6.12	172618	379416	9.84	755772	8.55
44 Leather	22826	7.53	41678	55547	3.59	71420	4.96
45 Footwear	283250	8.13	542711	750015	4.04	995425	5.46
46 Timber, F.	83633	5.14	126205	241417	8.11	425841	7.08
47 Paper	151979	5.00	23839	109196	19.02	413526	14.15
48 Rubber, P.	37488	7.15	66400	264008	17.25	883354	13.74
49 Other Man.	46449	7.11	82048	204781	11.43	455886	9.93
Tot. Manuf.	1639994	8.05	3122076	7280076	11.87	18521424	10.54

Our long-term projections of imports use, on the one hand, projections of GNP per head for both the Eastern European and the group of reference countries (the same as those used in the exports projections) for the year 2010 (these projections are based on Rollo and Stern, 1992, supplemented by complementary projections derived from the Kravis *et al.* set of statistics, see Kravis, Summers and Heston, 1988) and, on the other hand, the relationship just established. The projected import structures for the year 2010 are thus determined, for each Eastern European country, as a weighted mix of the import structures of the reference countries. The weights are given by the formula:

Table 3.11. *Distance from total EC import structure, manufacturing, 1988–90 (measure as used on p. 78)*

Hungary	Poland	Czecho.	Bulgaria	Romania	USSR	Yugo.
3.371 606	3.304 031	5.269 147	4.721 357	3.762 459	4.858 143	1.988 682

Table 3.12. *Relationship between distance in import structure from total EC exports and level of development*

Dep. variable: Distance from EC import structure
Regressor: GDP/Pop in 1985
Data Source: Kravis, Summers and Heston (1988)

Constant	9 234.81
Std err of Y est	2 679.99
R^2	0.419
No. of observations	19
Degrees of freedom	17
X coefficient(s)	− 1 266.61
Std err. of coeff.	361.35
T-ratio	3.51

Data	GDP/Pop	Distance
Austria	9 023	1.445823
Switzerland	10 670	1.109208
Finland	9 266	1.541039
Sweden	9 780	1.430149
Denmark	10 893	1.196869
Spain	6 385	2.069718
Portugal	3 622	1.828976
Greece	4 511	2.22261
Turkey	2 521	2.738768
Israel	6 183	5.938709
Egypt	1 197	3.032227
Iran	3 884	3.545099
Korea	3 034	5.151653
Japan	9 363	2.408773
Taiwan	3 556	2.712993
Malaysia	3 351	3.275756
Philippines	1 364	3.932764
India	757	7.659656
Brazil	3 253	4.27359

$$\omega^{c'} = |1 - | \, (GNP/head)^{c'} - (GNP/head)^{ee}) \, / \, (GNP/head)^{c'} ||$$

where c' refers to the reference country and ee to the Eastern European country in question. Table 3.13 presents the weights of the different reference countries for each Eastern European country in order to determine its import structure for the year 2010. The resulting import structures are presented in table 3.14.

Summary of results

This chapter has described a methodology to analyse the processes of short-run East-West European integration in both the short and the long run. For the longer run we have outlined a scenario of East-West European integration which corresponds to a successful economic transformation in all Eastern Europe including the former Soviet Union (EEFSU) countries and successful trade integration between all European economies.

The principal assumption behind the projections is that, by 2010, all the EEFSU countries will be at or approaching the levels of economic and trade performance currently displayed by those market economies which have fairly recently joined the European Community or border on the Community. By associating each EEFSU economy with those economies most closely approximating its employment structure we hope to have identified areas of long-run comparative advantage. We also take into account each country's size and location, the current quality of its exports and the relative starting date at which its economic reform process is firmly established. We will now present some summary results of the analysis.

Long-term export projections

Figure 3.6 summarises the interim results for exports from the whole of manufacturing industry in each EEFSU country. It shows multifold increases in most countries' shares of EC imports between 1987 and 2010. For the EEFSU as a whole, market penetration rises from 2% to 8.5%.

Experience is however likely to vary greatly between countries. In 1987, the former USSR provided only a minute share (0.6%) of the manufactured goods imported by the EC. Allowing for the size of the former USSR, and its employment structure, quality and expected technological catch-up, however, produces an expected increase in market share to 2.6% by 2010. By contrast, the market share of ex-Yugoslavia is projected to rise only from 0.7% to 1%. Relative to its modest projected position in 2010, its current market share benefits greatly from its relatively advanced trade integration with the EC.

Table 3.13. *Weights for target import structures*[a]

	Hungary	Poland	Czecho.	Bulgaria	Romania	USSR	Yugo.
Austria	0.109	0.075	0.115	0.076	0.068	0.067	0.069
Switzerland	0.055	0.031	0.060	0.031	0.023	0.023	0.024
Finland	0.101	0.069	0.107	0.069	0.061	0.061	0.062
Sweden	0.085	0.055	0.090	0.055	0.047	0.047	0.048
Denmark	0.048	0.025	0.052	0.025	0.017	0.017	0.018
Spain	0.196	0.146	0.204	0.147	0.139	0.139	0.140
Portugal	0.137	0.216	0.126	0.215	0.213	0.213	0.214
Greece	0.166	0.197	0.156	0.197	0.189	0.189	0.190
Turkey	0.101	0.187	0.089	0.185	0.243	0.243	0.235
Sum	1	1	1	1	1	1	1

Note: [a] Derived from the formula on p. 107.

(a)

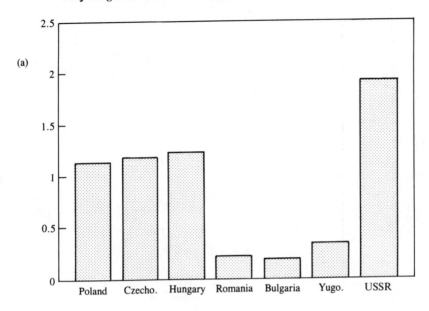

(b)

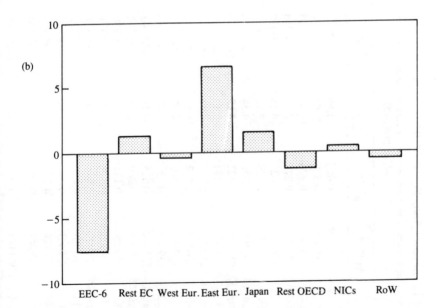

Figure 3.6 Changes in EEFSU shares in total EC imports, total
manufacturing, 1987–2010

Table 3.14. *Imports from EC, 1987–91*

			Czechoslovakia		
NACE	M87	g^{8891}	g/gec	M91	
Met. ex. 21	3 799	−0.067	1.56	2 879	
Met. pr. 22	80 119	0.329	29.91	249 940	
Min. ex. 23	3 003	0.876	19.47	37 195	
Min. pr. 24	39 030	0.221	3.75	86 748	
Chemic. 25	376 736	0.022	0.58	410 999	
Fibres 26	16 864	0.104	−2.42	25 052	
Met. man. 31	43 994	0.356	4.34	148 742	
Mech. eng. 32	637 559	0.121	1.89	1 006 799	
Office 33	48 958	0.474	5.39	231 107	
Elec. eng. 34	232 764	0.2	3.92	482 659	
Motor 35	36 515	1.152	11.88	783 142	
Transp. 36	7 027	1.169	4.47	155 528	
Instrum. 37	39 413	0.22	2.82	87 313	
Food/Dri. 41	113 102	0.025	0.47	124 843	
Food/Dri. 42	6 996	0.269	2.72	18 142	
Textile 43	76 256	0.142	2.58	129 700	
Leather 44	4 222	0.8	21.62	44 321	
Foot./Clo. 45	25 477	0.441	7.88	109 851	
Timber 46	10 501	0.458	5.59	47 453	
Paper 47	23 421	0.362	5.93	80 596	
Rubber 48	34 126	0.278	3.81	91 035	
Other 49	48 261	0.295	4.76	135 730	
Tot. Manuf.	1 908 143	0.191	2.94	4 489 774	

NACE	MX1987	MX1991	MX1995	MX2000	MX2010	diff9587	diff1095	diff1087
Met. ex. 21	0.20	0.06	0.06	0.06	0.06	-0.14	-0.00	-0.14
Met. pr. 22	4.20	5.57	5.79	6.07	6.62	1.59	0.83	2.42
Min. ex. 23	0.16	0.83	0.75	0.64	0.43	0.59	-0.31	0.27
Min. pr. 24	2.05	1.93	1.96	1.99	2.05	-0.09	0.10	0.01
Chemic. 25	19.74	9.15	9.83	10.67	12.36	-9.91	2.53	-7.38
Fibres 26	0.88	0.56	0.60	0.64	0.74	-0.29	0.14	0.14
Met. man. 31	2.31	3.31	3.44	3.59	3.89	1.13	0.46	1.59
Mech. eng. 32	33.41	22.42	20.77	18.70	14.57	-12.64	-6.20	-18.85
Office 33	2.57	5.15	4.85	4.48	3.73	2.28	-1.12	1.17
Elec. eng. 34	12.20	10.75	10.76	10.78	10.82	-1.43	0.05	-1.38
Motor 35	1.91	17.44	16.41	15.12	12.54	14.50	-3.87	10.62
Transp. 36	0.37	3.46	2.99	2.40	1.21	2.62	-1.78	0.84
Instrum. 37	2.07	1.94	1.93	1.92	1.89	-0.13	-0.04	-0.17
Food/Dri. 41	5.93	2.78	3.45	4.28	5.94	-2.48	2.49	0.01
Food/Dri. 42	0.37	0.40	0.47	0.56	0.74	0.11	0.26	0.37
Textile 43	4.00	2.89	3.59	4.47	6.23	-0.40	2.64	2.23
Leather 44	0.22	0.99	0.94	0.88	0.75	0.72	-0.18	0.53
Foot./Clo. 45	1.34	2.45	2.77	3.17	3.96	1.43	1.20	2.63
Timber 46	0.55	1.06	1.16	1.30	1.56	0.61	0.40	1.01
Paper 47	1.23	1.80	2.05	2.38	3.02	0.83	0.97	1.79
Rubber 48	1.79	2.03	2.45	2.98	4.03	0.66	1.58	2.25
Other 49	2.53	3.02	2.98	2.94	2.84	0.46	-0.14	0.31
Tot. Manuf.	100.00	100.00	100.00	100.00	100.00			

Table 3.14. (cont.)

			Hungary	
NACE	M87	g^{8891}	g/gec	M91
Met. ex. 21	3 872	−0.099	2.30	2 552
Met. pr. 22	1 171 149	0.033	3.00	133 133 395
Min. ex. 23	3 802	0.109	2.42	5 751
Min. pr. 24	35 127	0.26	4.41	88 537
Chemic. 25	452 448	0.018	0.47	485 914
Fibres 26	49 980	−0.121	2.81	29 837
Met. man. 31	54 844	0.193	2.35	111 094
Mech. eng. 32	501 632	0.115	1.80	775 327
Office 33	35 445	0.367	4.17	123 774
Elec. eng. 34	202 062	0.092	1.80	287 326
Motor 35	71 555	1.12	11.55	1 445 385
Transp. 36	7 290	0.435	1.78	30 913
Instrum. 37	38 395	0.169	2.17	71 702
Food/Dri. 41	60 088	−0.048	−0.91	49 355
Food/Dri. 42	5 523	0.183	1.85	10 817
Textile 43	227 207	0.083	1.51	312 562
Leather 44	53 771	0.069	1.86	70 220
Foot./Clo. 45	45 960	0.548	9.79	263 915
Timber 46	11 207	0.53	6.46	61 412
Paper 47	59 607	0.18	2.95	115 565
Rubber 48	69 935	0.093	1.27	99 810
Other 49	63 731	0.201	3.24	132 594
Tot. Manuf.	2 170 630	0.14	2.15	4 707 756

NACE	MX1987	MX1991	MX1995	MX2000	MX2010	diff9587	diff1095	diff1087
Met. ex. 21	0.18	0.05	0.06	0.06	0.06	−0.12	0.00	−0.12
Met. pr. 22	5.40	2.83	3.63	4.63	6.62	−1.77	2.99	1.22
Min. ex. 23	0.18	0.12	0.19	0.27	0.44	0.01	0.25	0.27
Min. pr. 24	1.62	1.88	1.92	1.96	2.06	0.30	0.14	0.44
Chemic. 25	20.84	10.32	10.76	11.30	12.39	−10.09	1.64	−8.45
Fibres 26	2.30	0.63	0.66	0.68	0.74	−1.65	0.08	−1.56
Met. man. 31	2.53	2.36	2.69	3.10	3.92	0.16	1.23	1.39
Mech. eng. 32	23.11	16.47	16.08	15.59	14.62	−7.03	−1.46	−8.49
Office 33	1.63	2.63	2.86	3.16	3.75	1.23	0.88	2.11
Elec. eng. 34	9.31	6.10	7.11	8.37	10.88	−2.20	3.77	1.57
Motor 35	3.30	30.70	26.84	22.00	12.33	23.54	−14.50	9.04
Transp. 36	0.34	0.66	0.77	0.92	1.21	0.44	0.43	0.87
Instrum. 37	1.77	1.52	1.60	1.70	1.90	−0.17	0.30	0.13
Food/Dri. 41	2.77	1.05	2.05	3.30	5.81	−0.72	3.76	3.04
Food/Dri. 42	0.25	0.23	0.33	0.46	0.73	0.08	0.39	0.47
Textile 43	10.47	6.64	6.56	6.47	6.28	−3.90	−0.28	−4.19
Leather 44	2.48	1.49	1.34	1.15	0.76	−1.14	−0.57	−1.71
Foot./Clo. 45	2.12	5.61	5.26	4.83	3.98	3.15	−1.29	1.86
Timber 46	0.52	1.30	1.36	1.43	1.58	0.85	0.21	1.06
Paper 47	2.75	2.45	2.58	2.73	3.03	−0.17	0.45	0.28
Rubber 48	3.22	2.12	2.53	3.04	4.06	−0.69	1.53	0.84
Other 49	2.94	2.82	2.83	2.84	2.87	−0.11	0.04	0.07
Tot. Manuf.	100.00	100.00	100.00	100.00	100.00			

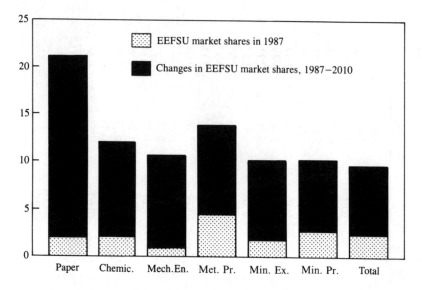

Figure 3.7 Changes in EEFSU shares in total EC imports, 1987–2010, of industries with highest market share growth

The Central European economies of Poland, ex-CSFR and Hungary are expected to gain substantial increases in EC market share as they become much more like other advanced European economies. Hungary's share, in particular, is expected to rise sevenfold from 0.2% to 1.4%.

The aggregate projections, however, conceal substantial differences between industrial sectors. Some sectors in some countries are already producing output at quality close to that of the major Western nations; others lag a long way behind. In some sectors, the orientation has been so firmly towards former CMEA members that, despite conversion problems, the scope for penetrating EC markets in a successful reform scenario may be sufficient for them to exceed the growth rates of sectors which have already been competing effectively. In addition, some sectors tend to be more open than others to competition from outside Europe.

Figure 3.7 displays the six industries which we expect to benefit most under the optimistic scenario. They are ordered by the size of the change in the EC market share for their own sector. The strong performance of these industries reflects relatively weak starting positions as a result of past patterns of specialisation and trade within the former CMEA.

Industries which show high relative growth in market penetration are thus the Paper industry, Chemicals, Mechanical Engineering, Metal and Mineral Products and Mineral Extraction.[12] On average, their share of EC

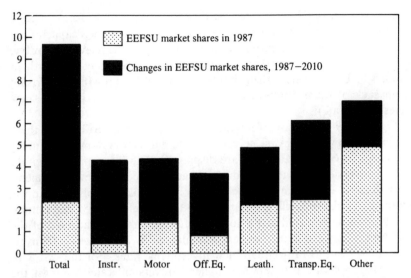

Figure 3.8 Changes in EEFSU shares in total EC imports, 1987–2010, of industries with lowest market share growth

markets rises from 2% to 11%. Only in the Paper industry is the EEFSU projected, on the basis of the results, to achieve a market share above 15% by 2010.

Compared with the 7 percentage points rise in average EEFSU penetration of EC markets over the period, some industries are projected to lag substantially. Figure 3.8 picks out the six slowest performers for the period up to 2010 as a whole. A rise from only 0.5% to 4.5% is projected for Instrument Engineering, despite its particularly low starting level. Other relatively poor performers are Office Equipment, Leather, Motor Vehicles, Transport Equipment and Other Goods. Implicit in the analysis is the assumption that most EEFSU countries will be at a comparative disadvantage in these sectors because the relative quality of their exports and features of their industrial structure mean that, like other neighbouring countries, they will continue to face particularly severe competition in these sectors from the older members of the EC or other parts of the world.

Short-term export projections

In our short-term projections (up to 1995) we concentrated on supply-side considerations. The issue is how fast additional export capacity for EC markets can be brought onstream. We assumed that some capacity previously used for CMEA trade can be converted (the greater the previous emphasis on intra-CMEA trade – particularly exports to the former USSR – the slower this process will be) and we also assumed that new capacity can be added (the higher the current 'quality' attained in the relevant industry, the more attractive that sector will be to new investment). Growth in exports to EC markets is then simply the sum of the growth rates arising from each of these sources (the 'conversion' growth rate plus the 'new investment' rate).

Figures 3.9–3.11 show, for Hungary, Poland and CSFR, how these projected growth rates vary across the different sectors of manufacturing industry (20 NACE categories are displayed). The lower panels identify both 'conversion' growth rates (darker shaded areas) and 'new investment' growth rates. The assumptions behind our methodology imply that exports from most industries will grow at rates in the range of 5–10% per annum. Looking in more detail at the lower panels we can see that most of the differences between industries can be explained by differences in 'conversion' growth rates rather than 'new investment' rates. For the CSFR in particular, we can also see that higher 'conversion' rates amongst the heavier industries (NACE categories 22–37) lead to higher average growth rates overall despite generally lower 'new investment' rates than in the lighter industries.

These high conversion rates reflect, in the main, the relatively higher levels of export capacity directed toward intra-CMEA trade in 1987. The upper panels in figure 3.9 show that, for Czechoslovakia, over 85% of exports in NACE categories 31–37 went to other EEFSU countries in 1987. Although we assume that this concentration itself implies lower effective speed of conversion (even slower if a high proportion of intra-EEFSU trade went to the former Soviet Union) the higher levels of available export capacity in 1988 dominate the calculations.

The different considerations underlying the projections of short-term rather than long-term export growth mean that the relative performance of different industries may vary considerably over time.

Concluding remarks: confronting the methodology with actual results

Chapter 2 analysed in some detail trade developments after 1989. It also applied a factor-intensity model to explain past trade specialisation patterns between East and West European economies and their current trends. We have seen that the explanatory power of such a model was rather high in explaining current East-West inter-industry specialisation. The problem with relying purely on such a traditional comparative advantage/relative factor endowments type of model is that it does not

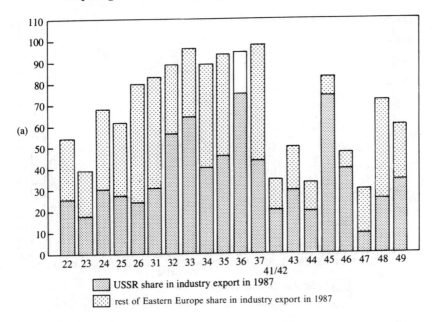

USSR share in industry export in 1987

rest of Eastern Europe share in industry export in 1987

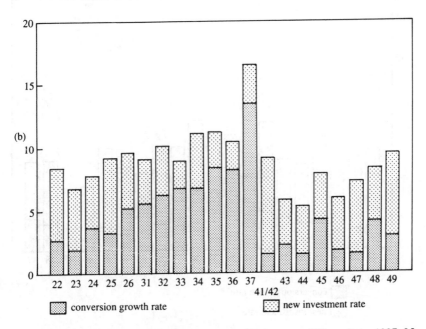

conversion growth rate   new investment rate

Figure 3.9 Czechoslovakia, annual growth of exports to EC markets, 1987–95

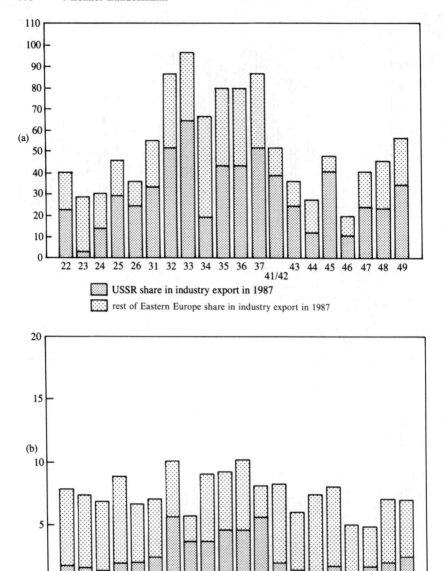

Figure 3.10 Hungary, annual growth of exports to EC markets, 1987–95

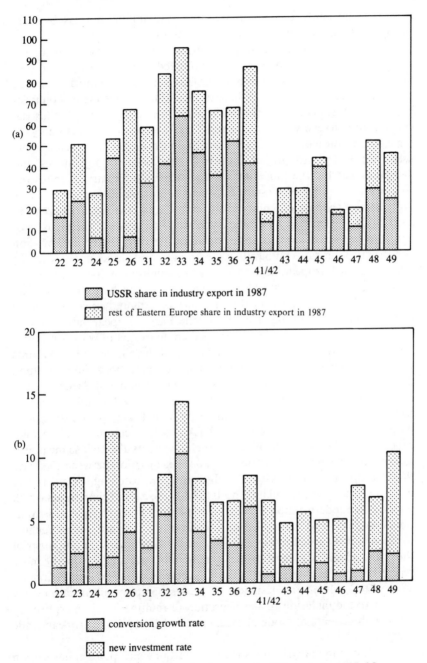

Figure 3.11 Poland, annual growth of exports to EC markets, 1987–95

consider sufficiently the possibility of a catching-up process by East European economies (or of a sub-set of these).

The analysis in this chapter, in contrast, has described a relatively extreme scenario of catching-up, which implied that the most advanced of the CEE economies will occupy market share positions (taking due account of size, distance, etc.) similar to those of West European reference countries by the year 2010. However, the model also allowed a pattern of industrial specialisation to evolve in the long run, i.e. convergence does not imply the same composition of exporting industries. In the model presented we only used two factors to project industrial specialisation advantages and disadvantages for the long run, i.e. the current proximity of industrial structures to a range of Western European economies and relative quality ('technology') gaps in different industries relative to the 'quality leaders' in each industry. There is no doubt much scope to improve the analysis of long-run patterns of specialisation, including the use of further information concerning long-run comparative advantages and disadvantages of the different East European economies. Factor-intensity analysis of the type presented in chapter 2 (see also Aiginger, 1993) can be part of such an extension; furthermore, detailed studies on strengths and weaknesses in the qualification and training structure of the East European labour forces (such as in Nesporova, 1993) or detailed comparisons of wage structures (see, e.g., Peneder, 1993) as well as analyses of the differential constraints which the underdeveloped capital market institutions impose upon different types of industrial activities (see, e.g., Bonin and Székely, 1994) can all contribute to such an analysis. Over time, as the rather negative results indicated when the factor-intensity model was applied to explain patterns of specialisation between EFTA and EC economies, one would expect a model based on relative factor endowments also to lose the power to explain the evolving structure of trade specialisation between East and West European economies if and as the former are 'catching-up' in terms of developmental levels (in all its aspects) and as the capital constraints which impede the modernisation process of these economies in spite of institutional change and strengths in human infrastructure are somehow overcome. If the catching-up scenario becomes dominant for a number of the (more advanced) East European economies we would expect the more recent theories of international trade (such as Grossman and Helpman, 1990, 1991) which are designed to analyse patterns of intra-industry trade with the inclusion of the operation of multinational enterprises to become the dominant mode of explanation of East-West European trade integration.

Our short-run analysis of trade reorientation which put emphasis upon the 'historical legacy' of large export capacities which were previously oriented towards CMEA markets and which then had to find new sales outlets seems to have been borne out by the facts. See, for example, the cross-section regression analysis presented in table 2.11 (p. 61) which showed the strong relationship between relative export growth rates over the period 1989–91 and the relative exposure of different industries to CMEA export markets prior to 1987. The use of the separate methodologies to analyse the short-run process of trade reorientation and the longer-run process of catching-up and evolving patterns of specialisation led to a picture which indicated that the export growth pattern which we observed immediately after the impact of trade liberalisation and the collapse of intra-(ex-)CMEA trade relationships might not be a good predictor of the longer-run patterns of export growth. Similarly, the dramatic shifts in the composition of imports reflect once-for-all adjustment patterns which do not indicate a trend. We think that current developments support these elements underlying our analysis.

Notes

I wish to thank Anna Hont, Jon Shields and István Székely for their splendid collaboration on earlier versions of the projections reported in this paper. I also want to thank István Ábel, László Halpern, Geoffrey Horton, David Newbery and John Stern for their comments on a previous draft of this chapter.

1 At a later date it may be desirable to adjust the reference countries so that they all have the same expected population as the CSFR, which we take as our reference Eastern European country. This can be done by scaling the trade share of each country by the ratio of the (total) manufacturing export share, correcting for population alone (but not level of development) to its actual export share. Note that the relation between export share and population is non-linear.

2 The group of reference countries includes both more or less industrially advanced Western European economies. The distance in current industrial structures relative to the different Western European economies therefore reveals the current level of development as well as the pattern of specialisation of each Eastern European country relative to each Western European country. It thus gives an indication of the location of each Eastern European country in the spectrum of more or less developed economies of an integrated Europe. It is true that specialisation structures as revealed by current information are affected by past development strategies of the socialist economies and their position within CMEA trading structures, and that these features will become less relevant in shaping the Eastern European countries' industrial structures in the future. Nevertheless, we assume that some of the past legacy will continue to shape specialisation of Eastern European economies in the future, although the boundaries of such specialisation are defined by the group of (Western

European) reference economies. In our analysis, we used employment structures as proxies for output structures since value added data for Eastern European economies were, and still are, affected by relative price distortions.

3 See e.g. the recent group of studies commissioned by the European Commission, forthcoming in *European Economy* (Buigues, ed., 1994).

4 From 1988 onwards Eurostat has adopted the Combined Nomenclature (CN) as a basis for its trade classification. Hence any use made of detailed Eurostat trade statistics after 1988 in this chapter adopts this classification.

5 This figure can of course be adjusted downwards if we wanted to assume, say, an 85% catching-up in the mean; in this case all the other countries will automatically be adjusted downwards as well.

6 Geoffrey Horton (London, NERA) remarked that the fact that we already scaled the different countries' overall market shares up or down by their current levels of total manufacturing exports makes this additional scaling factor superfluous. However, we should remember that the 'size' scaling factor referred to differences in total manufacturing export capacity, while the global 'quality' adjustment factor makes use of relative 'quality gaps' observed in exports to EC markets only. This indicator for a 'technology gap' with respect to exports in this important segment of export trade in advanced Western markets would not be sufficiently taken account of if only the 'size' variable (referring to overall export capacity, a large proportion of which went to CMEA markets) were used for global adjustment.

7 The help of István Székely in this work is gratefully acknowledged.

8 To do it absolutely properly we should use a mapping at a 6–8-digit level.

9 We reproduce here and in tables 3.10 and 3.14 the results for only two of the CEE economies in order to reduce the number of printed tables; the full set of tables is available in Landesmann (1993).

10 In our algebraic forecasting model we analyse only two distinct periods, 1987–95 and 1995–2010, with only average growth rates considered for each period. Figure 3.5 presents a more general description of the catching-up process as it shows continuous variations in growth rates until convergence of CEE with average EC import growth rates is achieved in the very long run. In a stylised way figure 3.5 shows the initial boost which CEE export growth to the West obtained from the process of trade reorientation of large export capacities previously oriented towards CMEA markets. After this period, assumed to be concluded by 1995, the model assumes that export growth is entirely dependent upon the building up of 'new export capacities'. The double-peaked shape of export growth which results and which is shown is – at least so far – compatible with the initially very high and then declining export growth rates observed for CEE economies after 1990.

11 Parameter λ is thus itself a non-linear function of QP_j to arrive at a pattern of a catching-up process as described by figure 3.5.

12 Mineral Extraction excludes energy-producing materials but includes, for example, building materials and phosphates.

References

Aiginger, K., 1993. 'Chancen und Gefährdungspotentiale der Ostöffnung: Konsequenzen für die österreichische Wirtschaft', *WIFO Research Report*, Vienna

Berndt, E. R. and Fuss, M. A., 1986. 'Productivity measurement with adjustments for variations in capacity utilization and other forms of temporary equilibrium', *Journal of Econometrics*, 33, 7–29

Bonin, J. P. and Székely, I. P. (eds.), 1994. *The Development and Reform of Financial Systems in Central and Eastern Europe*, London: Edward Elgar

Buigues, P. and Ilzkovitz, F., 1992. *Economic Interpenetration between the EC and Eastern Countries*, DOC. II/528/91-EN, Commission of the European Communities

Buigues, P., Ilzkovitz, F. and Lebrun, J. F., 1991. 'The sectoral impact of the internal market by industrial sector: the challenge for the Member States', *European Economy*, special edition, 2, 133–137

CEPR, 1990. 'Monitoring European Integration. The impact of Eastern Europe', *Annual Report*, London: CEPR

Chenery, H. and Syrquin, M., 1975. *Patterns of Economic Development, 1950–70*, Oxford: Oxford University Press

Collins, S. M. and Rodrik, D., 1991. 'Eastern Europe and the Soviet Union in the world economy', Washington DC, Institute for International Economics (May)

Englander, S. and Mittelstädt, A., 1988. 'Total Factor Productivity: Macroeconomic and Structural Aspects of the Slowdown', *OECD Economic Studies*, 10 (Spring)

Grossman, G. M. and Helpman, E., 1990. 'Comparative advantage and long-run growth', *American Economic Review*, 80, 796–815

1991. 'Quality ladders in the theory of growth', *Review of Economic Studies*, 58, 43–61

Halpern, L., 1992. 'The effect of costs and subsidies on trade reorientation in Hungary, 1981–90', *Structural Change and Economic Dynamics*, 3(1)

Hare, P. and Hughes, G., 1992a. 'Industrial policy and restructuring in Eastern Europe', *Oxford Review of Economic Policy*, no. 1

1992b. 'The international competitiveness of industries in Bulgaria, Czechoslovakia, Hungary and Poland', *Oxford Economic Papers*, forthcoming

Hulten, C.R., 1986. 'Productivity change, capacity utilization and the sources of efficiency growth', *Journal of Econometrics*, 33, 31–50

Kravis, I., Summers, R. and Heston, A., 1988. 'A new set of international comparisons of real product and price level estimates for 130 countries, 1950–1985', *Review of Income and Wealth*, 34(1)

Křovák, J. and Macourková, E., 1992. 'Structural change in the Czechoslovak Economy', Paper presented at the ACE Workshop on 'Industrial Restructuring and Trade Reorientation in Eastern Europe', Prague (April)

Landesmann, M., 1991. 'Industrial restructuring and the reorientation of trade in Czechoslovakia', *European Economy*, Special edition 2

1993. 'Scenarios for East-West integration', in H. D. Kurz and T. Heuss (eds.), *United Germany and the New European*, London, Edward Elgar, pp. 264–326

Landesmann, M. and Székely, I., 1991. *Industrial Restructuring and the Reorientation of Trade in Czechoslovakia, Hungary and Poland*, CEPR Discussion Paper, 546, London: CEPR

Nesporova, A., 1993. 'Preconditions of the industrial restructuring in the skill, professional and age structure of the labour force in the Czech Republic', Prague, mimeo

Peneder, M., 1993. 'Kosten- und Produktionsstruktur der Industrie in den Ländern Ost-Mitteleuropas', in K. Aiginger (1993)

Rollo, J. and Stern, J., 1992. 'Optimistic and pessimistic development scenarios for Eastern Europe and the former Soviet Union', mimeo, National Economic Research Associates, London

Verspagen, B., 1991. 'A new empirical approach to catching-up or falling behind', *Structural Change and Economic Dynamics*, 2(2)

Part Two
Country studies

4 Deindustrialisation or reindustrialisation? On the future of the eastern German economy

Klaus-Dieter Schmidt and Petra Naujoks

Introduction: how do you merge a socialist and a capitalist economy?

The transition experiment of eastern Germany seems to support the pessimistic view that the 'jump into the market' is not a textbook case for which solutions are easily available (Csaba, 1992). Although, according to recent figures, it is likely that the economy has turned the corner, there is no reason to believe that the crisis is over. It has now been accepted that the time needed to restructure a Soviet-type economy must be measured in decades rather than in years.

At first glance, the results of three years of economic unification look disappointing, as major industries continue to decline. In terms of employment it has lost three-quarters of its productive capacity (figure 4.1), and there is no sign of a reversal. The Treuhandanstalt has an uphill task in attempting to restructure the core of the old industries by privatisation; its portfolio still consists of 1000 industrial companies with 270 000 employees. The great majority of these companies operate at a large loss, and without financial support they would have no chance of survival.

If the prospects are so worrying, has the German shock therapy failed? Is eastern Germany on its way to becoming a depressed area, a Mezzogiorno in Central Europe? Or can it catch up with the western German economy, and if so, how quickly? Is the recent deindustrialisation an 'accident' which could have been avoided, or is it the pre-stage to a reindustrialisation – the necessary correction of a biased production structure inherited from the past? Will other Central and East European countries sooner or later experience a similar decline of production and employment?

When searching for an answer, it must not be overlooked that eastern Germany is a special case. The task is not only to transform its economy from a centrally planned system into a market system but also to integrate it into another economy which has a different level of development, of factor endowment and of international competitiveness. What will happen

127

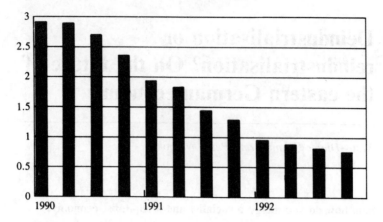

Figure 4.1   Employment in eastern German manufacturing[a], 1990–2, mn
[a] Enterprises with 20 or more employees.
Source: Statistisches Bundesamt; own calculations.

if they merge? From the theory of integration we would expect the following (Siebert, 1990):

(i) Both economies will try to exploit their comparative advantages. On the basis of given factor endowment, specialisation pattern and productivity differential the outcome will be an extension and diversion of bilateral trade. In the short term the superior economy will display its comparative advantages in tradables and will have a huge export surplus. The inferior economy will have an import deficit which must be financed by foreign capital or transfers from abroad.

(ii) Both economies will experience a process of structural change – adjustment in their trade and production structures in line with their long-run comparative advantages. The size of this adjustment will depend on the extent of distortion. In the short run the inferior economy will experience deindustrialisation, but in the long run reindustrialisation is likely. Where trade and production structures are identical (albeit of different efficiency levels) an intra-industry specialisation should emerge, leading to complementary structures in each of the two economies.

(iii) Both economies will export excess mobile resources: the superior economy tends to be relatively rich in capital and technology while in the inferior economy labour and land are plentiful. The transfer of mobile factors of production is an important vehicle in the adjustment process: in the short run it prevents bottlenecks in the factor markets, in the long run it eliminates differences in productivity, in real wages and profits.

So far there is no room at all for disappointment. The collapse of the eastern German economy is fully congruent with standard economic theory which predicts that in these circumstances things must become worse before they can get better.

The crucial point is that the model is based on the assumption that factor prices are determined by relative scarcity; huge wage differences exist which reflect the backwardness of the former socialist economy and, hence, the gap in productivity. In reality, however, real wages in eastern Germany are rising rapidly, faster than productivity (Schmidt and Sander, 1993). At present, effective wages in east German manufacturing have reached 66%, while labour productivity does not exceed 40% of the west German level. From this we can conclude that unit labour costs are roughly 50% higher while all other costs are nearly the same. The prospects for many eastern German firms are gloomy.

The heritage of the past: what can be kept?

From the beginning it was clear that the east German economy would undergo a deep transformation – as have other former socialist economies. Manufacturing was expected to shrink and services to expand (Bode and Krieger-Boden, 1990). As industrial production and employment were much higher, and service production and employment much lower than the 'normal pattern' in Western countries, it was reasonable to assume that the shares in output and labour input would come closer to the western German level. As table 4.1 shows, this projection has been confirmed by experience: the share of industrial production fell sharply – even more drastically than anyone predicted. In 1992 the relative weight of manufacturing in the sectoral composition of production amounted to only 17%, a loss of 21percentage points from 1989 onward. From the west German pattern a relative weight of about 30% could have been expected.

How can this 'overshooting' be explained? In order to understand the debate it is necessary to recall the state of east German industry after the fall of the wall: the overwhelming majority of companies had been totally unable to compete with Western companies. This was not only due to the shortcomings of all Soviet-type economies, such as low product quality and low productivity, but was also the result of the import substitution, intra-bloc specialisation philosophy practised by the CMEA countries. Historically, there was a complementary division of labour between the eastern and western parts of Germany: the steel and shipbuilding

Table 4.1. *Comparison of production and employment structures of eastern and western Germany, 1989 and 1992, %*

	Production					
	eastern Germany			western Germany		
	1989[a]	1992	Change[b]	1989	1992	Change[b]
Agriculture, forestry and fishing	2.1	1.6	−0.5	1.7	1.3	−0.4
Mining, energy, manufacturing & construction *of which:*	54.1	32.7	−21.4	40.4	38.1	−2.3
Manuf.	37.9	16.9	−21.0	31.9	30.4	−1.5
Trade & trans.	17.8	15.5	−2.3	14.5	14.3	−0.2
Services	12.1	26.2	+14.1	29.8	33.0	+3.2
Government & non-profit organisations	13.9	23.9	+10.0	13.6	13.4	−0.2

	Employment					
	eastern Germany			western Germany		
	1989	1992	Change[b]	1989	1992	Change[b]
Agriculture, forestry and fishing	10.0	5.2	−4.8	3.7	3.2	−0.5
Mining, energy, manufacturing & construction *of which:*	44.5	35.8	−8.7	39.8	38.5	−1.3
Manuf.	.	.	.	31.4	.	.
Trade & trans.	16.8	19.9	−3.1	18.6	19.1	+0.5
Services	9.2	15.3	+6.1	18.0	19.8	+1.8
Government & non-profit organizations	19.5	23.8[c]	+4.3	19.9	19.4	−0.5

Notes:
[a]In DM and Western prices.
[b]Percentage points.
[c]Including persons in job-creation programmes.
Source: Statistisches Bundesamt.

Table 4.2. *Comparison of employment structures, manufacturing, GDR and the FRG, 1989, %*

| | Shares | | Deviation[a] |
	GDR	FRG	GDR against FRG
Tot. Manu.	100	100	
of which:			
Oil refineries, plastic manuf.	4.8	5.4	−0.6
Stone, sand and clay industries	5.1	3.8	+1.3
Iron and steel industries,			
non-ferrous metal industry	5.6	7.6	−2.0
Metal products	8.2	7.0	+1.2
Chemic. industry	5.9	8.2	−2.3
Eng.	15.2	14.0	+1.2
Vehicle building	7.2	14.5	−7.3
El. eq.	14.1	15.6	−1.5
Precision engineering, optical,			
watches	1.9	1.9	±0
Wood processing	4.5	3.5	+1.0
Paper and board	1.6	2.2	−0.6
Printing	1.3	2.5	−1.2
Leather and leather products,			
textiles, clothing	12.8	6.0	+6.8
Food, drink and tobacco	9.1	6.3	−2.8
Manuf.			
Basic products	29.6	32.0	−2.4
Capital goods	38.4	46.0	−7.6
Consumer goods	20.2	14.2	+6.0

Notes:
[a]Percentage points.
Source: Bode and Krieger-Boden (1990).

industries, for example, were mainly located in the west, the chemical industry and the textile industry in the east. As a consequence of the autarky strategy of the GDR the eastern German industrial structure became more and more a duplicate of the western German one. A comparison of the employment structures of the GDR and the FRG industry on a 2-digit level shows that both were very similar (table 4.2). The only significant differences were in Vehicle Building (where the share in the FRG was twice as high as in the GDR) and in the manufacture of Leather, Textiles and Clothing (where the reverse was true). Because of this, the

Table 4.3. *Sectoral structure of intra-German trade, 1989, %*

	Sales	Purchases
	of the GDR	
Food, drink and tobacco	3.8	7.7
Mineral fuel	11.3	4.7
Chemical products	12.4	14.5
Engineering and vehicles	11.4	34.2
Wood products and furniture	4.9	0.2
Textiles	12.4	4.6
Iron and steel	9.4	10.4
Precision engineering and optical goods	0.6	1.0

Source: Statistisches Bundesamt; own calculations.

weight of the capital goods sector in the GDR was somewhat lower, and the weight of the consumer goods sector somewhat higher, than in the FRG.

Meanwhile this large degree of identity in industrial structures is more of a burden than an advantage for east German industry. In open Western market economies with identical factor endowment and technology, identical patterns are not exceptional, but these economies have a high degree of intra-industry specialisation, not only in production, but also in exports and imports of manufactured goods. The bilateral trade between the GDR and the FRG, however, had only a slight bearing on this matter. The GDR exports were predominantly basic material and consumer goods while imports were mainly capital goods. Textiles, chemical products and mineral fuel amounted to roughly 35% of total exports to the FRG in 1989 (table 4.3). It is evident that the GDR had no comparative advantage in these fields: the export of textiles (most of them of low quality) was heavily subsidised, and the export of chemical products and mineral fuel was profitable only on the basis of cheap crude oil imports from the Soviet Union.

The low competitiveness of GDR industry was also reflected in the terms of trade in intra-German trade: according to the calculations by Schmieding and Stehn (1989) the ratio of the GDR export prices to import prices (in DM) was on average roughly 1:3 (table 4.4). It is remarkable that the ratio was 1:4 in the consumer goods sector and even 1:5 in the capital goods sector. The price ratio was nearly the same as the productivity ratio, which has been estimated to range between 1:3 and 1:4 on average.

It should be noted that between 1980 and 1989 the price ratios declined substantially – by almost the same amount in all market segments. Consequently, the domestic resource costs incurred by GDR firms in

Table 4.4. *Price ratios in intra-German trade, 1980 and 1989[a]*

	1980	1989
Tot. industry	0.56	0.36
of which:		
Basic products	0.64	0.42
Investment goods[b]	0.34	0.22
Consumer goods	0.44	0.26

[a] Average DM values of FRG purchases divided by the average values of sales of the respective class of goods.
[b] Without shipbuilding, aircraft and spacecraft, finished buildings.
Source: Stehn and Schmieding (1990).

Table 4.5. *Domestic resource costs in eastern German industry in trade with Western and Eastern countries, 1989*

	Costs in Marks of earning 1	
	D Mark	Transferrubel
Industry	3.73	4.65
of which:		
Energy	2.08	3.16
Chemicals	4.11	5.93
Metallurgy	3.22	7.63
Machinery	3.59	3.62
Transport equipment	3.46	3.35
Electronics	4.82	3.44
Textiles	3.70	6.45
Furniture, toys, etc.	4.22	4.55
Glass, ceramics, paper	3.33	4.65
Food, beverages	4.09	8.00

Source: Akerlof *et al.* (1991).

selling their products on world markets rose. Akerlof *et al.* (1991) calculated the shadow exchange rates at which the firms would have been competitive: in Marks per DM earned in exports to non-socialist countries it averaged 3.73 in 1989; and in Transferrubels, earned in exports to non-socialist countries, it was 4.65. However, these rates varied widely across and within sectors. The costs in Marks of earning a DM ranged from 2.08 in the energy sector to 4.82 in the electronics sector (table 4.5).

Table 4.6. *Trade with Western countries of the GDR and the FRG in classes of goods, 1987, structure in %*

	GDR[a]		FRG[b]	
	Exports	Imports	Exports	Imports
Resource-intensive goods	28.2	17.7	7.3	21.6
Labour-intensive goods	28.8	17.5	20.0	23.0
Capital-intensive goods	17.7	17.8	28.8	18.6
Easy-to-imitate research-intensive goods	10.8	14.3	15.5	16.6
Hard-to-imitate research-intensive goods	13.2	32.4	28.4	20.2

Notes:
[a] Trade with OECD countries including intra-German trade.
[b] Trade with industrialised Western countries.
Source: Stehn and Schmieding (1990).

Domestic resource costs are a good indicator of the viability of east German industrial firms under free trade. The total collapse of electronic industries (the conglomerate 'Mikroelektronik/Robotron' needed to spend 7.17 Marks in order to earn one DM) demonstrates the predictive power of these figures.

The low competitiveness of east German industry is also reflected in the composition of its trade with all Western countries. The structure of exports as well as of imports was more comparable to those of a less developed country than to those of an industrialised country. The export side was dominated by resource-intensive and labour-intensive goods, and the import side by research-intensive goods. The contrast with the export and import structures of the FRG was striking (table 4.6).

In early post-unification plans there was little understanding of the state of east German industry; indeed there was a widespread feeling that it would be possible to restructure and modernise the old socialist conglomerates in a relatively short period of time. The enormous productivity gap was thought to result from the general backwardness of the industrial sector in a Soviet-type economy – not only production techniques and product quality, but also the specialisation pattern. It has now become evident that east German industry must be totally built up from scratch; it makes no sense to stop or to delay the decline.

The recent trends: between collapse and revival

Our analysis shows that east German industry is suffering an adjustment crisis. From recent statistical figures we can conclude that it is midway between collapse and revival. While in some branches production has not yet reached the bottom line, in others it has already turned up. The question arises how these different 'trends' should be interpreted. Are they an indicator for the long-term prospects of different branches, or do they simply reflect their different short-term market conditions? A closer examination of relevant statistical figures may cast some light on the matter.

Production

During the last two years east German industry experienced not only a dramatic contraction but also a considerable change in its sectoral structure. At first glance (table 4.7), the results look surprising:

- On an aggregated (2-digit) level, capital goods industries have become the main losers in the unification process; they lost about one-fifth of their shares in production. Initially, these industries had been expected to be amongst the winners. However, against strong international competition they have lost nearly all their foreign and domestic markets. Only the manufacture of constructional steel increased its share as a result of the building boom in eastern Germany.
- The share of consumer goods industries has stabilised. This is mainly due to gains in the printing industry which benefited from a heavy demand for printing material and from high investments by west German publishers.
- There has been an increase in basic product industries' share. This is largely explained by favourable demand conditions and the relatively high competitiveness of branches such as the stone, sand and clay industry. Many basic products are produced only for local markets where they are needed to modernise the infrastructure.
- Industries producing food and drink have been the 'champions' – they were able to increase their share from 13% to 18%. Due to the relatively high competitiveness of these goods before unification these industries have been amongst the first to be privatised. After modernising their plants most of the firms could increase their competitiveness.

From this, it could be concluded that the changes in the production structure have been more coincidental than systematic. A closer examination, however, reveals a clear-cut pattern: the losers have been the

Table 4.7. *Production structure of eastern German manufacturing, by branches, 1990–2, %*

	1990	1991		1992		
	II	I	II	I	II	Change[a]
Tot. Manuf.	100	100	100	100	100	
Manuf. of basic products	22.4	25.1	26.2	28.2	26.3	+3.9
of which:						
Oil refineries	2.2	4.0	4.2	4.5	4.4	+2.2
Stone, sand & clay						
industries	4.8	3.9	5.1	6.2	8.0	+3.2
Iron & steel industry	2.6	3.0	2.3	2.5	3.4	+0.8
Foundries	1.6	1.5	1.2	1.2	0.9	−0.7
Chemic. industry	8.3	9.4	10.1	10.1	7.2	−1.1
Manuf. of capital goods	53.4	45.2	44.9	40.2	42.8	−10.6
of which:						
Constructional steel	5.2	7.5	9.6	10.4	12.4	+7.2
Eng.	23.6	18.3	18.5	12.6	11.1	−12.5
Vehicle building	3.3	2.9	2.1	2.5	3.2	−0.1
El. eq.	15.7	11.5	11.1	10.8	12.1	−3.6
Precision engineering,						
opticals, watches	2.4	1.1	0.6	0.6	1.5	−0.9
Metal products	1.1	1.9	1.8	2.3	2.0	+0.9
Manuf. of consumer goods	11.6	12.2	12.0	13.5	12.8	+1.2
of which:						
Wood processing	2.3	2.8	2.5	2.9	2.7	+0.4
Printing	1.6	2.5	3.1	3.5	3.5	+1.9
Textiles	3.0	2.1	1.8	1.7	1.3	−1.7
Food, drink and tobacco	12.6	17.6	16.9	18.3	18.1	+5.5

Notes:
[a] Percentage points.
Source: Statistisches Bundesamt; own calculations.

producers of tradables where the market is characterised by high competition from west German and other non-domestic suppliers. The winners have been among those industries producing goods for local markets – because these products are easily perishable, because their transport costs are high relative to their value, or because they are needed immediately, for example, for the newspaper industry. In these markets strong competition need not be feared, because it is not worth transporting the products.

Markets

At the moment the main markets for east German industry are found within east Germany. In 1992 the share of sales to foreign markets to total sales was only 15%, no higher than in 1991, which is extremely low for such a small economy (table 4.8). In fact, the export performance is even weaker than these figures suggest; more than 60% of exports go to the former COMECON partners, massively pushed by export credits and producer subsidies. Eastern Germany has lost almost the whole of its export bases, in contrast to the other Central and East European reform countries which have been very successful in entering Western foreign markets.

Low competitiveness, especially in Western markets for tradables, is also reflected in the relatively low importance of sales to west Germany. Sales of engineering products, for example, are almost negligible. The only industry with a promising future which has reached a significant share of sales to west Germany is the automobile industry. This is mainly due to the new assembly plants of Volkswagen and General Motors which serve both east and west German markets. In the iron and steel industry and in the textile and clothing industry, however, the prospects are gloomy. Their high share of sales in west German markets is not an indicator of competitiveness. Many firms are only – temporarily – 'prolonged workbenches' of west German producers.

Performance

The need to improve competitiveness, in international as well as in domestic markets, forced east German industry to raise productivity levels. In 1992 the turnover per employee (as a rough measure of labour productivity) nearly doubled (table 4.9) due to a reduction of employment. The greatest jump was accomplished by the automobile industry when General Motors and Volkswagen started their new assembly plants. The textile industry was also able to achieve above-average productivity gains, mainly by closing down a great number of unprofitable plants. The stone, sand and clay industry profited from favourable demand conditions created by rising east German construction activity; increased demand could be satisfied with fewer workers.

Despite these remarkable improvements in productivity east Germany is still lagging behind. For industry as a whole, 1992 turnover per employee was only one-third of the level in western Germany. While the productivity gap in basic goods industries was below average and in capital goods industries it was near the average, in the consumer goods industries it was substantially higher than average. The textile and clothing industries were

Table 4.8. *Sales structure of eastern German manufacturing, 1991 and 1992*

1991

| | Sales (mn DM) | | | Ratio to total sales of sales to: | |
	Total	Foreign Markets	Western German Market	Foreign Markets	Western German Market
Tot. Manuf.	86 664	13 658	.	0.16	.
of which:					
Stone, sand & clay industries	2 917	31	109	0.01	0.04
Iron & steel	3 654	1 032	608	0.28	0.17
Eng.	13 169	3 664	331	0.28	0.03
Vehicle building	3 869	371	720	0.10	0.19
Shipbuilding	1 420	834	4	0.59	0.00
El. eng.	7 682	895	703	0.12	0.09
Chemic. industry	8 857	2 156	1065	0.25	0.12
Textiles	1 782	282	408	0.16	0.23
Clothing	594	61	257	0.10	0.43

1992

| | Sales (mn DM) | | | Ratio to total sales of sales to: | |
	Total	Foreign Markets	Western German Market	Foreign Markets	Western German Market [a]
Tot. Manuf.	84 863	12 369	.	0.15	.
of which:					
Stone, sand & clay industries	4 537	37	189	0.01	0.04
Iron & steel	2 779	686	743	0.25	0.27
Eng.	10 704	2 977	257	0.28	0.02
Vehicle building	5 434	436	1431	0.08	0.26
Shipbuilding	1 548	758	303	0.49	0.2
El. eng.	7 650	745	704	0.10	0.09
Chemic. industry	7 751	1 831	1159	0.24	0.15
Textiles	1 451	251	339	0.17	0.23
Clothing	673	44	154	0.07	0.23

Note:
[a] December values estimated.
Source: Statistisches Bundesamt; own calculations.

Table 4.9. *Turnover per employee, selected branches of eastern and western German manufacturing, 1991 and 1992, DM*

	1991			1992		
	east	west	ratio[a]	east	west	ratio[a]
Tot. Manuf.	52 902	261 342	0.20	98 264	268 453	0.37
of which:						
Stone, sand & clay industries	53 625	261 244	0.21	134 183	261 389	0.51
Met. pr.	71 367	271 030	0.26	107 521	261 089	0.41
Eng.	42 289	199 097	0.21	66 773	203 771	0.33
Vehicle building	47 822	318 866	0.15	136 176	325 320	0.42
Shipbuilding	49 636	234 667	0.21	89 569	230 919	0.39
El. eng.	36 152	202 828	0.18	79 884	215 927	0.37
Chemic. industry	70 438	336 544	0.21	111 703	345 363	0.32
Textiles	20 769	204 453	0.10	53 182	209 326	0.25
Clothing	15 677	176 590	0.09	33 895	184 500	0.18

Note:
[a] Turnover per employee in eastern Germany divided by turnover per employee in western Germany.
Source: Statistisches Bundesamt; own calculations.

those with the least favourable productivity level.

It is a matter of simple arithmetic that east German industry as a whole operates at heavy losses. In 1992 the deficit amounted to 15% of total sales, whereas in west Germany a surplus of 3–4% is normal (figure 4.2). Thus, one can conclude that only a small number of firms are profitable. Average losses of the Treuhandanstalt accounted for roughly 30% of total turnover in 1992. Some branches such as electrical engineering or tool engineering reported losses of more than 50% of sales (figure 4.3).

A company which makes losses has – in the short run – two possibilities: it can try to increase prices, or to increase productivity by cutting manpower. In eastern Germany these strategies are now open to only a limited extent:

- The position of companies in price competition is still extremely weak (table 4.10). Producer prices in Eastern Germany remained almost stable in 1991–2. The only branch able to increase prices slightly was the food industry which produces mainly for local markets where competition is lower than elsewhere.

Table 4.10. *Producer price indices of eastern and western German manufacturing, 1991 and 1992, 1989 = 100*

	eastern Germany		western Germany	
	1991	1992	1991	1992
Tot. Manuf.	58.6	58.7	102.3	105.1
of which:				
Basic goods	51.8	51.4	100.2	99.0
Capital goods	64.8	64.2	105.8	108.7
Consumer goods	52.0	52.1	105.2	107.1
Food, drink, tobacco	67.4	69.9	101.9	105.5

Source: Statistisches Bundesamt; own calculations.

• Employment is now approaching the 'bottom line'. Jobs in management and maintenance, for example, are in some ways comparable to fixed overheads; some production jobs may become obsolete if continuous automated processes are used. Under such circumstances manpower can be reduced only by closing down entire production units.

Many companies will be unable to improve their performance without help. It is therefore a matter of the greatest urgency that private investors are found for the companies currently owned by the Treuhandanstalt. What is needed are investors with the ability to modernise production plants, restructure the product range and improve sales figures. In February 1993 only 40% of industrial firms were completely privatised, 25% were in liquidation, 12% were still on offer for sale. It is not surprising that the share of Treuhand companies in liquidation is highest in the leather, textile and clothing industry. Neither is it surprising that in the stone, sand and clay industry, the printing industry, and the food, drink and tobacco industry, only a handful of companies are still to be privatised (table 4.11).

The prospects: some benchmarks for a projection

What can we learn from the facts presented? We find an ongoing decline of industries producing goods saleable in international markets and a revival of industries producing goods for local markets. That is exactly what we could expect in the short run: an economy in which incomes are mostly based on external transfers must have a relatively large non-tradable sector. However, this cannot be a scenario for the long run. In a small open economy the expanding industries of the future must be found mainly

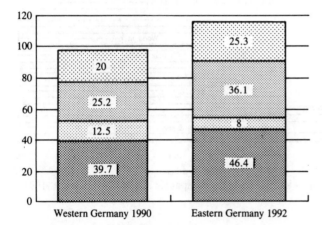

□ overhead costs

▨ personnel costs

□ costs of offshore
   production and of
   merchandise for sale

▨ material costs

Figure 4.2 Cost structure in eastern and western German manufacturing, 1990
and 1992, % of gross output
Sources: Statistisches Bundesamt; Institut für Wirtschaftsforschung Halle.

amongst those which are able to produce competitive tradables. These are
exactly those which are currently in decline.

It is hard, if not impossible, to predict precisely which branches will rise
and which will decline. The figures for sectoral growth and decline over the
last three years do not supply sufficient information about the direction and
the scale of adjustment necessary to overcome the crisis. The period is too
short to calculate a numerical projection of long-term trends. This is a big
challenge for forecasters. They must solve their problem in the framework
of a more general evaluation of the diverse economic and political factors
which may be relevant for development; the computer can only give limited
assistance. At present only some benchmarks for such a projection can be
provided.

General prospects

There are good reasons to argue that – despite all the existing substantial
handicaps – the transformation and integration of the east German

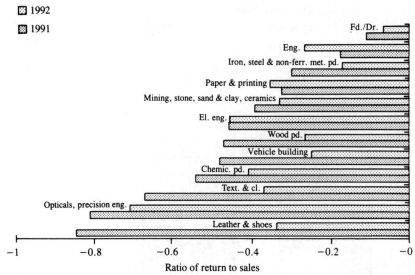

Figure 4.3 Return on sales of Treuhand companies in selected branches, 1991 and 1992
Source: Treuhandanstalt.

economy will be successful. The dramatic decline of the industrial sector was inevitable in the short run – as a precondition for a catch-up in the long run. It is by no means justifiable to argue that the area is on the way to becoming Germany's Mezzogiorno.

This optimism, of course, cannot be based purely on reasoning but must be supported by facts:

- The most encouraging sign is the huge private, and public, investment. Although a lot of investment projects are still blocked by several bottlenecks (by the privatisation process and by the sluggish establishment of the administrative machinery) investment in the productive capacities and the physical infrastructure is rising steadily. In 1993 fixed capital investment of 131 bn DM is expected, compared to 109 bn DM in 1992 and only 83 bn DM in 1991 (Arbeitsgemeinschaft Deutscher Wirtschaftswissenschaftlicher Forschungsinstitute, 1993). Significant parts of the capital stock have been completely renewed, and investment projects incorporate the most modern technologies. The east German telecommunication system will soon be of a higher standard than the one in west Germany.
- Another positive factor is the growing transfer of knowledge, as the result of privatisation and investment from Western firms. In many cases

Table 4.11. *State of privatisation of eastern German manufacturing, by branches, February 1993*

| | Total enterprises | | Of which % [a] | | |
| | | | | In Treuhand ownership | |
	No.	(%)	Completely privatised	In liquidation	To be privatised
Manuf.	5494	100	40.1	24.9	12.8
of which:					
Chemic. industry	254	4.6	43.7	22.8	16.1
Plastic, rubber & asbestos industry	177	3.2	37.3	27.7	7.3
Stone, sand & clay industry, fine ceramics	455	8.3	55.6	14.5	7.9
Iron, steel and non-ferrous metal industry, foundries, steel forging	246	4.5	38.2	21.1	22.4
Constructional steel	202	3.7	38.1	14.4	17.3
Eng.	1105	20.1	42.9	20.6	17.0
Vehicle building industry	360	6.6	55.0	15.3	11.4
Precision engineering, opticals, watches	79	1.4	36.7	32.9	8.9
Metal products, musical instruments, toys, jewellery	324	5.9	28.4	32.4	11.7
Wood processing	502	9.1	31.5	28.7	11.8
Paper and board, printing	239	4.4	51.0	24.3	8.8
Leather and leather products	170	3.1	17.6	50.0	12.9
Textiles, clothing industry	520	9.5	17.9	40.2	18.7
Food, drink and tobacco	861	15.7	47.4	23.9	5.9

Note:
[a] Difference: already closed down, given to the former owner or to municipalities, partly privatised.
Source: Treuhandanstalt.

the old management was replaced completely; management deficiencies in the former socialist firms proved to be one of the most important bottlenecks in the restructuring process.

One can consequently expect that a number of companies and industries in eastern Germany are going to grow strongly in the near future when huge investments in fixed and human capital materialise in production and employment. The expected completion of the two new car plants of Volkswagen and General Motors in Saxony and Thuringia in 1993 should push production figures in the automobile industry to some hundred thousand units annually. Recent statistics suggest that the adjustment process is well under way in other branches also.

Sectoral dualisation

Due to public subsidies for capital and labour there will emerge a dual economy in the industrial sector. On the one hand the government pushes private investment by a generous aid package (which amounts to an effective rate of subsidisation of between 30% and 50%), so that new plants (mostly built up from scratch) will be highly capital-intensive, probably with a much higher degree of automation than in the west. On the other hand, the government backs employment by directly financing several labour market measures, and indirectly by pressing the Treuhandanstalt to open its 'deep pockets' for loss-making firms. Consequently, it delays the decline of the old industries (steel, shipbuilding, textiles) which face gloomy long-term prospects. Basically, this dualisation will be in many respects a duplicate of the development in western regions in the 1970s and 1980s. However, while the sunset regions in the west were left with still tolerable unemployment rates of 10–15%, the rock bottom of unemployment in the east must be expected to amount to more than 20–25% of the labour force for a long time (Paqué, Soltwedel *et al.*, 1993).

It is not possible to predict the emerging sectoral structure of east German industry in detail. Its modern part cannot simply duplicate west German industry. Huge subsidies on investment encourage the development of capital-intensive production facilities. It was not inevitable that the German automobile industry decided to establish two ultra-modern new plants in Saxony and Thuringia – even though it is normal to relocate production to low-wage countries. Currently, it is hardly possible to reach definite conclusions in this respect.

Regional agglomeration

Within eastern Germany it can be expected that the industrial heartlands of the pre-war period in Saxony, Saxony-Anhalt, Thuringia and South

Brandenburg will have the best prospects for reindustrialisation. Notwith-standing chronic structural problems, they are attractive locations for investment. The most important advantage of these regions is that they are geographically well placed at the crossroads between Europe's West and East. With the re-establishment of trade and transport links to the East, the artificial handicaps will disappear. The most likely winner will be the area south of the capital, Berlin, which is becoming the seat of the German government. Many firms may relocate their headquarters from Munich, Frankfurt or Cologne where they moved after the Second World War. However, due to their relatively high wages compared to neighbouring regions to the east – especially Bohemia, Moravia and Silesia with their formidable industrial tradition – they will be no place to establish 'prolonged workbenches'. The new automobile plants of Volkswagen and General Motors, for example, are not restricted to pure assembly lines, but include the manufacturing of parts and components as well. Moreover, they will include cheap input suppliers in Central East European countries in their facilities network. As a consequence, a new 'borderline economy' will emerge based on the division of labour between low-wage and high-wage countries.

Industrial networks

Recent trends in manufacturing can be characterised as an ongoing process of internationalisation, specialisation, diversification, decentralisation and tertiarisation (Klodt and Schmidt, 1988). Producers are searching for new organisational forms for sourcing, production and sales. Special attention is being paid to new concepts such as 'lean production', i.e. aiming to lower the degree of vertical integration. In order to implement the new concepts they need an efficient network of suppliers. Those must be located in the vicinity of the plants guaranteeing 'just in time' production. With the exception of the automobile industries, the new concepts have not yet fully materialised.

Eastern Germany could become a place for practical experiments in a big way. Typical candidates for network production are the chemical industry, the automobile industry and the iron and steel industry. Consequently, the Treuhandanstalt's strategy is to enable such links to be established. In the chemical industry it tries to restructure and privatise bundles of enterprises which are strongly interrelated. In these cases it digs deep into its pockets in order to preserve the agglomerational advantages of well developed industrial networks.

Policy conclusions: what are the lessons for other former socialist economies?

The German experience may offer some insights into the general problems of transforming the countries of Central and Eastern Europe from command to market economies. Although there are considerable differences – eastern Germany is in the best of all circumstances because it enjoys massive support from the western rich brother – there are also similarities. Like the other former socialist economies east Germany suffers from all the well known shortcomings of a command economy, especially low competitiveness. Confronted with common problems, policy makers in Central and Eastern European countries can draw some lessons from how east German enterprises are responding to the introduction of a market-based system.

First lesson: the decision in favour of the 'big-bang' strategy was politically determined and fully justified. In many respects, however, this strategy has proved to be less optimal for the transition from a command to a market economy. Restructuring enterprises takes time, and time appears to be the scarcest factor in the process of political and economic unification of the two parts of Germany. In contrast, the other former socialist economies have the opportunity to buy time. They can fix their exchange rate low enough to stimulate exports and to put the brakes on imports – there is always an exchange rate making domestic enterprises internationally competitive. Thereby, they can maintain low real wages as long as necessary.

Second lesson: the decision in favour of the 'big-bang' strategy is more costly in the short run than a gradualistic strategy. However, in the long run it may turn out to be cheaper. It is true that competition from outside accelerates the collapse of the old system, but it also stimulates the process of reallocation. Despite its apparent weakness in the face of foreign competition, opening up the economy to foreign trade is essential. There is indeed no transformation without change. Without change – especially in the production structures – only slight improvements can be expected.

Third lesson: restructuring a former socialist economy is a formidable challenge.

- It requires splitting and privatising state enterprises. A government agency will never be able to make enterprises fit for the market; it quite often reacts in the wrong way. Restructuring needs an 'iron hand' because plant closures and employment losses are unavoidable.
- It requires considerable new capital from financially strong investors. At present, this type of investor can only be found abroad, so nothing should be done to put limits on the scale of foreign ownership. It is a

reasonable expectation that much foreign investment will involve the creation of new enterprises rather than the restructuring of old ones with all their problems.

- Restructuring requires new management. The shortage of qualified managers is perhaps the most important constraint for existing firms – even more important than the shortage of capital. Therefore, a strong foreign partner is required who either helps on the production side (e.g. by installing modern technologies) or helps with a highly developed network of outlets that can be used to stimulate sales activities.

- Restructuring requires new patterns of specialisation, redirecting production to products in open and internationally linked markets. Former centrally planned economies are known for their distorted trade structures unrelated to comparative advantages; trade flows within the former COMECON have consequently diminished dramatically. It is useless to complain about the collapse of traditional markets within the CMEA area.

Note

An earlier version of this chapter was presented at the ACE-Workshop on Industrial Restructuring and Trade Reorientation, Vienna, WIIW (27–29 March 1993). The authors wish to thank their colleagues Klaus-Werner Schatz and Birgit Sander for helpful comments.

References

Akerlof, G., Rose, A., Yellen, J. and Hessenius, H., 1991. 'East Germany in from the cold: the economic aftermath of currency union', *Brooking Papers on Economic Activity*, 1, 1–105

Arbeitsgemeinschaft Deutscher Wirtschaftswissenschaftlicher Forschungsinstitute, 1993. 'Die Lage der Weltwirtschaft und der deutschen Wirtschaft im Frühjahr 1993', Kiel (29 April)

Bode, Eckardt and Krieger-Boden, C., 1990. 'Sektorale Strukturprobleme und regionale Anpassungserfordernisse der Wirtschaft in den neuen Bundesländern', *Die Weltwirtschaft*, H. 2, 84–97

Csaba, László, 1992. 'After the shock: some lessons from transition policies in Eastern Europe', Kopint-Dators *Discussion Papers*, 8 (October)

Institut für Wirtschaftsforschung Halle, 1993. Konjunkturbericht H. 1/93, Halle

Klodt, H. and Schmidt, K-D., 1989. 'Weltwirtschaftlicher Strukturwandel and Standortwettbewerb', *Kieler Studien*, 228 Tübingen

Paqué, K-H., Soltwedel, R. *et al.*, 1993, 'Challenges ahead. Long-term perspectives of the German economy', *Kiel Discussion Paper*, 202/203, Kiel (March)

Schatz, K-W. and Schmidt, K-D., 1992. 'Real economic adjustment of the Eastern German economy in the short and in the long run', in Horst Siebert (ed.), *The Transformation of Socialist Economies*, Symposium 1991, Tübingen, pp. 369–94

Schmidt, K-D. and Sander, B., 1993. 'Wages, productivity and employment in Eastern Germany', in A. Ghanie Ghaussy and Wolf Schäfer (eds.), *The Economies of German Unification*, London and New York, 60–72

Siebert, H., 1990. 'The economic integration of Germany – an update', *Kiel Discussion Papers*, 160 a (September)

Stehn, J. and Schmieding, H., 1990. 'Spezialisierungsmuster und Wettbewerbsfähigkeit: Eine Bestandsaufnahme des DDR-Außenhandels', *Die Weltwirtschaft*, H. 1, 60–77

5 Stabilisation, crisis and structural change in Hungary

András Blahó and László Halpern

Economic performance in Hungary experienced conflicting trends in 1991–92. Overall economic activity declined, unemployment quintupled, the rate of inflation, though down on the previous year, remained high, and the budget deficit increased. On the other hand, the level of foreign exchange reserves and the balance of payment outperformed even the most optimistic forecast. Privatisation and the inflow of foreign investment eased the crisis, but their effect on efficiency and restructuring is still rather limited.

The government's economic programme anticipated a radical turn-around in 1992: the first sizeable drop in the rate of inflation since the beginning of economic transformation, and an end to economic decline. The figures for 1992 show that these targets were only partly achieved: the rate of inflation was reduced, but the expected economic growth has not yet materialised. Prospects for industrial restructuring remain bleak and there are no signs of a quick economic recovery.

Economic crisis and restructuring

The downward economic trend of 1990 continued into 1991 and 1992. Consumption, investment, and exports decreased, while imports remained at their 1990 level, so production levels also declined. The current account balance was positive, in spite of the huge loss in terms of trade due to the collapse of the CMEA, an indisputable success that helped to maintain the credibility of Hungary on international capital markets and made possible the financing of Hungary's foreign debts with favourable terms. However, the simultaneous increase of the rates of inflation and of unemployment show that a concerted effort must be made to stabilise the economy.

As a result of a lower than expected level of revenue on the one hand, and steadily increasing expenditures dictated by inflation and the creation of new administrative bodies on the other, the budget deficit was much higher

Table 5.1. *Macroeconomic indicators, 1989–92*

	1989	1990	1991	1992[a]
	Year-to-year rate of change, %, at constant prices			
Ind. output	−1.0	−9.2	−19.1	−9.8
GDP	0.7	−3.5	−11.9	−5.0
Consumption	0.8	−2.7	−5.3	−3.0
private	2.3	−3.6	−5.8	−2.5
public	−6.3	2.6	−2.7	−4.0
Investments	7.0	−7.1	−11.6	−7.5
Exports	1.2	−5.3	−5.0	1.0
Imports	1.8	−4.3	5.0	−7.0
PPI	15.4	22.2	28.5	15.5
CPI	17.0	28.9	35.0	23.0
Budget deficit[b]	2.8	0.0	3.9	7.1

[a] Preliminary data, Ministry of Finance.
[b] As a share of GDP in percentage at current prices.
Source: Main indicators of economic development, 1983–1989, (CSO)
Budapest, *National Bank of Hungary Monthly Report* 1993/1.

than officially forecast. Nonetheless, the fiscal expansion characterising this period did not translate into inflationary pressure because of an unexpectedly high level of private saving. Though new enterprises mushroomed and privatisation continued, their effect remained very modest.

Production

The decline in production was deeper than the government expected: GDP declined by 3.5% in 1990, 11.9% in 1991, and about 5% in 1992 (see table 5.1). As a result, the level of real GDP in 1992 was equal to that in 1980. Industrial gross output in real terms fell by 19.1% in 1991, though variation was immense: large firms (over 300 employees) experienced a fall of 23.2%, while medium-size firms (between 50 and 300 employees) declined by 4.3%. Small firms' (below 50 employees) output was up 50.1%, but their share remained marginal: 6.1% of industrial gross output, 7.0% of industrial employment, and only 3.1% of export sales of industry. The large firms produced the vast majority of the industrial output, 84.1%, employed 76.1% of the industrial labour force, and exported 88.1% of the industry's exports.

The recession had uneven effects on different industries: the energy sector was not really hit, while there were certain manufactured goods whose

Table 5.2. *Structure of industrial production, %, 1980–91*

	1980	1989	1990	1991
Mines	8.1	5.7	5.6	6.4
El.	5.7	6.2	7.0	8.2
Met.	9.1	10.5	9.1	7.8
Mach.	23.5	24.8	20.8	17.2
Chemic.	18.6	18.5	20.5	21.3
Building materials	3.5	3.1	3.3	2.8
Light industry	13.7	12.4	12.6	11.5
Food processing	16.7	17.8	21.1	24.3
Others	1.1	0.8	0.6	0.5
Total	100.0	100.0	100.0	100.0

Sources: Statistical Yearbook 1989 (CSO) Budapest, 1990; *Monthly Bulletin of CSO*, Budapest (1992)2.

production fell dramatically (steel, coaches, audio tape recorders) due to the CMEA demand shock. The production of some other industrial consumer goods remained stable, and there were no large falls in foods and beverages. The accelerating decline in fertiliser production was due to the collapse of the CMEA and to the weakening financial position of agricultural cooperatives.

Industrial structure did not change substantially between 1980 and 1989; only the diminishing share of mining is worth mentioning (see table 5.2). Since 1989, however, quite an important shift can be observed even at this very aggregated level, though mainly as a result of the uneven effects of the recession mentioned above. The energy sector – mainly electricity – increased its share compared to 1980, and the share of chemicals and food processing grew at the expense of metallurgy and machinery which lost more than 7 percentage points within two years.

There was no industrial sector which increased its production at constant prices in 1991, and the only sector showing positive growth in 1990 was electricity, up 0.2% (table 5.3). The decline of metallurgy and machinery was 45% compounded in the last two years. Industrial labour productivity fell only by 0.4% in 1990, that is, labour lay-offs kept pace with the decline of output volume (see table 5.4). In 1991, however, when the fall in industrial production was 21.5%, labour productivity declined by 9.4%, which meant that the unit labour requirement increased by more than 12%. Nonetheless, the increase in the level of unemployment was five times higher than in the previous year.

Table 5.3. *Industrial production, year-to-year change, %, at constant prices, 1988-91*

	1988	1989	1990	1991
Mines	-3.7	-5.2	-11.8	-10.9
El.	0.1	2.2	0.2	-8.0
Met.	4.3	4.4	-19.0	-32.7
Mach.	0.0	0.2	-16.2	-34.9
Chemic.	1.3	-3.9	-5.4	-18.5
Building materials	1.6	-1.6	-5.0	-33.0
Light industry	0.2	-4.8	-11.7	-24.9
Food processing	-2.5	1.0	-0.9	-9.7
Total	0.0	-1.0	-9.2	-21.5

Source: Monthly Bulletin of CSO, Budapest (1992) 2.

Table 5.4. *Industrial labour productivity, year-to-year change, %, 1988-91*

Production per employee	1988	1989	1990	1991
Mines	1.5	3.0	6.7	6.0
El.	-2.0	3.3	-2.7	-2.9
Met.	9.7	13.6	-1.2	-17.5
Mach.	2.2	1.6	-7.7	-11.7
Chemic.	0.8	-6.1	-1.4	-12.1
Building materials	4.0	0.2	-0.4	-23.2
Light industry	4.2	-4.5	-1.9	-13.2
Food processing	-1.2	0.8	2.5	-2.8
Others	3.2	-2.0	-2.3	-14.0
Total	2.7	0.7	-0.4	-9.4

Source: Monthly Bulletin of CSO, Budapest (1991) 12.

Within the 13% decline in overall industrial employment there were sizeable variations across sectors: ranging from 6.8% in food processing to 18.2% in metallurgy. Employment in agriculture fell by 23.9%, and in construction by 22%. The overall decline in employment induced a substantial change not only in the branch structure of industrial production but also in the size structure of industrial firms: large firms dismissed 19.3% of their labour force, compared to 1% in medium-sized firms.

Table 5.5. *Unemployment, 1990–92*

	Rate	Total[a]	Of which (%) Blue collar Skilled	Semi-skilled	Unskilled	White collar
1990	1.9	79 521	27.4	21.8	30.7	20.1
1991	7.5	406 124	33.2	23.9	26.2	16.7
1992	12.3	663 027	35.0	23.4	25.2	16.4

Note:
[a] Registered unemployed persons.
Source: Monthly Bulletin of CSO, Budapest (1993)4.

Capacity utilisation deteriorated in 1991: basic equipment in large firms was in use for only 41.8% of time compared to 53.2% in 1989. It was worse in machinery, light industry and food processing, with rates of capacity utilisation of between 28% and 38%. The average number of shifts decreased from 1.60 to 1.26 within two years.

Agricultural production experienced a slow but steady annual 3% decline from 1989 until it fell to its 1980 level. However, in 1991 crops increased by 9%, just as in 1990, after zero growth in 1989, whilst animal husbandry decreased by 13–15% in 1991, further accelerating the fall in livestock.

On the whole the recession was not really abrupt: the monthly series shows a steady decline in 1990–91 with some acceleration in 1991, at least for firms with more than 50 employees. This trend has stopped, and industrial production varied around its 1991 November level in 1992.

Inflation and unemployment

The fight against inflation remained at the centre of economic policy. Nonetheless, it accelerated to 35% in 1991, compared to 29% in 1990, a fact explained by the elimination of a large part of the remaining consumer price subsidies, further price liberalisation and import price pressure due to the trade reorientation. Monthly CPI figures show that in the last two years the major part of the annual inflation occurred in the first quarter, and some deceleration can be observed. The average monthly inflation rate was 5.4% in the first quarter of 1991 and only 1.5% during the following three quarters. In 1992, a significant reduction took place as the rate fell to 23%, mainly as a result of the anti-inflationary exchange rate policy.

Table 5.6. *Changes in the number of economic organizations, 1988–92*

Year	No. of organisations at beginning of period	Foundation	Liquidation	Of which: without legal successor
1988	9 597	1 445	231	87
1989	10 811	4 669	245	166
1990	15 235	14 867	632	202
1991	29 470	24 275	989	314
1992	52 756	18 052	1 422	419

Source: Monthly Bulletin of CSO, Budapest (1992) 2; (1993) 2.

Unemployment increased very rapidly in 1991, reaching 7.5% in December, five times the level of the previous year (see table 5.5), then increased at a somewhat slower rate in 1992, reaching 12.3% by the end of 1992. The structure of unemployment by qualification shows a higher increase in the skilled workers' group, due to the fact that the export fall hit mainly the metallurgy and machinery industries. Regional distribution was very uneven; the highest rate observed was in Szabolcs-Szatmár-Bereg county and in Nógrád county, both in the North-East region, and it remained relatively low in Budapest.

Budget deficit

The 1991 gap between actual and forecast budget deficit was mainly due to the fact that actual revenues were 7–8% less than planned. Revenues from corporate income tax, import duties and VAT were less than expected, and the 2–3% reduction on the expenditure side could not fully compensate for this fall in revenues. The retention of some consumer price subsidy on energy, and the increased costs of administration impeded a more drastic reduction. In 1992 the budget deficit soared to an unprecedented level: 7.1% of GDP.

Households increased their money savings by 30.7% on average. They preferred convertible currency deposits to the national currency deposits, so that the former increased by 85.2% and the latter by only 15.8%. The stock of household credits decreased by 33.7%, because of early repayment of mortgages due to a radical cut in mortgage rate subsidies. A large number of households liquidated their mortgage by paying back 55% of the nominal value, instead of accepting the alternatives, i.e. to pay the market interest rate after a 50% reduction of the mortgage, or to pay about the half of the market interest rate for the whole amount of outstanding credit.

The financial position of the enterprises *vis-à-vis* the commercial banks did not change, their credit increased by 18%, their debit by 21.8%. The NBH published a list of 716 enterprises, the bill of exchanges of which were not to be rediscounted. The amount of (involuntary) interenterprise (or trade) credit of these insolvent firms increased by 96.2% in 1991.

Privatisation and institutional changes

In 1991, foreign direct investment in the form of buying a privatised firm or raising the share capital of a newly privatised firm reached USD 900 m, which amounted to almost half of all foreign direct investments in Hungary. This amount is roughly equal to 9% of the equity of the transformed – commercialised and/or privatised – companies. Foreign participation in joint ventures was 40% on average. The State Property Agency (SPA) approved the transformation of 316 companies. Privatisation has already affected more than 10% of the state-owned firms, and 20% of the national assets have been transformed (commercialised). In 1992, the structure of privatisation revenues was: 25.9% sold for cash paid in HUF, 13.5 for (HUF) credits, and 60.6 for cash paid in convertible currencies. The original total book value of already transformed firms was HUF 725bn which was valued at HUF 1385bn in the share capital of newly incorporated companies.

The large privatisation programme failed, leading to a further decentralisation of privatisation. The role of domestic investors in privatisation remained rather limited, partly because the special credit schemes were not attractive enough. Privatisation has been accelerated by new credit facilities, and by possibilities for employees' stock ownership (ESOP).

Different types of enterprise form flourished, the most popular being limited liability. The creation of new enterprises was very intensive (see table 5.6), especially in December, due to the special tax reliefs which ceased to exist at the end of that month. The very low number of liquidations shows that the necessary effects of the deep recession will come later, enhanced by new bankruptcy regulations and new accounting rules.

The number of non-registered, individual entrepreneurs was 632 000. If this number is compared to the level of industrial employment, which was about 909 000, it is clear that Hungary became the heaven of the entrepreneur, even if the large number of shadow firms established only to benefit from tax reliefs is taken into account.

Foreign trade and structural change in Hungary

Foreign trade has played an important role in the Hungarian economy since the reform[1] process started in 1968. This reform, however, did not greatly change trade orientation; major transformations only took place after 1979. A large proportion of trade was carried out with the CMEA countries, and within this group about 50% of the trade was with the Soviet Union. Foreign trade policy was implemented by a number of highly specialised foreign trade organisations (FTOs), and all foreign trade transactions were subject to licensing. Foreign exchange payments were highly centralised and regulated.

Trade with CMEA economies was based on annual protocols of deliveries and paid in transferable roubles, and was exempt from customs tariffs. As CMEA foreign trade prices remained distorted relative to world market prices, a system of taxes and subsidies was introduced by the central authorities in order to ensure somewhat similar trade prospects both in rouble transactions and in hard-currency trade. Until 1988, the enterprises involved in CMEA-related trade flows received full and almost automatic compensation from the budget for the difference in the two kinds of trade profitability. From 1988 onwards the central authorities tried to tighten the loose financial discipline inherent in rouble trade regulations. The forint was appreciated against the transferable rouble and other measures, including administrative ones, were taken to curb rouble exports.

Starting on 1 October 1989 the National Bank of Hungary stopped encashing transferable roubles earned on above-quota exports into forint. In the first quarter of 1990, CMEA export licences were withdrawn and new licences were issued monthly, depending on trade developments. During the meeting of the Executive Committee of the CMEA in Sofia in mid-1990, the decision was taken to abolish transferable rouble accounting in intra-regional trade as from 1 January 1991. Although contracts signed before that date remained in force throughout 1991, a substantial part of trade was now conducted in hard currency, mostly in US dollars. In the case of Hungary, export deliveries contracted in 1990 in transferable rouble could be implemented until the end of March 1991. The CMEA officially closed down as from 28 June 1991.[2]

Trade development since 1988

The impact of domestic recession was the most significant. This exerted a downward pressure on imports, which have generally been contracting in volume. The volume of exports to Eastern Europe alone fell by about 40% in 1991 (see table 5.7), forcing many companies to find new, Western

Table 5.7. *Foreign trade indicators for Hungary, changes in volume and terms of trade, %, 1988–92*

	1988	1989	1990	1991	1992[a]
Exports					
Rouble trade[b]	0.4	−6.0	−26.1	−44.4	0.3
CMEA	0.9	−7.0	−22.5	...	3.5
Hard-currency trade	12.3	5.0	9.3	19.5	−1.7
Developed economies	13.9	9.0	12.1	21.7	...
Developing economies	−0.1	0.0	−5.3	5.6	...
Total	6.8	0.3	−4.1	−4.9	1.8
Imports					
Rouble trade	2.9	−6.9	−17.8	−43.4	1.9
CMEA	0.5	−7.0	−11.1	...	1.8
Hard-currency trade	−2.8	7.1	2.7	30.3	−5.9
Developed economies	−3.9	11.1	−3.5	32.5	...
Developing economies	14.5	−5.3	41.9	8.7	...
Total	−0.3	1.1	−5.2	5.5	−7.6
Terms of trade					
Rouble trade	3.3	3.7	3.2	−37.2	2.7
CMEA	4.8	3.8	3.6		1.9
Hard-currency trade	1.8	2.2	−1.6	−10.4	−3.8
Developed economies	−0.2	1.5	0.1	...	...
Developing economies	4.3	5.9	−11.6	...	...
Total	2.4	2.8	0.4	−19.2	−2.3

Notes:
[a] Preliminary data. Volume development was derived using 1992 January–September price indices of external trade published in *Statisztikai Havi Közlemények* (Budapest) 12–3 (1993), p. 81 (price indices) and p. 59 (value indices). Note that from 1992 on, the CSO no longer publishes foreign trade data by foreign exchange.
[b] 'Rouble' volume in this respect means trade volume development with Eastern Europe, including the former Soviet Union.
... Not available.
Source: Statisztikai Évkönyv, 1990 (Budapest) (1991), pp. 188–9 for volume data; p. 206 for terms of trade data. Final data for 1991: *Gazdaságstatisztikai Évkönyv, 1991* (Budapest) (1993), pp. 206–7.

Table 5.8. *Hungary: value and structure of foreign trade, 1988–93, billion US$[a]*

	1988	1989	1990	1991	1992	1993[b]
Exports						
World	10.00	9.67	9.55	10.23	10.64	1.81
Former socialist countries	5.06	4.58	3.60	2.41	2.48	0.45
Eur.-6	1.70	1.53	1.05	0.71	0.67	0.20
Soviet Union	2.76	2.43	1.93	1.37	1.40	0.25
Developed market economies	3.95	4.17	5.03	6.94	7.58	1.23
Developing market economies	0.99	0.92	0.92	0.86	0.57	0.11
Imports						
World	9.37	8.86	8.62	11.45	11.08	2.52
Former socialist countries	4.59	3.93	3.19	2.75	2.80	0.62
Eur.-6	1.75	1.52	1.26	0.79	0.90	0.18
Soviet Union	2.34	1.95	1.64	1.75	1.87	0.42
Developed market economies	4.06	4.37	4.53	7.62	7.73	1.76
Developing market economies	0.72	0.56	0.90	0.90	0.47	0.13
Balance						
World	0.63	0.81	0.93	−1.22	−0.44	−0.71
Former socialist countries	0.47	0.65	0.41	−0.34	−0.32	−0.17
Eur.-6	−0.05	0.01	−0.21	−0.08	−0.23	0.02
Soviet Union	0.42	0.48	0.29	−0.38	−0.47	−0.17
Developed market economies	−0.11	−0.20	0.50	−0.68	−0.15	−0.53
Developing market economies	0.27	0.36	0.02	−0.04	0.10	−0.02

markets. The same factors must have worked to stimulate exports in the face of the slackening of domestic markets, but unfortunately, detailed foreign trade statistics – especially in rouble and non-rouble breakdown – are available only until 1990.

Of external developments which affected foreign trade flows during this period, the abrupt dissolution of the CMEA trade and payment system was most important. The collapse of intra-Eastern European trade, which had started to dwindle already in 1987, certainly contributed to the decline of the domestic economy. As a result, Hungarian exports fell by 4% in real terms in 1990, by 5% in 1991, and showed a slight increase of 1.8% only in 1992 (see table 5.7). Imports contracted by 5% in 1990, grew by 5.5% in 1991, and declined by 7.6% in 1992. The trade balance deteriorated in 1991: there was an estimated $1.2 bn trade deficit compared to an almost $1 bn surplus in 1990. The trade deficit in 1992, however, decreased to $0.4 bn.[3]

Table 5.8. (*cont.*)

Exports	(percentage shares)					
World	100.0	100.0	100.0	100.0	100.0	100.0
Former socialist countries	50.6	47.4	37.7	23.5	23.3	24.9
Eur.-6	17.0	15.8	11.0	6.9	6.3	11.1
Soviet Union	27.6	25.1	20.2	13.4	13.2	13.8
Developed market economies	39.5	43.1	52.7	67.8	71.2	68.0
Developing market economies	9.9	9.5	9.6	8.4	5.4	6.1
Imports						
World	100.0	100.0	100.0	100.0	100.0	100.0
Former socialist countries	49.0	44.4	37.0	24.0	25.3	24.6
Eur.-6	18.7	17.2	14.6	6.9	8.1	7.1
Soviet Union	25.0	22.0	19.0	15.3	16.9	16.7
Developed market economies	43.3	49.3	52.6	66.6	69.8	69.8
Developing market economies	7.7	6.3	10.4	7.9	4.2	5.2

Notes:
[a] Forint/US dollar rates: 1988: 50.41; 1989: 59.06; 1990: 63.20; 1991: 74.73; 1992: 79.2565; 1993:1: 85.333. Forint/transferable rouble rates: 1988: 26.00; 1989: 28.25; 1990: 27.50; 1991: 27.50. US dollars/transferable rouble cross-rates: 1988: 0.5157; 1989: 0.4783; 1990: 0.4351; 1991: 0.3680. From 1991 on the former GDR is included in the 'Developed market economies' group of countries. Shares are based on data in current US dollars.
[b] 1993: 1 are from *Statisztikai Havi Közlemények* (Budapest), 4 (1993), p. 60. Growth is 1993: 1 over same period in 1992.
Source: Külkereskedelmi Statisztikai Évkönyv, (Budapest), *Központi Statisztikai Hivatal* (various years). For 1991 see *Gazdaságstatisztikai Évkönyv, 1991* (Budapest) (1993), pp. 206–7.

Early reports on the first quarter of 1993 showed a $0.7 bn trade deficit (see table 5.8).

Falling trade volumes: reorientation from Eastern to Western markets

At the time of writing, trade developments can be reviewed only in value terms which partly hide real developments. Measurement and data reliability problems were especially acute in 1991,[4] but 1992 was not a year without statistical problems, either[5] (see Mink, 1993, p. 14). For foreign trade, 1991 was clearly the year of competition; liberalisation exceeded the 90% level,[6] the level of tariffs was reduced further, and consequently, about 70% of industrial production faced direct foreign competition (Kádár, 1991). About half of the remainder represents the food industry, where liberalisation could, and would, come at a later stage after negotiations with the EC, EFTA and the GATT Uruguay Round (Koczka, 1991). Items which cannot be liberalised in the long term (materials causing environmental damage, weapons, precious metals, etc.) amount to an additional 2–3%.

In the course of 1991, several enterprises complained about 'threats' to their domestic markets from liberalised imports. Competitive enterprises have been calling for more 'up-to-date and fine-tuned' (Oblath, 1992; Török, 1992) means of market protection.

The most important boost to exports came from trade with the EC, where exports reached $4.7 bn in 1991, a 48% increase on 1990.[7] In 1992, exports to EC countries continued to grow by 13.3% in dollar terms. Trade with former CMEA countries declined: in 1991 exports dropped by 33% followed by a nearly 3% increase in 1992. Imports declined by 14% in 1991, but slightly increased in 1992 by nearly 2% (see table 5.8). By contrast, trade with the developed market economies increased strongly in 1991, with export growth of some 38% (dollar terms), and import expansion of 68%.

Hungary started to reduce trade relations with the former CMEA countries well before the systemic change, at which point trade declined sharply. The share of trade with former socialist countries[8] shrank from 55% in 1987 to 23% in 1992 in exports and from 52% to 25% in imports (see table 5.8). The share of exports to Eastern European former CMEA countries decreased by more than two-thirds between 1987 and 1991 (17% and 6%, respectively). The share of the Soviet Union in Hungarian exports and imports plummeted from 33% (1987) to 13% (1992), and from 28% to 17%, respectively. The dollar value of imports from the USSR has been on the increase since 1990, even though its volume declined. This is perhaps the most striking result of the switch to convertible currencies in trade with the USSR. On the other hand, values of exports to the same market measured in dollars diminished sharply in 1991 and was only slightly higher in 1992, reflecting both the expected impact of price changes due to the switch-over from rouble to dollar trade and the import cuts on the Soviet side. As a result, Hungary developed trade deficits with the USSR in both years.

1992 data show that the reorientation from Eastern to Western markets continued. Some preliminary trade data for the first quarter of 1993 show a substantial increase in export shares with other Eastern European econo-mies. This increase, however, was only enough to 'regain' the export share of the region attained in 1990 (see table 5.8). Import shares of these economies – including the former USSR and its successor states – have continued to decline through the first quarter of 1993.

An important result of trade reorientation has been the reduced importance of large-scale firms in both rouble and non-rouble exports, and the increase in the importance of medium- and small-scale enterprises in this respect.

Factors in the collapse of intra-CMEA trade

Three key elements have to be analysed: the dissolution of the CMEA as a trading system; macroeconomic policies and policy changes in Hungary; and international developments.

Perhaps the most important influence on trade with former CMEA countries came through the terms-of-trade effect. This effect manifested itself by a surge in the value of Hungarian imports from the USSR in 1991 coupled with a fall in the volume. Import cuts were not very significant as Hungary had already substantially reduced imports of so-called 'soft' goods in the years 1988–90. The elimination of transferable rouble payments[9] warranted an immediate rationalisation and restructuring of trade. Non-essential trade flows have been cut back, with domestic producers and consumers shifting to Western markets in search of cheaper and more reliable sources of supplies. The trade diversion effect was stronger on the import side, leading to a further drop in demand for products from former CMEA countries. It is questionable whether the substantial increase in exports to the market economies was realised by shifting sales away from the former CMEA markets or from the domestic market. Partial evidence discussed above suggests the latter, thus trade diversion was less important, although not insignificant, on the export side.

The effect of domestic contraction is quite straightforward. GDP fell by about 19% in 1990–92. Imports from former CMEA countries, however, fell well above average in 1990–2 combined. Hungary has been transformed into a demand-constrained economy, and the fall in the volume of imports from other Eastern European countries may to a significant degree be attributed to domestic recession induced by the stabilisation programme(s).

Finally, trade with former CMEA countries was also adversely affected by international developments, German unification being the most important. The immediate effect of German unification in 1990 was a massive cancellation of trade contracts by east German firms, further complicating the trade situation in the region. Previously, the GDR had been an important trading partner for Hungary, second only to the USSR.

Exchange rate policies and trade

Monetary authorities, by giving the highest priority to fighting inflation, followed the policy of real appreciation of the national currency, i.e. the forint was devalued by 18.2% to the US dollar in 1991, while the going domestic inflation rate (CPI) was about 35%. This trend continued into 1992, when the forint devalued by only 6.1%. Apparently following the same policy, the NBH devalued the national currency in the first half of 1993 by 6%, though the pressure for a change in the policy was mounting, as the first quarter of 1993 witnessed a substantial decline in the volume of Hungarian exports, coupled with a surge in imports.

Several observers considered this decline in exports to be a temporary phenomenon;[10] others, however, have been arguing the contrary: as the sources for a continued export growth have been exhausted, additional export promoting measures, including devaluation of the forint, are needed (Oblath, 1993, p. 14). The proponents of the first view favoured the exchange rate policy of the NBH which allows the forint to slightly appreciate. Others, however, have been calling for a strong devaluation so that the 'dormant' resources of exports might be revived. They emphasised that the continuing real appreciation of the national currency might lead to serious recession, and worsening balance of trade, especially as imports are liberalized.

Although, owing to the lack of detailed company and trade statistics for 1991–2, it is still quite difficult to provide any serious empirical evidence supporting either side of this debate, it appears that the competitiveness of the Hungarian export and import substitution sectors has worsened. In other words, the fall in export performance which began in the last quarter of 1992 and continued in the first months of 1993 is not transitory. Competitive pressures, coming through both exports and import substitution, seem to reveal structural weaknesses in the Hungarian trade sector. Without taking other measures aimed at theses structural problems, devaluing the forint in order to increase the level of exports might not only be inflationary but could lead to other negative consequences for the domestic economy.

Changes in foreign trade structure, 1988–92

Hungarian trade statistics up to 1990 provide an opportunity to analyse trade structure in two different ways: by groups of countries, i.e. 'Former CMEA countries', 'Developed market economies', and 'Developing countries' , and by type of foreign exchange – transferable rouble and non-transferable rouble. For 1991, such data are not available. There are about 48 product groups for which complete export and import data are available for the years 1988–91.[11]

Hungarian exports to former CMEA countries underwent substantial changes between 1988 and 1991. As table 5.9 shows, shares of Materials, Semi-finished Products and Spare Parts increased significantly, while those of Machinery, Transport Equipment and Other Capital Goods decreased by a very large margin. It is very likely that this trend continued in 1992. There was a sharp increase in the shares of raw materials for the food industry, livestock, and processed food products (from 19.5% in 1988 to 38.4% in 1991); and a similar increase in the share of the food industry (from 11% to 25.8%, respectively).

In exports to developed market economies, the share of Materials, Semi-finished Products, and Spare Parts somewhat declined, after a slight increase up to 1990. The share of Machinery, however, slightly increased, from 7.3% in 1988 to 8.4% in 1991. The major change in structure was the spectacular increase in the share of industrial consumer goods that took place mainly in 1991, attributable to Textiles, Clothing and Footwear and Pharmaceuticals. On the other hand, raw materials for the food industry, and food industrial products declined (see table 5.9).

With the exception of agricultural and food products, changes in the structure of exports to developing economies showed a pattern similar to that of exports to former CMEA countries. The share of the product group Materials, Semi-finished Products, Spare Parts increased (from 45% in 1988 to 50.6% in 1991), that of Machinery and Equipment decreased (from 31.9 to 28.8%, though with some fluctuation).

Analysing the commodity pattern of Hungarian exports by types of foreign exchange, the main findings correspond to those based on country groupings.[12] Because of changing destinations, the structure of total exports has changed significantly: the share of Materials and Semi-finished Products has increased in the last four years, mostly due to increased exports to the market economies. Machinery and Equipment and other capital goods gave about 13% of the total exports, almost exactly half the 1988 share.[13] The predominant factor behind this development is the dramatic decline in the share of this product group in exports to former CMEA countries. The decline would have been even steeper had exports to developed market economies not increased.

The structure of imports from the former CMEA countries also underwent substantial changes in the years 1988–92. Energy resources and electricity had a substantially higher share in 1991 than in 1988. The obvious explanation for this development is related to the fact that energy supplies from within the former CMEA area – mostly from the USSR – have been accounted for at world market prices and in hard currency from

Table 5.9. *Commodity pattern of Hungarian exports and imports by groups of countries, 1989–91, % of total*

	Former CMEA countries			Developed market economies			Developing economies		
	1989	1990	1991	1989	1990	1991	1989	1990	1991
Exports									
Materials, semi-finished products, spare parts	26.0	23.0	29.8	45.0	45.8	39.3	49.4	54.2	50.6
Raw and base materials	4.1	4.6	11.0	12.5	12.9	8.8	13.4	13.1	11.2
Semi-finished products	12.6	10.5	14.0	28.3	28.2	23.2	31.9	37.8	31.0
Spare parts	9.3	7.9	4.8	4.3	4.7	7.3	4.1	3.3	8.1
Machinery, transport equipment, other capital goods	39.4	35.2	18.8	7.7	8.8	8.4	23.0	25.5	28.8
Complete factory, other equipment	3.4	2.8	0.0	0.2	0.2	0.0	3.5	3.2	0.0
Transport equipment	10.5	10.8	9.9	0.9	1.3	1.2	3.0	1.9	12.6
Telecommunication machines, goods	6.7	4.7	1.0	0.3	0.4	1.0	0.7	7.2	3.9
Industrial consumer goods	14.7	15.3	12.0	17.8	18.5	28.0	10.4	8.9	9.2
Clothing, footwear, household textiles	5.8	5.0	2.9	9.2	9.1	15.6	2.2	1.4	1.6
Furniture	0.3	0.3	0.2	1.4	1.4	1.7	0.0	0.0	0.0
Raw materials for food industry, livestock, processed food products	19.4	25.8	38.4	25.0	23.0	22.2	17.2	11.3	11.3
Agricultural products, live animals	8.4	7.9	12.6	6.3	5.3	5.8	8.7	5.2	4.7
Products of the food industry	11.0	17.9	25.8	18.7	17.7	16.4	8.5	6.1	6.6
Total	100.0	100.0	100.0	100.0	100.0	100.0	100.0	100.0	100.0

Imports

Energy resources, electricity	24.2	27.4	47.1	0.5	0.3	1.2	0.3	35.5	42.1
Materials, semi-finished products, spare parts	37.8	35.9	33.9	63.8	58.5	40.5	36.0	19.0	14.4
Raw and base materials	14.1	12.7	16.8	9.3	7.7	6.1	17.2	7.2	4.2
Semi-finished products	16.2	15.5	15.0	35.2	31.4	25.8	14.5	5.7	6.9
Spare parts	7.5	7.8	2.2	19.2	19.4	8.6	4.2	6.1	3.3
Machinery, transport equipment, other capital goods	17.9	14.8	6.0	20.0	22.4	27.3	3.3	4.3	8.1
Complete factory, other equipment	0.7	0.8	0.0	0.8	1.2	0.0			
Transport equipment	4.3	4.3	2.0	0.5	0.6	2.8			
Telecommunication machines, goods	2.9	1.6	0.3	2.7	2.5	3.3	1.5	3.2	2.4
Industrial consumer goods	16.8	16.9	8.4	10.1	13.5	27.0	11.8	11.6	23.4
Clothing, footwear, household textiles	3.9	3.4	2.5	2.6	3.7	11.0	6.6	6.1	11.4
Furniture	0.7	0.5	0.5	0.0	0.1	0.5			
Raw materials for food industry, livestock, processed food products	3.3	5.0	4.6	5.6	5.3	4.0	48.5	29.7	29.3
Agricultural products, live animals	0.9	1.6	0.9	1.2	1.7	1.4	16.8	9.2	12.1
Products of the food industry	2.4	3.3	3.7	4.4	3.6	2.6	31.7	20.5	17.0
Total	100.0	100.0	100.0	100.0	100.0	100.0	100.0	100.0	100.0

Source: Based on *Külkereskedelmi Statisztikai Évkönyv, 1990* (Budapest), *Központi Statisztikai Hivatal* (1991) pp. 62–3. For 1991,*Gazdaságstatisztikai Évkönyv, 1991* (Budapest) (1993).

1991 onwards. Former, advantageous supply contracts have not been renewed. This change in itself immediately increased the share of this product group. There is a dramatic decline in the share of Machinery and Equipment in imports: from 18% to 6%. There was a slight increase in raw materials for food industry, and the food industry proper (see table 5.9).

The high share of Materials and Semi-finished Products in imports from developed market economies in 1988 (68%) declined to 41% by 1991, a remarkable development indeed. In the same period the share of Machinery and Equipment increased from 17.1% to 27.3%, contributing to the necessary technological change in the Hungarian economy. Similar increase has occurred in the product category of Industrial Consumer Goods. Analysing the commodity pattern of Hungarian imports by types of foreign exchange reveals similar tendencies.

For imports as a whole, three distinct features are noted: the decline in the share of Materials, Semi-finished Products; the gradual increase in the share of imported Machinery and Equipment (17% in 1988, 20% in 1991); and a large increase in the share of Industrial Consumer Products (from 12% in 1988 to 22% in 1991). These developments are most likely due to the change in the structure of imports from the developed market economies that happened after substantial trade liberalisation.

Changes in industrial exports, 1988–92

Exports of industrial products have always played a predominant role in total exports, accounting for around 90%.[14] Economic decline hit industry the hardest, putting it under pressure to restructure and reorient its trade. As table 5.10 shows, industrial exports were on the rise for the first two years of the period but declined in both 1991 and 1992. The structure of industrial exports reflected the uneven changes across industries. The export share of Engineering declined from 42% in 1988 to 30.3% in 1992; light industry's share was practically unchanged, while that of the chemical industry increased by 7 percentage points. The food industry was the other industrial sector which was able to increase its share in total industrial exports (from 15% to 20%) up to 1991 but suffered a serious decline (3 percentage points) in 1992.

Declining gross production and increasing exports was tantamount to increased export ratios (exports over gross output of the sector) in metallurgy (increase from 30% to 43%) and light industries. The engineering sector, chemical industry and food industry, however, showed lower export ratios in 1992 compared to 1988.

Non-rouble exports of metallurgy, both ferrous and non-ferrous, increased from 1988, and had about a 16% share in overall non-rouble industrial exports in 1990 (see table 5.11). Engineering, chemical industry and light industry had to accept a declining share. Since final 1991 data in this distribution are not available, it is estimated that some of the sub-sectors in engineering, such as Other Machinery, Electrical Machinery and Instruments, might have increased their shares in 1991.

It is indeed revealing that all the main industrial sectors witnessed a growing non-rouble export share of gross production. Whereas in 1988 about 17% of industrial production was exported to hard-currency countries, in 1990 this had risen to 21%. Recalling a 38% increase of exports to developed market economies in 1991 (see table 5.8), a substantial share of which came from industry, one can estimate the 1991 share of non-rouble export sales in total industrial production at about 25%.

Hungary's rouble industrial exports have been decreasing since 1988 as a share of total industrial exports (see tables 5.10 and 5.11). Metallurgy, engineering and light industry all had lower shares in 1990 than in 1988, but the chemical industry, mostly due to pharmaceuticals, and the food industry increased their shares in overall industrial exports. As a result, only about 8% of industrial gross production was sold on rouble markets in 1990 compared to 13% in 1988. All industries showed declining export ratios over gross production between 1988 and 1990. Recalling the fact that no rouble-dominated export contract was allowed after 1 January 1991, we can presume that in 1991 the overall share of rouble industrial exports in gross industrial production might have declined further, probably to 2–3%.

The value of industrial imports expressed in current forint grew by 95.2% between 1988 and 1992 (see table 5.10). Metallurgy, engineering (especially machinery and equipment, telecommunication equipment and instruments), and light industries showed high increases in value terms. Imports of the chemical industry in 1992, however, were down on 1991.

All commodity groups except light industry had a smaller share in total industrial imports in 1992 than in 1988. The share of light industry in overall industrial imports increased steadily between 1988 and 1992, reaching 20% by the end of the period. Industry as a whole showed an import ratio of 43.2% in 1992 compared to about 30% in 1988.

Balance of payments

Despite expectations of a heavy deficit due to the massive terms of trade loss, the current account balance changed little in 1991 and 1992. It was positive in 1991[15] and slightly negative in 1992 (see table 5.12) due to a positive balance of tourism, large interest payments and rather high inflow

Table 5.10. *Total industrial exports and imports of Hungary, 1989–92*

	In current forint (billion)				Structure (%)				Ratio of exports (imports) over gross output in (%)			
	1989	1990	1991	1992	1989	1990	1991	1992	1989	1990	1991	1992
Exports												
Metallurgy	56.6	68.4	68.1	47.0	11.0	12.4	11.1	9.8	30.6	37.0	43.2	42.5
Engineering	203.2	187.9	203.0	128.0	39.4	34.2	29.2	30.3	48.2	44.8	45.7	46.0
Machinery & equipment	62.3	58.3	49.5	35.8	12.1	10.6	7.1	8.5	56.0	47.1	36.3	44.0
Transportation machinery	52.4	45.5	47.3	32.6	10.1	8.3	6.8	7.7	56.0	59.8	52.0	57.1
Electrical machinery	14.8	16.4	32.2	18.1	2.9	3.0	4.6	4.3	26.7	28.6	53.0	37.4
Telecommunication equipment	32.1	28.2	38.4	16.0	6.2	5.1	5.5	3.8	42.9	42.2	70.1	33.1
Instruments	32.9	29.6	16.4	9.6	6.4	5.4	2.4	2.3	75.1	64.7	35.2	23.9
Chemical industry	95.3	102.3	134.1	103.9	18.5	18.6	19.3	24.6	29.6	26.6	29.2	23.8
Heavy industry, total	364.5	369.7	422.9	292.9	70.6	67.3	60.8	69.2	30.7	28.6	29.3	23.1
Light industry, total	64.9	69.9	127.4	57.0	12.6	12.7	18.3	13.5	30.2	29.9	51.8	22.0
Lumber, furniture industry	9.2	11.5	19.7	…	1.8	2.1	2.8	…	41.2	51.1	84.9	…
Textile industry	21.7	21.3	25.4	15.1	4.2	3.9	3.7	3.6	30.0	29.7	39.9	33.3
Leather, fur & shoe industry	13.3	13.7	28.6	9.0	2.6	2.5	4.1	2.1	43.7	45.4	96.0	33.3
Textile clothing	15.7	18.2	44.9	17.6	3.0	3.3	6.5	4.2	62.6	65.9	132.8	42.7
Other industrial products	2.3	4.5	4.0	0.9	0.4	0.8	0.6	0.2	17.3	35.0	28.2	4.9
Food industry	84.2	105.2	141.1	72.3	16.3	19.2	20.3	17.1	27.8	27.2	31.9	15.1
Total	515.9	549.3	695.4	423.1	100	100	100	100	30.0	28.5	32.4	21.1

Imports

Metallurgy	35.0	29.9	50.8	51.8	6.9	5.7	6.1	6.0	18.9	16.1	32.2	46.8
Engineering	202.7	216.5	313.5	279.1	40.0	41.2	37.7	32.2	48.0	51.7	70.6	100.4
Machinery & equipment	73.5	76.5	83.3	89.7	14.5	14.6	10.0	10.3	66.0	61.9	61.2	110.3
Transportation machinery	42.1	46.4	65.6	52.8	8.3	8.8	7.9	6.1	45.1	61.1	72.1	92.5
Electrical machinery	14.2	14.9	25.8	28.0	2.8	2.8	3.1	3.2	25.7	25.9	42.4	57.9
Telecommunication equipment	32.5	38.5	59.2	34.8	6.4	7.3	7.1	4.0	43.4	57.6	108.0	71.9
Instruments	13.2	12.2	53.3	36.1	2.6	2.3	6.4	4.2	30.2	26.8	114.4	90.0
Chemical industry	110.5	105.6	140.9	122.9	21.8	20.1	16.9	14.2	34.9	33.4	44.6	54.6
Heavy industry, total	414.8	432.0	643.2	693.8	81.8	82.3	77.3	80.0	34.9	33.4	44.6	54.6
Light industry, total	58.9	58.2	142.4	173.3	11.6	11.1	17.1	20.0	27.4	24.9	57.9	66.9
Lumber, furniture industry	7.4	7.3	11.4	7.3	1.5	1.4	1.4	0.8	32.9	32.7	49.1	30.3
Textile industry	23.2	20.0	65.8	53.7	4.6	3.8	7.9	6.2	32.0	27.9	103.3	118.3
Leather, fur & shoe industry	6.4	7.1	19.1	...	1.3	1.4			20.8	23.7	64.1	...
Textile clothing	4.7	6.2	17.6	21.5	0.9	1.2	2.1	2.5	18.8	22.5	52.1	52.2
Other industrial products	4.5	5.6	12.2	50.5	0.9	1.1	1.5	5.8	33.6	43.1	85.9	277.5
Food industry	28.7	29.4	33.9	40.3	5.7	5.6	4.1	4.6	9.5	7.6	7.7	8.4
Total	506.9	525.1	831.8	867.1	100	100	100	100	29.5	27.2	38.8	43.2

Notes: Data for 1992 are preliminary and partly estimated based on the latest available official trade statistics. See *Statisztikai Havi Közlemények* (Budapest), 2–3 (1993), pp. 61–2.

Source: *Statisztikai Évkönyv, 1990* (Budapest); *Központi Statisztikai Hivatal* (1991). For 1991 see *Gazdaságstatisztikai Évkönyv, 1991* (Budapest) (1993), *Központi Statisztikai Hivatal* (1993), pp. 232–3.

Table 5.11. *Non-rouble and rouble industrial exports of Hungary, 1988–90, billion forint and %*

	Exports in current forint (billion)			Structure of exports (%)			Export ratio of production (exports/gross output)		
	1988	1989	1990	1988	1989	1990	1988	1989	1990
Non-rouble trade									
Metallurgy	34.08	50.26	64.15	13.7	16.2	16.1	25.2	27.2	35.0
Engineering	64.28	71.87	96.89	25.8	23.2	24.3	17.0	17.0	23.1
Machinery & equipment	23.71	27.32	35.33	9.5	8.8	8.8	25.3	24.5	28.6
Transportation machinery	10.32	10.39	15.29	4.1	3.3	3.8	11.6	11.1	20.1
Electrical machinery	7.79	10.30	13.51	3.1	3.3	3.4	15.7	18.7	23.6
Telecommunication equipment	10.64	10.90	15.65	4.3	3.5	3.9	15.6	14.6	23.4
Instruments	6.85	6.68	8.68	2.8	2.2	2.2	17.9	15.2	19.0
Chemical industry	56.59	70.66	81.28	22.7	22.8	20.4	19.9	21.9	21.2
Heavy industry, total	160.50	199.41	251.76	64.5	64.3	63.0	15.2	19.3	23.0
Light industry, total	37.91	44.57	55.79	15.2	14.4	14.0	19.5	21.4	22.8
Lumber, furniture industry	6.87	8.00	10.38	2.8	2.6	2.6	24.6	24.2	26.7
Textile industry	1.51	1.93	2.22	0.6	0.6	0.6	2.3	2.7	3.1
Leather, fur & shoe industry	11.43	13.59	15.95	4.6	4.4	4.0	37.4	44.6	52.8
Textile clothing	6.53	7.69	10.08	2.6	2.5	2.5	28.9	30.7	36.6
Other industrial products	1.41	1.57	3.76	0.6	0.5	0.9	10.9	11.2	29.3
Food industry	49.11	64.80	88.09	19.7	20.9	22.1	19.5	21.4	22.8
Total	248.94	310.36	399.41	100.0	100.0	100.0	16.5	18.1	20.7

Rouble trade

Metallurgy	6.41	6.37	4.20	3.3	3.1	2.8	4.6	3.4	2.3
Engineering	124.06	131.34	90.96	63.4	63.9	60.7	32.7	31.1	21.7
Machinery & equipment	33.33	34.97	22.95	17.0	17.0	15.3	35.5	31.4	18.6
Transportation machinery	42.03	41.97	30.18	21.5	20.4	20.1	47.2	44.9	39.7
Electrical machinery	4.15	4.46	2.93	2.1	2.2	2.0	8.4	8.1	5.1
Telecommunication equipment	21.01	21.23	12.56	10.7	10.3	8.4	30.7	28.3	18.8
Instruments	21.26	26.21	20.89	10.9	12.8	13.9	55.5	59.8	45.7
Chemical industry	21.39	24.69	21.00	10.9	12.0	14.0	7.5	7.7	5.5
Heavy industry, total	154.43	165.06	117.97	79.0	80.3	78.7	14.6	16.1	10.8
Light industry, total	20.56	20.37	14.07	10.5	9.9	9.4	3.0	3.7	2.7
Lumber, furniture industry	0.84	1.23	1.06	0.4	0.6	0.7	12.5	11.2	7.4
Textile industry	8.21	8.11	5.30	4.2	3.9	3.5	22.1	18.4	11.9
Leather, fur & shoe industry	6.74	5.62	3.58	3.4	2.7	2.4	15.8	16.0	11.3
Textile clothing	3.56	4.02	3.10	1.8	2.0	2.1	10.6	9.5	6.0
Other industrial products	0.69	0.74	0.75	0.4	0.4	0.5	5.4	5.5	5.8
Food industry	19.87	19.37	17.11	10.2	9.4	11.4	7.9	6.4	4.0
Total	195.56	205.55	149.91	100.0	100.0	100.0	13.0	12.0	7.8

Source: Statisztikai Évkönyv and *Központi Statisztikai Hivatal* (**Budapest**) various years. The *Gazdaságstatisztikai Évkönyv, 1991* (*Központi Statisztikai Hivatal, 1993*) have now discontinued publishing trade data by foreign exchange.

Table 5.12. *Balance of payments of Hungary in convertible currencies,*
US$ mn, 1990–2

	1990	1991	1992
Exports	6,346	9,258	10,028
Imports	5,998	9,069	10,076
Trade balance	348	189	−48
Travel, net	345	560	590
Government expenditures, net	17	63	78
Investment income			
receipts	230	297	420
expenditures	1,644	1,628	1,636
net	−1,414	−1,331	−1,216
Direct investment income, net	−24	−32	−45
Unrequited transfers, net	727	860	859
Services, net	302	67	103
Labour and property income, net	18	−20	9
Other current payments, net	−28	−9	110
(1) Current account balance	127	267	324
(2) Medium- and long-term capital			
account	204	3,070	432
Liabilities	280	1,668	−894
inflow	2,827	4,077	2,204
outflow	2,547	2,409	3,098
Assets	−76	−57	−145
Foreign direct investment	311	1,459	1,471
(3) Basic balance ((1)+(2))	331	3,337	756
(4) Short-term capital			
account, net	−893	−617	5
Liabilities	−569	−758	−152
Assets	−324	141	157
(5) Overall balance ((3)+(4))	−562	2,720	761

Source: Monthly Bulletin, NBH (1993/1)

of foreign exchange in the form of unrequited (unilateral) payments. The high unrequited payments can be explained by the relatively liberal environment for foreign exchange deposits and operations, by the turbulent situation in the neighbouring countries, and to a certain degree by tax evasion by Hungarian exporters.

Foreign direct investments increased substantially, reaching a level of around US$ 1.5bn. This contributed to the accumulation of the international reserves which now cover 5.3 months of imports (compared to 2.3 at the end of 1990), in spite of the very dynamic increase of imports. The debt service ratio (the sum of interest and principal repayments divided by exports) decreased to 40.4%, still very high by international standards, but less alarming than the 62.4% observed in 1990.

Gross foreign debt was US$ 22.6bn at the end of 1991, showing an increase of US$ 1.4bn throughout the year. A US$ 900mn net credit was the main factor behind the 1991 increase. A part of this rise can be attributed to the exchange rate movements in favour of those currencies in which the Hungarian debts are denominated. In 1992, however, gross foreign debts declined by US$ 1.2bn.

New hope: Association agreements with the EC

The EC is perhaps the most important market and a vital source of foreign direct investment not only for Hungary but also for Eastern Europe as a whole. Almost 50% of Hungarian exports were sold in EC markets in 1992, and imports from EC countries have been substantially liberalised. On 16 December 1991 the EC signed Association agreements with Czechoslovakia, Hungary and Poland. The trade protocol of the agreements came into effect in March 1992. Most quotas have been abolished and many tariffs will be removed over the next two to five years.

There is much protectionism to dismantle. The export structure of Hungary in relation to the EC is as follows: agricultural products 25%; textiles and clothing 15%;[16] steel industry 5%; general industrial products 55% (Farkas, 1992). Agriculture, textiles, iron and steel together account for 45% of exports. All have traditionally faced high levels of EC protection. Hungary has been particularly hurt by the high level of EC agricultural protection; tariffs levied under the CAP have practically doubled the price of Hungarian agricultural exports.

Textiles, apparel and iron and steel exports have faced only modest tariffs; protection has been applied through non-tariff barriers instead. Half of Hungarian textile exports to the EC have faced quantitative restrictions under the MFA. Barriers to iron and steel exports to the EC take the form of quotas.

Much of this EC protection will survive the Association agreements, at least until 1996. Trade liberalisation will be slower for certain 'import-sensitive' sectors – textiles and apparel, iron and steel – and no liberalisation is in sight for agricultural exports.[17] Member countries required these exceptions, despite the small size of Eastern European exports to the EC. Completely free trade with Eastern Europe would be expected to reduce the output of the industries mentioned above by a mere 2–4% in EC countries (Messerlin, 1992).

The Association agreements eliminated all quantitative restrictions in regard to Hungarian industrial exports (save for textiles). Over 70% of these products have now become duty-free, and remaining duties will be reduced to zero in stages, in five to six years. According to the original Agreements – there were some changes accepted at the Copenhagen summit of European Community leaders (21–22 June 1993) – customs duties for steel will be reduced by 20% in the first stage and fully eliminated in five years.[18] QRs on textile exports will be lifted in five years under a schedule to be specified later. Textiles manufactured under contract have now become duty-free, and customs duties for other textiles reduced by 29%. These duties will be eliminated in six years. As far as agricultural products are concerned, both sides grant one another mutual preferences. In the next three years, the EC will reduce customs duties for Hungarian exports by 20% per annum. The quotas of farm products falling under preferential treatment will be raised by an annual 10% over the next five years. Hungary grants much smaller preferences in agricultural imports than it receives.

Changes accepted in Copenhagen to the timetable of proposed improvements in the conditions of the Association agreements are as follows:[19]

- Duties on imports on sensitive basic industrial products will be abolished after two years, instead of four.
- Duties on imports of industrial products covered by the consolidation of the General System of Preferences (GSP) abolished after three years instead of five.
- Quotas and ceilings for the above will be raised by 25% instead of 15% for Hungary.
- Levies/duties on farm product quotas reduced by 60% six months earlier than foreseen and a 10% increase in quotas planned from the third year onwards applied six months earlier.
- Elimination of duties on textiles after five years instead of six.
- Abolition of duties on steel products at the end of the fourth year instead of after the fifth.

Export opportunities might be curtailed by the special conditions agreed to in the agreements. Any reduction of duties on Hungarian products can only be given for products containing at least 60% Hungarian value added. What exactly is considered 'originating material' from Hungary is detailed by complex legal regulations. The issue of origin is further complicated by the so called 'cumulation' rule, when the final product contains components from different countries. Manufactured products, assembled in Hungary but containing parts produced abroad, might very well be excluded from the agreement, depending on the place of origin.

This, of course is a common problem in all agreements concerning preferential treatment, where the aim is to avoid opening a back door to third-party exports into the free-trade area. In other words, the agreements have many provisions which may seriously undermine trade liberalisation. Article 30 allows the trade barriers to be re-erected in order to safeguard a threatened domestic industry and prevent 'serious disturbances in any sector of the economy or difficulties which could bring about serious deterioration in the economic situation of a region' (Messerlin, 1992).

Although the results of the Association agreements have to be acknowledged, much needs to be done in order to ensure better access for Hungarian products into the EC. Tensions over steel, textile and especially farm produce have been rife between the European Community and Hungary. Hungarian representatives pointed out how government procurement procedures, national production standards, and commodity-specific taxation improve the position of the Western domestic industries, and at the same time neutralise the competitive edge of outside, including Hungarian, suppliers. The Hungarian government welcomed the modification of the agreement, but pointed out unfair trade practices by some of the EC member countries with regard to agricultural trade.

The issue at stake is the threat of Western agricultural exports to former CMEA countries, mostly to Russia. Hungary has been using its comparative and competitive advantage to export large volumes of grain to these markets. The switch to hard-currency trade accounts, and prolonged droughts for two years in a row, have already made the prospects for agricultural exports precarious. In addition to these problems, Hungary claims that France is selling wheat in the Baltic countries at half the cost, namely, at subsidised prices. In addition, according to the state secretary at the Agriculture Ministry, Germany increased its subsidised exports of beef to the former USSR. Hungary's beef exports to these markets have fallen to a tenth of their 1980s level. It is almost certain that such tense relations between the EC and Hungary will continue for some time.

Perspectives and conclusion

Although the Hungarian case, at least until 1993, was widely regarded as one of the few success stories of economic transformation in Central and Eastern Europe, the gradualist success story (Dervis and Condon, 1992), the period between 1990 and 1992 can only be regarded as years of survival and beginning of structural change. The economy survived the longest and deepest recession of its post-war history, but major structural changes necessary for a longer-term recovery and growth did not take place.

In spite of the substantial decline in GDP, income and consumption,

Hungarian economic policy makers were fairly successful in maintaining a relatively stable domestic macroeconomic environment and a remarkably stable external position of the country. The rate of inflation was kept at manageable levels, the current account balance, at least until 1993, remained positive, international reserves reached comfortably high levels, and net foreign debts declined. A reorientation in exports from Eastern to Western countries took place.

Moreover, institutional and legal reforms progressed in an impressively fast manner: in spite of the serious problems the Hungarian economy experienced during this period, the process of economic transformation was remarkably smooth. As a consequence, the image of the country abroad improved substantially, resulting in a steady inflow of FDI and a relatively easy access to international private capital markets.

While all this was undoubtedly a major achievement, one could observe several warning signs of possible future problems. On the macroeconomic level, the budget deficit was increasing rapidly reaching alarmingly high levels by 1993. As the policy was to finance the budget deficit domestically, it pushed up real lending rates and mopped up available long-term finance.

High real lending rates were also due to the lack of certain financial reforms. Reflecting the collapse of former CMEA markets and the subsequent decline of domestic demand, a rapidly increasing number of enterprises experienced financial difficulties. While new bankruptcy, banking and accounting regulations forced banks to reclassify their portfolios, policy makers failed to come up with a loan consolidation scheme that could have coped with this situation. As banks got very little help in coping with the fast increasing stock of bad loans that had resulted from this process, they had to recover the costs of building up the necessary bank reserves by widening the margin between lending and borrowing rates.

Therefore, while real deposit rates declined (in fact turned negative), real lending rates reached unbearably high levels for enterprises. This situation discouraged both saving and investment. Until mid-1993, increasing private saving could to some extent counterbalance the rapid increase in the budget deficit; since then, the damaging repercussions of the above process have become painfully clear.

With fast declining investment and a relatively slow pace of privatisation, structural changes in the economy, as pointed out in the analysis presented above, were confined to the uneven decline across sectors. The lack of new investment and affordable enterprise finance also meant that changes in the product structure of production and exports were very limited. Hungarian producers remained trapped in outdated production technologies and product structures. Hungarian products consequently fetched low prices on foreign and domestic markets and, perhaps even more important, Hungarian exports became very vulnerable to any recession in Western European economies. Developments in 1993, in particular the sizeable decline in Hungarian manufactured exports, clearly show the importance of this point.

The lack of affordable finance also hindered the expansion of the private sector, in particular the development of newly emerging private enterprises. In fact, increasing real lending rates started to threaten previously fast expanding and successful private firms, as well.

As a consequence, besides the budget deficit, the steeper than expected increase of unemployment became the major concern for policy makers. Unemployment can be cured only by economic growth which mainly depends on the speed of the restructuring process, while the elimination of the persisting budget deficit would require a major reform of the expenditure side of the state budget (social security system, health, education and administration). However, there are no signs of an investment boom in the near future; the volume of non-residential construction will not recover soon. Households will continue their very cautious approach by keeping a relatively high level of precautionary savings, preparing themselves for any possible circumstances.

Under conditions of deep domestic economic recession Hungary was unable to compensate for a 60% decline in its CMEA-related exports. The US$ 2 bn loss in exports to former CMEA economies could only partially be offset by the US$ 1.2 bn increase in exports to Western market economies. The 'demand shock' in the Eastern trade has been reinforced by the 'supply shock' coming from the West (Kádár, 1992). The high level of import liberalisation, the 20% reduction in the average level of tariffs and the more than 50% increase in dollar-denominated imports created a competitive domestic market, with plenty of opportunity for consumers to buy.

The collapse of the CMEA trade and payments system has forced Hungarian exporters to try hard to upgrade their existing product range for Western markets. For some companies the competition proved over-whelming, for others it was a stimulating factor. Many Hungarian economists caution that overstretched companies have redirected as much production as they can and the issue is now whether the pace of export growth to the West is sustainable or not (Köves, Lányi and Oblath, 1993).

The Association agreements with the EC, though fairly important regarding the integration of the Hungarian economy into the Union, provide an annual increase in exports of only about US$ 100–200 mn. This should be increased, for the major stimulus to economic growth and the reduction in unemployment must come from the foreign trade sector through an expansion of exports.

The positive results achieved so far are endangered by the deleterious tendencies pointed out above. The government had to modify its targets for 1994–6 as no general breakthrough is expected. Only a slow and painful recovery can be expected during economic transition in Hungary.

Notes

The views expressed here are András Blahó's own and do not necessarily reflect those that may be held by the United Nations Secretariat.

1 The reform carried the name New Economic Mechanism.

2 More precisely, as was pointed out by one of the referees, it was decided to close down the CMEA within 90 days, pending resolution of the ownership of CMEA headquarters.

3 For the current foreign trade values in forint see *Magyar Hírlap* (Budapest, 13 February 1992), p. 11. For final statistics see *Statisztikai Havi Közlemények* (Budapest), 2–3, pp. 43–44, *Központi Statisztikai Hivatal* (1992) for the year 1991 and *Statisztikai Havi Közlemények* (Budapest), 2–3 (1993), pp. 59–62 for preliminary final 1992 data.

4 One part of these problems has to do with the changed character of payment in intra-regional trade; the other with the new system of trade statistics collection. Contrary to the past years, trade data from 1991 onwards are based on *customs statistics*. The inexperience of customs agents in this field and the inadequate computerisation of data processing is clearly discernible behind confusing and sometimes conflicting trade data.

5 One particular issue concerned the statistical accounting of imported textiles, and clothes manufactured later in Hungary and exported with high value added content.

6 Government Decree No. 112 (23 December 1990) rendered the pursuit of foreign trade a virtual individual right. More than 60% of all goods may be exported and almost 90% may be imported without permits.

7 Within this, the share of Germany is $2.8 bn, an increase of 61% over 1990.

8 Members and non-members of CMEA.

9 This was called the transferable rouble clearing system.

10 See the discussion in the Budapest weekly *Figyelö* between G. Oblath, A. Szentgyörgyvári, T. Erdös, L. Halpern, J. Neményi and E. Czelnai, 13, 15, 16, 18, 20 (1993).

11 Unfortunately, these product groups could not be analysed based on groups of countries and/or groups of foreign exchange, for 1991 data were published not in the customary *Foreign Trade Yearbook* format but in the *Gazdaságstatisztikai Évkönyv, 1991* (Budapest). This important publication was published only in early 1993!

12 There are differences, however, for exports to 'former CMEA countries' contain dollar trade to these economies, as well, and 'Rouble accounts' exports do not.

13 Most of this sharp decline happened in 1991.

14 The actual shares of industrial exports in total exports for the years 1988–91 are as follows: 90.3%; 90.3%; 89.3%, and 92.7%, respectively. See *Külkereskedelmi Statisztikai Évkönyv, 1990* (Budapest), *Központi Statisztikai Hivatal*, (1991), p. 79. For 1991 see *Gazdaságstatisztikai Évkönyv, 1991* (Budapest), *Központi Statisztikai Hivatal* (1993), pp. 210–11.

15 Figures here refer to the balance of payments statistics compiled by the NBH. As the figures show, there was a substantial discrepancy between customs clearance-based trade statistics compiled by the Ministry for International Economic Relations and the payments-based balance of payments figures for exports and imports. In this section, we use the latter.

16 Within this group, 5% is the share of 'bérmunka'. In this type of cooperation, textiles are imported into Hungary and sewn into final clothing products. Hungary thereby exports value added 'only'.

17 An eloquent analysis of the agricultural issues concerning the Association agreements is given by Varga (1992).

18 The EC expects voluntary exports restrictions from Hungary.

19 These improvements have been suggested to be part of all Association agreements. Where Hungary specifically is mentioned, that obviously refers only to that country.

References

Csaba, L., 1992. 'How to survive trade reorientation and liberalization? (the example of Hungary)', paper presented to the European Bank for Reconstruction and Development conference on 'Eastern European Trade Policy Issues' (26–27 March)

1993. 'Economic consequences of Soviet disintegration for Hungary', in I. P. Székely and D. M. G. Newbery (eds.), *Hungary: An Economy in Transition*, Cambridge: Cambridge University Press, pp. 27–43

Dervis, K. and Condon, T., 1992. 'Hungary: An emerging gradualist success story?', paper presented at the symposium 'Making Markets: Economic Transformation in Eastern Europe and the Post-Soviet Republics', Council on Foreign Relations, Cambridge, MA (12–13 February)

Farkas, Z., 1992. 'Mit tartalmaz az Európai Közösséggel kötött társasági szerzödés? Beszélgetés dr. Juhász Endrével, a Nemzetközi Gazdasági Kapcsolatok Minisztériuma föosztályvezetöjével', *Külgazdaság*, 36(3), 46–57

Kádár, B., 1991. *Népszabadság* (Budapest) (19 December), 4

1992. 'Visszatekintés és elórepillantás', *Külgazdaság,* 36(3), 4–10

Koczka, L., 1991. 'Lassubb import liberalizáció 1992-ben.', *Figyelö* (24 October), 29

Köves, A., Lányi, K. and Oblath, G., 1993. 'Az exportorientált gazdaságpolitika feltételei és eszközei 1993-ban', *Külgazdaság*, 37(5), 4–22

Messerlin, P., 1992. *Restrictions on OECD Imports from Eastern Europe*, Institute d'Etudes Politiques de Paris (March)

Mink, M., 1993. 'Ez sem az igazi', *Figyelö* (Budapest) (24 June)

Oblath, G., 1992. 'Veszélyes vizeken', *Figyelö* (Budapest) (7 May)

1993. 'A leértékelés nem jó vagy rossz', *Figyelö* (Budapest) (3 June)

Török, Á., 1992. 'A strukturális alkalmazkodás iparvédelmi eszközei I – II', *Külgazdaság* 36(3 and 4), 21–33 and 29–41, respectively

Varga, Gy., 1992. 'A magyar agrárpolitika és a közös piaci csatlakozás', *Külgazdaság* 36(3), 58–64.

6 Industrial restructuring in Czechoslovakia after 1989

Alena Nešporová

The initial conditions of economic transformation in Czechoslovakia

In analysing and understanding the outcome of the economic transformation processes taking place in the economies of the Central and Eastern European countries (CEE countries), account must be taken of the similarities and differences in initial economic and institutional conditions. These conditions are very important in explaining the eventual impact of economic policy mixes and single policy instruments, the social costs of transition, as well as prospects for future development.

Despite only moderate growth through the 1980s, the Czechoslovak economy's overall level of development was widely regarded as being higher than those of Hungary and Poland, and considerably higher than those of the USSR, Romania and Bulgaria. A detailed comparison of the per capita net material product across the CMEA countries that was carried out by the Statistical Commission of the CMEA in 1983 and 1988 found NMP per head to be 20–30% higher for Czechoslovakia than for Hungary and Poland. This gave policy makers in Czechoslovakia more room to manoeuvre, and it cushioned the inevitable social costs of transformation.

Another advantage enjoyed by Czechoslovakia was its relatively stable internal and external equilibria. Gross foreign debts in convertible currencies amounted to US$ 7.9 bn (US$ 510 per capita) in 1989. Poland's gross debt was more than double that, and Hungary's almost four times as great. Net foreign debts were practically zero, though the quality of a considerable proportion of development loans in the former CMEA countries was very low. Unlike Hungary and Poland, the debt service ratio (around 19%) was acceptable in World Bank terms.

Two main components of internal equilibria are the consumer goods market and the state budget. On the whole, the consumer goods market was in equilibrium (Charemza, 1991) though, due to price distortions and import restrictions in certain segments of this market – such as consumer electronics, household appliances and some luxury goods – there were clear signs of excess demand. Consequently, suppressed inflation, forced substitution and monetary overhang stemming from shortage of consumer goods was minimal. Official records showed an average annual CPI inflation of around 2% which, together with hidden inflation not reflected in official statistics, remained within a 3–5% per annum level. Throughout the whole post-war period (and, indeed, during the inter-war period) rather tight monetary and fiscal policies were pursued. Consequently, at the beginning of the economic transformation, the state budget was balanced and the accumulated internal state debt was less than 1% of GDP. Incomes policy ensured that nominal wages increased more or less in line with labour productivity growth. In this respect too, Czechoslovakia differed from Poland and Hungary.

On the other hand, distortion in the structure of production, employment and industrial assets was perhaps greatest in Czechoslovakia. Though the share of agriculture was not so different from that typical in developed market economies, the country was certainly overindustrialised and, what is worse, industrial activity was concentrated in resource-intensive, low value added industries (such as heavy chemistry, metallurgy, mining, heavy engineering, building materials). These industries were not only inefficient but also created immense long-term ecological problems. In general, the dependence of industrial production on CMEA export markets, in particular on Soviet markets, was overwhelming.

On the surface, the structure of trade with the USSR appeared very advantageous for Czechoslovakia. The less competitive manufactured goods ('soft products') produced by Czechoslovakia were mainly exchanged for oil, natural gas and raw materials from the USSR, that is, for goods which were easy to sell on international markets. However, this trade had an enormous lock-in effect on the Czechoslovak manufacturing industries. The importers of manufactured goods in the USSR did not demand (in fact, in most cases resisted) any product innovation and exerted no pressure on Czechoslovak producers to increase their cost efficiency. Perversely, deterioration in terms of trade gave an impetus for Czechoslovak producers to increase the volume of their production, further locking the country into an obsolete economic structure and further increasing the extent of ecological disaster created by industry. The increase in the share of trade with the USSR made Czechoslovakia very vulnerable to any disruption in this market, and thus it is not surprising that when the disintegration of the Soviet economy started to take place Czechoslovakia was worse hit than countries where the process of gradual trade reorientation had started earlier (Csaba, 1992).

Another important disadvantageous factor for Czechoslovakia was the very high level of concentration in the economy and the almost complete lack of a private sector. The economy was characterised by huge SOEs (Newbery, 1990), even in sectors where enterprises are predominantly small-size units in market economies (for example, in services). Cooperatives had the same characteristics as SOEs. Entrepreneurship was suppressed, it could survive only in the (semi- or illegal) second economy, the size of which, however, was substantially less than in Poland or Hungary. This overcentralised and rigid structure survived until the beginning of economic restructuring in 1990, and, as subsequent sections will show, changed very slowly thereafter. The situation in this respect was much more favourable in Poland and Hungary where, in the second half of the 1980s, private activities were given more opportunities and other partial reform steps were also taken, creating a much better general climate for economic transformation.

Reform steps after 1989

In August 1990, the government's programme for economic restructuring was passed by the Federal Parliament. This programme had three pillars: (a) quick privatisation of state assets, (b) liberalisation of prices, and (c) liberalisation of foreign trade. The two last elements were based on the internal convertibility of the national currency (convertibility on the current account). The main priority for macroeconomic policy was to maintain the internal and external stability of the economy by means of tight monetary and fiscal policies.

Although the package described above was introduced in January 1991, some preliminary measures were already in place by 1990 in order to facilitate changes in the following year. First of all, the state budget was amended to eliminate the budget deficit. Items on the expenditure side, mainly production subsidies for state enterprises and agricultural cooperatives, were cut back. Investment finance was decentralised and enterprises were given the right to make investment decisions. Food price subsidies were removed and the corresponding gain was channelled to households in the form of transfers. The national currency was devalued in three steps from 15 CSK/US\$ to 28 CSK/US\$, that is, by 46%. The most important step, however, was the creation of the legislative and institutional framework for economic transformation. In this process, the fundamental institutions of a market economy were created.

The main shock to the Czechoslovak economy in 1990 was of domestic origin, as changes in CMEA markets were not yet significant. The inflationary expectations of producers and consumers created by policy

Table 6.1. *Macroeconomic indicators of the CSFR, 1990 and 1991*
indices in %, constant prices, the same period of the previous year = 100

Indicator	1990					1991				
	I	II	III	IV	I-IV	I	II	III	IV	I-IV
GDP	.	.	.	.	99.6	97.0	87.3	78.5	74.8	84.1
NMP (produced)	102.6	101.1	95.8	96.8	98.9	95.3	82.3	74.8	71.2	80.5
NMP (domest. used)	107.4	106.8	104.4	104.7	95	70.7	56.7	52.9	67.6	
Private consumption	109.9	110.1	99.5	101.0	104.8	74.0	61.4	64.2	68.5	67.0
Investment (gross)	108.2	96.6	99.4	98.6	100.0	87.7	73.1	67.8	60.1	70.1
Rate of unemployment[a]	0.1	0.2	0.6	1.0	.	2.3	3.8	5.6	6.6	.
Consumer prices	103.4	103.9	114.1	118.4	110.0	154.7	168.5	156.3	148.7	153.8

Note:
[a] The ratio of officially registered unemployment to employment in December 1989, %.
Source: Federal Statistical Office, *Statistical Bulletins.*

proposals, including price liberalisation and subsidy reduction, induced an unprecedented upsurge in demand for production and consumption durables and for storable production and consumption non-durables (e.g. raw materials and intermediates). This process accelerated in the course of the year, destabilising domestic consumer goods markets and lifting the investment rate to an all-time high.

The yearly and quarterly values of some of the main macroeconomic indicators for 1990 are presented in table 6.1. Though the values for the whole year show a stagnating economy, the quarterly figures clearly reveal a tendency to continuous decline. The decline in 1990 is mainly attributable to the supply side: logistical problems, irregularities in deliveries of domestic and in the import of production inputs, and significant cuts in the imports of some raw materials and energy (crude oil, iron ore, etc.). The only market where domestic producers had to face a demand constraint was processed food after the removal of price subsidies in July 1990. The domestic demand for investment goods and raw materials was very strong, resulting in an upsurge in imports. This forced the government abruptly to devalue the national currency in order to avoid a serious deterioration in the trade balance, although the original plan had been to devalue at the time of the launch of the reform package described above. In spite of this measure, the gap between NMP produced and domestically used turned out to be rather large for the year as a whole, and widened throughout the year. The foreign trade deficit reached 10% of imports. The figures for the whole year reveal a reduction in public consumption, on the one hand, and an increase in private consumption and investment, mainly into input inventories, on the other.

Another result of inflationary expectations was a rapid decline in household savings, whilst due to the rather strict incomes policy pursued by the government, nominal incomes increased by only 7.2% (of which nominal wage incomes rose 3.5%), while consumption expenditures increased by 15.4%. As a result, savings, for the second time in the post-war history of the country, fell in absolute terms.

Reorientation of foreign trade started to take place in 1990. Trade shares with developed market economies increased substantially (in exports from 31.2% to 42.3%, in imports from 31.1% to 42.4%), though this was partly a result of German reunification. The share of developing countries remained practically unchanged, while the share of the former CMEA countries diminished (in exports from 60.8% to 49.3%, in imports from 62.3% to 51.4%). Due to the structure of intra-CMEA trade discussed above, imports declined slightly less than exports.

In January 1991, reform was started by liberalising prices and foreign trade and by introducting internal convertibility of the national currency. In addition a programme of small privatisation aimed at the selling off of approximately 40 000 small business units (shops, restaurants, hotels, workshops, or smaller enterprises) was launched. By the end of the year the records showed 14 200 units privatised in the Czech Republic (of which 88% were sold in auctions, 11% to the leaseholders, and 1% in the form of restitution), and 7300 units in the Slovak Republic. The so called 'large privatisation' was carried out in two phases in 1992–94, the majority by means of a rather controversial voucher scheme.

The first 'wave' of privatisation started on 18 May 1992 with the offer of 1491 enterprises having a total book value of CSK 300 mn. This phase terminated at the end of 1992 when 93% had been sold, of which 65% was by vouchers, 15% remained in the National Property Fund, 12% was transformed into the capital participation of the state in financial institutions, 3% were sold to foreign firms and 5% were restituted to former owners or their heirs. The second 'wave' will be carried out in compliance with the original plan in the Czech Republic, but Slovakia will develop a different scheme. In the Czech Republic about 900 companies will be offered for sale, but only one-third of their value will be distributed to the population as prize vouchers.

The restrictive macro-policy had three pillars: credit control (with credit and interest rate ceilings), subsidy reduction, and wage control (with penalty taxes on above-target wage increases). The budget was planned to be balanced, though the targets on several items on the revenue side (turnover taxes, profit taxes, and income taxes) rested on rather shaky ground. In order to protect socially vulnerable groups and to avoid poverty on a massive scale, a social safety net was created under which certain social benefits, mainly old-age pensions, were indexed, minimum wage and minimum income levels were set, and an unemployment benefit scheme was set up.

Price liberalisation resulted in a price jump much higher than expected, mainly because the monopolistic structures of production and trade were preserved. Households reacted to this price jump by reducing their demand for goods and services, and making use of their pre-liberalisation hoarding of industrial goods and non-perishable foodstuff. Retail trade turnover declined by 40% in real terms. In the first quarter of the year, the decline in real wages was 32%, compared to the same period in the previous year. Surprisingly, however, consumer demand remained sluggish throughout the whole year, though real wages and other incomes partly recovered later in 1991. Consequently, real savings increased substantially. The price shock caused by liberalisation was absorbed by April, and from May, month-on-month CPI inflation was less than 1%. Although towards the end of the year inflation somewhat accelerated, the average month-on-month rate remained below 2%.

High real interest rates, resulting from high nominal rates and declining inflation, gave an impetus to saving. The incremental saving ratio (change in savings/change in incomes) in national currency-denominated instruments increased by 8.2 percentage points to 8% (in 1990 savings in crown-denominated assets fell), and if assets in convertible currencies are also taken into account, it increased by 9 percentage points to 10.2%. This increase in saving was mainly attributable to precautionary motives, fear of unemployment and poverty under the weak social security system, though a part of it may create a financial basis for future business ventures. This change in the saving behaviour of the population has important implications for macro-policies, for the effects of incomes policies and of fiscal stimulation.

The decline in consumer demand had a widespread impact on production: consumer goods output declined substantially, in spite of the rapid increase in the inventories of finished goods; then, with a lag, this spread to other industries, resulting in diminishing demand for investments.

The other important source of disruption was the collapse of the CMEA and the intra-regional trade flows in CEE. The devastating impact of this trade contraction concentrated on industries with a high exposure to CEE markets, such as textiles, clothing, leather, engineering, and electronics.

As the figures in table 6.1 show, economic contraction accelerated throughout the year. While in the first quarter (compared to the same period of the previous year) GDP was down by only 3% and industrial output by 10.4%, the figures for the fourth quarter are 25.2% and 33.9% respectively. As a result of demand contraction and foreign trade liberalisation, the economy was gradually turned into a demand-constrained economy, abandoning the long-lived system of central planning characterised by supply constraints.

The importance of different factors in causing or explaining the economic collapse observed across the whole region, and in particular in Czechoslovakia, is fiercely debated. Perhaps economic transformation cannot be achieved without a decline in economic performance. This process has neither historical precedent, nor economic theory to guide practice. Delays or failures in creating some parts of the new legal and institutional framework inevitably lead to problems in other parts of the economy. Discussions in the economic literature draw attention to many such issues, for example, the underdeveloped financial system and its implications for capital allocation and enterprise performance. However, restrictive monetary and fiscal policies seemed to deepen the economic depression more than was necessary by suppressing domestic demand.

Credit ceilings imposed by the government and the Central Bank froze credits in real terms in the first months of 1991 well below their level in 1990, so enterprises became illiquid and were unable to meet their payment obligations. An illiquidity chain developed rapidly throughout the whole corporate sector affecting one-quarter to one-third of net material product. This phenomenon, widely termed 'queueing', can only partly be explained by lack of financial discipline and proper bankruptcy regulations. A major part was evidently caused by the abrupt fall in the money supply at the beginning of the period, catching not only inefficient firms but also firms with a good sales record. Though the government tried to mitigate the impact of 'queueing' by injecting an additional CSK 50 bn into the economy through the commercial banks (as a matter of fact, only 28.5 bn was actually used for this purpose, the rest was retained by the banks), this measure turned out to be inadequate.

The very high nominal interest rates, which were appropriate during the period of rapid price increase in the first few months of 1991, proved to be counterproductive after inflation had been brought down. The result was a massive slump in investment and an entry barrier to newly emerging private firms.

The excessive curtailing of domestic demand by tight monetary and fiscal policies had repercussions on the economy throughout the course of the year. Though the government argued that economic decline had been mainly caused by external factors (the collapse of CMEA markets), foreign trade was, in fact, a stabilising factor. Sales figures for industry as a whole show that in 1991 sales of consumer goods to domestic markets decreased by 29.5% in real terms, sales to the state for public consumption by 22.3%, to other domestic enterprises for production uses by 37.6% and for investment uses by 42.8% (all figures refer to sales in real terms, year-to-year). On the other hand, export sales fell only by 4.8% in real terms.

Another very important factor of disruption was what one can call the 'pre-privatisation agony' of state-owned firms before the first wave of 'large' privatisation in May 1992. Enterprises were obliged to prepare privatisation projects which competed with projects prepared by potential investors, or by other groups in the Ministry for the Privatisation of State Property. Many managers expected personal gains from their participation in the process through their personal contacts with potential investors or the managements of privatisation funds. They also had a strong interest in avoiding any conflict with employees due to lay-offs, which led them to pay workers from funds intended for investment purposes. This was the main reason why the increase in unemployment was moderate, though production declined rapidly. Naturally, this development had a damaging effect on the future prospects of the enterprises involved. In many cases, firms were mismanaged on purpose, so as to drive down the market value of the assets to the benefit of potential investors. This practice raises the question whether concentrating on ownership (privatisation) rather than on management control is an appropriate strategy.

The lack of proper finance for enterprises was an additional factor hindering economic restructuring and investment. The newly created commercial banks were cautious in placing new loans, in many cases because of the lack of proper procedures for, and experience with, evaluating credit applications. The lack of a government industrial policy further aggravated the crisis, leaving the economy with gloomy prospects for the short and medium run.

Besides containing inflationary pressures, the other successful element of the macroeconomic policy pursued by the government was foreign trade and balance of payments. The country achieved a positive balance of payments, amounting to US$ 950 mn (of which US$ 360 mn was in convertible currencies and US$ 590 mn in non-convertible currencies). This was much better than expected at the beginning of the year, although it was partly attributable to lower than expected oil prices on world markets. The trade balance in convertible currencies was negative (US$ −447 mn), but this was offset by a massively positive balance of services.

In 1992 economic growth remained negative – GDP fell by 7% in constant prices. However, in the course of the year some positive tendencies occurred stemming from substantial recovery of domestic demand, both in the investment and the consumer goods markets, so that the gap between GDP in corresponding quarters of 1991 and 1992 was narrowed. In the last quarter, for the first time since 1989, GDP rose by 3% on the same period for the previous year. Although industry was not so successful, signs of an upturn were visible, especially in construction where production increased by 12.6%.

Other economic indicators recorded good results, too. The consumer price index reached 111.5, producer prices grew by 8.4%, and real wages grew by 9.3%, although they were still 17% below their 1990 level. The foreign trade balance was favourable in the first part of the year when it achieved a surplus of US$ 850 mn, but in the second half-year the stimulating impact of the devaluation on exports was exhausted and enterprises rapidly increased their imports in advance of the splitting of Czechoslovakia. Total imports went up by 9.7% while exports decreased by 1.3%.

However, this recovery will be negatively influenced by three factors occurring in 1993: the split-up of Czechoslovakia will dampen trade between the new republics as well as production cooperation amongst enterprises; the implementation of the law on bankruptcies is expected to affect many enterprises; the global economic recession will have an adverse effect on the export expansion of both republics – an expansion that is necessary to enable them to overcome their temporary problems. A downward swing will therefore be repeated in 1993 and an eventual recovery postponed once more.

Economic structure in 1989

Economic shares in production, employment and investment were highly distorted in the 'socialist' period compared to market economies. The factors behind this were not only Marxism and confrontation ideology but, over time, strong economic lobbies gained political influence which kept the economic structure stable with only slow changes, regardless of economic inefficiency.

This well known fact is demonstrated by the national indicators in table 6.2 and industrial indicators in table 6.3. Even if there are certain mismatches in the numbers (especially the GDP shares due to distorted relative prices and the statistical problems of separating other sorts of production from the main production in enterprises), the global tendency is

Table 6.2. *Branch structure of the Czechoslovak economy, 1989, shares in*
%

	GDP	Employment	Investment
Agriculture	8.8	11.6	13.4
Industry	49.6	37.7	42.2
Construction	8.4	10.2	4.3
Services	33.2	40.5	40.1

Source: Statistical Yearbook of the CSFR (1991).

Table 6.3. *Branch structure of Czechoslovak industry, 1989, shares in %*

	Gross output	Employment	Investment
Fuel ind.	4.1	7.9	10.0
Prod. of el. energ.	4.0	2.8	16.8
Iron metallurgy	9.5	6.3	4.9
Non-ferr. metallurgy	2.8	2.0	2.1
Chemic. ind.	12.9	5.9	10.0
Eng.	22.0	6.3	18.4
Electrical eng.	10.4	7.2	6.9
Metal-proc. ind.	5.6	3.5	
Building materials	3.1	3.5	2.9
Wood-processing ind.	2.8	4.1	2.1
Paper and pulp ind.	2.0	1.6	2.6
Glass, ceramics, china	1.5	3.0	1.7
Textile ind.	4.5	7.2	4.4
Garment ind.	1.4	3.1	0.7
Leath. and shoe ind.	2.2	3.6	1.2
Printing	0.7	1.0	1.1
Food-processing ind.	14.4	7.3	9.3
Total	100	100	100

Source: Statistical Yearbook of the CSFR (1991).

clear. The share of industry in production, investment and employment
was very high. The share of agriculture in investment was excessive
(although it declined in the second half of the 1980s) relative to its output
share.

Within the industrial sector, heavy industry accounted for 30% in gross
output and 34% in employment. Mechanical engineering alone created

10% of total employment in Czechoslovakia, rising to 15% if electrical engineering and metal-processing industry are included.

The tertiary sector was underdeveloped both in the use of inputs as well as in its contribution to the national product, even taking into account artificially low output prices and the fact that many service activities took place within the industrial sector (e.g. recreation and health care facilities within enterprises, etc.). Producer services, in particular, were strongly undervalued; they took place mainly within larger enterprises and some, such as marketing, hardly existed at all. Financial services played a passive accounting role in the economy and did not influence real economic conditions.

Since transport and housing accounted for more than half of total service investment (although both branches suffered from the rundown of basic assets) other services attracted even lower investment than the aggregated figures would imply.

The significant differences in input intensity and output efficiency, even among manufacturing branches, were only partly related to specific technological features. Non-technological factors played a very important role and created presumptions for the perpetuation of structural distortions at least in the near future, as has been proved in the present phase of the transition period. Enormous differences among enterprises within the same industry give clear evidence of the importance of non-technological factors behind varying efficiency. While value added per worker varied over a range of 1:7 among West European industrial enterprises, in Czechoslovakia, according to Kolanda and Kubista (1990), the range was 1:60, and still failed to exert sufficient pressure to close down extremely ineffective enterprises. The main non-technological factors were strong political lobbying by some industries (in particular mining, energy production, metallurgy, electrical and mechanical engineering, petrochemicals and agriculture), which secured an inflow of investment and other subsidies, and substantial sales assistance from the state. The quality of management and of staff, as well as tradition, affected economic performance.

The same factors played a role in export performances. The shares of export in total production of individual industries varied both in size and in orientation towards market economies and the CMEA markets (see table 6.4).

Engineering and light industry exported the highest proportion of output, in spite of poorer access to investment and other state subsidies, but the engineering, clothing and leather industries were most dependent on the CMEA markets, and thus most vulnerable.

As for the commodity structure of Czechoslovak foreign trade at the end of the 1980s, there was a clear difference between the two territories. In

Table 6.4. *Share of exports in manufacturing production in Czechoslovakia, 1988, %*

	Total export	To CPEs	To other
Manuf.	20.4	12.3	8.1
Of which			
Engineering	27.6	21.6	6.0
Iron metallurgy	20.0	11.7	8.3
Non-ferrous metal.	9.8	7.3	2.5
Chemical ind.	19.0	7.6	12.1
Paper and cellulose	18.9	3.2	15.7
Wood-processing	28.1	12.1	16.0
Glass, china, ceramics	38.1	13.1	25.0
Textile	25.1	10.5	14.6
Garment	44.1	32.7	11.4
Leather and shoes	30.5	20.9	9.6
Food prod.	6.6	1.5	5.1

Source: Kolanda and Kubista (1990).

relation to the centrally planned economies (CPEs) Czechoslovakia played the role of a developed country with high shares both of machines and consumer goods in exports which were exchanged for raw material and energy, and less for finished goods (this type of exchange was even more marked in trade with the USSR). But its trade with developed market economies (ME) was just the opposite, as table 6.5 shows.

Structural developments since 1989

Structural change in basic economic branches in the period 1989–91 are presented in table 6.6. Agriculture was already caught by recession in 1990. The decline of demand after the elimination of food subsidies led to a large reduction in investment and animal stocks. The fall in production was, however, only partly due to lack of demand; the main factor was the effect of bad weather on the harvest. In 1991 both state and cooperative farms faced the combined effect of sharply reduced state subsidies and lack of demand due to high prices of foodstuffs in shops (farm prices barely changed). In addition to falling production, investment was cut to less than one-half of its 1989 volume, further reducing animal stocks and rapidly decreasing efficiency so that the future development of this industry was seriously endangered.

Table 6.5. *Czechoslovak foreign trade in 1989, SITC classification*

Class	Export			Import		
	Total	ME	CPE	Total	ME	CPE
0 (Foodstuffs)	4.6	10.1	1.1	6.9	11.9	3.9
1 (Beverages)	0.4	0.3	0.4	0.7	0.7	0.7
2 (Raw material)	3.7	6.1	2.1	8.8	13.5	5.9
3 (Mineral fuels)	5.2	9.1	2.7	17.3	2.6	26.2
4 (Oils and fats)	0.1	0.3	0	0.4	0.8	0.1
5 (Chemicals)	7.6	11.2	5.2	9.3	16.5	5.0
6 (Interm.prod.)	22.4	32.7	15.8	10.4	11.2	9.9
7 (Mechanics)	44.4	20.9	59.5	36.9	35.8	37.6
8 (Manuf.prod.)	9.7	8.5	10.4	6.2	6.2	6.1
9 (Other)	2.0	0.7	2.7	3.0	0.8	4.4
Total	100	100	100	100	100	100

Source: Statistical Yearbook of the CSFR (1991)

Construction also suffered from demand problems in 1990. There were several factors behind this: increasing enterprise investment demand concentrated mainly on machines and equipment, and the share of construction investment fell. Public expenditure for big public construction projects was also reduced, as were subsidies for housing construction. In 1991 this branch faced a very deep fall in demand both from state enterprises and from the general population. Building material prices as well as construction prices increased very sharply and a worsening financial situation, together with very uncertain prospects, led to deep cuts in investment. Subsidies and credits for housing construction also ceased to be as generous as in the past, and private investment in this field was very modest. Although construction employment declined rapidly, labour productivity fell by 22.7%. Many building firms survived only by increasing exports of their capacities – mainly to Germany. In 1992 construction slightly recovered; available statistics do not, however, provide precise information on this.

The construction sector also underwent substantial organisational shifts – the largest in the economy. Big enterprises were divided into smaller units. While at the end of 1990, 17.3% of all enterprises had more than 1000 workers, 41.1% between 500–1000 workers and 29.6% between 200–500 workers, by December 1992 this had changed to 3% for the biggest enterprises, 10% for the second group and 40% for the third group. However the smallest firms accounted for only 7.2% of total employment and 9.3% of production, whilst the group of enterprises with more than

Table 6.6. *Structural change in the Czechoslovak economy, 1989–92, changes in %, at constant prices, previous year* = 100

Branches	Output[a]			Investment			Employment		
	1990	1991	1992	1990	1991	1992	1990	1991	1992
Agriculture[b]	96.1	91.6	87.4	91.5	5.0	n.a.	97.7	83.2	86.6
Industry	96.5	74.5	85.8	115.5	74.6	n.a.	96.5	94.7	92.8
Construction	94.4	74.4	111.1[c]	83.7	80.2	n.a.	100.8	96.2	96.4
Services	103.3	n.a.	n.a.	106.6	76.9	n.a.	101.3	95.4	101.7

Notes:
[a] Gross output in the Material Product System (MPS) in constant prices.
[b] Without forestry.
[c] Only output by own workers of construction enterprises.
n.a. not available.
Source: Statistical Yearbook of the CSFR (1992) and *Statistical Yearbook of the CR* (1993).

1000 workers still accounted for more than a third of the construction industry, and employed 28.5% of its workers. Of total production, 12% was within the private sector.

The tertiary sector as a whole developed relatively well in 1990, although there were great differences among individual service branches. Social services faced increasing financial problems, but private entrepreneurs went into business in many service activities. With the exception of health care and education, all state and cooperative organisations shed labour. Investment in service branches more or less stagnated except for health care (up 63%), trade (up 21%), education (up 12%), telecommunications (up 17%) and transport (down 5.5%). An acceleration in investment, employment and profits occurred in banking (the workforce increased by 9.2%, investment by 257%), tourist services (employment up 19%) and personal and repair services (employment up 23%, and together with tourist services, investment up 41%).

In 1991, the economic depression, combined with large cuts in public expenditure (in real terms) in social services and transport, affected the performance and employment of the tertiary sector. Employment in education and health care slightly increased, but investment fell substantially. Research and development faced large reductions both in staff and in investment. The same problems occurred in transport and communication (more in investment than in staff). The only branches with high increases in employment and investment were banking, consulting agencies for producers and governmental (central and local) bodies.

The ownership structure of retail trade and personal services underwent large shifts: significant employment losses in state and cooperative enterprises (in both branches by more than 25%) were balanced by increases in the private sector. The private sector accounted for 64% of retail and catering by December 1992. Many private businessmen, however, operate in the secondary economy which has increased enormously, especially in services, in the last two years. Investment in these branches in the state and cooperative sectors fell. Although private investment has increased to 12.7% in 1992, in no case could it compensate for the fall in public investment.

The structure of the tertiary sector, which includes both official and unofficial private enterprises, has shifted towards producer services (banking, insurance, consulting, accounting, etc.), trade and personal services (repair services are included in industry), and the civil service necessary for a market economy. On the other hand the shares in transport, culture, housing services, research, etc. are falling rapidly. Economic competition and longer-term depression will lead to other significant shifts in services in the near future.

The bias in statistical data due to inadequate methodology is obvious when comparing the official data based on enterprises with more than 100 employees, and estimates of employment including the small private sector. In 1991 official statistics registered 11.8% of workers in agriculture, 39.7% in industry, 6.5% in construction, and 42.0% in services, i.e. a deterioration of the employment structure for 'productive' branches. The same estimates including small firms show a clear shift from 'productive' to 'non-productive' branches: agriculture 9.5%, industry 35%, construction 8.8% and services 46.7%. If the shadow economy is included, the shift would be even greater, but no data are available.

Industry underwent a slight decline in 1990 both in terms of gross production and in employment, so that labour productivity remained stable (see table 6.7). The industries most affected were those which depended on imports from the CPEs (chemistry and non-ferrous metallurgy) and those which faced weaker demand (building materials and fuels due to increasing prices). Consumer goods industries developed relatively well, as did metallurgy. Investment varies greatly from industry to industry, partly due to previous plans and unfinished construction, partly induced by the inflationary expectations of enterprises and population. Enterprises invested all their financial means regardless of efficiency, in many cases to the detriment of solvency. This approach contributed to the increasing mutual indebtedness of enterprises. Investment activity was quite independent of the economic performance of individual branches.

The situation changed dramatically in 1991. Falling demand for consumer goods hit consumer goods industries just at the beginning of 1991. The deepest decline occurred in the textile, clothing, leather and shoe industry, and in the food industry. Also non-ferrous metallurgy, electrical engineering and building materials faced great sales problems. On the other hand, heavy industrial branches experienced practically no problems, though during the second quarter of 1991 they also registered a fall in output, but they still developed well in comparison to light industry (except for paper and pulp, still stagnating). The decline of demand increased in investment goods industries – engineering and construction.

In the second half-year, i.e. with a six-month delay, the depression spread into primary production (heavy industry). While both engineering and light industry fell by more than 40% below their outputs of the previous year, the decline of primary production appeared now also around 30%.

Over the year, mining and electrical energy production registered the best results, but the food industry, paper and pulp industry and iron metallurgy were also above average. Non-ferrous metallurgy, engineering, building materials and traditional branches of light industry fell well below the industrial average.

Table 6.7. *Structural shifts in Czechoslovak industry, 1989–91*
(changes in per cent, the same period of the previous year = 100)

Branches	Gross output 1990	Gross output 1991ᵃ	Deliveries in 1991 for export	Deliveries in 1991 for domestic market	Investment 1990	Investment 1991	Employment 1990	Employment 1991ᵃ
Total ind.	96.5	75.3	95.2	70.5	115.5	73.6	96.8	87.7
Of which:								
Fuel industry	93.3	94.5	158.8	121.4	82.5	78.6	95.2	91.1
Prod. of el. energy	97.8	96.4	67.5	.	119.7	79.4	100	96.4
Iron metallurgy	99.2	78.0	124.1	21.4	130.4 ⎫ 193.7		97.2	90.7
Non-ferrous metl.	94.5	56.8	164.4	42.7	144.3 ⎭		94.6	79.2
Chemical ind.	91.3	77.2	92.0	84.3	138.2	93.0	97.6	90.3
Mech. engineering	96.7	69.7	84.6	53.5	110.4 ⎫ 55.0		96.4	87.5
Electrical engineering	96.3	61.0	69.9	48.0	87.6 ⎭		97.1	81.7
Metal processing ind.		66.4	95.7	67.9	107.7		96.9	87.8
Building materials	93.9	67.3	119.6	62.9	126.4	66.7	95.0	83.9
Wood-processing ind.	97.9	74.5	98.3	69.1	157.6	66.4	97.5	87.3
Paper and pulp	100.9	81.5	120.5	63.8	216.9 ⎫		97.8	91.3
Glass, china	101.2	74.1	93.3	52.9	90.2		96.5	90.7
Textile ind.	100.4	64.7	98.9	50.5	117.9 ⎬ 48.3		97.1	82.5
Garment ind.	95.2	60.0	72.6	47.3	152.4		96.7	86.7
Leather ind.	98.5	63.3	74.3	48.8	106.6		97.1	87.2
Printing	107.8	73.1	99.7	73.8	86.9 ⎭		96.6	91.2
Food ind.	98.0	83.4	115.5	82.3	100.4	76.1	98.5	89.6

Note: ᵃData for 1991 cover industrial enterprises with more than 100 employees. Only total gross industrial output also includes estimates for smaller enterprises. Data for output and investments are given in constant prices.
Source: Statistical Yearbook of the CSFR (1991); Federal Statistical Office, *Statistical Bulletins.*

Export performance in all industrial branches was much better than performance on the domestic market and was partly compensated for the very negative effects of low domestic demand. In fact serious export problems appeared only in engineering, electronics and clothing and leather industries.

Table 6.8. *Industrial indicators, 1992*
(indices to 1991 in %)

Industry	Production (in const. prices)	Employment	Labour productivity	Total sales	Sales for export
Total	86.3	88.2	97.7	88.6	85.6
Of which:					
Coal mining	86.5	88.9	97.3	88.5	99.6
Manufacturing	85.4	87.8	97.2	87.6	84.8
Food industry	93.0	95.6	97.2	95.0	82.8
Textile industry	86.3	87.2	98.9	87.9	93.4
Leather industry	86.0	92.6	92.9	92.3	84.1
Wood-processing	78.6	91.2	86.3	80.4	93.5
Paper and printing	96.8	88.6	109.3	96.7	107.9
Chemical industry	90.7	90.5	100.2	93.9	102.0
Building materials	94.0	90.5	103.8	98.2	119.1
Metallurgy	81.4	87.1	93.5	87.3	101.7
Mech. eng.	75.1	86.9	86.4	82.0	66.4
Elec. eng.	71.0	80.0	88.8	70.4	66.0
Motor vehicles	73.3	87.4	83.8	74.5	57.3

Investment activity showed clearly inherited advantages from the past. While consumer industries were forced to reduce their investment by more than half, and engineering by almost as much, metallurgy doubled its investment. The chemical industry could afford to maintain its investment volume, and the reduction in mining and energy production was less than the average for the whole industry. Despite falls in employment levels, overmanning increased; labour productivity increased only in mining and energy production.

Data for 1992 are given in table 6.8. Although they are not fully comparable with those in table 6.7 (statistical methodology is undergoing major changes) some tendencies are evident. Industries such as chemicals, building materials, textiles, leather and food processing were not greatly affected by the 1991 recession, and are now leading the recovery. In contrast, mechanical and electrical engineering and automobiles could not cope with the new conditions, and recorded a continuous decline. Industries with good export performances fared better than those depending on the home market, indicating that export-led growth is the only feasible strategy for such a small country. Labour productivity was closely correlated with economic performance and increased in the three most successful branches. Labour hoarding is thus typical of the less successful industries.

One explanation for these developments is the short lag of raw materials and energy production linked with the demand for consumer and investment goods. The second factor is the temporary boom of metallurgical goods, but most important is the gap between short-term and long-term comparative advantages within the Czech economy. In the short run, past investment policy means that primary production is more competitive than more sophisticated industry and achieves better results, though to the detriment of the environment. Already there are pressures to introduce Western production techniques, and in the longer run, as ecological costs are taken into account, these industries will become non-competitive. On the other hand, enterprises producing medium-sophisticated products which will need investment in the near future are threatened with bankruptcy due to their temporary sales problems and secondary insolvency. Their production has fallen and, without a selective export-oriented government policy, many of them will not survive.

It is clear that the wide production spectrum inherited from the past represents an untenable burden for the economy and must be narrowed down to products and branches which could become competitive in the future. The problem is finding a method to stimulate their development and overcome the big gap between short- and longer-term prospects.

The commodity structure of Czechoslovak foreign trade for the period 1989–91 is given in table 6.9.

While the commodity structure of both exports and imports experienced no significant changes in 1990, substantial changes occured in 1991 due to territorial shifts in foreign trade and a rapidly increasing share of payments in convertible currencies. Export shares of machines fell sharply compared to intermediate products, raw materials and foodstuffs. The same shift occurred in imports. The commodity structure of foreign trade changed in the same direction as the structure of industry. 1992 saw a continuation of this trend: shares of intermediate products and chemical exports rose again; import shares of machines returned to their previous level.

Conclusion

It is difficult, if not impossible, to differentiate between structural shifts due to economic depression and shifts resulting from the unequal development potential of different branches. Nevertheless, the first alternative is likely to be the prevailing factor in the present period. Apart from banking, retailing, some household services, tourism and catering, other service branches are still declining or, at best, stagnating. The branch structure of

Table 6.9. *Czechoslovak foreign trade, 1989–92*
(shares in %)

Commodity group	Export				Import			
	1989	1990	1991	1992	1989	1990	1991	1992
Total (US$)	14 440	11 882	10 961	11 280	14 277	13 106	10 528	12 856
Agricultural products	4.4	4.6	8.7	8.5	7.2	5.8	7.3	7.3
Raw material	3.4	3.1	5.2	6.3	8.1	7.4	10.0	6.2
Fuels	2.8	4.3	4.2	4.4	19.4	18.9	29.1	21.1
Chemicals and intermediate products	28.4	29.0	41.1	45.4	18.6	18.7	18.6	19.9
Machines	48.9	46.7	28.0	22.8	37.1	35.9	27.8	36.6
Other manufacturing products	12.2	12.3	12.7	12.6	9.5	13.2	7.1	8.7

Source: Kubalek, J. (1992a).

industry has become even more resource-intensive – metallurgy, heavy chemicals, mining and building materials further increased their share to the detriment of light industry and more value added industries such as high-technology engineering, electronics, etc. Even though the fall in production of textiles, clothing, food and other consumer goods has recently moderated, their production levels will remain well below their pre-1989 levels, as these industries are now faced with Western protectionist policies. One would guess that in the future, Western firms will transfer their production capacities into CEE countries to benefit from lower labour costs. So far, however, there is little sign of this happening; it would be politically sensitive, both due to increasing unemployment in the West and to the uncertain political situation in the East.

The first stage of the transformation process with the introduction of basic systemic changes and macroeconomic stabilisation has already been completed. The most urgent task now is to promote economic recovery and industrial restructuring both at the macro-level and in enterprises. Recent structural changes, especially in industry, have emerged as a result of past investment activity and also comparative advantages due to the impact of recent macroeconomic and reform measures. But these will be of a shorter-term character for several reasons: labour costs are expected to rise rapidly, there are limited domestic resources of energy and raw materials which do not allow any further price advantages since prices of imported energy resources and materials (from the ex-USSR) have already reached, or will soon reach, world level. It is thus important to undertake policies which could assist the development of a viable future production pattern based on longer-term comparative advantages. This should be the content of structural and industrial policies formulated as an integral part of a comprehensive economic strategy.

An effective, market-consistent industrial policy should be primarily export-oriented, promoting sound projects in enterprises rather than whole industries and using instruments such as export credits, export premiums and export guarantees within a competitive framework. Another part of industrial policy is the promotion of small- and medium-sized enterprises able to create new jobs and fill market gaps and niches. The policy should ensure broader availability of credits and credit guarantees for new entrepreneurs as well as tax reliefs for the starting period but, apart from financial assistance, also provide assistance in technological and business development (dissemination of new technologies by special – at times publicly supported – technology centres and technology parks, provision of business training and counselling, etc.).

A well developed financial and technical infrastructure is clearly a necessary condition for successful business performance and economic growth. It requires large investments into telecommunications, highways, air transport, etc. Public investment or private investment with state assistance in infrastructure would not only improve the level of provision but also give a stimulus to supplier industries and create new jobs. Industrial policy will need a strong regional dimension to compensate for a very unequal distribution of positive and negative effects of economic transformation among regions, combining promotion of local initiatives with tax concessions and other fiscal stimulative instruments for those regions which are most hit by economic recession.

The large reallocation of labour – both sectoral (now especially from the secondary to the tertiary sector and inside the tertiary sector) and territorial – is unavoidable. Until now, state labour market institutions put a lot of effort into developing a whole range of labour market policies primarily aimed at job creation in small businesses and, to a lesser extent, public works. So far, only limited attention has been paid to retraining as there is little interest on the part of employers and jobseekers. However, in a situation of mass labour reallocation there should be much more emphasis on training and retraining for new skills as basic instruments for increasing labour flexibility. Even if future demand for particular skills is not yet fully known, some of these are obvious: managerial and business skills, accounting, financial operations, marketing, foreign languages, computer skills. The educational system must be redesigned in order to be more flexible, to react quickly to the emerging needs of the labour market. Educational and training facilities should closely cooperate with enterprises and entrepreneurs so as to adjust training courses to the demand for newly skilled workers and to retraining and redeployment within enterprises.

International experience of countries and regions undergoing substantial structural change (including relatively successful developments in some regions of ex-communist Europe) shows that the process of restructuring is relatively smooth when all the important players in the region, i.e. the state administration, self-governing bodies, employers, workers, educational facilities and other institutions, participate actively in designing and implementing the economic and social development strategy and are prepared to bear responsibility for their own failures. Up to now such cooperation seems to take place at least at the macro-level in the Czech Republic; at the regional level, the delay in deciding upon and establishing a new territorial–administrative division of the country still represents a significant obstacle for such mutually beneficial collaboration; however, this should be solved in the near future. Such cooperation represents a substantial comparative advantage for the country and good promise for further economic development.

Appendix: Enterprise sector behaviour and performance
Alena Buchtíková, Jiří Křovák and Eva Macourková

Introduction

While systemic and economic changes at the macroeconomic level were significant during the first, stabilisation stage of the transformation process, it would be interesting to investigate how far and in what respects these processes affected the behaviour of enterprises in the period 1990–2. Our analysis represents only a first attempt to describe emerging shifts in the enterprise sector as basic indicators were available only in nominal terms reflecting also huge changes due to price liberalisation. The first section investigates changes in the enterprise sector as a whole while the second tries to give an insight into its structure by branch.

Enterprise sector behaviour

We make use of an enterprise dataset provided by the Czech Ministry of Finance. In this section we will use the aggregated information for the

Table 6.A1. *Matrix of correlations of selected indicators*

	Revenues	Profit	Credits	Deposits
Profit	0.6031	- cor. coefficient		
	(24)	- sample size		
	0.0018	- significance level		
Credits	0.5467	−0.1179	- cor. coefficient	
	(24)	(24)	- sample size	
	0.0057	0.5832	- significance level	
Deposits	0.1130	−0.5857	0.5639	
	(24)	(24)	(24)	
	0.5990	0.0026	0.0041	
Indebtedness	0.6962	−0.0403	0.9268	0.6281
	(24)	(24)	(24)	(24)
	0.0002	0.8517	0.0000	0.0010

Source: Own calculations based on table 6.A3.

enterprise sector as a whole. We selected the following indicators to describe the situation of the enterprise sector over the period 1990–2: (i) revenue, which is thought to show the ability of the firms to produce and market their products; (ii) profits, measuring cost efficiency; (iii) outstanding credits, indicating claims on enterprise assets and finance costs; (iv) indebtedness and bank deposits, indicating liquidity. The correlation matrix of the selected indicators is given in table 6A.1 (see the raw data in appendix tables 6A.3 and 6A.4, which follow the discussion of enterprise sector behaviour on pp. 209–10). Table 6.A5 gives the codes used in the classification of branches.

The highly significant positive correlation of bank credits with total indebtedness is to be expected as growing indebtedness requires new credits. It is the relationship of credits and indebtedness on the one hand, and deposits on the other which deserves attention. High positive correlations of deposits with both credits and indebtedness (even higher with total indebtedness) indicates that enterprise managements were unwilling, rather than unable, to repay their debts. While total indebtedness in December 1991 amounted to CSK 165 bn, and credits to CSK 476 bn, the banks' deposits of enterprises reached CSK 113 bn. Though there is no information available on the distribution of indebtedness and deposits among individual companies, this fact seems to support the interpretation of the elastic band which interenterprise and bank credit provided to the enterprise sector. The increase in deposits accelerated much more sharply at the end of 1991 than the increase in indebtedness, probably in anticipation of privatisation.

Enterprise sector performance by branches

Changes in industrial composition of the Czechoslovak economy and the effectiveness of individual industries are analysed in this section on the basis of the latest Czech classification of economic activities. The data for individual years are not directly comparable, due to the changes in the number of companies included in the respective databases. However, the analysis of performance dynamics makes sense because the data on performance presented below reflect averages for the branches.

For the following analysis, two groups of indicators are used (the full set of calculated indicators are contained in Buchtíková, Macourková and Křovák, 1993):

Group A indicators (in thousand CSK)

Assets (average) = remaining value of fixed assets + investment assets + means of payment and cash + bonds and obligations + debts outstanding + inventories + future costs + other assets.

Profit = revenues – total costs.

Cash flow = profit + depreciation + change in reserves – activated material – increase in stocks of unfinished and finished production – (profit tax + other payments) – contribution to companies' funds – other use of profit.

Value added = profit + labour costs + interest + depreciation + contribution to companies' funds + payroll tax.

Revenues = sales + activated material + sales of inventories and fixed assets + increase in stocks of unfinished and finished production + price differences + extra revenues.

For the analysis of efficiency of branches, the following group B indicators are used:

Group B indicators (%)

PA = profit/assets.
CFA = cash flow/assets.
VAA = value added/assets.
PS = profit/sales.
CFS = cash-flow/sales.
VAS = value added/sales.

Table 6.A2 *Average ranking of selected branches*

Places in AR	group A 1989	group A 1990	group A 1991	group B 1989	group B 1990	group B 1991
1	25	21	22	73	53	53
2	21	25	21,25	78	79	21,75
3	22	22	21,25	74	83	21,75
4	11	61	37	91	45	22
5	37	11	23	45	76	12
6	61	37	62	82	75	36
7	26	62	26	76	61	45, 83, 87
8	33	26	41, 61	22, 87	87	45, 83, 87
9	53	27	41, 61	22, 87	78	45, 83, 87
10	23	33	53	61	66	32,76
11	41, 51	53	27, 30	33	21	32,76
12	41, 51	23	27, 30	75	12	82
13	27	41	51	36	82	63
14	62	51	–	63	34	38
15	–	–	–	34	63	66, 79
16	–	–	–	13	85	66, 79
17	–	–	–	11	29	43
18	–	–	–	53	71	–
19	–	–	–	85	13	–

Note: For a list of codes used in the classification of branches see table 6.A5.
Source: Own calculations based on data supplied by the Ministry of Finance.

The datasets were taken from the Ministry of Finance of the Czech Republic. For every year, all branches were ranked in descending order by each indicator.

In order to evaluate the different rankings and thus make both the intersectoral and intertemporal comparisons easier, the following methodology was applied. Branches ranked below 10 for more than one indicator in a given year were eliminated. A single entry between the first 10 ranks was considered chance and eliminated. For the group of selected branches only, which are the 'best' in the sense of selected indicators, an average ranking AR was calculated (see table 6.A2).

As can be seen from table 6.A2, by far the largest branch is engineering. It reports the largest values of all the Group A indicators, except for cash flow, in both 1989 and 1990. The situation was similar in 1991. Its position in average ranking is biased by the untypical value of cash flow. The other large branches are fuel; energy; chemicals and rubber. These results are more or less as expected, and confirm the importance of these industries for the Czechoslovak economy.

However, there are some figures which need more detailed explanation. It happened several times that a branch reporting high profits reported negative cash flow at the same time. This is the case for engineering; electrotechnical; metal processing; building and civil engineering; and other branches. This phenomenon can be explained by an analysis of the cash flow. Let us examine the case of engineering in 1989 (the figures are in million CSK).

$$\text{Cash flow} = 18\,832 + 8532 + 1070 - 11\,153 - 153 - 347 - 15\,715 - 6705 - 324$$
$$= -5963$$

There are three basic factors making the cash flow negative in spite of relatively high profits:

- A low depreciation rate in engineering, compared with other branches and the average of the industry. One of the reasons is the age structure of fixed assets in this branch.
- An extraordinarily high value of the subtracted activated material. Engineering, as well as other branches with negative cash flow and positive profits, belongs to those branches which in a CPE were to the highest degree 'self-sufficient' self-suppliers. Due to the unreliability of external supplies, the engineering companies mostly produced inter-mediate products themselves. This tendency became stronger in the pre-transition and transition period when the existing chains of suppliers and sub-suppliers were gradually disintegrating. The other possible explanation lies in deliberate shifts by the companies between individual categories of stocks. In accounting, the companies shifted the stocks of unfinished and finished production into the activated material category. This manoeuvre helped the companies to obtain cheaper operating credits. Another reason for the increase in the activated material was the efforts of management to maintain the employment level which, with a steep decline in the demand for final production, was possible only by increasing production of intermediate goods.
- An extraordinarily high value of the subtracted profit tax and other payments. The corporate profit tax rate, which was 75% for most of the companies in 1989, was lowered to 55% in 1990. The profit tax was paid from profits inclusive of subsidies. However, subsidies were abolished in 1990 which, together with a lowered corporate profit tax rate, led to the decrease in the weight of this item in cash flow.

The results of this empirical analysis may be surprising in some way. There are in general three reasons for this:

* Profit in this definition does not include subsidies while profit tax is levied on profits inclusive of subsidies.
* Other payments before 1991 were a part of a redistributive process within branches; they can mean additional taxation for profit makers, or additional subsidies for loss makers.
* Activated material is a company's own intermediate product. Under the system of 'do-it-yourself' production in many of the Czechoslovak (especially industrial) branches, its weight is unusually high by Western standards.

The time period under study is too short to allow any firm generalisations. However, the analysis of size and output indicators between the three years confirms features observed earlier in Czechoslovakia's economic structure. The role of heavy industries such as fuel, energy, iron and steel, and chemical and rubber in the economy has further increased. The explanation is that the decline in demand first hit the consumer goods producing branches, and then the heavy industries that provide them with inputs. Also the social impact of the decline has not been so significant in the heavy industries as their production is less labour-intensive.

Substantial increases are recorded in the shares of both domestic and foreign trade in gross output. It was not, however, until 1991 that substantial changes in the economic structure began to take place due to the effects of price liberalisation. The branches benefiting most from price liberalisation were food, iron and steel, and metal processing.

The analysis of the group B indicators, i.e. the branch efficiency indicators, shows that the most efficient branches in 1989 were hotel industry (82); energy (22); textiles (33); printing (36); water supply (13); and agriculture (11). It is necessary to point out that water supply and agriculture were heavily subsidised branches in 1989. Over 1989 and 1990, substantial shifts in the efficiency of the branches can be observed. In 1990, the most efficient branches were communications (53); recreational services (83); domestic trade (61); publishing activities (66); fuel (21); forestry (12); hotel industry (82); and, rather surprisingly, clothing (34); wood processing (29); and water supply (13). Their efficiency increased either in absolute terms (in the case of communication, recreational services, publishing activities and others), or in relation to branches with an absolute decrease in efficiency such as energy (in the case of textile, domestic trade and others), or in both.

The branches that benefited from economic reform expectations, from the opening up of the economy, from increased tourism, and from newly found freedoms are mostly service-oriented branches. Telecommunications benefited most from the unprecedented expansion of contacts with the outside world. Recreational services, domestic trade and the hotel industry benefited from the unprecedented inflow of foreign visitors (both tourists and businessmen) to a newly discovered free country in the centre of Europe, as well as from an adjustment of prices to European standards. Publishing activities benefited from the freedom of the press, from the need to publish once prohibited books, as well as from the increase in prices. The fuel industry benefited mainly from price increases given the unreliability of supplies of crude oil and gas from the ex-Soviet Union.

In 1991, the most efficient branches were telecommunications (53), fuel (21), energy (22), forestry (12), printing (36), recreational services (83), glass, china and ceramics (32), and hotel industry (82). The branches that benefited most from price liberalisation were fuel, energy, printing, glass, china and ceramics, frozen food and tobacco. The branches that lost most were domestic trade, publishing activities and clothing. The reason was depressed domestic demand in the case of domestic trade and publishing activities and the decline in external demand in the case of clothing.

The results of this enterprise-based analysis confirm the conclusions of the previous macroeconomic analysis. The smallest decrease in output was recorded in the heavy industries such as fuel, energy, chemicals and rubber, while light industries suffered significant decreases in output. The shift in efficiency was towards service-oriented branches such as recreational services, hotel industry, domestic trade, communications, those activities benefiting from regained freedoms (publishing activities, communications, the hotel industry and recreational services), and those benefiting from price increases (fuel, hotel services and to some extent domestic trade). The price liberalisation introduced in 1991 more or less continued the trends in efficiency indicators started in 1990. It is clear that, apart from the anticipated boom in non-social services, most enterprises so far have just followed a short-term strategy of utilising existing advantages either inherited from the past or temporarily emerging due to the impact of reform measures without there yet being much evidence of longer-term industrial restructuring.

Raw data and industrial classifications

Table 6.A3. *Economic indicators of the enterprise sector, 1990–2, monthly data, bn CSK*

Month	profits	revenue	credits	deposits	indebt.	unempl.
January 1990	8.282	99.746	434.1	66.1	6.51	0.01
February	7.735	98.981	434.6	63.2	8.7	0.1
March	12.241	114.797	429	64.4	11	0.1
April	8.235	101.740	433.6	59.5	14.4	0.1
May	10.987	112.112	435.3	66	16.12	0.1
June	13.483	112.327	432.9	67.3	14.45	0.2
July	3.897	96.134	441.5	64.8	16.47	0.3
August	10.433	100.026	445.1	61.5	20.15	0.4
September	12.716	114.078	440.4	57.1	24.91	0.6
October	11.101	115.155	438.7	52.7	33.89	0.8
November	13.075	124.514	436.3	52.9	40.75	0.9
December	11.391	126.204	435.9	57.4	47.77	1
January 1991	26.264	145.403	433.7	50.5	79.64	1.5
February	25.455	158.129	453.3	55.1	73.56	1.9
March	23.324	155.703	458	61	76.73	2.3
April	20.329	140.731	477.4	60.7	93.44[a]	2.8
May	11.614	143.892	485.4	64.4	107.52[a]	3.2
June	15.537	151.239	489.7	60.7	124.31	3.8
July	7.327	121.126	500.4	66.7	132.7[a]	4.58
August	11.896	133.308	502.3	78.1	141.63[a]	5.12
September	10.021	134.377	500.5	75.5	147.18	5.64
October	10.397	136.483	504.2	80.6	153.75[a]	5.99
November	8.990	139.564	506.3	94.4	159.87[a]	6.31
December	−1.304	133.867	476.1	112.6	165.1[a,b]	6.61
January 1992	N.A.[c]	N.A.	462.7	78.3	N.A.	7.10
February	N.A.	N.A.	463.5	82.8	N.A.	6.90
March	N.A.	N.A.	463.1	72.3	170.52	6.50
April	N.A.	N.A.	464.7	72.5	N.A.	6.00
May	N.A.	N.A.	449.2	75.8	N.A.	5.60
June	N.A.	N.A.	439.8	72.5	162.25	5.50
July	N.A.	N.A.	427.0	77.1	N.A.	5.40
August	N.A.	N.A.	428.6	77.0	N.A.	5.30
September	N.A.	N.A.	426.6	70.7	154.59	5.20
October	N.A.	N.A.	421.3	81.1	N.A.	5.10
November	N.A.	N.A.	420.5	79.9	N.A.	5.00
December	N.A.	N.A.	413.2	91.9	N.A.	5.10

Notes:
[a] These figures are based on smoothed time series of real indebtedness.
[b] The figure for December 1991 is the estimate of corporate indebtedness from the Federal Ministry of Finance which was used to calculate the smoothed series; the corresponding figure in 1992 was 170.73.
[c] N.A. Not available due to the splitting of Federal statistical bodies to separate Czech and Slovak bodies.

Table 6.A4. *Economic indicators of the enterprise sector, 1990–2, quarterly data, bn CSK*

Quarter	profits	revenue	credits	deposit	indebt.	unempl.
1:90	28.258	313.524	429.0	64.4	11.00	0.10
2:90	32.705	326.179	432.9	67.3	14.45	0.20
3:90	27.046	310.238	440.4	57.1	24.91	0.60
4:90	35.567	365.873	435.9	57.4	47.77	1.00
1:91	75.043	459.235	458.0	61.0	76.73	2.30
2:91	47.480	435.862	489.7	60.7	124.31	3.80
3:91	29.244	388.811	500.5	75.5	147.18	5.64
4:91	18.083	409.914	476.1	112.6	170.73	6.61
1:92	35.641	370.903	463.1	72.3	170.52	6.50
2:92	22.161	297.545	439.8	72.5	165.25	5.50
3:92	29.100	N.A.[b]	426.6	70.7	154.59	5.20
4:92	30.000[a]	N.A.	413.2	91.9	N.A.	5.10

Notes:
[a] Estimated.
[b] N.A. Due to the number of organisational changes connected with the splitting of the Czech and Slovak Federal Republic, monthly data for profits and revenues for 1992 and quarterly data in revenues and indebtedness for the second half of 1992 are not available.

Table 6.A5. *Codes used in the classification of branches*

Code	Branches
11	Agriculture
12	Forestry
13	Water supply
21	Fuel industry
22	Production of electric power and heat
23	Iron and steel industries
24	Non-ferrous metallurgy
25	Chemical and rubber industries
26	Engineering
27	Electrotechnical industry
28	Building materials industry
29	Woodworking industry
30	Metalworking industry
31	Pulp and paper industry

Table 6.A5. (*cont.*)

32	Glass, china and stoneware industries
33	Textile industry
34	Clothing industry
35	Leather, boot-and-shoe and furrier industries
36	Printing industry
37	Food industry
38	Frozen food and tobacco industries
39	Other industrial activities
41	Building and civil engineering
43	Geological activity
45	Design activity
51	Transport
53	Communication
61	Domestic trade
62	Foreign trade
63	Supply and sales of goods
64	Supply of agricultural goods
66	Publishing activities
71	Res. & development in agriculture, forestry & water supply
72	Research & development in basic industry
73	Research & development in consumer's and food industry
74	Research & development in building
75	Research & development in transport and communication
76	Research & development in commercial activities
77	Fundamental science
78	Research and science services
79	Services in research and development
81	Housing
82	Hotel industry
83	Recreational services
84	Personal services
85	Education
86	Cultural services
87	Medical and other health services
88	Social care
91	Other services
92	Banking
93	Insurance
95	Public administration, courts and arbitrage
96	Security and national defence
97	Social organisations' activity

References

Buchtíková, A. and Flek, V., 1993. 'The impact of deconcentration and indirect industrial policy on structural development and export performance in the Czech Republic', Prague: Czech National Bank, Institute of Economics

Buchtíkowá, A., Macourková, E. and Křovák, J., 1993. 'Enterprise sector behaviour and performance', paper written for the ACE workshop on 'Industrial Restructuring, Trade Reorientation and East-West European Integration, March

Charemza, W., 1992. 'Alternative paths to macroeconomic stability in Czechoslovakia', *European Economy*, special edition, 2, 41–56

Csaba, L., 1993. 'Economic consequences of Soviet disintegration for Hungary', in I. P. Székely and D. M. G. Newbery (eds.), *Hungary: An Economy in Transition*, Cambridge: Cambridge University Press, 27–43

Hahn, F., 1992. 'Cash-flow der Industrie 1991 von Konjunkturflaute erfasst', *Monatsberichte*, 1, WIFO, Vienna: 34–40

Havelec, J. and Buchtiková, A., 1991. 'Hodnoceni uspesnosti a likvidity cs. podnikove sfery' (Evaluation of performance and liquidity of the enterprise sector), Prague: Institute of Economics

Hrnčíř, M. and Klacek, J., 1991. 'Stabilisation policies and currency convertibility in Czechoslovakia', *European Economy*, Special edition, 2, 17–39

Kolanda, M. and Kubista, V., 1990. 'Cost, performances and behaviour of enterprises in Czecho-Slovak manufacturing on world markets in the eighties', Prague: Institute for Forecasting

Kubalek, J., 1992a. 'An analysis of development tendencies in external economic relations of the CSFR in the period 1989–91', Prague: Institute for Forecasting
  1992b. 'Analysis of the transition to a market economy in the CSFR including alternative considerations about further progess', Prague: Institute for Forecasting

Landesmann, M., Nešporová, A. and Székely, I., 1991. 'Industrial restructuring and the reorientation of trade in Czechoslovakia', *European Economy*, 2

Macourková, E. and Buchtíková, A., 1992. *The Privatisation Process in Central Europe: Czechoslovakia*, London: Central European University Press

Nešporová, A., 1993. 'Preconditions of industrial restructuring in the skill, professional and age structure of the labour force in the Czech Republic', paper presented to the ACE workshop on Industrial Restructuring, Trade Reorientation and East-West European Integration, Vienna (WIIW, November 26–28.

Newbery, D. M. G. (1990): 'Tax reform, trade liberalisation and industrial restructuring', *European Economy*, 43, 67–95

7 Economic transition and industrial restructuring in Bulgaria

*Rumen Dobrinsky, Nikolay Markov, Boyko Nikolov
and Dimiter Yalnazov*

The background of the economic transition in Bulgaria

By the time political change had begun in November 1989, the Bulgarian economy had slid into deep economic crisis. Declining economic growth, not officially recognised by the Bulgarian statistics, resulted from the massive distortions which are typical of a centrally planned economy, and the bunching of external shocks in the second half of the 1980s.

After 1989 the Bulgarian economy entered a period of prolonged depression caused by major structural adjustments. Although all Central and Eastern European (CEE) countries inherited similar macroeconomic and structural problems from the system of central planning, their magnitude varied greatly and Bulgaria has several particular problems.

Short-sighted industrial strategies

Throughout the 1980s, when other CEE countries were reducing their dependance on CMEA trade, 75% of Bulgaria's trade was with CMEA countries, of which 55–60% was with the USSR. This meant that the collapse of CMEA was a major factor in Bulgaria's economic crisis.

Heavy dependence on CMEA was not simply a market strategy, but influenced important long-term strategic decisions affecting the whole structure of the economy. Many large-scale investment projects which were launched in this period (especially in ferrous metallurgy, heavy machinery and electronics) were specifically designed to produce exports for the USSR.

In the 1980s the central authorities continued to boost fixed investments in the hope of arresting the decline in the rate of economic growth. In fact, this only contributed to further overheating of the economy. As is typical

213

with central planning, new investments were allocated very inefficiently, so contributing to the decrease in the return on investment and the productivity growth rate. For example, the electronics industry was developed in a way that isolated it from other branches of Bulgarian industry and from Western competition in final products. Intermediate products were bought in using convertible currency, and final goods were sold for transferable roubles. Other industries that suffered in the same way were perfumery and cosmetics, ready-made clothing, leather industry, pharmaceuticals and food processing. Besides, most exports to the CMEA region turned out to be heavily dependent on imports of inputs and intermediates from the West.

The industrial structure of the economy was created without consideration of the country's endowments. This is especially true for the excessive growth of highly energy-intensive industries such as metallurgy, heavy machine building, the chemical industry, pulp and paper industry, and construction materials. In addition, agriculture was allowed to decline from the 1970s and in the 1980s the output of many of the main products and livestock started to decline in absolute terms.

Foreign indebtedness

Quite unexpectedly, even to the international financial community, Bulgaria accumulated a huge foreign debt in a relatively short period (1986–9). During the first Eastern European debt crisis in the early 1980s the country had been able to solve its debt problems quite successfully and for a long time had the reputation of being a reliable debtor.

One of the main reasons for the rapid growth of foreign debt was the deterioration in the terms of trade after 1984 following the decline in the world price of oil (oil products based on Soviet oil were a substantial share in Bulgarian convertible currency exports). On the other hand the ruling elite was reluctant to give up ambitious and prestigious investment projects. The result was an increasing deficit in the balance of trade which was financed through heavy international borrowing from foreign commercial banks.

All this, combined with sluggish overall economic performance, incompetence and mismanagement of foreign borrowing, brought about the accumulation of a large foreign debt with an extremely poor maturity structure. This put great pressure on repayment of the principal in certain years. For example, roughly 40% of the liabilities of the Bulgarian Foreign Trade Bank, which was at that time responsible for about 80% of the foreign debt, was scheduled to be due in 1990 (Bulgaria, 1990).

The situation was aggravated by the mismanagement of the rescheduling problem. Without undertaking any preliminary negotiations with her creditors in March 1990, Bulgaria abruptly and unilaterally declared suspension on the servicing of her foreign debt. This decision undermined international confidence in Bulgaria and limited the potential sources of external financing for economic reform.

Domestic macroeconomic imbalances

The magnitude of macroeconomic distortion in Bulgaria was second only to that in the ex-USSR. The economy had accumulated huge suppressed inflationary pressures in the form of monetary overhangs which devastated the domestic market. The long-held policy of 'soft' budget constraints, the lack of tight credit discipline, combined with the pervasive practice of vast redistribution of income through the state budget, widespread subsidisation of loss makers, and wage growth exceeding the growth of labour productivity, contributed to the almost complete disintegration of the monetary system. The amount of accumulated forced savings by 1989 exceeded 25 bn leva, or about two-thirds of the country's NMP. This caused constant shortages of raw materials and consumer goods which went hand in hand with overemployment in the labour market.

Economic policies and performance in the transition period

The economic reform process

Economic policy in Bulgaria after the change in political regime has been to a large degree chaotic and incoherent. One of its main deficiencies was the reluctance of policy makers to define any form of clearly stated long- or even medium-term objectives. The long-term goals rarely went beyond a vague formulation of a 'social market economy' without portraying even its broadest outlines. On the one hand this is the outcome of political instability and economic uncertainty which prevailed in this period; on the other it reflects the still unsettled state of society and its unreadiness to face and cope with the new realities.

The most comprehensive economic policy package in the period since 1990 was the stabilisation programme launched in February 1991 and coordinated with the International Monetary Fund (Letter of Intent, 1992). Similar to the stabilisation programmes of Poland and (then) Czechoslovakia, it included an almost complete price liberalisation; liberalisation of foreign trade; establishing of a uniform and market-determined (floating) exchange rate; liberalisation of the interest rates; demonopolisation and restructuring of state-owned enterprises (Avramov, 1993). Actually 1991 was the year when the most significant economic changes took place in Bulgaria.

Apart from this a number of legislative and institutional reforms have been implemented in this period. Among the important economic legislative acts with an impact on the process of industrial restructuring are:

- Commercial Law (a company code), passed in May 1991, which sets the rules of establishing commercial entities.
- Law on Foreign Investment, passed in May 1991, amended in January 1992, which regulates (quite liberally) the economic activity of foreign economic entities in Bulgaria.
- Restitution laws, passed in December 1991 – January 1992, which made possible the restitution of urban real estate and industrial properties (nationalised during communist rule) to previous owners or their inheritors.
- Privatisation Law, passed in April 1992, which regulates the process of transformation of state-owned enterprises into private companies.
- Law on the Bulgarian National Bank (BNB), passed in June 1991, which establishes a two-tier banking system in the country and transforms the BNB into an independent Central bank.
- Law on Banks and Credit Activity, passed in March 1992, which regulates commercial banking activity in the country.
- A new Labour Code, passed in November 1992, which replaced a similar code acting under the old regime and aimed at regulating labour relations in a market environment.

Several new institutions were created as a direct consequence of some legislative acts: the Privatisation Agency; the National Land Council; Liquidation committees of agricultural cooperatives, the Council for Social Partnership (a kind of tripartite committee), etc. Other new institutions were formed following governmental decisions: the National Labour Office (which is supposed to regulate and stimulate employment); the Bank Consolidation Company (whose goal is to transform about 60 small-sized state-owned commercial banks into 10 larger-sized banks). Yet a third type of newly emerging institutions are self-organised ones, which appear under the newly passed legislation: commodity exchanges (acting in many Bulgarian cities) and stock exchanges.

The performance of the real economy

After a period of slow growth in the second half of the 1980s, Bulgaria entered a prolonged depression in 1989. The extent of the crisis was unprecedented for a peace-time economy: in 1990 GDP plummeted by 9.1% which was followed by a further 11.7% in 1991 and 7.7% in 1992 (table 7.1).

Table 7.1. *Bulgaria, selected indicators of economic performance, average annual rates of change, % unless otherwise indicated, 1989–93*

	1989	1990	1991	1992	1993[a]
Gross domestic product	−2.1	−9.1	−11.7	−7.7	−4.8
industry	−0.3	−12.5	−18.6	−11.0	...
agriculture	−2.4	−3.7	7.7	` 7.7	...
services	−5.4	−4.3	−11.3	−3.3	...
Gross fixed capital formation	−7.5	−18.5	−19.9	−1.5	−9.0
Private consumption	1.6	0.3	−15.1	−7.8	...
Total employment[b]	−2.3	−6.1	−13.0	−12.7	...
Registered unemployment					
(1000 persons, end period)	...	65.1	419.1	576.9	626.1
Unemployment rate					
(% of labour force, end period)	...	1.7	11.1	15.6	16.4
Consumer prices	...	23.8	338.5	91.3	74.0
Average wages and salaries[b]					
nominal	8.7	31.8	165.7	113.8	60.8
real	...	6.5	−39.4	11.8	−7.6
Money supply (M1)	15.2	24.0	24.2	40.7	27.3
Money supply (broad money)	10.5	16.1	118.0	52.5	53.1
Central interest rate					
(annual compound rate, %)	4.5	4.5	61.4	60.9	57.9
Average lending interest rate					
of commercial banks (short term)					
(annual compound rate, %)	...	...	67.8	74.0	78.3
Exchange rate					
(leva/US$, period average)	1.7	2.6	16.7	23.3	27.8
Exports of goods[c]	−7.8	−19.9	−37.7	6.7	0.9
Imports of goods[c]	−7.1	−24.5	−51.7	30.5	3.0

Notes:
[a] Preliminary.
[b] Without private sector.
[c] Based on current US$.
... Not available.
Sources: Statistical Yearbooks of Bulgaria; Annual Reports of the Bulgarian National Bank; News Bulletins of the Bulgarian National Bank; *Monthly Bulletins* of the National Statistical Institute.

Preliminary figures for 1993 indicate that negative growth has continued. After several years of consecutive decline Bulgarian GDP had by 1993 dropped to about 70% of its pre-crisis level.

The main factor behind the disastrous performance of the economy in

1991 was the disintegration of the CMEA and the loss of traditional markets, especially of the Soviet market. All CEE countries were hurt by this, but none more than Bulgaria because of her total dependance on CMEA trade. Apart from that Bulgaria suffered additionally from her debt crisis and the mismanagement of the rescheduling problem: the debt crisis practically cut the country off from international financial markets.

The tough measures of the stabilisation programme gave an additional dimension to stagnation. One of the main reasons behind this was the inability of the large (state-owned) industrial enterprises (SOEs) to adjust to the changing market environment. Since the start of the transition Bulgaria has followed a restrictive monetary policy, discontinuation of almost all subsidies (with no industrial or export promotion policies in place) and liberalisation of foreign trade. One of the goals of this policy was to make enterprise more responsive to demand-side changes and to introduce competitive pressures necessary for the restructuring of the domestic economy and for the establishment of non-monopolistic equilibrium prices. The experience of past years indicated that there existed serious systemic factors which set limits to the possible speed of market adaptation of the Bulgarian enterprises. The loss of traditional ex-CMEA markets; disturbances in the supply of some inputs; the lack of marketing and managerial skills as well as of experience to operate in a highly competitive environment; the malfunctioning and imperfect domestic markets; the complete lack of incentives for enterprise managers and the general resistance to change are only some of the factors which impeded the process of restructuring and adjustment.

Although the recession affected the whole economy, its depth varied across the main economic sectors (table 7.1). Like all other CEE countries, Bulgaria was overindustrialised. Industry, which accounted for 70% of the gross output and 58% of the net material product in 1988, suffered most from the crisis. By 1992 real industrial gross output had plunged by more than 45% of its 1988 level. Construction was the second most sensitive sector, contracting by some 55% of its 1988 level.

Agriculture also suffered deeply from the adjustment. The causes of the crisis in this sector were however of a different nature. During the totalitarian regime agriculture in Bulgaria underwent several stages of involuntary reorganisation but land was never formally nationalised and agriculture retained some form of cooperative organisation. The land reform initiated in 1990 took the form of a bill on the restitution of land which was adopted in 1991 and amended in early 1992. This amendment mandated the liquidation of all existing (Soviet-type) agricultural cooperatives and the disposition of their assets (land, livestock, machinery, etc.) to the previous owners or their heirs. This element of the agrarian reform in Bulgaria also seems to have been overdone and it affected agricultural output adversely.

The process of restitution turned out to be cumbersome and had a number of negative side effects. The establishment of ownership rights was impeded by the lack of proper documentation, the migration of the population in this period (40–50 years) and disputes among the claimants. This turned out to be a serious obstacle to the speedy restitution of land. In the meantime a kind of ownership vacuum exists; while the process is underway the land is to be managed by the interim liquidation committees which, however, have no incentives for efficient performance. The cooperatives-in-liquidation are suffering and many of their assets are being ruined. As reported by the National Statistical Institute (*Tekushta stopanska konyunktura*, 12, 1993), by the end of 1993 only 12.7% of the agricultural land subject to restitution had formally been returned to the old owners; another 25.2% was returned conditionally, until formal procedures are finalised.

The restitution of other assets such as machinery revealed a number of abuses by authorised officials. When livestock was restituted a large number of animls were immediately slaughtered due to problems with feeding. All these side effects of the agrarian reform affected agricultural output adversely.

The tertiary sector on the aggregate level was least affected by the crisis. This is mainly due to the development of the private sector which penetrated some of the existing services (such as trade and banking) and expanded into some new areas (law firms, financial and business consulting, etc.).

There have also been substantial changes in employment (table 7.1); however, the figures need more specific treatment. According to official statistics total employment in the state-owned and cooperative sector declined by some 1 700 000 persons over the period 1988–91 (mid-period estimations); the officially registered unemployment by the end of 1992 was 577 000. So there are about 1 200 000 people who are not covered by these statistics. The main factors which contributed to this development were:

- Emigration from the country.
- Newly emerging private firms (so far over 200 000 have been registered).
- Liquidation of the agricultural cooperatives in 1992; after liquidation former coop members who received land are considered to be self-employed and no longer included in the figures.

In spite of these high levels, unemployment in Bulgaria has obviously not yet reached its peak. The level of open unemployment (at least in 1991 and 1992) lagged behind the level of output contraction (table 7.1) which is a sign that labour hoarding is still taking place, presumably in the public sector. Besides, one has to take into consideration that a major restructuring and privatisation of the Bulgarian industry is still ahead which will almost certainly cause a further growth in the level of unemployment.

The effect of these developments has to be taken into account in analysing the employment situation, but it is evident that there was more inertia in the response of employment to the adjustment process than in the response of other economic factors. There are many reasons for this:

- The lack of legal bankruptcy procedures (no SOE has been declared bankrupt yet, though in a purely market environment there could have been many), which would enable the financial system to reallocate resources; in this situation, the only way to stop an unprofitable activity is by administrative closure.
- The lack of clear industrial strategy and policy of all governments in office during that period, and their reluctance (for populist reasons and also due to the existence of extremely powerful trade unions) to start closures and lay-offs in industries which obviously have no future.
- The existing labour legislation, which gives wide protection to employees and very little power to managers to shed labour.

In this situation a new type of 'hidden' unemployment developed. Faced with the impossibility of firing employees some companies kept their excess labour formally employed but without paying them (most often this takes the form of unpaid leave). Unemployment pressure has thus accumulated which, sooner or later, will become open unemployment.

Turning to investment (table 7.1), due to the lack of proper price information for the period under consideration, very little can be said about changes in real terms. A very rough estimate based on the industrial price index (see p. 222) suggests that total investment in real terms in 1992 may have contracted by as much as 70–80% from the 1988 level and no recovery has been under way since that time. All sectors are severely affected, but the biggest losers are industry, agriculture and transportation. Only in relative terms are the sectors of 'Construction' (mainly due to inertia of previously launched projects) and 'Trade' better off.

Monetary adjustments and inflation

The main targets of monetary policy since the start of the transition have been to achieve macroeconomic stabilisation by reducing macroeconomic disequilibria, and tight control over the money supply to compensate for inflationary pressures in the economy (Guenov, 1993; Gueorguiev and Gospodinov, 1992). The Bulgarian National Bank (BNB, the central bank of the country) in general has conducted a restrictive monetary policy since 1991. It uses two main instruments of control over the money supply: credit ceilings and the central interest rate. At this stage the instruments of direct monetary control still prevail over the market-based instruments.

The most important monetary policy instrument in Bulgaria currently is credit ceilings. Credit ceilings were introduced as a part of the stabilisation programme of 1991 and provided an easy-to-handle means of controlling the growth of money supply. They set an upper limit to the commercial loans denominated in national currency, which are allocated by commercial banks during a certain time span. Credit ceilings are determined individually for each commercial bank; when they are exceeded, a penalty is imposed on the bank in the form of higher reserve requirements.

The aggregate credit ceilings which were set by the Central bank on the total commercial credit expansion in the economy amounted to a growth rate of 52% in 1991 and 29% in 1992 (BNB, 1992; 1993). As compared to the inflation rate in this period such targets speak of a rather restrictive monetary policy and especially in 1991 they made it possible to bring money supply under control in the face of 3-digit inflation (table 7.1).

The central interest rate is a more powerful tool in Bulgaria than the Central bank discount rate usually is, due to the fact that almost all prices in the banking sector are usually directly linked to the central interest rate. In turn, this is due to the high level of dependence of commercial banks on refinance from the BNB. In 1991–2 the Central bank implemented a flexible interest rate policy in an attempt to match its sometimes conflicting monetary policy goals regarding money supply, inflation and exchange rate (the central interest rate was changed several times in that period).

Actual macroeconomic performance shows somewhat mixed results (table 7.1). The growth of the money supply in 1991–2 was successfully kept at rather a low level. This was achieved both by restricting the demand for new money and by stimulating absorption of excess personal cash holdings by the banking system, partly through the attractive time deposits and partly by stimulating the purchase of state-owned flats by tenants. The quarterly figures of the money supply reflect the almost astonishing outcome that the monetary system was able to absorb the huge open inflation in that period with an almost negligible expansion of the money supply (M1 actually shrank in the first half of the year). Apart from reflecting the deep economic decline this is also evidence of the magnitude of the accumulated monetary overhang at the start of the stabilisation programme.

However, credit expansion was slowed only at the expense of severely restrictive interest rates: the central interest rate, with some fluctuations, followed an upward trend to hit a high of 54% in the last quarter of 1991, whilst commercial bank interest rates reached levels of the order of 65–70%. These rates were a barrier to economic activity and it is no surprise that in such an environment investment activities came to a standstill.

In analysing the restrictive character of the money supply and of interest rates, one should bear in mind the big differentials in the dynamics of the price structure. The rate of inflation as measured by CPI was a 3-digit number in 1991 because of one-time price adjustment at the beginning of 1991; in the second half of 1991, and throughout 1992, monthly inflation was of the order of 3–5% (the yearly CPI inflation in 1992 was nearly 80%). In this period the average real commercial interest rate appears to be slightly negative in terms of CPI. However the average rate of change of the producers' price index (PPI) in 1992 was a mere 40.1% (*Ikonomikata na Bulgaria*, National Statistical Institute, 1993). So for many industrial producers the interest rate in this period was highly positive and restrictive.

On the other hand allocation of available credit resources in 1991–2 was further distorted by crowding-out of commercial credit and this can at least partly be attributed to the impact of credit ceilings. If a bank manages its credit portfolio by minimising its risk exposure, and having the alternatives to allocate limited resources, it is likely to increase the relative share of the less risky government securities and decrease the relative share of commercial credits, thus directly creating a crowding-out effect. The actual data confirm that crowding-out has increased: the share of the government in total borrowings denominated in BGL increased from 19.1% in 1991 to 27.8% in 1992 (BNB, 1993).

Recent price developments indicate that Bulgaria is experiencing a persistent inflation which is probably going to be a medium-term phenomenon. The sources of inflation in the country currently appear to be mostly of cost-push type. Government-controlled prices (energy, fuels and some utilities) were significantly increased on several occasions after 1991. What is even more important is the expectations of economic agents which induce them to make precautionary price adjustments in anticipation of such increases.

Another major cost-push inflationary factor is the level of nominal wages. At first, at the start of the stabilisation programme, restrictive wage policy was selected as one of the nominal anchors (together with the control over the growth of money supply). This restrictive policy was successful only in the first half of 1991. Then gradually it started to erode, partly under pressure from trade unions, partly via a loosening of control in some public sectors, and partly under the general instability of the monetary system (Nenova, 1993). Throughout 1992 the level of real wages changed little and in 1993 wage policy was loosened further. Indexation of wages in the public sector was practically reintroduced in 1993, compensating for 90% of price increases which added to the inflationary pressures. The floating exchange rate and the chronic budget deficit also contributed to the persistence of high inflation.

Exchange rate adjustments

Exchange rate adjustments play a very significant role in the Bulgarian transition process. However, again the results with respect to exchange rate and its impact are rather mixed. In 1991 the Bulgarian lev became internally convertible (in essence current account convertibility was introduced) at a market-determined floating exchange rate. The multiple exchange rates (which existed before) were abolished and a uniform market-determined exchange rate (under a floating regime) was established. All importers were granted the right to purchase foreign exchange from commercial banks (at the current market rate) in quantities necessary for the specific transaction. Exporters could either keep their foreign exchange earnings in foreign exchange deposits or could sell them on the market. Local residents were granted the right to purchase certain quantities of foreign exchange for travelling purposes and were allowed to open foreign currency accounts in local commercial banks without the necessity to prove the origin of the currency.

After a very high one-time depreciation immediately after its liberalisation at the beginning of 1991 the lev started to appreciate in real terms which continued throughout 1992 and the first half of 1993 (table 7.1). However, at the end of 1993–beginning of 1994 in the course of several months the lev collapsed, depreciating in nominal terms by nearly 80% (a real terms depreciation of about 40% for the period). The exchange rate crisis resulted from the combined effect of inconsistent policies, deteriorating balance of payments in 1993 and malfunctioning markets. Throughout most of 1992 and 1993 the *ex post* combination of nominal exchange rate dynamics and nominal interest rates translated into a violation of the interest rate arbitrage which created the conditions for financial speculations (Dobrinsky, 1994). On the other hand this development may be regarded as a compensatory adjustment (albeit of a crisis type) of the exchange rate after the real appreciation of the lev in the previous 18 months.

The most significant deficiency of the floating exchange rate policy in a transition economy like Bulgaria is the lack of transparency about its future dynamics which increases considerably the risk for all economic agents operating with foreign exchange. Under the general uncertainties about the economy due to its transitory nature, the floating exchange rate becomes another source of inflation even when the exchange rate is appreciating in real terms. This can again be explained by the expectations of economic agents. The uncertainty about the future level of the exchange rate, created by the floating mode, acts in favour of precautionary price adjustments which, in turn, translate into persistent inflation.

Fiscal adjustments

The stabilisation programme also envisaged substantial changes in fiscal policy including reducing of income redistribution through the state budget; cutting the fiscal deficit; reducing the level of monetising of the budget deficit by increasing the role of government bonds. This translated into a substantial restructuring of the budget (table 7.2).

On the expenditure side the most significant change was the abolition of almost all subsidies; on the other hand the emergence of unemployment brought about the necessity to increase social security spending (the social safety net). At the same time the restructuring of the revenue side was based on an overoptimistic view of future economic performance, so the target for a balanced budget could not be met (table 7.2).

A tax reform introduced in 1991 also contributed to the relative reduction of the budget revenue:

• Profit tax rates which had varied from 15% to 95% were replaced by a flat 40% rate, reducing the overall tax burden on enterprises.
• The turnover tax rates were also made more uniform and neutral (three basic rates of 0%, 10% and 22% were introduced) and the overall effect amounted to a reduction of the indirect tax burden.

But probably the most destructive macroeconomic impact of the high budget deficit resulted from the failure to introduce non-inflationary financing of the deficit. In accordance with the acting regulations not more than 50% of the voted budget deficit could be financed by direct credit from the Central bank; the rest had to be financed by government securities.

However, with underdeveloped financial markets and high uncertainties about the interest rate, the only marketable securities were short-term (3–6 month) Treasury bills. Practically the only participants in the market are the commercial banks. But one of their incentives to buy securities is to use them as collateral for refinancing from the Central bank. When they do so this results in the further monetisation of the budget deficit, fuelling inflation in the economy. Another negative impact of the high deficit is the deterioration of the expenditure structure, resulting in increasing relative shares of consumption-related expenditures and declining shares of investment expenditures.

Table 7.2. *Breakdown of the Bulgarian state budget, % of GDP, 1989–93*

	1989	1990	1991	1992[a]	1993[a]
Total revenue	57.9	52.8	43.5	39.6	38.5
Tax revenue	49.3	42.4	39.9	32.6	...
profit taxes	23.2	17.9	17.5	9.2	...
income taxes	4.1	4.2	3.8	5.6	...
turnover taxes and excises	11.2	9.0	7.4	8.5	...
duties	0.8	1.0	1.6	...	...
social security instalments	9.6	9.6	9.5	9.3	...
others	0.3	0.7	0.1	...	...
Non-tax revenue	8.6	10.4	3.6	7.1	...
Total expenditure	58.5	62.0	58.8	45.6	49.7
Non-interest expenditure	55.4	52.5	40.3	34.7	...
salaries and allowances	4.7	5.5	6.7	..	...
current expenses	14.5	12.2	9.7	13.3	...
national security	4.9	4.8	4.1	...	...
investments	5.5	3.1	2.0	4.9	...
social security	10.4	12.0	13.6	14.6	...
subsidies	15.5	14.9	4.2	1.8	...
Interest expenditure	3.1	9.5	18.5	11.0	...
domestic	0.0	0.7	6.2	9.3	...
foreign	3.1	8.8	12.3	1.7	...
payable	3.1	4.6	0.4	1.7	...
unpayable	0.0	4.2	11.9	...	...
Primary surplus/deficit $(-)$[b]	2.5	0.3	3.2	...	...
Cash surplus/deficit $(-)$[c]	−0.6	−4.9	−3.4	−6.0	−11.2
Total surplus/deficit $(-)$[d]	−0.6	−9.1	−15.3	−6.0	−11.2

Notes:
[a] Preliminary data; different breakdown of aggregate since 1992.
[b] Total revenue *less* non-interest expenditure.
[c] Primary surplus/deficit *less* domestic and payable foreign interest expenditure.
[d] Total revenue less total expenditure.
... Not available.
Sources: Reports of the Ministry of Finance; *News Bulletins* of the Bulgarian National Bank.

It should be noted that the breakdown of the budget presented in table 7.2 does not contain the due servicing of the foreign debt (see p. 226). If the foreign debt had been serviced the public sector borrowing requirement would have been much higher. The delays in the introduction of a major tax reform (some parts of it were finally voted in 1993) also affected the fiscal situation in the country adversely.

The balance of payments and foreign debt

The unresolved foreign debt issue has been one of the bottlenecks in Bulgarian economic performance since March 1990 when Bulgaria suspended the servicing of her foreign debt. This abrupt and unilateral suspension undermined international confidence in Bulgaria and limited the country's access to the international financial markets. Since 1990 the country fell into serious external financial isolation, just at the period when international finance was badly needed for the process of economic restructuring. It is estimated that since that time Bulgaria has been able to raise just about US$ 2 bn external financial resources, but only from international financial institutions and governments. The main sources of funding were: US$ 644 mn from the IMF, US$ 455 mn from the World Bank, ECU 115 mn and US$ 161 mn from EBRD, ECU 226 mn from the EIB and US$ 594 mn from the EU and G-24.

The external isolation affected Bulgarian trade adversely (no access to short-term trade credits) and had a negative impact on investors' confidence in the creditworthiness of the country. As per estimations of the governmental committee on foreign investment the cumulative value of foreign investments in the country in 1990–3 amounted to about US$ 220 mn, which is much lower than the corresponding figures for any other CEE country.

There have been a number of difficult negotiations with foreign creditors, and progress in dealing with the Paris Club and the London Club debt differed substantially. In 1991 and in 1992 Bulgaria managed to sign two partial rescheduling agreements with the Paris Club and restarted servicing this debt (which is, however, only a minor portion of the total). As regards London Club banks, some progress was made only in 1993, when a preliminary debt rescheduling and reduction agreement was reached which was finalised in 1994.

The situation with foreign debt and the results of the ongoing negotiations with creditors to a large extent determine the situation with Bulgaria's balance of payments (table 7.3). Since 1991 the balance of payments also experienced some changes but they were not so dramatic due to the stagnation of the capital account. In analysing the recent trends one should also bear in mind some peculiarities in the reporting of the Bulgarian balance of payments (see appendix, p. 239).

In general the current account of the balance of payments in the recent years followed the *de facto* balance of trade. Net services deteriorated due

Table 7.3. *Balance of payments in convertible currencies, US$ mn, 1988–92*

	1988	1989	1990	1991	1992
Current account balance[a]	−840.0	−1306.0	−1152.0	−76.9	451.5
Trade balance	−972.0	−1199.0	−757.0	−32.0	484.5
exports of goods, fob	3539.0	3138.0	2615.0	3737.0	5093.0
imports of goods, fob	4511.0	4337.0	3372.0	3769.0	4608.5
Services, net	54.0	−170.0	−503.0	−114.0	−75.9
receipts, of which:	849.0	908.0	734.0	455.5	883.4
shipments	340.0	311.0	202.0	199.4	361.3
travel	229.0	224.0	237.0	43.7	49.2
interest	79.0	125.0	105.0	55.6	125.1
other	201.0	248.0	190.0	156.8	347.8
payments, of which:	795.0	1078.0	1237.0	569.5	959.3
shipments	220.0	203.0	151.0	213.2	393.0
travel	22.0	55.0	159.0	127.9	23.1
interest paid[b]	442.0	680.0	793.0	83.7	201.2
by BFTB	415.0	639.0	752.0	35.9	135.8
by commercial banks	27.0	41.0	41.0	47.8	65.4
other	111.0	140.0	134.0	144.7	342.0
Transfers, net (private)	78.0	63.0	108.0	50.1	39.8
receipts				104.4	111.0
payments				54.3	71.2
Interofficial unrequited					
transfers				19.0	3.1
Capital account	1882.0	596.0	137.0	115.0	−31.5
Direct investment in Bulgaria,					
net			4.0	55.9	41.5
Medium- and long-term loans,					
net	2139.0	712.0	−67.0	−48.1	42.1
drawings				108.0	232.4
repayments				156.1	190.3
Loans extended, net	−445.0	−167.0	200.0	294.9	32.5
Developing countries, net				92.4	23.4
drawings				12.1	3.7
repayments				104.5	27.1
Yamburg pipeline[e]				202.5	9.1
Short-term debt, of which:				−187.7	−147.6
deposits and loans				−85.2	53.0
clearing account with					
ex-USSR				−102.5	−197.5
clearing account with					
Russia[d]					−3.1
Other capital	188.0	51.0			

Table 7.3. (*cont.*)

Errors and omissions	−385.0	276.0	97.0	6.8	−20.6
Overall balance	657.0	−434.0	−918.0	44.9	399.4
Change in reserves (incr:-)	−595.0	430.0	888.0	−44.8	−399.4
gross BNB reserves	−595.0	430.0	888.0	−358.0	−575.1
gold of BNB ($300 per oz)					
foreign exchange of BFTB				−51.5	−128.4
foreign exch. of commerc. banks				−213.4	−85.3
use of IMF credit				385.6	217.2
EC loan				192.5	172.2
Valuation adjustment	−62.0	4.0	30.0		

Source: News Bulletin, Bulgarian National Bank.
Notes:
[a] Includes transactions in convertible currencies with former CMEA.
[b] Payments of interest are on cash basis for 1991 and 1992.
[c] Includes repayment by former USSR in natural gas.
[d] Includes balance in clearing account.

to the fact that some sectors such as 'transportation' and 'tourism' went into deficit. The most substantial drop occurred in 'tourism' (it plunged in 1991 by some US$ 200 mn as compared to 1990) as a result of the closing-down of the currency shops (one of the controversial measures of the stabilisation programme aimed at preventing the dollarisation of the economy) whose revenue used to be reported under this item. A positive development in 1991–2 was the increase in foreign reserves which had been almost wholly depleted in the course of 1990.

The bulk of the financing of the balance of payments deficit was accomplished by extending the moratorium on foreign debt servicing. Bulgaria is a heavily indebted country whose foreign debt by the end of 1992 had reached US$ 12,952 mn, which is roughly 152% of GDP or 296% of export revenue (*News Bulletin of the Bulgarian National Bank*, 9, 1992). The current situation of the Bulgarian economy suggests that the country will not be solvent even in the medium term. It is thus likely that the foreign debt problem will continue to be one of the acutest problems for the country for years ahead.

The agreement on the foreign debt problem will have a very positive impact on the Bulgarian economy, mainly in easing access to international financial markets and, eventually, in increasing the inflow of foreign investment. However, it must also be pointed out that due to the tiny foreign reserves of the country a deal with the London Club banks will be impossible without the active participation of the IMF and the World Bank. This, in turn, is conditional on the progress of economic reforms and systemic transformation.

Industrial restructuring and reorientation of trade

Market adaptation of industry

Bulgaria has not advanced substantially in the process of industrial restructuring and trade reorientation. The adjustment that has taken place so far has mainly been the outcome of trade reorientation after the collapse of the CMEA. A period of two or three years is very short to trace any investment-induced industrial restructuring, especially in an economy which is in deep crisis. Moreover, implementation of institutional changes were very slow as none of the governments in office in this period had a clear long-term industrial strategy and thus a consistent industrial policy.

An important element of the Bulgarian reform was the restructuring of large monopolistic state-owned enterprises, in line with the Law for Protection of Competition. In 1991–2 most of the large companies which enjoyed a monopolistic position (apart from the natural monopolies) were broken down into smaller, independent and competing units. This, together with the liberalisation of foreign trade, contributed to the process of demonopolisation and development of competitive industrial structures in the country. In the period after 1992 the speed of reform markedly slowed, partly due to internal political instability.

On the other hand, privatisation proceeds very slowly, affected adversely by a combination of factors. One serious obstacle to the speeding-up of the privatisation process was the actual philosophy of the Law on Privatisation voted in 1992. It set quite rigid lines for the privatisation process, presuming predominantly commercial sales of SOEs to potential investors. Experience since the adoption of the law has shown that the chances of this privatisation method in Bulgaria being viable are not very high. Domestic private capital is scarce and foreign investors (as already mentioned) have not shown much interest in Bulgarian enterprises (as compared to the Central European transition economies). Last but not least, domestic political instability and frequent change of governments also affected the process of privatisation adversely.

By the end of 1993, 113 privatisation deals had been accomplished and another 611 deals were in preparation (National Statistical Institute, *Tekushta stopanska konyunktura*, 12, 1993). However, the majority of successful privatisation deals have comprised small enterprises or shops. Most of the few large-scale privatisation projects were marred by scandals such as suspicion of undervaluation, delays in payments by investors, juridical obstacles, etc.

The current Law on Privatisation is also obscure with respect to which government body would exercise ownership rights in the process of privatisation of SOEs as well as the actual planning of the privatisation process (if any). This caused tension and rivalry (instead of cooperation) between different institutions involved in the privatisation process. It is expected that the law will be amended to allow for some form of mass privatisation (the combination of schemes applied in the Czech Republic and Poland is envisaged).

Bankruptcy procedures are also lacking: no SOE has been closed down for inefficiency. The only change which was initiated in 1991–2 was the breaking down of large monopolistic companies into smaller units. However these transformations were performed in haste and very often without solid validation.

If we turn now to the performance of individual industrial sectors (table 7.4) we can note that the significant structural changes which have taken place since 1989 are mostly the result of differential effects of the recession on industrial sectors. This is clearly visible if we compare the indices of gross output across sectors.

The Iron and steel industry was hit by cuts in imports of ferrous ores as a result of the CMEA disintegration, and demand for iron and steel fell drastically due to the decline in other sectors such as Machinery and Construction. Moreover, iron and steel prices marked the highest jump across sectors (table 7.4) as a result of previous distortions and rising production costs; this development further hit effective demand. Output in Non-ferrous metallurgy manifested a similar trend for similar reasons, though the drop was not so large because of continuing exports of metals to other markets. In absolute terms the worst affected sector was Machinery and Electronics, the largest sector of Bulgarian industry, accounting for more than 30% of its output in 1989, and designed mainly for exports to the ex-USSR.

A vicious circle was generated between these sectors and the energy sector: primary materials and energy were imported from the USSR to produce machinery for export to the USSR, so that more materials and energy could be imported. The main problem of this trade was the very low value added content of the manufactured products. Under market conditions economic links of this type have no chance of survival and most probably the fast decline of these industries will be irreversible, at least until they shrink to their 'natural' shares in industry.

Table 7.4. Gross output, by industrial sectors, 1988–92

Sectors	Structure of gross output in constant prices of 1990, %					Indices of gross output, 1988=100				Price indices of gross output, 1990=100	
	1988	1989	1990	1991	1992	1989	1990	1991	1992	1991	1992
Production of electricity and thermal power	4.35	4.28	4.69	5.69	6.70	98.2	89.0	82.9	74.9	613.8	1018.5
Coal mining	0.93	0.93	1.04	1.24	1.37	99.9	92.0	84.4	71.5	811.8	1229.1
Extraction of petroleum and natural gas	0.04	0.04	0.04	0.04	0.05	105.9	87.6	78.4	73.5	491.6	1238.8
Iron and steel industry (incl. extr. of ores)	4.81	4.69	3.46	2.47	2.84	97.3	59.5	32.5	28.7	1082.8	964.2
Non-ferrous metallurgy (incl. extr. of ores)	2.55	2.57	2.32	2.19	2.55	100.4	75.0	54.4	48.4	665.6	1071.5
Metal proc., manuf. machin., el. and electronic equip.	30.72	29.80	27.86	26.33	21.95	96.7	74.8	54.3	34.7	303.9	465.8
Chemic. industry and oil refining	14.10	14.34	12.87	13.80	13.60	101.4	75.3	62.1	46.9	609.4	899.5
Manuf. of building materials	2.79	2.67	2.68	2.20	2.34	95.3	79.0	50.0	40.8	419.8	612.2
Wood sawing and processing	2.39	2.45	2.62	2.79	3.05	102.0	90.4	73.9	61.9	366.1	578.4
Pulp and paper industry	1.20	1.14	1.12	1.05	1.36	95.3	77.1	55.4	55.0	741.7	712.3
Glass and ceramic industry	0.88	0.88	1.06	1.13	1.14	99.5	99.4	81.0	62.9	385.0	719.1
Textile and knitting industry	5.01	5.29	6.29	5.65	6.45	105.3	103.7	71.6	62.6	290.7	439.9
Manuf. of ready-made clothes	1.69	1.74	2.26	2.46	2.61	102.7	110.5	92.6	75.2	220.9	331.9
Leather and shoe industry	1.31	1.49	1.54	1.72	1.92	113.3	96.8	83.0	71.3	275.0	491.1
Printing industry	0.43	0.50	0.60	0.85	0.95	113.8	114.6	124.3	106.1	364.0	227.5
Food industry	24.36	24.63	26.84	27.60	28.31	100.8	90.9	71.8	56.5	341.9	555.7
Other industry	2.45	2.57	2.72	2.79	2.81	104.7	91.7	72.3	55.8	195.3	280.7
Industry total	100.00	100.00	100.00	100.00	100.00	99.8	82.3	63.2	49.3	411.7	628.6
Total manufacturing	94.69	94.75	94.24	93.03	91.88	99.9	82.5	62.5	47.3	394.0	590.9

Sources: Statistical Yearbook of Bulgaria; Statisticheski Izvestiya (Statistical Reports) of the National Statistical Institute.

At the other extreme the most successful industry appears to be Printing, the only sector which experienced growth during the three years (table 7.4). The explanation is quite simple. This is a very tiny sector, operating mainly within the domestic market (table 7.5); after the transition to a pluralistic democracy the demand for information grew, so driving the growth of the printing industry.

Most of the other sectors: Food, Forestry and the light industries (Textiles, Apparel, Glass and ceramics, Leather and shoes) managed partly to substitute their CMEA markets for new ones and in general performed above the average for industry as a whole. As to the important sector Chemical industry and oil refining, it is a mix of two differently performing sub-sectors: the strongly affected oil refining and the relatively less affected chemical industry, which is largely based on local resources.

From the dynamics of prices across sectors (table 7.4), one can trace the process of price adjustment in the economy. These figures indicate really big differentials in relative sectoral prices caused by the distorted price structure which the country inherited from the past. Another impact of price dynamics is the different exposure of sectors to monetary policy: some sectors enjoyed negative real interest rates, whereas others had to cope with highly positive ones.

Bulgarian industrial output shrank substantially. The average capacity utilisation in the Bulgarian (state-owned and cooperative) industry in 1993 is reported to have been 57%; only 23.5% of all industrial enterprises reported a positive growth of sales in 1993 (National Statistical Institute, *Tekushta stopanska konyunktura*, 12, 1993). The financial situation of the state-owned and cooperative industry has been deteriorating: on the aggregate level all industrial sectors were performing at a loss by 1993. However, it would be premature to say that Bulgarian enterprises function under 'hard' budget constraints. Owing to leaks and inconsistency in the existing legislation (mainly the lack of bankruptcy legislation) many enterprises were able to find alternative sources of finance in spite of their losses. In 1992 and 1993 it was mainly the defaulting on commercial bank credits which led to the snowballing of bad loans.

Trade performance

The most dramatic structural changes since the start of the transition took place in the trade sector. Up till now the national statistics have not provided foreign trade data for this period in real terms but even the current price data (table 7.6) provide good evidence on these developments.

Bulgarian trade in the 1970s and 1980s was rather unevenly distributed. Apart from the heavy dependence on CMEA it was marked by imbalances

Table 7.5. *Exports and imports, by industrial sectors, 1988–91*

	Structure of exports by sectors, %				Export ratio (gross output), current prices, %			Structure of imports by sectors, %				Import ratio (gross output), current prices, %		
	1988	1989	1990	1991	1989	1990	1991	1988	1989	1990	1991	1989	1990	1991
Production of electricity and thermal power	0.3	0.2	1.6	2.7	1.1	6.5	10.6	3.2	3.0	3.1	7.8	17.4	12.8	24.6
Coal mining	0.0	0.0	0.0	0.0	0.0	0.0	0.0	2.6	2.6	3.1	7.1	55.1	57.8	76.8
Iron and steel industry (incl. extr. of ores)	2.5	2.0	1.7	3.6	16.1	9.1	18.5	6.1	5.3	4.6	2.6	41.6	25.9	10.5
Metal proc., manuf. machin., el. and electronic equip.	63.7	62.8	61.9	32.1	43.8	42.0	54.6	44.9	46.1	49.8	17.6	30.5	34.9	24.0
Chemic. industry and oil refining	10.4	10.9	10.9	29.3	18.0	15.9	47.5	8.1	7.8	7.1	8.7	12.2	10.8	11.3
Manuf. of building materials	0.4	0.4	0.5	0.7	2.5	3.4	10.4	0.7	0.7	0.7	0.6	4.0	5.1	7.4
Wood sawing and processing	0.8	0.8	0.8	1.7	7.2	5.9	22.8	0.5	0.4	0.3	0.3	3.5	2.5	3.0
Pulp and paper industry	0.2	0.2	0.2	0.4	4.4	3.1	6.7	1.3	1.4	1.4	2.7	30.5	24.1	37.7
Glass and ceramic industry	0.2	0.2	0.2	0.5	5.5	3.0	17.0	0.2	0.2	0.2	0.1	4.0	2.9	2.2
Textile and knitting industry	1.6	1.6	1.5	3.1	7.6	4.6	26.0	2.3	2.5	2.2	2.4	11.2	6.8	15.9
Manufacture of ready-made clothes	1.5	1.5	1.7	1.1	16.8	14.5	28.3	0.2	0.2	0.3	0.3	1.7	2.7	5.7
Leather and shoe industry	0.9	0.9	0.8	0.9	13.3	10.2	25.8	0.3	0.4	0.3	0.2	4.8	4.2	3.6
Printing industry	0.1	0.1	0.1	0.1	5.1	3.7	3.4	0.2	0.3	0.3	0.1	11.8	10.6	2.0
Food industry	13.3	12.8	13.3	19.4	13.3	9.4	28.0	3.8	4.1	3.4	4.5	4.0	2.5	5.2
Other industry														
Industry total	100.0	100.0	100.0	100.0	22.7	18.9	33.1	100.0	100.0	100.0	100.0	21.5	19.6	26.6
Total manufacturing	95.6	94.3	93.6	93.0	22.5	18.8	34.6	68.6	69.3	70.6	39.9	15.7	14.6	11.9

Source: Statistical Yearbook of Bulgaria.

Table 7.6. *Structure of exports and imports, by commodity groups, %, current US $, 1988–92*

a Exports

Commodity groups	1988	1989	1990	1991	1992
Industrial machinery and equipment	52.7	49.4	50.1	30.5	16.9
Fuels, mineral raw materials and metals	11.8	14.2	12.6	10.5	21.2
Chemical products, fertilisers and rubber	5.4	5.5	6.3	11.0	11.6
Building materials and details	1.6	1.6	1.7	1.0	1.7
Raw materials and products (exc. foodstuffs)	3.0	3.5	3.2	3.5	6.9
Live animals (not for slaughter)	0.0	0.2	0.3	0.1	0.3
Raw materials for the food industry	3.3	3.5	4.2	5.7	9.9
Processed food products	10.9	10.9	10.6	15.2	12.1
Industrial consumer goods	9.9	10.2	9.4	21.7	19.4
Productive operations (not classified)	1.3	0.9	1.6	0.6	–
Total	100.0	100.0	100.0	100.0	100.0

b Imports

Commodity groups	1988	1989	1990	1991	1992
Industrial machinery and equipment	33.9	35.5	39.7	16.3	26.0
Fuels, mineral raw materials and metals	35.4	33.8	33.1	58.5	44.0
Chemical products, fertilisers and rubber	8.1	7.0	6.5	4.9	9.2
Building materials and details	1.1	1.0	0.9	0.7	0.7
Raw materials and products (exc. foodstuffs)	8.5	8.0	6.9	7.4	7.7
Live animals (not for slaughter)	0.0	0.1	0.1	0.0	0.1
Raw materials for the food industry	4.7	5.9	2.6	3.6	1.1
Processed food products	1.6	2.1	2.3	3.9	5.7
Industrial consumer goods	5.8	5.9	7.4	4.4	5.4
Productive operations (not classified)	0.8	0.6	0.6	0.3	–
Total	100.0	100.0	100.0	100.0	100.0

Sources: Iznos i Vnos (Exports and Imports), *Quarterly Bulletin of the National Statistical Institute; Statisticheski Izvestya* (Statistical Reports) of the National Statistical Institute.

by trading partners. One specific feature of Bulgarian foreign trade was the chronically negative balance of trade with the developed market economies for which the country tried to compensate by trade surpluses in convertible currencies with some developing countries. This risky strategy (which was to a large extent linked to the exports of armaments) was only successful till the middle of the 80s.

The disintegration of the CMEA was a severe blow to the economy of the country: in current US$ total exports from Bulgaria in 1991 plunged to 45% of their 1988 level whereas total imports contracted to 33% of their 1988 level. 1992 experienced some recovery of trade flows, but they still remained far below their pre-crisis level. In both exports and imports the most affected commodity group was Industrial Machinery and Equipment.

Foreign trade regulations also underwent substantial changes after 1990. Bulgaria entered the transition period with trade regulations which were very far from anything which is common in developed market economies and much needed to be done in this respect. A major reform of trade regulation was implemented in the period 1990–2 (see appendix, p. 239).

Regarding trade performance it must be emphasised that, besides the factors already discussed, there was another reason for the disastrous performance: the lack of an institutional infrastructure such as export credit facilities facilitating foreign trade. The fund for foreign trade which was established at the end of 1991 is not yet operational, and is still very poorly endowed. Besides, none of the waves of reform included export promotion measures (on the contrary, for some periods export taxes were imposed) which confirms the comment made above about the lack of industrial policy.

As also indicated above the most affected commodity group is Industrial Machinery and Equipment whose share both in exports and in imports was reduced by some 30 percentage points in 1992 (table 7.6). In value terms this represents a drop in exports of 80% as compared to the 1988 level. Imports of industrial machinery and equipment also plunged in 1991, but recovered slightly in 1992 (table 7.6). This was a direct consequence of the disintegration of the CMEA as exports and imports of machinery constituted the bulk of the trade flows in this market.

Relatively less affected were exports of Chemical Products, Industrial Consumer Goods (mainly textiles, apparel and shoes) and to some extent Processed Food, where the country either maintained some share in the Soviet market or managed to switch to new markets.

The dynamics of the structure of exports (table 7.6) clearly manifests the trend towards a composition of exports, with an increasing weight of commodities whose production relies on natural endowments (e.g. chemicals, food) or on comparative advantages such as cheap labour in labour-intensive sectors (textiles, apparel, shoes, etc.).

On the other hand the changing import structure exposes the country to imported raw materials and fuels (58.5% of total imports in 1991 and 44%

in 1992). This is an area where a strategic diversification will have to be looked for in the future.

Traditionally, the geographical distribution of trade was largely distorted by the extreme orientation to the ex-CMEA market. Besides, as already pointed out, trade within specific market segments was marked by serious structural imbalances. Bulgaria used to record chronic deficits in trade with developed market economies and large surpluses in trade with ex-CMEA countries, exclusively due to trade surpluses with the ex-USSR. The situation changed dramatically with the disintegration of the CMEA when the countries of the region turned to trade in convertible currencies at world market prices. Under these circumstances, most traditional Bulgarian exports (this especially concerns manufactures) were no longer competitive on the ex-Soviet market especially in the light of the economic problems which the newly established states faced themselves. On the other hand shrinking domestic demand and financial problems in Bulgaria caused serious reduction of imports.

The most dramatic changes took place in the direction of trade (table 7.7). The disintegration of CMEA caused the export share of Eastern Europe to drop by over 50 percentage points in 1992 compared to 1990; the drop in import share was 40 percentage points. However, the ex-USSR, despite a huge fall in trade in absolute terms, remained Bulgaria's largest trading partner, following a transitory clearing agreement denominated in US$ which was signed in 1991 (a similar agreement was signed with Russia in 1992).

However, Bulgaria had a painful experience with the implementation of this agreement. At first it was announced by the Bulgarian government that the current US$ market rate would be applied to settle payments with exporters and importers from the USSR. This motivated many Bulgarian companies to start exporting, whereas imports from the USSR were irregular and had long delays. By the middle of the year Bulgaria had already accumulated a substantial positive trade balance with the USSR which, owing to the clearing payments system which was linked to the budget, started to impose strong monetary pressure on the latter and created a threat to macroeconomic stability. Faced with the impossibility of finding a more reasonable solution, the government in August 1991 drastically cut the clearing dollar exchange rate. However, this measure turned most of the Bulgarian exporters into loss makers and demotivated any further expansion of exports to the USSR.

The process of trade reorientation which was taking place in 1991–2 was mainly a redirection from CMEA to other European markets. In terms of export and import shares trade with the EC shows the biggest increase. The Trade and Cooperation agreement between Bulgaria and the EC signed in

Table 7.7. *Structure of exports and imports, by countries and groups of countries, %, in Bulgarian lev, 1988–92*

Country	Exports					Imports				
	1988	1989	1990	1991	1992	1988	1989	1990	1991	1992
Total	100.0	100.0	100.0	100.0	100.0	100.0	100.0	100.0	100.0	100.0
Eastern Europe	75.3	76.8	76.4	54.9	24.2	67.9	65.8	68.1	46.4	28.8
Poland	4.1	3.8	2.6	2.1	2.3	5.0	4.8	5.0	1.1	0.8
Romania	2.0	2.0	3.9	1.8	2.6	2.1	1.9	1.3	0.4	2.7
CIS	62.5	65.2	64.0	49.8	17.9	53.5	52.9	56.5	43.2	22.8
Hungary	2.0	1.4	1.5	0.4	0.7	1.9	1.3	0.7	0.4	0.6
CSFR	4.6	4.3	4.4	0.9	0.7	5.4	4.9	4.6	1.2	1.9
OECD	6.4	8.0	11.9	26.3	42.3	15.5	17.1	21.6	32.8	46.5
EC	4.6	5.5	7.9	15.7	30.8	9.7	10.3	16.3	20.7	32.6
United Kingdom	0.7	0.9	0.6	1.9	3.0	1.0	1.1	1.7	3.6	1.9
Germany	1.0	1.1	4.2	4.8	10.0	4.9	6.4	10.4	7.0	12.8
Greece	0.9	1.3	0.8	2.2	4.3	0.3	0.4	0.3	0.9	5.9
Spain	0.2	0.3	0.2	0.5	0.6	0.2	0.2	0.2	0.5	0.4
Italy	0.7	0.6	0.8	2.7	5.3	1.1	1.4	1.9	4.2	5.3
France	0.3	0.5	0.5	1.4	2.4	0.7	1.0	0.7	2.1	2.8
EFTA	1.2	1.5	1.5	3.4	3.3	3.5	3.8	3.2	7.8	6.7
Austria	0.2	0.3	0.4	1.0	1.2	1.6	1.5	1.6	4.7	3.2
Switzerland	0.8	1.0	0.8	1.6	1.3	1.4	1.7	1.3	2.1	2.2
USA	0.2	0.6	1.7	3.4	1.7	0.9	1.5	0.6	2.9	3.0
Arab countries	7.0	4.2	6.1	8.3	7.9	4.5	4.8	4.3	4.5	7.7
Other	11.3	11.0	5.6	10.5	25.7	12.2	12.3	6.0	16.2	16.9

Sources: as table 7.6.

January 1991, and the Association agreement of March 1993, will undoubtedly play a significant role. Exports to the USA in 1991 also increased, both in relative and in absolute terms, after the country was granted most favoured nation (MFN) status, but fell back in 1992.

At the same time one should bear in mind that there is a marked difference in the sectoral composition of the trade flows with the East and with the West, and especially in the structure of exports. Thus the Eastern market 'hits' – mechanical and electrical engineering and data processing machinery, responsible for about 60% of Bulgarian manufacturing exports to the ex-CMEA in 1988 – had a modest 13.6% share in the manufacturing exports to the EC. By the end of the period under consideration these differences started to diminish, mainly due to the drop in exports to the East – the corresponding figures for 1992 were 22.0 and 11.5%.

At the other end of the spectrum are the Metal processing and Footwear and clothing sectors: in 1998 their share in the total manufacturing exports to the ex-CMEA was a modest 4.8% whereas that in the EC market was 23.5%. In 1992 these figures were 12.9% and 39.0%, respectively. Within the manufacturing sectors only the sector of food processing and to some extent chemical industry can be regarded as outliers of this tendency.

It is important to note also that there was very little (if any) substitutability in Bulgarian manufacturing exports to the Eastern and to the Western market. One can say that, judging by technical and quality standards, the products going to the West and those going to the East, within one and the same sector, were completely different products. This is now one of the main difficulties (together with the lack of managerial and marketing skills) in the attempt to reorient some of the trade flows to the West: basically this requires a complete restructuring of the whole production process, starting from the technologies and the fixed assets and ending with the retraining of the workforce. In view of the implied investment requirements this is hardly possible on a large scale.

Judging from the character and the magnitude of the changes that have already occurred, it would seem that the major part of trade reorientation has already taken place, and changes in the future will be more evolutionary in character.

Conclusion

Although not so much in the public eye in the West as the frontrunners of Central Europe, Bulgaria has firmly stepped onto the road of radical reform. As compared to them, due to the degree of overindustrialisation and the level of dependence on trade with the former CMEA as well as to the extent of macroeconomic imbalances, the transition process will be longer and more painful. There is an obvious necessity to speed up the process of reform, especially in areas such as industrial strategy and policy; privatisation; dealing with the problem of the foreign debt, which may have a strong impact on macroeconomic stabilisation; and developing the institutional infrastructure needed by a market economy which is still lacking in the country.

The implementation of infrastructural laws and economic policy in Bulgaria faces problems due to domestic political instability which causes delays in the reform process. The achievement of credibility of economic policy could also speed up the economic transformation in the country.

Appendix: methodological note and time schedule of Bulgarian trade reforms

Methodological notes on the Bulgarian balance of payments

Owing to methodological and statistical imperfections the Bulgarian balance of payments should be analysed rather cautiously. In comparison with other indicators and data in the chapter it should be borne in mind that table 7.3 refers only to the balance of payments in convertible currencies, and that there is a separate rouble balance. So the trade figures in table 7.3 are trade in convertible currencies and are not directly comparable to the trade figures in tables 7.5–7.7.

The trade balance in the balance of payments is reported on a cash basis and differs substantially from trade statistics which are reported on a customs basis (p. 232). One significant difference is due to the lags in payments and, for example, the positive trade balance (on a customs basis) of 1991 appears in the balance of payments only in 1992 (table 7.3). In addition, it should be noted that in 1992 the BNB changed its method of reporting the balance of payments statistics (debt service is now reported only on a cash basis and not on an accruals basis) so there is not full comparability of this data in table 7.3.

Further caution is needed as in 1991 there were three types of trade with ex-CMEA countries:

(1) Trade in transferable roubles (although formally abolished there were still a number of such transactions performed on the basis of previous commitments as well as settlements of pending balances).
(2) Trade under the clearing agreement between Bulgaria and the ex-USSR determined in US$ (but applying a different exchange rate – see p. 236).
(3) Trade based on cash payments in convertible currencies.

The trade figures reported in table 7.3 include (2) and (3) and do not include (1). If the clearing-based trade with the ex-USSR is also excluded, total exports in 1991 would be valued at US$ 2664.9 mn and total imports would be US$ 2811.4 mn (*News Bulletin of the Bulgarian National Bank*, 3, 1992).

The reform in Bulgarian trade regulations

Trade regulations went through three main phases in the period after 1989:

• Partial liberalisation of foreign trade and devaluation of the national currency; no substantial change in import tariffs (1990).

- Full liberalisation of foreign trade (in the sense of the rights to perform foreign trade operations); introduction of a floating exchange rate; introduction of the harmonised system of duty tariffs (Tariff, 1991; Tariff, 1992) together with some provisional, transitory trade measures (1991–2).
- Abolition of most of the provisional measures and introduction of a comprehensive set of trade regulations (1992–3).

The latest trade regulations (introduced by the government in June 1992 and modified slightly in 1993) include the following measures:
On the imports side:

- A number of commodities are subject to import registration: these include alcoholic beverages, fuels and electricity, pulp and paper, fabrics, footwear and clothing, ferrous and non-ferrous metals, some chemicals for agricultural use.
- A set of commodities is subject to import licensing: pharmaceuticals, tobacco products, radioactive and other environmentally hazardous material, explosives, precious metals and some others.
- Import quotas were introduced for a limited number of commodities: tobacco, citrus fruits, bananas, ice cream and, seasonally, for tomatoes and cucumbers.
- Import tax is imposed on certain commodities: meat and preparations of meat, some dairy products, grapes, apples, processed fruits, perfume and toilet preparations, luxury automobiles.
- Some commodities are granted temporary tariff relief by either eliminating the existing tariffs (medicinal children's foods, pharmaceutical inputs, agricultural machinery, pesticides and fertilisers) or by applying a reduced tariff rate (sugar and sugar substitutes, rice, salt, pharmaceuticals).

On the export side:

- Some commodities are subjected to mandatory registration (in principle it cannot be an obstacle to exporting, but the procedure is rather bureaucratic and time-consuming): these include live animals, dairy products, vegetable oils, wine and alcoholic beverages, fuels and electricity; ferrous and non-ferrous metals.
- Some commodities are subjected to export licensing, such as: tobacco and tobacco products, precious metals, wood (logs), scrap of ferrous and non-ferrous metals, historic articles of art, pharmaceuticals, radioactive materials, explosives, etc.

- Some (mainly agricultural) commodities were subjected to domestically set export quotas: live animals for breeding; wine grapes; wheat and wheat flour; sunflower seeds; raw hides and skins.
- A number of commodities are subjected to export price controls by setting lower limits on export prices: live animals, meat, cheese, sunflower seeds, wool, fuel wood.
- In a further move later the export quotas were replaced by export taxes on the same commodities.

References

Avramov, R., 1993. 'The limits of macroeconomic stabilisation of an economy in transition: the case of Bulgaria', *MOST*, 1, 63–87

BNB, 1992. *Bulgarian National Bank Annual Report, 1991*, Sofia

1993. *Bulgarian National Bank Annual Report, 1992*, Sofia

Bulgaria, 1990. 'Bulgaria. Crisis and Transition. Volumes I and II', *World Bank Report*, 9046–BUL (October)

Dobrinsky, R., 1991. 'Bulgaria in the wake of the moratorium on the foreign debt payments', *Bulgarian Quarterly*, 1, (3) (Winter)

1994. 'Exchange rate policy and macroeconomic stabilisation: lessons from the Bulgarian exchange rate crisis of 1993', paper presented at the Conference on 'Transition from the Command to the Market System: What Went Wrong and What to Do Now?', Sofia (22 February)

Guenov, K., 1993. 'The monetary policy in 1992: instruments and results', Agency for Economic Coordination and Development, Sofia (April)

Gueorguiev, N. and Gospodinov, N., 1992. 'The monetary policy: mechanisms and results', Agency for Economic Programming and Development, Sofia (March)

Letter of Intent, 1992. Letter of Intent of the Bulgarian Government to the IMF of 14 February 1991, *Information Bulletin of the Bulgarian National Bank*, 4 (February)

Nenova, M., 1993. 'Wage regulation: the Bulgarian experience in 1991–1992', Agency for Economic Programming and Development, Sofia (April)

Tariff, 1991. 'Customs Tariffs', Republic of Bulgaria, Central Tariff Department, VEKOTRON, Bulgarian Chamber of Industry and Trade

1992. 'Customs Tariffs', Ordinance 35 of the Council of Ministers of 26 February 1992, Sofia

8 Economic reforms and structural change in Poland

Lucja Tomaszewicz and Witold Orlowski

Introduction

The Polish economic reforms since 1989 have been widely reviewed in the literature (see e.g. Gomulka (1992), Schaffer (1992), Calvo and Coricelli (1992) and also Berg and Sachs (1992). Most of the papers were devoted to the discussion of the so-called Balcerowicz Plan, its aims and the economic problems which arose after its implementation. The papers all concern, in general, the Polish path of transformation to a market economy, but most of them concentrate on macroeconomic issues of the transition. In contrast, this chapter will focus on industrial structural change, an issue which was less emphasised in the first batch of studies on the transition of the Polish economy. There are basically two reasons why less attention was paid to structural changes: the first was the minor role of industrial restructuring in the Polish reforms, this being seen as closely linked with privatisation and left to enterprises themselves; the second was that the effects of restructuring of the economy are not immediate. In fact, the recession might have strongly influenced and also restricted the pattern of structural adjustment. The enormous expansion of interenterprise credit, the lag of financial restructuring, coupled with a lack of detailed analysis of the determinants of efficiency of different sectors, are the main restrictions on industrial restructuring. Moreover, with a very low level of investment really decisive changes cannot be expected.

In the first, shorter, section of the chapter we will briefly outline the macroeconomic context, and suggest a sequence of the main factors responsible for the fall in industrial production. In the second section, changes in industrial structure (gross output and employment) and foreign trade are analysed in the light of statistical data for the period 1989–92. It is concluded that structural changes in output and employment mirror the changes in final demand for domestic products caused by adjustments of domestic to world prices, growing foreign competition, and decline of

242

demand from the ex-CMEA. This conclusion should be slightly modified, because the development of small private industry over the years 1990–2 brought noticeable changes, especially within the foodstuffs industry. The changes of export structure are, of course, mostly due to the expansion of trade towards the Western countries and a collapse of trade with the former CMEA. The industries most affected are electrical and mechanical engineering, where a decline of export shares in all markets is observed. On one side, the change in shares of different imported goods over 1990–2 resulted from a sharp decline of consumers' demand (in 1990), a drop in intermediate goods and growing demand for the most competitive products, i.e. chemicals, wood and paper, light and electronic industries.

Towards economic stability: the Polish economy, 1990–3

The starting point: the economy after the turn

The first democratic government that took power in Poland in August 1989 inherited an economy in a state of decline: falling production, massive shortages of goods, financial indebtedness and, probably most important, hyperinflation rising to 55% per month (in October 1989; the annual inflation rate in the year December 1988–December 1989 was 640%). All these phenomena reflected longer-term problems of the real economy: inefficient, non-competitive industry; massive external and internal debt (the latter reflected in the liquidity overhang of the household sector); an extremely inefficient system of economic regulation (both on the macro-economic and the microeconomic levels); a distorted structure of employment, fixed capital and production, leading to imbalances and inflationary pressures.

The Polish economy at the end of 1989 was, without doubt, the weakest in Eastern Europe – excluding the USSR. No other country except Yugoslavia suffered hyperinflation, the scale of economic disequilibria and the level of excess demand were much higher than in the other countries, market-oriented reforms were far less advanced than in Hungary or Yugoslavia, Poland had very large foreign debt and a particularly high debt service-to-exports ratio.

The stabilisation programme

The Polish stabilisation programme (the 'Balcerowicz Plan') was introduced on 1 January 1990. Its main tasks were the following:

- to create a free market for goods and services through almost complete price liberalisation;

- to fight hyperinflation through tough monetary and wage policy;
- to eliminate shortages of goods through the sharp reduction of domestic demand;
- to restore financial and macroeconomic equilibria;
- to open the economy through the internal convertibility of the currency and import liberalisation.

At the same time Poland had to initiate long-run policies for creating an organisational framework for a modern market economy, through privatisation, restructuring production, and trade reorientation.

The stabilisation programme was implemented by the government in conditions of broad social acceptance. The reduction of domestic demand was achieved through the strict control of wage rises that led to a temporary 45% drop in the real wage in January–February 1990, linked to an extremely high interest rate (the basic rate of interest in January 1990 was 43% per annum, then dropped quickly to about 34% in the second half of the year). Careful preparations were made for opening the economy: in order to facilitate this, a massive devaluation of the domestic currency took place (between October 1989 and January 1990 the zloty was devalued by 380%). The system of central rationing of convertible currencies was abolished, and internal convertibility implemented. Finally, a provisional system of heavy taxation was introduced to achieve budgetary equilibrium.

Achievements of the stabilisation programme, 1990–1

All these tough measures, and especially the restrictive monetary policy, led to a remarkable success in reducing inflation rates. After two-digit monthly inflation rates in January–February 1990 they fell to 3–5% in the following months; there followed a second, much weaker, price shock which took place in January 1991. The prices of raw materials imported from the USSR increased dramatically. To avoid the revival of high inflation it was necessary to increase interest rates once more, and to depress consumer demand through a decrease of the real wage. Finally, the inflation rate dropped to approximately 3–4% monthly in May–June 1991, and to 0% in July–August. As the policy of elimination of the remaining subsidies was continued, the current account deteriorated 16 months after the beginning of the stabilisation programme and the fixed exchange rate policy was dropped. Inflation rates stabilised at 3% per month (43% per annum) by the end of 1991 and remained at this level throughout 1992.

A major achievement of the stabilisation programme was the successful management of aggregate demand leading to a restoration of economic equilibrium. The centrally planned economy with an overwhelming shortage of goods was astonishingly quickly replaced by a system of free circulation of goods and services creating the basis for a free market; excess demand was replaced by excess supply.

The liberalisation programme proved its effectiveness in creating an open economy. In 1990 Poland achieved an unexpectedly radical improvement in the balance of trade. A 45% increase of exports to Western countries (and especially to EC countries) was accompanied by relatively modest imports (the officially published data concerning Polish imports in 1990 certainly underestimate their magnitude). Eventually, a trade surplus of US$ 2.2 bn was achieved (the surplus on the current account was US$ 0.7 bn), and the US$ 1 bn Stabilisation Fund supplied by Western countries to help Poland to support currency convertibility remained untouched.

The fixed exchange rate policy, successfully implemented in 1990, reached its limits of usefulness by mid-1991. As the terms of trade between foreign and domestic production were changing in favour of imports and the logic of the open economy did not allow a significant tariff increase nor the implementation of any other form of protectionism, Polish imports started to grow rapidly in 1991. The stable exchange rate together with a still high inflation meant, in fact, a real revaluation of the Polish zloty which discouraged exports. Eventually, the deterioration of the current account (the negative current account of US$ 1.7 bn in the first half of 1991) forced the Polish National Bank to gradually devalue the zloty. This policy was continued throughout 1992. On the other hand, tariffs increased and a turnover tax was imposed on many imported, especially consumer, goods.

The problems connected with trade with the former CMEA countries, and above all with the former USSR, proved to be much more difficult to solve. The massive Polish trade surplus in 1990 (the last year of the CMEA-based rouble trade) should be seen as defeat rather than success, as roubles paid to Polish exporters could not be exchanged for goods or hard currency and Polish imports from the USSR were sharply reduced (see also the analysis of the Soviet trade shock in Berg and Sachs, 1992). The introduction of hard-currency trade between Poland and the USSR changed the situation dramatically. The value of Polish imports (particularly oil and gas) in 1991 increased considerably. At the same time the USSR, as a result of its own liquidity problems and overwhelming economic crisis, sharply reduced its imports from Poland. The only positive element in this phenomenon was the acceleration of the Polish foreign trade reorientation towards the EC and other Western markets: the role of the USSR as the first Polish trading partner in the eighties passed into history (the share of trade with the USSR in Polish foreign trade was historically about 40%, and fell to 13% in 1991). This process continued in 1992 mainly due to the deterioration of economic conditions in the former USSR.

Some final remarks should be made about long-run policies. Privatisation of the economy proceeded, except for heavy industry, surprisingly quickly. This was due particularly to the fast growth of the Polish private sector (always much stronger than in many other Eastern European economies). Two years after the installation of the democratic government, the last obstacles to private entrepreneurship were eliminated. The share of private sector industrial production increased to about 20% (retail trade to 75%, construction to 40%). In agriculture the private sector in Poland had always played a much more important role than the collectivist or state-owned one. However, the programme of massive privatisation in industry that was to be implemented in 1992 was finally accepted by Parliament only in May 1993 (in March 1993, the Sejm refused to accept fairly liberal government proposals, but two months later it agreed to a modified proposal which, at the request of the trade unions, increased the role of employee representatives). Thus, contrary to official forecasts, such a delay did not locate Poland on the path of a fast change of ownership structure.

Much less can be said about the restructuring of production. A shift of resources between different sectors of the economy could be seen as the result of the uneven decline in the rates of capacity utilisation. However, with a very low level of investment, one could hardly expect a really decisive change.

The recession and the social costs of the transition

The austerity policy proved its effectiveness in stopping inflation and restoring economic equilibrium. Nevertheless, the price that Polish society paid for this success was extremely high:

- the real wage fell in 1990 by more than 24% and did not significantly grow in 1991 (2% increase); it further declined in 1992 (by 3.5%);
- Polish GDP fell in 1990 by 12% and by 7.5% in 1991; however, in 1992 it has shown a slight increase (official figures are between 0.5% and 2%) despite a deep drop in agriculture due to a severe drought;
- production of state-owned industry was down by 25% in 1990 and by 12 % in 1991; it started to grow in the second half of 1992 (between 2% and 4%);
- unemployment rocketed, reaching 2.2 mn at the end of 1991 and 2.5 mn in 1992.

The basic economic indicators for Poland 1989–1992 are presented in table 8.1.

Table 8.1. *Key macroeconomic indicators for Poland, 1989–92 (previous year = 100)*

Annual data	1989	1990	1991	1992
GDP	100.2	88.4	92.5	102.0
Industrial output	99.5	75.8	88.1	104.2
Personal consumption	100.1	84.8	110.5	100.9
Investment outlays	97.6	89.9	92.0	100.6
Exports	100.2	113.7	97.6	107.7
Imports	101.5	82.1	137.8	104.2
Price index of indust. output	312.8	722.4	148.1	128.5
Consumer price index	351.1	685.8	170.3	143.0
Trade in convertible currencies (US $ mn)				
Trade balance	240.0	2214.0	51.0	512
Current account	−1843.0	716.0	−1359.0	−269
Trade in non-convertible currencies (roubles mn)				
Trade balance	978.0	6608.0	408.0	...
Current account	1104.0	7121.0	520.0	...
Unemployment rate (%, end of year)	0.0	6.3	11.8	13.6
Budget surplus (+) or deficit (−) (% of GDP)	−3.0	+0.4	−3.8	−6.1

Quarterly data	1992				1993
	I-III	IV-VI	VII-IX	X-XII	I-III
Industrial output	98.7	100.1	104.5	108.4	94.3
Exports	94.8	107.1	99.8	103.3	...
Imports	81.5	102.0	118.3	120.2	...
Price index of indust. output	106.4	108.2	105.9	106.6	107.7
Consumer price index	112.7	109.1	107.5	109.9	109.4
Trade in convertible currencies (US $ mn)					
Trade balance	385.0	561.0	73.0	−507.0	−370.0
Current account	133.0	256.0	−110.0	−548.0	−680.0
Unemployment rate (%)	12.1	12.6	13.6	13.6	14.2

Note:
... Not available
Sources: SYP, 1990, 1991, 1992; *SB* (1990–3); HZ (1992); Ps (1991).

The drop in industrial production in 1991 was due to :

- the reduced supply of money (introduced to avoid the revival of hyperinflation);
- high interest rates (the average level was 54%) which, together with pessimistic expectations about the recession, made investment fall by 8%;
- the contraction of CMEA trade (above all the direct effects of decrease of exports to the USSR);
- the growing competitiveness of imported goods that hit demand for domestic production.

The year 1991 led, after the dramatic adjustment of 1990, to a drop in economic activity. An increase of FDI (estimated on the level of US$ 1 bn) was not sufficient to compensate for the internal and external factors that hit industrial output.

The fall of CMEA trade demonstrated the extent to which some regions of Poland were economically dependent on the Soviet market; broad financial assistance that would allow the restructuring of production seemed to be necessary to compensate for the negative effects of the change. At the same time, the recession caused a serious financial crisis: budget revenue fell significantly, and the government lacked funds to help enterprises to modify their production structure. The fall of exports to the USSR was not fully compensated by the increase of exports in 1991 to other markets: either the products that were exported were not competitive enough (for example, a large part of machinery, transport equipment, electronics), or the markets of the developed countries remained closed to the growth of exports (textiles, food, steel and metallurgy). Finally, together with the growing imports and the terms-of-trade deterioration with the USSR, this led to a serious deterioration of the 1991 current account. The situation improved slightly in 1992 as total exports showed a considerable increase and imports seemed to rise more slowly. However, discrepancies in foreign trade statistics were discovered. It is claimed, in fact, that total imports were higher than the inflows of foreign currency reported by the banks.

The problems with export markets, together with the deep recession in Poland and the growing competition of imports, led to a dramatic fall in the rentability of the Polish state-owned firms: the gross profits-to-sales ratio fell from almost 30% in 1990 to 5% in 1991 and to 2% in 1992. Several branches of the economy began to run deficits and the number of firms on the edge of bankrupcy increased rapidly. The process may have some positive aspects (it can eventually speed up privatisation); in the short run, however, it caused a rapid growth of unemployment. The growing social costs of the process of transition resulted in a growth of social and political tensions.

At the beginning of 1992, monetary policy was slightly relaxed and the zloty was significantly devalued. Together with the activities that were undertaken to improve the budgetary balance, it led to increased inflation. The only unquestionably positive result of this policy was the growth of exports and the decrease of imports that finally led to an improvement of the balance of trade and the current account.

Changes in industrial structure and foreign trade, 1989–92

Changes in industrial structure

The industrial structure in 1989 was the result of 40 years of an industrial policy aimed at forcing autarky and economic independence (hence, coal, other mining industries, and metallurgy dominated). It was targeted on developing manufacturing export-oriented industries within the division of labour of the former CMEA countries with an emphasis on electrical and mechanical engineering industries related to the military complex, and light industry. Hence, the structure of employment (value added figures were unavailable until recently) was dominated by coal and power branches (16%), electroengineering and metallurgy (37%), light industry (16%) and food processing industry (10%).

It must be emphasised that branches were modernised in the mid-seventies. Due to the crisis of the early eighties and low investment levels in the following years (including constraints imposed on imports of new technology) the technical level of industry's equipment generally became poor, negatively affecting its competitive position.

The coal industry was considered the most strategic branch as for many years it guaranteed independence in fuel supplies (imports of oil and gas from the former USSR) and was a major export commodity (only weakly dependent on import deliveries) supporting the balance of payments. The negative feature was that the structure of fuels used in Polish industry was inefficient, and major industries are still dependent on coal supplies. The organisation of the coal industry was characterised by a high degree of centralised decision making, enjoyed a monopolistic position, and was heavily subsidised. After 1989 the subsidies were systematically reduced, forcing an increase in coal prices. The coal pits are concentrated in one geographical area (Silesia), thus constraining production and the closure of less efficient mines would lead to enormous, localised unemployment. Also employment in many associated services sectors would be badly affected. The process of employment reduction, however, has already started (see

Table 8.2. *Dynamics of gross output and employment, 1990–92*

	Gross output (1989 = 100) (const. prices)			Employment (1989 = 100)		
	1990	1991	1992	1990	1991	1992
Coal	67.9	68.5	62.8	88.6	79.6	75.7
Fuel	83.4	71.2	79.5	99.6	92.6	94.8
Energy	90.8	86.1	80.9	101.7	102.0	102.6
Basic met.	87.0	66.2	64.0	94.4	91.7	82.5
Non-ferrous met.	78.0	61.5	58.0	97.2	110.0	104.7
Met. processing	71.9	63.2	68.3	88.6	87.1	81.9
Eng.	85.0	67.9	63.0	89.7	81.6	68.9
Prec. instruments	83.5	62.3	68.5	91.4	83.6	68.2
Transp. eq.	78.0	51.6	63.7	91.9	84.4	74.5
Electrotechnics	82.2	68.5	73.5	92.3	78.3	63.7
Chemic.	75.9	65.7	70.1	91.0	92.9	86.4
Min.	79.0	77.0	77.0	94.7	95.4	90.8
Wood processing	70.4	70.3	81.2	85.5	107.1	105.5
Paper and pulp	79.5	77.9	84.5	91.5	87.3	78.0
Light	64.7	56.3	58.6	88.0	84.1	73.3
Food processing	73.9	74.5	77.6	97.5	110.3	113.9
Other	63.3	56.0	66.2	76.1	56.3	52.2
Total	76.2	67.1	70.0	90.8	88.2	81.5

table 8.2). The share of employment in the coal industry declined systematically over the years 1989–91, but increased again in 1992, indicating that it is only the beginning of a deep structural decline (see table 8.3).

The electroengineering industry was one of the fastest developing industries in the 1970s. It was a leading export industry and its products, which included military equipment, were mainly delivered to the former CMEA countries. Its technological level deteriorated over the 1980s and its capacities were highly underutilised. In 1989 this industry accounted for more than 32% of total employment. Its activities declined in 1990 but to a lesser extent than industry generally. In 1991 and in 1992 exports of machinery equipment to the former USSR declined dramatically (see pp. 253–5) and the opening of the Polish economy, with an almost complete lack of tariff protection, brought about a high inflow of competitive imports, mainly of consumer durables (electronic equipment, cars, etc.). Hence, the industries' shares declined both in gross output and in employment: the latter to 30% in 1991 and to 28% in 1992, and it seems

Table 8.2. (*cont.*)

	Gross output/Employment (1989 = 100)			Employment (prev. year = 100)	
	1990	1991	1992	1991	1992
Coal	76.6	86.1	82.9	112.3	96.4
Fuel	83.7	76.9	82.6	91.9	109.0
Energy	89.3	84.4	78.7	94.5	93.5
Basic met.	92.1	72.2	76.7	78.4	107.4
Non-ferrous met.	80.3	56.0	55.3	69.7	99.0
Met. processing	81.2	72.6	83.6	89.4	115.0
Eng.	94.8	83.3	91.6	87.8	109.8
Prec. instruments	91.4	74.5	100.4	81.6	134.7
Trans. eq.	84.9	61.2	86.1	72.7	139.8
Electrotechnics	89.1	87.4	115.7	98.1	132.0
Chemic.	83.4	70.7	81.2	84.8	114.8
Min.	83.5	80.7	84.6	96.8	105.0
Wood processing	82.4	65.6	78.0	79.6	117.4
Paper and pulp	86.9	89.2	107.5	102.7	121.4
Light	73.6	66.9	79.9	91.0	119.4
Food processing	75.8	67.5	68.4	89.1	100.9
Other	83.2	99.4	127.0	119.5	127.6
Total	83.9	76.1	85.8	90.7	112.9

Sources: SYP (1990, 1991, 1992); *SB* (1990–3).

that this process will continue. A similar pattern of change can be observed in the cases of the fuel industry and basic metals.

Light industry comprises textiles, clothing and footwear, and belongs to a group of industries with a long and successful tradition. Its share reached nearly 16% in total industrial employment in 1989. In the 1970s, being one of the important exporting industries, it was modernised and enlarged. By 1989 its equipment was outdated and the quality of its products was considerably below Western European standards. The textile industry is geographically concentrated (the largest centre being in Lodz), whereas the clothing industry is spread all over the country. The textile industry in particular has tended to decline over the period 1989–92 both in terms of activity levels and in shares in gross output and employment. The latter declined by 14%, causing a higher rate of unemployment in areas with textile industry concentration. The major reasons for the decline were falling domestic demand (especially in 1989) due to lower real incomes and

Table 8.3. *Branch structure of Polish industry, shares %, 1989–92*

	Gross ind. output						Employment			
	1989	1989	1990	1991	1992	1992	1989	1990	1991	1992
	curr. prices 1990	const. prices 1990	curr. prices 1990	const. prices 1990	curr. prices 1990	const. prices 1990				
Coal	3.6	4.9	4.3	5.0	5.8	4.4	12.1	11.8	10.9	11.2
Fuel	5.0	7.2	7.8	7.6	8.7	8.2	1.3	1.5	1.4	1.6
Energy	2.9	4.5	5.3	5.8	7.0	5.2	2.9	3.3	3.4	3.7
Basic met.	6.3	7.7	8.7	7.6	4.7	7.1	3.6	3.7	3.7	3.6
Non-ferrous met.	4.2	5.4	5.5	5.0	2.6	4.5	1.5	1.6	1.9	1.9
Met. processing	4.3	4.2	3.9	3.9	4.7	4.1	6.0	5.8	5.9	6.0
Eng.	7.4	6.7	7.4	6.7	4.5	6.0	10.4	10.3	9.6	8.8
Prec. instruments	1.2	0.9	1.0	0.8	0.9	0.9	1.8	1.8	1.7	1.5
Transport eq.	7.5	7.2	7.3	5.5	5.9	6.6	8.0	8.1	7.6	7.3
Electrotec.	5.5	4.6	4.9	4.7	3.9	4.8	6.0	6.1	5.3	4.7
Chemic.	8.8	9.7	9.6	9.5	9.2	9.8	6.8	6.9	7.2	7.2
Min.	3.4	3.6	3.6	4.1	4.2	3.9	5.1	5.3	5.5	5.7
Wood processing	3.3	2.8	2.6	2.9	4.4	3.3	4.1	3.8	5.0	5.3
Paper and pulp	1.3	1.4	1.4	1.6	1.3	1.2	1.1	1.1	1.1	1.1
Lighting	11.9	8.5	7.1	7.1	7.1	7.2	15.6	15.2	14.9	14.1
Food processing	21.8	18.8	18.0	20.7	23.2	21.0	10.1	10.9	12.7	14.1
Other	2.1	1.9	1.6	1.6	2.1	1.8	3.6	3.0	2.3	2.3
Total	100	100	100	100	100	100	100	100	100	100
Tot. previous year = 100		99.2	77.1	87.5	104.2			96.9	90.8	97.1	92.3

Sources: SYP (1990, 1991, 1992), *SB* (1990–3).

the imports of cheap footwear and clothing from the Far East, and of expensive, high quality products from the West. Competition thus negatively affected domestic production in 1991, particularly in the wake of the relative import price fall due to the stabilisation of the dollar/zloty exchange rate. At the same time demand from the former CMEA countries declined without compensating exports to other countries. Similar factors affected 'other' industries (table 8.3).

The coal, metal processing and wood industries, on the other hand, which showed declining shares in 1990, improved their position in 1991 and 1992, mainly as a result of expanding exports to Western countries. The same applies even more to the energy, non-ferrous metals and minerals industries whose share was increasing over the whole period. Foodstuffs have a special position – employment increased over the whole period and, since 1991, its share in output has also risen. The chemical industry shows an opposite trend – in 1991–2 output shares were declining, whereas employment increased, which may be due to changes in the product mix (pharmaceutical industry shares have declined).

Generally, a majority of these changes can be attributed to two factors – on the one hand is the 'external shock' caused by the decline in exports to the former USSR and other CMEA countries in 1991 and in 1992 only partly compensated for by the increase in exports to other countries. On the other hand, because of the stable exchange rate policy, the imports in 1991, especially of consumer goods, increased. Hence, structural changes in output and employment can be attributed to changes in the final demand for domestic products, partly the result of real income losses and partly due to growing foreign competition, and the steep decline of demand from the former CMEA. While the output mix has changed, productive capacity has not adjusted in the same way, as scrapping has been delayed and new investment declined. This conclusion should be slightly modified to allow for the impact of small private firms developing over the years 1990–2, most noticeably in the foodstuffs industry. Thus major structural changes still lie ahead.

Changes in export and import structures

Data on this subject are included in table 8.4. Notice first that in the years 1989–91 the value of exports increased only slightly (in US$). As we have mentioned before, the shares of exports to the CMEA countries declined dramatically, from 35% in 1989 to 22.2% in 1990, which was due mostly to an expansion of trade towards Western countries, and then to 17% in 1991 which was mostly due to a collapse of trade with the former CMEA. As for the USSR, Poland's most important trading partner, the shares declined from 21% in 1989 to 11% in 1991, whereas for Hungary and Czechoslovakia only a slight decline was noticed – from 7% to 5%. The decline in exports to the former CMEA did not affect all industries in the same way, in fact fuel, metal products, wood and paper, and food and agricultural products all increased their export shares to the CMEA countries. A decline of export shares was characteristic of electrical and mechanical engineering products in all markets (except for the former USSR where this share was rising up until 1990). These changes had a clear

Table 8.4. *Structure of Polish exports, 1989–91*

		Production of industries								Con-struc-tion	Prod. of agri-culture	Tot. in US $ mn
	Tot.	Fuel and energy	basic met.	electr. eng.	chemic.	wood and paper	light	food				
A. Industrial composition (%) for each export market												
Tot.												
1989	100	9.6	10.5	38.4	10.5	2.9	5.5	9.6	5.9	4.1	13466.1
1990	100	10.6	15.0	30.0	12.2	3.7	6.1	9.7	5.0	4.3	13626.8
1991	100	11.4	16.1	22.7	11.8	6.0	5.9	9.9	4.8	6.5	14493.7
CMEA												
1989	100	7.0	3.6	61.8	10.1	0.5	3.0	1.4	9.1	2.0	4688.5
1990	100	5.3	5.6	60.8	10.1	0.4	5.4	2.3	6.6	2.0	3006.4
1991	100	11.1	5.2	38.2	18.2	0.5	3.9	5.8	7.1	7.2	2449.0
Other than CMEA												
1989	100	11.0	14.1	25.9	10.7	4.2	6.9	14.0	4.2	5.3	8777.6
1990	100	12.1	17.7	21.3	12.8	4.6	6.3	11.8	4.6	4.9	10620.5
1991	100	11.4	18.3	19.5	10.5	7.1	6.3	10.7	4.3	6.3	12044.7
B. Geographical composition of exports (%) for each industry												
CMEA												
1989	34.8	25.2	11.9	56.0	33.5	6.2	18.7	5.0	53.4	17.1	–
1990	22.1	11.0	8.2	44.8	18.2	2.4	19.5	5.3	28.7	10.3	–
1991	16.9	16.5	5.5	28.4	26.1	1.4	11.1	10.0	25.0	18.9	–
Other than CMEA												
1989	65.2	74.8	88.1	44.0	66.5	93.8	81.3	95.0	46.6	82.9	–
1990	77.9	89.0	91.8	55.2	81.8	97.6	80.5	94.7	71.3	89.7	–
1991	83.1	83.5	94.5	71.6	73.9	98.6	88.9	90.0	75.0	81.1	–

Sources: SYP (1990, 1991, 1992); **P**s (1991)

impact on the decline in the shares of these industries in domestic output, as did the increase in competitive imports, especially in the year 1991. We comment on these changes below.

Information about imports is presented in table 8.5. In the past the industrial structure of imports was determined to a large extent by the constraints imposed in the late eighties on imports of consumption and investment goods. Imports of agricultural products and processed food were exceptionally high, however, because of high domestic demand caused by subsidised food prices.

In 1990 imports declined considerably because of the fall in domestic demand and an unfavourable exchange rate. On the other hand, the policy of stable exchange rates in 1991 (the import prices increased by 26% compared with a 70% domestic rate of inflation) encouraged imports. The shares of imports from Hungary and Czechoslovakia had already declined in 1990; total imports from the former CMEA countries showed a steady decline in shares from 32% in 1989 to 20% in 1991. There were differences across ex-CMEA countries. The share of imports from the former USSR grew from 18% in 1989 to 29% in 1990 due to the relative oil price increase, and declined to 15% only in 1991 because of a collapse caused by a sharp change from transferable roubles to convertible currency. Electroengineering imports, which are linked to investment activities, had the largest shares in total imports; they fluctuated around 37%. The imports from the non-CMEA countries, however, increased from 62% in 1989 to more than 80% by 1992 as the purchase of machinery equipment from the former CMEA countries declined dramatically to 20%.

The recession brought about a general decline of imports in 1990; of intermediate inputs because of the decline in economic activity, and of foodstuffs (and agricultural products) due to a sharp decline of consumers' demand (as the result of an increase in relative prices). The radical increase of imports in 1991 (both in nominal and real terms) changed the shares once again. The shares (and volumes) of foodstuffs increased once more, then stopped and reversed because of an increase of tariffs and a turnover tax on imported commodities introduced in the last quarter of 1991 and kept over 1992. Because of the further decline in investment activities the shares of electroengineering and basic metal products declined. This process may be reversed in the future as the economy starts to expand.

Concluding remarks

So far, economic stabilisation has had absolute priority in Polish policy towards transformation, and industrial restructuring received little attention. Despite the changes in industrial structure, restructuring in the

Table 8.5. *Structure of Polish imports, 1989–91*

	Tot.	Fuel and energy	basic met.	electr. eng.	chemic.	wood and paper	light	food	Con-struc-tion	Prod. of agri-culture	Tot. in US $ mn
				Production of industries							
A. Industrial composition of imports (%) for each trading partner											
Tot.											
1989	100	12.7	8.7	37.0	15.0	1.2	1.9	7.6	9.1	4.6	10277.3
1990	100	21.8	7.7	40.7	11.9	1.2	1.4	5.2	6.7	1.4	8160.0
1991	100	20.2	4.2	36.3	12.6	1.6	2.4	6.2	10.2	3.1	14292.7
CMEA											
1989	100	29.6	8.0	43.9	7.1	1.5	1.8	3.4	2.1	0.5	3308.6
1990	100	56.1	9.4	25.3	3.8	0.8	0.5	1.4	1.2	0.3	2060.0
1991	100	56.7	5.6	20.3	6.7	1.1	0.7	2.4	4.8	0.7	2866.2
Other than CMEA											
1989	100	4.6	9.1	33.8	18.8	1.1	2.0	9.6	12.4	6.5	6968.7
1990	100	10.2	7.1	45.9	14.7	1.3	1.7	6.4	8.6	1.8	6100.0
1991	100	17.3	6.7	37.9	16.8	1.2	2.1	4.3	10.3	1.5	11426.5

B. Geographical composition of each imported commodity (%)

CMEA

Year											
1989	32.2	75.3	29.6	38.2	15.2	40.1	31.0	14.3	7.6	3.7	—
1990	25.2	64.9	31.0	15.7	8.0	17.5	9.2	7.1	4.5	4.7	—
1991	20.1	56.5	26.8	11.2	10.7	13.3	6.3	7.8	9.5	4.3	—

Other than CMEA

Year											
1989	67.8	24.7	70.4	61.8	84.8	59.9	69.0	85.7	92.4	96.3	—
1990	74.8	35.1	69.0	84.3	92.0	82.5	90.8	92.9	95.5	95.3	—
1991	68.7	36.5	69.9	82.1	87.2	85.4	91.9	87.4	95.0	96.3	—

Source: SYP (1990, 1991, 1992). Ps (1991).

Table 8.6. *Activities of state-owned and private sectors, 1991–3*

	1991		1992		I–III 1993	
	State-owned sector	Private-owned sector	State-owned sector	Private-owned sector	State-owned sector	Private-owned sector
Sold production of industry (%)	75.8	24.2	69.0	31.0	68.1	31.9
1990 = 100	80.5	125.4	...	...	...	...
Output of construction (%)	44.8	55.2	23.3	77.7	17.4	82.6
1990 = 100	81.0	132.5	...	...	...	...
Transport services (%)	76.3	23.7	60.7	39.3	58.2	41.8
1990 = 100	80.6	130.9	...	...	...	...

Source: 'Rzeczpospolita' (6 February 1992), SB (1990–3).
... Not available

broader sense involves the creation of an institutional framework characteristic of a market economy. However, the stabilisation programme might constrain structural adjustment. As a result of the recession and the lag in financial restructuring, an enormous expansion of interenterprise credit appeared.

In the newly emerging market economies the problem of reconstruction is extremely complex. Where different areas of the economy are interdependent and complementary, it is not easy to decide which changes should play a lead role in the process. However, there are some structural changes that clearly play the primary role, and some are consequential or play a secondary role. Generally, there is no doubt that in the newly emerging market economies priority should be given to changes in the property structure, determining directly or indirectly many other structural adjustments: in the structure of production and in efficiency, in social stratification and the structure of consumption, in the structure of monetary–financial flows, in the needs for organisational and institutional changes in the economy, etc. In table 8.6 the shares of private- and state-owned activities in industry, construction and transport services are shown. The large fall in the activities of the state-owned firms is accompanied by a significant growth of the private sector. The share of activities of the private sector in industry and transportation is, however, still less than half of total activity in these sectors. The most significant share of the private sector (mostly small firms) is observed in domestic trade.

The main obstacle to the privatisation of large SOEs, apart from the technical difficulties connected with the valuation of firms, was the problem with the legislative procedure, the existence of monopolies and sometimes unsettled property rights of former owners. It should be noticed that SOEs were significantly subsidised. In 1989 subsidies amounted to 31% of the state budget. Privatisation will probably result in cutting the remaining subsidies and this process will be accompanied by new regulations broadly based on the new structure of taxes (value added tax, corporate income tax, personal income tax).

Growing unemployment on the one hand, and the expansion of the private sector on the other led to a polarisation of incomes and changes in the distribution of incomes. Social discontent in Poland caused by a worsening of the standard of living is one of the factors that can still decide the success or failure of the economic reforms. There is no detailed strategy for restructuring in a broad sense in any of the CEE economies. However, their general strategies, despite different sequencing of the transformation process, are very similar, as the basic structural features of the different national economies differ little.

In the production structure one can observe an excess of raw material-based and heavy industries, a deficiency of sophisticated processing industries, and a very low share of services. The consumption structure reflects a somewhat similar phenomenon: a very high share of food and a very low share of durables and services. The spatial structure of production, mostly created by the heavy industry zones, causes structural problems of employment, ecological threats, etc. Finally, the branch and occupational structure of employees, the structure of foreign trade, the organisational features of economic and social processes are mostly the consequence of the current pattern of property ownership and production. A major part of structural change is still lying ahead.

Appendix: economic policy scenarios and economic transformation, 1991–2000–simulations with a multisectoral model

Introduction

Macroeconomic models are a standard tool for investigating structural changes in market economies (see for example the INFORUM family of models described in Almon *et al.* (1974). Efforts were also undertaken to use them in the case of the centrally planned economy (CPE) (for the use of

INFORUM-type models for investigating CPEs see Orlowski and Tomas-zewicz, 1991); the overview of the other models for CPEs, including the works of Zalai, Simon, Sujan, Dobrinsky, Welfe, and the others can be found in Welfe (1991), Krelle (1989) and Zalai (1980).

The recent social and economic changes in Central and Eastern Europe created a new situation: models describing the centrally planned system cannot be used any more. At the same time, the construction of an appropriate macroeconomic model of an economy in transition meets the barrier of a lack of theoretical and methodological background. In this appendix we discuss some aspects of this problem and present an attempt to construct and use a multisectoral macroeconomic model for the Polish economy in transition.

Availability of data and new requirements

The use of multisectoral macroeconomic models for investigating struc-tural changes in the former CPEs in the transition period raises serious problems, starting with the availability of data, their reliability and usefulness for the analysis. The problems are common for the majority of countries in Central and Eastern Europe, although there exist differences among the statistical systems. The comments below refer, first of all, to the Polish situation. One of the main deficiencies of Eastern European statistics is that they underestimate the role of the process of income distribution and interactions between real and financial flows in the economy. This is obviously the result of the logic of a centrally planned economy in which the state control and interventon are identified with direct interference into the processes of production and distribution. The transformation process has thus to be reflected in appropriate changes of statistical practice of the Polish Central Statistical Office (CSO).

Statistical yearbooks published in 1991–2 show the efforts of the CSO to capture some of the financial flows, but the statistics are still 'biased' by the old-fashioned MPS statistical approach. Undoubtedly, the planned re-forms of the application of SNA (ESA variant) will take time.

It seems, however, that priority should be given to the temporary reorientation of statistical practice in order to collect data which are of crucial importance for analysing the Polish economy in the transition period. Such an approach would also allow us to measure economic indicators in these areas which are not a part of the SNA, but provide policy makers with valuable sources of statistical information. The transition period requires more data on firms, with more attention paid to the ownership structure, the monitoring of their revenues and expendi-tures, and financial performance in a broad sense.

Some global data on state and private enterprises concerning value added, gross output and material costs have been published. More detailed figures concern mainly state-owned enterprises. Information on flows between firms is scarce. The existing data mainly cover banks and security institutions. To facilitate the new requirements for statistical data some attempts have been undertaken by the Research Centre for Statistical and Economic Analysis of the Polish CSO to construct a so-called 'real and financial flows accounts' (see Zienkowski, 1990a).

The aim of these accounts is to show the relationships between production activities (output production and distribution) and the creation and redistribution of income. A considerable part of the Centre's efforts was devoted to the construction of a I–O table for 1987 within the SNA framework (see Zienkowski, 1990b). Another result of the Centre's investigations was the presentation of data collected in the form of a Social Accounting Matrix (SAM) for 1987. This consists of fairly disaggregated accounts for production activities (72 branches). Current accounts also comprise 8 accounts for consumption goods, 4 for capital investment, 10 institutional accounts grouping households according to income groups (8) and 2 accounts for ROW. Capital accounts are, in turn, divided into 8 institutional accounts while financial ones are divided into 5. No doubt the SAM is the most convenient form of simultaneous presentation of all real and financial flows within a given period; the SAM can therefore be viewed as a quantitative model for the economic system.

Economic models for a transition period

It is an extremely difficult and risky task to construct and use for simulation analysis a reliable macroeconomic model for an economy which is in transition. To some extent this is the result of methodological problems, although the instability of some economic processes does not make the choice of methodology any easier. The main problem, however, is the scarcity of statistical data. The data concerning the former periods describe a completely different type of economic system. On the other hand, the 'new' ones merely refer, as regards Poland, to a three-year period of transition to a market economy.

The past experiences of the former CPEs in macro-modelling based on time series data cannot be omitted when decisions on the choice of modelling technique for the transition period are being made. Among others, in the second half of the eighties, the authors of this chapter formed a multisectoral model of the Polish economy (see Orlowski and Tomaszewicz, 1991). The model was demand-oriented and, in some respects, described the behaviour and functioning of the economy of the years to come. The methodology of its construction was based on the analysis of the Polish economy in disequilibrium, in order to make possible (on the basis of available data) the estimation of stochastic equations, integrated with input-output relationships, generating the demand. Emphasis was put on the effective demand. This model was successfully used for a multivariant analysis of the stabilisation and development of the Polish economy in 1990–2. Although the model was demand-determined, the specification of equations – not only because of the inclusion of some supply constraints – reflected, to a great extent, the functioning of CPE.

The redesign of the model had thus to correspond to recent changes in the Polish economy. To do so, we decided to construct a model that would describe Poland in the coming years as a developed market economy. Let us characterise some of the problems of the functioning of our economy in a transition period, the ones which may be interpreted at the same time as arguments and counter-arguments for our decision.

Generally, we can assume that final demand determines production demand, and, eventually, output. However, in economic reality the mechanisms of a transformation of a demand increase into output are far from being perfect. The whole system works, therefore, under a much bigger risk of inflation increase than in the case of Western economies. A significant control over wages in the state-owned sector exercised by means of fiscal policy instruments still takes place. On the one hand, commercial-isation and privatisation of the state-owned sector are being introduced, on the other market imperfections still exist (monopolisation), above all in the state-owned sector. However, it can be claimed that in each economic sector the sensitivity to market signals (price, interest changes) increases systematically. Hence, these elements should be clearly emphasised in particular equations, i.e. the investment demand, savings, financial flows, etc.

More attention ought to be paid to the state budget and, consequently, taxes and subsidies should be isolated from the financial accumulation of enterprises. Other blocks concerning the financial flows should be also taken into consideration. This covers modelling of the banking system linked with capital and money markets. In the model presented below, being the basis for further research, we managed to solve the above-mentioned problems to only a limited extent. The changes in the functioning of the Polish economy practically cover only two years, so it is necessary to apply simplified and very often problematic methods of the quantitative description of economic processes. The incongruence of data on time series for different past periods with the current situation of the Polish economy makes us use the previous estimates of parameters carefully, even though those estimates were obtained by applying special methods of estimation. In the presented model we decided to use, whenever possible, the parameters estimated by methods of disequlibrium econometrics. In the remaining cases we calibrated parameters on the basis of the year 1990. Of course, 1990 data do not fully reflect the situation of a fully-fledged market economy. However, we assume that the parameters obtained for 1990 describe the situation of the transition period better than the parameters for previous years. An essential characteristic of our model is that it is based on the SNA and the SAM for 1987, from which the input-output table was taken.

A short description of the model

The model IMPEC91 disaggregates the economy into 22 branches. The branches are grouped into 3 categories, each treated differently in the model:

(a) Commercial branches (all branches except agriculture and non-material services).
(b) Agriculture.
(c) Non-commercial branches (services).

Appropriate bridge matrices join the 22 produced goods with the final demand for different groups of goods. Exports and imports are not disaggregated by countries (nor groups of countries) but only by goods.

Final demand equations

Personal consumption
The personal consumption block of the model consists of the standard LES functions (for details, see also Orlowski and Tomaszewicz, 1991); the estimation methods are described in detail in Orlowski (1991):

$$C_K = C^*_K + a(YP(1 - tax) - \Sigma_i C^*_i P_i)/P_k$$

where C = consumption, C^* = necessary purchases, YP = personal income, tax = tax rate, P = prices, a = distributions parameters, subscripts k, i = group of goods.

The values C^* and distribution parameters (a) were estimated on the basis of disequilibrium econometrics. The equation for savings is similar; however, in that case, there is no intercept (necessary purchase).

Investment demand
The investment demand is derived as the solution of the future profit maximisation problem. We assume that firms want to maximise the future profit (a difference between future sales and costs, including the cost of capital, i.e. interest rate) subject to a given technology of production (production function).

Under certain simplifying assumptions (first of all the stable price and wages relations – see Orlowski, 1991), we obtain a function that links the investment level with the interest rate (subscripts omitted):

$$I_{opt} = (aL^b/r)^{1/b}$$

where I_{opt} = optimal level of investment, L = employment in the period of making the investment decision, r = long-term interest rate, b = elasticity of production with respect to labour, a = parameter, making the investment decisions a function of the interest rate r. To capture the fact that in the transition period one can hardly assume producers to be perfect profit-maximisers, we have implemented in the model a formula for the investment demand that allows it to depend on the optimal level and on the output scale (the distribution parameter c was set to 0.5 level) (subscripts omitted):

$$I = c\,dX + (1 - c)\,I_{opt}.$$

The parameters of the equations were calibrated on the 1990 data basis (parameters d, a) or estimated (parameter b).

Exports equations
Exports are given by the standard demand-type equation (subscripts omitted):

$$E = aWE^b(Per/PW)^c$$

where E = exports, WE = world demand, P = domestic price, er = exchange rate, PW = world price.

Other final demand components
Inventory investment is assumed to be proportional to the value added level. Public spending is exogenous.

Demand for goods
As in the standard input–output-type models, the global demand for goods is calculated by multiplying the final demand vector by the appropriate matrix:

$$Q = (I - A)^{-1}F$$

where Q = vector of global demand for goods, A = I–O matrix, F = final demand vector (sum of vectors of personal and public consumption, investment demand, inventory investment and exports).

Demand for imports and domestic output

Once the final demand has been calculated and transformed into the total demand for goods (output), it is divided into demand for imported and domestically produced goods. To do so, we used the well known Armington formulation (see Armington, 1969) (subscripts omitted):

$$M/X = a(P/(PMer(1 + tar))^s$$

where M = imports of goods i, X = production, P, PM = import prices, s = elasticity of substitution, er = exchange rate, tar = tariffs.

Demand for labour and unemployment

The demand for production allows the calculation of the demand for labour from the inverted production function (subscripts omitted):

$$L = (X/aK^{(1-b)})^{(1/b)}$$

where L = labour, X = output, K = capital, a,b = parameters.

The difference between the sum of demand for labour by branches and the exogenously given labour supply gives the level of unemployment.

Income

Unfortunately, as we did not find any possibility of either calibrating or estimating the Phillips curve parameters, we had to use the following formula for the nominal wage:

$$W = a(X/L)^b P^c$$

where W = wage, X/L = average productivity of labour, P = price index.

The wage income (W multiplied by employment) played a decisive role in generating income in Poland. However, this is no longer true in the transition period. Other elements that are to be taken into account are:

• profit income – the share in the profits by branches proportional to the share of the private sector in the branch (exogenously given);
• social security payments – the exogenously given number of retired persons multiplied by the average retirement payment (proportional to wage) and the number of unemployed multiplied by the unemployment benefit (proportional to wage);

- farmers' income – a share in the value added of agriculture;
- other incomes – proportional to wage income.

The model also calculates the profits of firms, and the revenue and spending of the state budget.

Prices
Prices are calculated in the model on the cost-based formulation (which does not mean that they are not established by the free market (see Almon *et al.*, 1974). Such an approach, however, does not permit the link between the money supply and budget deficit or the price level.

The driving forces of the model
The model works in the following way:

- first, the consumer demand (driven by income), investment demand (driven by output level and exogenous interest rate), inventory investment (driven by output) and public demand (exogenously given) are calculated;
- then, the export demand (driven by the world demand and price relations) is derived;
- all the above components of the final demand are used to calculate the demand for goods (according to the I–O structure);
- total demand for goods is then divided between imports and the domestic production (depending on price relations);
- domestic output level determines employment, unemployment, wage level and profits;
- income is calculated;
- price level is determined (the inflationary loop links it to the average wage level);
- income and prices generated in this way are used to recalculate the final demand.

As can be clearly seen, the following driving forces of the model are exogenously given: world demand, labour supply, public spending. The main internal mechanism is the loop: productivity of labour–wage–income–output. The most important economic policy instruments are tax rates, tariffs, interest rates, and exchange rate.

The base run and simulation analysis experiments

The model was solved up to the year 2000. The most important trends in the base run are calculated to be:

(a) Dramatic adjustments in 1991: GDP falls by 10%. The very high interest rate (a real interest rate of 10 points) does not permit investment. The foreign trade balance deterioates. Inflation is still amounts to about 70%.

(b) Fast growth in 1992–4. Consumption grows even faster than investment. GDP annual growth is about 5%. Inflation gradually decreases.

(c) Stabilisation of growth after 1995 (around 4%) with a relatively modest inflationary pressure.

In table 8.A1 global indicators, being the results of simulation experiments until 2000, are shown. A short description of them is given below.

According to the aims of our study the simulation exercises were broken down into three areas.

A   In this group of experiments the impact of factors considered as internal on the production structure was investigated. The assumptions and the results (macro-variables) are the following:

(a) *Privatisation*: until 1995 half of the firms are privatised, and the subsidies are eliminated. The main assumption of the exercise is that the state-owned sector is loss making. The most important result of privatisation is, therefore, the elimination of public subsidies. One should be aware of the fact that we do not make any other assumptions about higher efficiency of private firms than state-owned ones in the exercise.

Results: With the cost-based price formula, the elimination of subsidies leads to a temporary increase of inflation. At the beginning consumption and investment fall, then consumption grows more rapidly than investments. In the medium and long period, however, it is net investment that gains more than personal consumption. A positive effect on the GDP can be observed.

(b) *Monetary expansion*: the active interventionist policy – interest rates (real) halved, public spending increased by 10%. In the exercise we try to answer the question about the efficiency of the standard interventionist policy tools, designed to increase the aggregated demand (investment and public spending directly, and consumption through the multiplier effect).

Results: Good effects on the production with an astonishingly small increase of inflation (let us recall, however, that in our price block formulation there is no link between inflation and budget deficit). Investment grows significantly in 1991, pulling the economy out of recession, therefore with a positive effect on unemployment.

(c) *Protection of agriculture*: tariffs on agricultural goods increased three times.

Table 8.A1. *Simulation experiments, results, in 1000 zloty, constant prices*

	1990	1991	1994	1997	2000	Annually 1990–2000	91–2000
MODEL IMPEC – Base run							
Personal Cons.	384.48	350.69	400.21	446.07	487.31	2.4%	3.7%
Net Invest.	163.48	157.48	178.81	203.21	228.91	3.4%	4.2%
Exports	132.50	105.92	127.77	152.83	183.07	3.3%	6.3%
Imports	113.43	110.93	118.19	128.21	137.51	1.9%	2.4%
GDP	700.68	632.21	732.42	833.25	937.73	3.0%	4.5%
Price Level	1.00	1.69	2.77	3.54	4.08	15.1%	10.3%
MODEL IMPEC – GDR option							
Personal Cons.	384.48	366.69	426.16	503.66	556.21	3.8%	4.7%
Net Invest.	163.48	178.96	184.05	210.68	237.27	3.8%	3.2%
Exports	132.50	104.96	75.50	82.42	99.11	−2.9%	−0.6%
Imports	113.43	117.42	144.36	165.51	175.51	4.5%	4.6%
GDP	700.68	674.05	692.30	799.06	902.40	2.6%	3.3%
Price Level	1.00	1.83	2.08	2.29	2.52	9.7%	3.6%
MODEL IMPEC – Monetary expansion							
Personal Cons.	384.48	366.69	409.91	459.11	508.90	2.8%	3.7%
Net Invest.	163.48	178.96	200.71	228.01	258.17	4.7%	4.2%
Exports	132.50	104.96	127.60	152.83	183.07	3.3%	6.4%
Imports	113.43	117.42	123.39	134.09	144.86	2.5%	2.4%
GDP	700.68	674.05	771.06	879.03	996.95	3.6%	4.4%
Price Level	1.00	1.83	3.01	3.83	4.41	16.0%	10.2%
MODEL IMPEC – Privatisation							
Personal Cons.	384.48	334.21	436.22	468.75	518.85	3.0%	5.0%
Net Invest.	163.48	151.78	188.80	210.99	240.03	3.9%	5.2%
Exports	132.50	105.42	127.86	153.01	183.41	3.3%	6.3%
Imports	113.43	107.04	124.66	132.23	142.85	2.3%	3.3%
GDP	700.68	612.08	774.86	861.79	978.09	3.4%	5.3%
Price Level	1.00	2.03	2.87	3.73	4.40	16.0%	9.0%
MODEL IMPEC – Protection of agriculture							
Personal Cons.	384.48	353.64	391.95	433.27	452.17	1.6%	2.8%
Net Invest.	163.48	160.33	185.84	210.85	231.50	3.5%	4.2%
Exports	132.50	112.68	155.37	185.51	222.51	5.3%	7.9%
Imports	113.43	109.66	113.48	123.34	129.99	1.4%	1.9%
GDP	700.68	647.05	765.72	867.98	953.17	3.1%	4.4%
Price Level	1.00	1.94	3.51	4.44	5.16	17.8%	11.4%

Table 8.A1. (*cont.*)

MODEL IMPEC – Austrian export structure						
Personal Cons.	384.48	371.21	400.13	445.26	489.10	2.4%	3.1%
Net Invest.	163.48	169.85	183.02	204.44	228.04	3.4%	3.3%
Exports	132.50	134.22	144.26	160.74	183.07	3.3%	3.5%
Imports	113.42	123.02	123.81	131.81	139.83	2.1%	1.4%
GDP	700.68	684.84	748.48	838.32	936.24	2.9%	3.5%
Price Level	1.00	1.64	2.90	3.68	4.16	15.3%	10.9%

MODEL IMPEC – German export structure						
Personal Cons.	383.48	371.03	399.26	443.90	487.52	2.4%	3.1%
Net Invest.	163.48	169.68	182.00	202.35	225.02	3.2%	3.2%
Exports	132.50	134.07	143.47	159.67	183.09	3.3%	3.5%
Imports	113.42	123.08	124.13	132.73	141.93	2.3%	1.6%
GDP	700.68	684.23	745.27	832.48	929.07	2.9%	3.5%
Price Level	1.00	1.64	2.90	3.67	4.15	15.3%	10.9%

Results: A positive effect on agricultural output and farmers' incomes. However, the costs of the protection are paid, first of all, by the domestic consumer. The effect on the GDP is U-shaped. First, GDP grows above its base-run level, then starts to fall, which means that the effect seems to be only temporary. Inflation is above its base-run level.

The second and third areas of analysis could be considered as the analysis of external challenges both in terms of opening up the Polish economy to the world market and in terms of the impact of changes in the exports structure of Poland.

B   Opening up the economy.
(d) *The GDR option*: the fast opening of the economy to the world market (in an east German style), with a 50% real appreciation of the zloty in 1992–5. The sense of this exercise is to investigate the effects of the liberal trade regime connected with a strong real appreciation of the domestic currency. We called the experiment the GDR option, as the best example of such a policy is east Germany after the monetary union; similar policies could, however, have been observed in other Central European countries as well (for example, in Poland in the first half of 1991).
Results: The decline is not as big as in the former GDR, but still significant. Positive effects on consumption and, to a smaller degree, on investment, are accompanied by a fall in exports and production. The

economic revival is postponed until after 1995; unemployment will grow until 2000. The current account deteriorates dramatically.

C   This group of experiments cannot be considered as a scenario analysis of the alternative economic policy. The experiments are performed to find out to what extent the output structure differences between Poland and the Western economies can be explained by the trade structure differences. To investigate it, we adjusted the Polish export structure in the year 2000 to the structures of Austrian exports in 1988 and German exports in 1988 (the last two structures were given – see *Polish Yearbook*, 1990 – in SITC, so they were transformed into model disaggregation with the use of the bridge matrices). Simulations are called Austrian export structure and German export structure, respectively.

Results: The results are similar in both experiments. Personal consumption, imports and price level are higher in 2000 than in the base run. At the same time net investment and the level of GDP is lower. Generally speaking, the changes are in favour of current consumption and somewhat unfavourable for future economic development (however, macroeconomic structures seem to be closer to Western ones). What should also be noticed is the fact that, in general, a much bigger change in macro-structures can be witnessed in the German exports experiment (due to the fact that the difference in exports structures between Poland and Germany was bigger than in the case of Austria). Another factor that is to be taken into consideration, however, is the difference of the export–GDP ratios among the three countries (the values of the ratio were about 31% in Germany (1989), 40% in Austria (1989) and only 20% in Poland (base run 2000)). What we investigated in the experiments is only the impact of the exports structure, and not the level of exports. Table 8.A1 shows the main results of the experiments.

Structural change in the economy

In Tables 8.A2 and 8.A3 structural changes in the Polish gross output under different scenarios are presented. Table 8.A2 shows that the base run does not create any dramatic change in the output structure. The simulation experiments, however, lead to much more distinct effects in this respect.

The privatisation experiment did not cause any significant change of the production structure compared with the structure from the base run. One can remember, however, that nothing was assumed in the scenario about the difference in the long-run efficiency between the private and state-owned sector, that may eventually lead to a different cost structure.

Table 8.A2. *Change in output structure from 1990 to 2000 (structure in various scenarios in 2000)*

	Base 1990	Base 2000	GDR option	Monetary expans.	Priva- tization	Prot. agric.	Austr. exp.	Germ. exp.
Fuel & energy	7.7	7.3	7.0	7.2	7.3	7.4	6.8	6.8
Metallurgy	5.7	5.4	4.6	5.4	5.4	5.8	6.1	5.4
Vehicles ind.	3.2	3.3	2.7	3.3	3.3	3.6	3.7	4.1
Machinery	8.0	8.2	6.7	8.1	8.1	8.7	8.8	9.2
Chemical ind.	4.6	4.5	4.1	4.4	4.4	4.6	4.5	4.8
Mineral ind.	2.3	2.3	2.4	2.3	2.3	2.3	2.3	2.3
Wood ind.	2.7	2.6	2.6	2.6	2.6	2.6	2.7	2.6
Light ind.	5.1	5.1	5.0	5.0	5.1	5.0	5.2	5.0
Food process.	10.5	10.9	11.2	10.7	11.0	10.6	10.2	10.3
Other manuf.	1.9	1.9	1.8	1.9	1.9	1.9	1.9	1.9
Construct.	11.0	11.3	12.0	11.8	11.3	11.3	11.5	11.2
Agriculture	10.8	11.6	11.6	11.5	11.8	11.6	10.7	10.7
Forestry	0.6	0.6	0.6	0.6	0.6	0.6	0.6	0.6
Transport	5.6	5.4	5.7	5.4	5.5	5.3	5.5	5.4
Commun.	0.5	0.5	0.5	0.5	0.5	0.5	0.5	0.5
Trade	8.5	8.2	9.1	8.2	8.3	7.8	8.3	8.3
Other material	3.0	2.9	3.2	2.9	2.9	2.7	2.9	2.9
Housing	1.2	1.1	1.3	1.1	1.1	1.1	1.1	1.1
Education	1.3	1.3	1.5	1.3	1.2	1.3	1.3	1.3
Health serv.	1.1	1.1	1.2	1.1	1.0	1.0	1.1	1.1
Oth. non-mat.	1.9	1.8	2.1	1.9	1.8	1.8	1.8	1.9
Social serv.	2.8	2.7	3.1	2.8	2.6	2.7	2.7	2.8
Tot. output	100.0	100.0	100.0	100.0	100.0	100.0	100.0	100.0

Nothing was assumed about demonopolisation, either. These phenomena can significantly influence the output structure of the Polish economy.

The interventionist policy in the monetary expansion experiment maintains the position of manufacturing industries; the clear winners are producers of investment goods (machinery, and construction). The protectionist policy of the protection of agriculture scenario leads to an improvement of the position of the primary sector of the economy, and that of the heavy industry.

The GDR option hits, first of all, manufacturing industries, except the ones that are particularly consumer-oriented (light and food processing industries). It is also building and trade that gain. The situation of services does not change significantly.

Table 8.A3. *Meaures of distance of output structures (OS) in experiments*

Gross output Structure	Polish structure Base run	Base run	Present Austrian structure	Present German structure
Dist. from: Experiments	1990 (1)	2000 (2)	(3)	(4)
Base run 1990	–	–	40.3	44.1
Base run 2000	3.6	–	42.0	45.3
Austrian exports	4.2	5.0	40.8	43.6
German exports	4.9	5.2	40.4	42.7
GDR	7.3	6.2	40.4	45.8
Privatisation	4.0	0.7	42.0	45.3
Monetary expansion	4.0	2.0	42.2	45.5
Protection of agriculture	4.1	2.6	42.8	45.3

The Austrian exports structure causes the changes of gross output structure towards the evident promotion of electromachinery and metallurgy industries.

The German exports structure significantly supports electromachinery and car industry.

The conclusions are presented in table 8.A3 where we compare the structural results obtained using the synthetic indicator (output structure indicator, OS). It covers the whole range of structural changes in the gross output under different cross-section comparisons. It has a form (Landesmann, 1991):

$$OS = \sqrt{\sum_i (SO_i^k - SO_i^L)^2 * SO_i^L}$$

where SO is the share of industry i in the total output in experiment K or L.

The first part of table 8.A3 shows the differences of the Polish production structure for different scenarios and different years. The second part shows the distances between the Polish structure of the gross output (under different scenarios) and the present gross output structures of Austria and Germany.

Columns (1) (change with respect to the Polish base run, 1990 solution) shows that the smallest change of the structure takes place in the case of the base run. The active macroeconomic policies (privatisation, monetary expansion, protection of agriculture scenarios) cause bigger differences. Exports structure changes result in an effect bigger than the macro-policies. However, the biggest change is due to the opening up of the economy (GDR option).

Column (2) (related to base run 2000) confirms the relatively low impact of internal factors on the structural change, and the importance of external ones (exports structure and opening up of the economy).

Columns (3) and (4) give the measures of the distance between the Polish output structure and those of Austria and Germany. Astonishingly, the base run and internal factors experiments cause the distance to be even greater than in 1990.

The only possibility of narrowing it is the reorientation of trade (the distance narrows in both experiments) and to some extent the opening up of the economy. A remark should be made about the comparison of the GDR option structure with the German one. Opening up of the Polish economy to the world market does not narrow the distances; the distance even increases with respect to the German economy. This is because the GDR option brings the deepest changes in the production structure but not necessarily in the desirable direction. The shares of the potential hi-tech industries are the lowest, of the food processing industry and services the highest. This means that the competitiveness of exports and production of the first group of products will deteriorate due to the appreciation of the zloty.

Generally, as was mentioned above, relatively greater changes of Polish gross output structure were obtained as a result of export structure adjustments than those due to internal economic policy factors. The analysis should be extended by introducing combined scenarios, all leading towards diminishing the distance between the production structure of Poland and Austria and Germany. These cumulative effects will, however, be investigated in the next phase after compiling a new version of the model.

Notes

The authors wish to thank Mr Michal Przybylinski for his valuable support in data collecting and presentation.
In preparing the appendix, we wish to acknowledge the valuable comments made by István Székely in cooperating with us in the ACE Project 'Industrial Restructuring, Trade Reorientation and East-West European Integration'.

References

Almon, C., Buckler, M. B., Horwitz, L. M. and Reimbold, T. C., *Interindustry* 1974. *Interindustry Forecasts of the American Economy*, Lexington, MA: Lexington Books

Armington, P. S., 1969. 'A theory of demand for products distinguished by place of production', *IMF Staff Papers*, 159–76

Berg, A. and Sachs, J., 1992. 'Structural adjustment and international trade in Eastern Europe: the case of Poland', *Economic Policy*, 14, 117–73

Calvo, G. A. and Coricelli, F., 1990. 'Stabilising a previously centrally planned economy: Poland 1990', *Economic Policy*, 14, 175–226

Dervis, K., de Melo, J. and Robinson, S., 1982. *General Equilibrium Models for Development Policy*, Cambridge: Cambridge University Press

Gomulka, S., 1992. 'Polish economic reform, 1990–1: principles, policies and outcomes', *Cambridge Journal of Economics*, 16(3), 355–72

HZ, Handel Zagraniczny, styczen-grudzien 1991 (*Foreign Trade*, January–December 1991), 1992, Central Statistical Office, Warsaw

Kornai, J., 1990. *A Road to a Free Economy*, New York: W. W. Norton

Krelle, W. (ed.), 1989. *The Future of the World Economy, Economic Growth and Structural Change*, Berlin: Springer Verlag

Landesmann, M., 1991. 'Industrial restructuring and the reorientation of trade in Czechoslovakia', *European Economy*, Special edition 2, 57–82

Mansur, A. and Whalley, J., 1984. Numerical specification of applied general equilibrium models: estimation, calibration, and data, in H. E. Scarf, J. B. Shoven (eds.), *Applied General Equilibrium Analysis*, New York: Cambridge University Press, 69–107

Orlowski, W. M. and Tomaszewicz, L., 1991. 'The INFORUM Model of the Polish economy', *Economic Systems Research*, 3, (1), 85–92

Orlowski, W. M., 1991. 'Fiscal and monetary policy options for the Polish economy in transition', University of Lodz, PhD Thesis (in Polish)

Ps, Prowizoryczny szacunek Produktu Krajowego Brutto w 1991 roku (Provisional Estimate of Gross National Product in 1991), 1991. Department of Statistical–Economic Research of the Central Statistical Office and the Polish Academy of Sciences, Materials and Studies, Warsaw

SB, *Statistical Bulletins, 1990–3*. Monthly, Central Statistical Office, Warsaw

Schaffer, M., 1992. 'The Economy in Poland', *Centre for Economic Performance Discussion Paper*, 67, London: Centre for Economic Performance

SYP, *Statistical Yearbooks of Poland*, 1990, 1991, 1992. Central Statistical Office, Warsaw

Welfe, W., 1991. 'Multisectoral econometrics models of the centrally planned economies and the disequilibrium', *Economics and Planning* 24, 203–6

Zalai, E., 1980. 'A non linear multisectoral model for Hungary: general equilibrium approach versus optimal planning approach', *IIASA Working Paper*, 8–148, Laxenburg

Zienkowski, L., 1990a. *Rachunek Przeplywow Rzeczowo-Finansowych (The Real-Financial Flows Account)*, ZBSE, Warsaw (in Polish)

    1990b. *Rachunek Przeplywow Rzeczowo-Finansowych: Macierz SAM dla Polski 1987 (The Real-Financial Flows Account: SAM for Poland 1987)*, ZBSE, Warsaw (in Polish)

Part Three

Enterprise analysis and policy issues

9 Microeconomic factors of trade reorientation in Hungary, 1981–90

László Halpern

Introduction

The collapse of regional integration of CMEA has dramatically changed the economic environment in which firms operate. According to standard assumptions a typical firm in a centrally planned economy (CPE) has slow, if any, price/cost responsiveness. This chapter aims at presenting the most important characteristics of these changes and some elements of enterprise reactions.

The general economic situation in Hungary can be understood from, for example, the OECD *Economic Surveys* (1991), but there is very little research on structural patterns of trade reorientation. The importance of these changes lies in the fact that most enterprises with significant exports were already operating under the previous regime, and their changing behaviour may be an indication of future patterns.

This chapter will combine time series and cross-sectional approaches. This twofold approach is the only way to analyse the problem of structural change and the evolution of the corporate sector simultaneously. Because trade reorientation from Eastern to Western markets mainly occurred in the late 1980s and early 1990s, it is impossible to verify empirically the specification of traditional trade models based on time series alone.

The chapter emphasises the trade performance of regularly exporting firms. The regular exporter position in this case does not necessarily imply efficiency imposed by foreign markets, since both rouble and dollar exports were heavily influenced by central regulation. The domestic market, which was sheltered from import competition by strict import licensing, might have compensated for losses in export activities. The sample contains 212 firms which exported in both rouble and dollar[1] trade in every year between 1981 and 1990. The chapter presents the general characteristics of the whole corporate sector, including small-scale firms. This will serve as a basis for the performance comparison of regular exporter companies.

The chapter is organised as follows. In the first section the corporate sector is analysed: the sales structure, the profit rate and the subsidy will be presented for the whole sector; the second section focuses on regularly exporting firms; the third section looks at disaggregated results. The sample was analysed by sector, profitability and asset-size breakdown. The fourth section provides some results of an econometric model which tries to synthesise the outcomes of the preceding sections. Finally, the main results are summarised.

The data

The database for our analysis covers the most important balance sheet and profit and loss accounts, and foreign trade activity for 212 firms, as well as aggregate indicators for the whole corporate sector. Firms were selected on the basis of their trade profile; a firm was included if it exported in both dollars and roubles in every year between 1981 and 1990. No newly born firms have been included in the sample due to lack of information; nonetheless, the principal goal, analysing the behaviour of those enterprises which already existed before large-scale trade reorientation, can be fulfilled. The analysis of the link between enterprise performance and institutional change – commercialisation or privatisation – is beyond the scope of this chapter.

Access to data from the Ministry of Finance was arranged through KOPINT-DATORG. Its main deficiency is the lack of price and foreign demand information at firm level so that only nominal variables are used, though aggregate price indices are applied.

It is unusual to have cross-sectional data for 10 years, but the price to be paid for this benefit was the difficulty of ensuring that the content of variables did not change over time. The analysis of relative profitability of different sales directions lies at the heart of the chapter, but it could not have been computed if one of the cost elements had been missing. Overhead costs were split among sales directions in the first four years as prescribed by economic regulation, but in the second half of the decade this rule was abandoned and the accounts contained only one aggregate overhead cost category. The method of breaking down overhead costs and its impact will be shown later.

Trade orientation of the corporate sector

In this section the sales, profitability, subsidy and price structures of the corporate sector will be presented, with attention focused on structural change between 1981 and 1990. Export reorientation from rouble to dollar

Table 9.1. *Structure of sales of Hungarian enterprises,[a] and annual increase in gross output,[b] 1981–90*

	1981	1982	1983	1984	1985	1986	1987	1988	1989	1990
Rouble	5.0	5.1	5.5	5.8	6.2	6.2	5.8	5.2	4.4	2.9
Dollar	6.3	6.1	6.3	6.5	6.6	6.0	6.5	7.4	8.1	8.4
Domestic	88.7	88.8	88.2	87.7	87.2	87.8	87.7	87.4	87.5	88.6
Gr. output	3.2	2.6	1.4	3.1	0.6	2.5	4.2	0.1	−1.2	−5.9

Source: KOPINT-DATORG data, CSO (Hungary) *Yearbooks*; own computations.
Notes:
[a] per cent of total at current prices.
[b] percentage increase at constant prices.

trade was accompanied by important modification in price, profitability and subsidy structures.

Enterprises had to meet the demand of three different markets: domestic, rouble and dollar foreign markets. Subsidies, wages, credit and hard currency import licence preferences were used as policy instruments, but in addition intermittent informal pressure was put on exporting firms. Our aim in this chapter is to reveal which elements of enterprise behaviour can be captured by an analysis mainly based on accounting data.

It is generally accepted that these accounts were heavily biased, despite threats of punishment for intentional disinformation, as accounts were very seldom audited by independent experts. Favourite techniques were manipulation of the cost breakdown, and postponement of profit declaration according to time preferences on profit tax payment.

This analysis will only use information supplied by the firms, which means that subsidy data will represent the importance of a sales direction for the central planner. The level of subsidy was a result of a game played between the government and the exporters' lobby; the relationship between export subsidy and export volume is not simple, as influential managers were most successful in obtaining subsidies for their exports. In any of these cases, directly or indirectly, the higher the export subsidy, the higher the export volume.[2]

Let us first show the global tendencies of the last decade with respect to gross output and the structure of sales for the corporate sector as a whole (table 9.1).

The gross output growth rate shows three different periods during the eighties (see table 9.1). In the earlier years a significant positive growth rate prevailed, while the response to the 1985 slowdown was an artificially

Table 9.2. *Profit-to-sales ratios for Hungarian firms, %, 1981–90*

	1981	1982	1983	1984	1985	1986	1987	1988	1989	1990
Rouble	10.0	11.2	10.9	10.5	20.6	17.6	18.5	13.1	8.1	3.0
Dollar	10.6	8.6	9.3	6.0	14.7	11.4	17.9	16.2	19.5	12.8
Domestic	9.4	9.0	9.0	8.4	8.1	9.0	9.6	7.7	7.8	7.8
Total	9.5	9.1	9.1	8.4	9.3	9.7	10.7	8.6	8.8	8.1

Source: KOPINT-DATORG data; own computations.

intensified economic growth in the following two years leading to a foreign indebtedness crisis. The very close relationship between growth and foreign indebtedness has been analysed in Halpern (1989). The third period began in 1988; the decelerating growth rate became negative in 1989.

The sales structure shows small increases in the shares of both components of exports in almost every year, especially in the rouble area for the first half of the 1980s. From a 6.2% peak level in 1985–6, rouble exports fell to 2.9% in 1990 as a result of the collapse of the CMEA. Between 1986 and 1989 dollar exports grew faster than the fall in rouble exports, the dollar exports' share increasing by more than 2 percentage points. The increase in the share of dollar exports was due to the decline in output, as the level of dollar exports fell slightly. Thus, in 1990, the increase in dollar exports could not offset the impact of the collapse of rouble exports.[3]

Our main question is: what was the consequence of the collapse of the CMEA market on cost structure and on subsidies; how did enterprises react? Our most important indicator is the profitability structure. How did income generation shift from rouble exports to dollar exports and domestic sales? 'Profit' is defined as the difference between sales income and costs for each sales direction. At enterprise level this profit corresponds to pre-tax profit.

In the 1980s the profitability structure by sales direction for the whole corporate sector changed quite dramatically (see table 9.2). In the first four years the profit/sales ratio for rouble exports was always above 10% but this was not so for the other two sales directions. It is important to know that in 1981 the highest profitability of dollar exports was due to the, so-called, simulated competitive price system. Price increases in the domestic market were authorised by the Price Office and, to simulate world market prices without import liberalisation, no permit was required to increase prices if certain rules were respected. The main rule was as follows: the profit margin achieved in dollar exports was the maximum margin to be

Table 9.3. *Subsidy-to-sales ratios for Hungarian enterprises, %, 1981–90*

	1981	1982	1983	1984	1985	1986	1987	1988	1989	1990
Rouble	12.2	12.3	13.5	14.8	15.3	14.8	18.5	16.3	6.9	15.5
Dollar	13.5	11.0	11.6	6.6	13.3	14.5	15.5	9.3	8.0	5.3
Domestic	1.5	1.2	1.2	0.9	1.9	2.5	2.2	2.8	2.1	1.2
Total	2.8	2.4	2.5	2.1	3.5	4.0	4.0	3.9	2.8	2.0

Source: KOPINT-DATORG data; own computations.

applied when calculating domestic sales prices on the basis of costs. This rule made it necessary to prescribe the method of computing overhead costs for different sales directions. It was obvious that dollar export revenues were partly financed by subsidies, as will be shown later, so the simulation of world market prices included the effect of subsidy policy.

The rules for cost-plus pricing for rouble exports were the same though the subsidisation was far more important than for dollar exports. The facts show that the rule was not so strictly respected; it had to work at enterprise level which gave room for manoeuvring and bargaining with the central planner for subsidies and price increase licenses.[4]

In 1985 the compulsory calculation of overhead costs was relaxed and the system of simulating world market prices was abandoned.[5] Nonetheless, the incentive to present higher export profitability has not yet disappeared, and export profitability has risen significantly due to the increased freedom of enterprises to reallocate costs.

Profitability of rouble exports dried up by the end of the decade, and from 1988 onwards dollar exports once more achieved the highest profit rate. The effect of subsidies on export profitability is shown in table 9.3. Until 1984 the subsidy ratio for both exports was higher than the profit ratio, though this occurred only three times in subsequent years. It is rather surprising that rouble exports were massively subsidised in 1990, but this can be explained by the coincidence of a sectoral shift of exports and increasingly differentiated sectoral subsidies in favour of those sectors which maintained most of their rouble exports. The trend of the improving profit ratio of dollar exports was broken in 1990 for which decreasing subsidy can only partly be blamed.

The effect of prices on profitability can be demonstrated at aggregate level. Price indices were computed on the basis of national currency, which includes exchange rate effects. Neither for export-oriented firms as a whole, nor for individual firms, were price data available.

Table 9.4. *Price increases according to directions of sales, %, year-to-year, 1981–90*

	1981	1982	1983	1984	1985	1986	1987	1988	1989	1990
Rouble sales	4.8	3.9	5.1	3.4	5.3	6.2	−2.5	−3.5	10.5	−0.5
Dollar sales	3.0	−1.5	4.9	5.5	1.2	−3.8	8.3	16.5	18.8	14.1
Dom. sales	6.2	5.8	5.6	5.2	4.8	3.3	5.6	10.2	14.9	26.6
Output	5.8	5.1	5.5	5.1	4.5	3.0	5.1	9.6	15.0	24.3
GDP	5.1	5.7	4.6	6.6	5.9	3.7	8.2	15.0	21.3	25.6

Source: CSO (Hungary) *Yearbooks.*

In the first five years, with the exception of dollar export sales, the general price increase was around 5% per annum (see table 9.4). The second half of the eighties shows considerable price differentiation as measured in 1986–9 prices of dollar exports; in 1990 domestic prices increased substantially faster than the average rate. The price indices of dollar exports show improvements in their relative attractiveness compared to rouble and domestic sales due mainly to real devaluation. The rouble export market suffered price decreases in 1987–8, and a 10% price rise in 1989 was enough to exceed the 1986 level by a mere 4%. In 1990 a further rouble export price drop occured. In addition to the effect of subsidies presented in table 9.3, it was widely known that for a long time rouble exports were very advantageous for exporting firms because of instantaneous payment guaranteed by the Hungarian government (irrespective of the time of the actual payment by the trading partner), the laxity of delivery schedules and lower quality standards compared with dollar markets. In early 1990 it was the government who had to intervene by introducing very strict export rationing to CMEA countries, especially to the USSR because of an increasing trade surplus.

Performance of regular exporters

This section presents sales, profitability and subsidy data for export-oriented firms. The analysis of the way in which this sub-set differs from the total corporate sector focuses on the question of how export reorientation influences profitability and subsidy ratios.

Table 9.5 shows the weight of the selected 212 firms in the corporate sector. A firm has been selected if it exported to both dollar and rouble areas in each year between 1981 and 1990. This set of firms can be regarded as main exporters. Their behaviour was investigated during the trade reorientation period which began in the second half of the 1980s and

Table 9.5. *Weight of regularly exporting firms as compared to the whole corporate sector, %, 1981–90*

	1981–8	1989	1990
Sales	18–20	19	16
Rouble sales	45–53	45	37
Dollar sales	44–49	48	36
Assets	18–22	17	17
Profit	16–24	21	14
Number of employees	18–19	19	19
Earnings	17–20	20	16

Source: KOPINT-DATORG data; own computations; tables 9.6–9.20 use the same sources.

Table 9.6. *Structure of sales of firms in the sample, %, 1981–90*

	1981	1982	1983	1984	1985	1986	1987	1988	1989	1990
Rouble	11.7	12.0	13.2	13.7	14.3	14.5	13.0	11.4	10.7	6.9
Dollar	12.9	12.4	13.0	14.6	14.7	13.8	14.8	18.2	20.1	22.2
Domestic	75.4	75.6	73.8	71.7	71.0	71.7	72.2	70.4	69.2	70.8

accelerated in 1989–90. Their diminishing role can be traced out in table 9.5. In the first 8 years they exported approximately half total exports in each direction. This decreased to below 40% in 1990 as their share in sales, profit and earnings diminished.

The characteristics of the sample may be different from those of the corporate sector as a whole. Our assumption is that the main reason for the difference lies in their export orientedness, which is why their performance will always be compared with the corporate sector. Comparing tables 9.1 and 9.6, the very dynamic increase of dollar export shares can be demonstrated. This fast increase was not enough to compensate for the collapse of the CMEA markets; the share of domestic sales increased in 1990 after a 3% decline since 1987.

The regular exporters had higher profitability than average firms (cf. tables 9.2 and 9.7), but this difference was more important in the first half of the decade (3–4%): in 1990 it was down to 0.9%. The main source of higher profitability was their profit rate in domestic sales, reflecting the higher than average bargaining power of these firms at home pricing (Halpern, 1992). Between 1981 and 1984 the regular exporters had higher profit rates

Table 9.7. *Profit rate of firms in the sample, %, 1981–90*

	1981	1982	1983	1984	1985	1986	1987	1988	1989	1990
Rouble	9.6	10.5	10.1	9.3	11.4	9.6	7.7	0.4	−7.9	−19.3
Dollar	15.0	11.8	12.0	13.1	14.2	6.1	11.8	11.7	16.4	9.3
Domestic	13.0	13.8	13.2	12.5	12.3	13.7	13.7	11.7	12.2	11.9
Total	12.8	13.1	12.6	12.1	12.5	12.0	12.5	10.2	10.8	9.0

Table 9.8. *Subsidy-to-sales ratios of firms in the sample, %, 1981–90*

	1981	1982	1983	1984	1985	1986	1987	1988	1989	1990
Rouble	14.0	13.2	14.1	15.6	16.0	13.9	15.7	13.5	2.9	4.6
Dollar	11.4	8.9	8.6	3.9	7.5	8.9	10.8	4.8	2.8	2.0
Domestic	−0.5	−0.8	−0.3	−0.7	0.9	2.1	0.5	−3.4	−3.2	−5.2
Total	3.1	2.4	3.1	2.5	4.3	4.9	4.4	0.4	−1.3	−2.8

on dollar exports than the average. However, from 1985 the reverse was the case.

The average subsidy was always higher for an average firm than for a regular exporter. This relation held, both for domestic sales and for dollar sales (cf. tables 9.3 and 9.8). Until 1985 the regular rouble exporters enjoyed preferential treatment, as the rouble export subsidy for the regular exporters was above average; after 1985, however, this was reversed.

Performance by asset size, profitability and branch

Three criteria have been chosen to investigate the structural characteristics of exporting firms: assets size, level of profitability and branches of production.

Disaggregation by asset size

Firms have been categorised by the size of their assets: small, medium and large. For the sake of comparability their size in 1990 was used for classification purposes.

The share of small and medium-sized firms declined in both exports, whilst large firms increased their share of dollar exports, mainly in 1989 and 1990 (see table 9.9). Somewhat counter-intuitively, there is an inverse

Table 9.9. *Export shares, by asset size, in the sample, %, 1981–90*

	1981	1982	1983	1984	1985	1986	1987	1988	1989	1990
Rouble										
small	11.1	10.3	10.6	10.7	10.5	9.8	8.7	9.0	9.8	9.3
medium	23.3	23.6	25.4	25.7	25.0	24.7	24.2	25.4	23.8	17.4
large	65.6	66.1	64.1	63.6	64.5	65.5	67.1	65.6	66.4	73.3
Dollar										
small	6.9	8.5	6.3	5.7	5.2	6.3	6.2	5.8	5.6	5.2
medium	21.1	19.1	18.4	17.6	19.1	18.2	17.0	16.6	14.0	10.5
large	72.0	72.4	75.3	76.6	75.7	75.5	76.8	77.6	80.4	84.3

Table 9.10. *Sales shares of firms, by asset size, in the sample, %, 1981–90*

	1981	1982	1983	1984	1985	1986	1987	1988	1989	1990
Small										
rouble	21.3	20.3	23.3	25.1	26.4	24.1	19.2	19.3	19.9	13.9
dollar	14.5	17.4	13.8	14.4	13.4	14.7	15.6	19.7	21.4	25.2
home	64.2	62.3	62.9	60.5	60.1	61.2	65.2	61.0	58.7	60.9
Medium										
rouble	14.8	15.6	18.6	19.2	20.2	20.1	18.3	18.2	16.7	9.9
dollar	14.7	13.1	13.3	14.1	15.8	14.0	14.6	19.1	18.5	19.1
home	70.5	71.3	68.2	66.7	63.9	65.8	67.1	62.7	64.8	71.0
Large										
rouble	10.2	10.5	11.1	11.5	12.0	12.5	11.4	9.5	8.9	6.1
dollar	12.3	11.9	12.9	14.8	14.5	13.6	14.8	17.9	20.4	22.5
home	77.5	77.7	76.0	73.7	73.5	73.9	73.9	72.5	70.7	71.4

relationship between the share of rouble export sales and the size of the firm in our sample: the smaller (larger) the firm, the larger (smaller) the share of rouble exports in total sales (see table 9.10). This means that smaller firms were more vulnerable to falling demand on CMEA markets. This relationship between the asset size and the role of exports was valid for the dollar exports until 1989 (1981 and 1985 excepted), but in 1989–90 the share of the dollar exports was higher in large firms than in medium-sized ones. Taking the rouble and dollar exports together the smaller firms were more export-oriented than the larger ones, but the difference diminished as size increased.

Table 9.11. *Profit rate of sales, by asset size, in the sample, %, 1981–90*

	1981	1982	1983	1984	1985	1986	1987	1988	1989	1990
Rouble										
small	12.1	13.0	12.9	11.3	12.6	12.8	12.6	4.0	−2.1	−6.5
medium	8.9	8.3	9.3	9.5	11.7	8.8	5.8	−1.9	−3.1	−5.4
large	9.4	11.0	10.0	8.9	11.1	9.4	7.8	0.7	−10.9	−25.0
Dollar										
small	11.8	9.0	−6.6	5.4	5.1	4.6	10.6	4.4	8.6	−0.3
medium	18.3	11.7	8.9	13.3	14.5	6.5	7.0	9.1	8.9	1.8
large	14.4	12.2	14.3	13.6	14.8	6.2	13.0	12.8	18.3	10.8
Domestic										
small	15.7	14.3	14.7	12.9	16.0	16.1	14.7	11.4	11.8	7.0
medium	8.2	9.8	9.6	7.8	12.0	14.0	15.4	12.7	11.7	7.8
large	13.8	14.6	13.8	13.5	12.2	13.5	13.3	11.6	12.3	12.8
Total										
small	14.3	13.0	11.2	11.4	13.6	13.6	13.6	8.5	8.3	3.3
medium	9.9	9.8	9.4	9.0	12.4	11.7	12.0	9.0	8.5	5.1
large	13.4	13.8	13.4	12.9	12.4	11.9	12.6	10.6	11.5	9.9

The overall profitability differences were very small between 1985 and 1987 (see table 9.11). Prior to this period the medium-size firms were the least profitable, and after that period the larger firms were significantly the most profitable. These profit differences came from lower rouble exports and domestic sales profit for medium-size firms in the first four years, and from the higher profit rates of dollar exports of large firms after 1987. It was only in 1990 that the large firms had a 5 percentage points advantage over the other groups in the profit rate of domestic sales, while their loss on their rouble exports was the heaviest at 25%.

Beginning with 1987 the overall subsidy was always higher for smaller firms, a fact mainly explained by the subsidies on domestic sales (see table 9.12). There is no clear relationship between the firm size and export subsidies, with the exception of rouble exports in the first five years when the larger firms had higher subsidies.

Sectoral analysis[6]

In the analysis below the following seven sectors are distinguished:

1. Energy and raw materials.
2. Machinery.
3. Chemicals.

Table 9.12. *Subsidy-to-sales ratios for firms, by asset size, in the sample, %, 1981–90*

	1981	1982	1983	1984	1985	1986	1987	1988	1989	1990
Rouble										
small	7.0	7.9	6.8	9.2	12.5	12.4	18.7	13.2	5.5	5.7
medium	12.7	12.2	12.8	15.3	15.2	16.0	17.7	14.5	11.5	16.3
large	15.5	14.2	15.8	16.8	16.8	13.3	14.5	13.2	−1.0	1.2
Dollar										
small	14.6	10.3	7.2	4.0	9.8	7.8	10.6	4.4	3.5	1.9
medium	9.5	8.2	8.4	5.5	5.8	9.6	12.7	9.1	5.5	4.7
large	11.6	9.0	8.7	3.5	7.8	8.8	10.4	3.8	2.2	1.6
Domestic										
small	2.7	0.9	1.9	1.1	3.6	4.5	2.7	6.0	7.2	7.6
medium	−4.9	−5.9	−5.6	−5.8	−3.4	−1.8	−2.2	0.6	2.1	−0.1
large	0.2	0.2	0.6	0.2	1.5	2.7	0.9	−4.7	−4.9	−6.7
Total										
small	5.6	4.1	3.8	3.7	6.9	7.0	7.5	7.2	6.1	6.0
medium	0.4	−0.7	0.3	0.6	2.4	4.0	4.4	5.1	4.4	2.7
large	3.5	3.0	3.6	2.9	4.6	5.0	4.1	−1.1	−3.0	−4.2

4. Light industry.
5. Food processing and agriculture.
6. Building materials and construction.
7. Services.

Rouble exports of the 212 firms in our sample are predominantly Machinery and Services; they accounted for 70–75% of total rouble exports (see table 9.13). The share of these two sectors behaved differently: the share of Machinery was around 38–39% until 1986, then it reached the peak level in 1988 with 44% and declined to 40% in 1990. Services reached their peak level (37%) in 1985 starting from 32% in 1981, declined to their lowest level (30%) in 1989, and in 1990 increased their share once more. The share of rouble export sales to total sales was still more than 22% for Machinery firms in 1990 compared with 35% in 1985 (see table 9.14). The share of rouble exports in the total sales for Service firms was above 21% in 1985, but dropped below 10% in 1990.

Dollar exports were more diversified than rouble exports; four of the seven sectors never fell below a 10% share. The share of the first two sectors exhibited similar behaviour in that, from 1985, they both increased at the

Table 9.13. *Export shares, by sectors, in the sample, %, 1981–90*

	1981	1982	1983	1984	1985	1986	1987	1988	1989	1990
Rouble										
Energ.	5.5	4.8	5.2	4.9	5.0	5.7	5.7	5.6	5.5	6.3
Mach.	38.8	39.1	38.6	39.3	38.3	37.8	40.8	44.0	43.1	40.4
Chemic.	8.4	8.5	8.4	8.6	8.8	8.3	8.1	8.9	9.0	10.6
Light	8.1	7.9	6.8	6.6	6.6	6.5	6.6	6.5	6.4	5.3
Foods	6.3	6.5	4.7	4.6	4.4	5.0	4.4	5.0	5.1	2.7
Build.	0.7	0.5	0.4	0.5	0.4	0.6	0.9	0.8	0.7	0.6
Servi.	32.2	32.6	35.9	35.6	36.6	36.2	33.4	29.1	30.3	34.1
Total	100.0	100.0	100.0	100.0	100.0	100.0	100.0	100.0	100.0	100.0
Dollar										
Energ.	17.9	16.1	17.7	17.4	14.8	15.2	15.6	18.4	21.6	23.2
Mach.	14.6	14.3	13.8	12.7	11.8	13.2	13.1	13.7	13.3	14.1
Chemic.	14.0	15.0	19.7	22.4	24.6	20.8	23.3	22.5	23.6	24.2
Light	5.9	5.8	6.6	6.0	5.9	7.0	7.6	6.8	6.3	5.8
Foods	15.9	16.6	12.6	14.4	15.5	10.8	7.7	9.5	7.1	4.2
Build.	0.7	1.0	0.9	1.1	0.7	0.8	0.8	0.9	0.8	0.9
Servi.	31.0	31.2	28.7	26.0	26.8	32.2	31.9	28.2	27.4	27.7
Total	100.0	100.0	100.0	100.0	100.0	100.0	100.0	100.0	100.0	100.0

expense of food processing, though energy increased most rapidly. The share of dollar exports in total sales rose in all sectors, with the important exception of food processing (see table 9.14). Firms in every branch except food processing became more outward-oriented in the second half of the 1980s.

The energy and raw materials industry always had the highest profit rate – sometimes around 30% – and only in one year was it below 20% (see table 9.15). The chemical industry also had high – above 10% – profit rates after 1987, due to the higher profitability of domestic sales. The profitability of exports was rather volatile, with substantial changes from one year to the next and across industries. The profitability of dollar exports in 1990 fell in the first three branches and in Food processing, but increased in Construction and for Services. The most surprising profit figures can be found in rouble exports of energy and raw materials in 1989 and 1990: −135% and −172%, respectively, which means that the costs of these exports were at least twice the value of export sales.

The overall subsidy level was not very different across branches, chemicals excepted, due to heavy taxation of domestic sales of fuel from

Table 9.14. *Sales shares of firms, by sectors, in the sample, %, 1981–90 total sales of firms in the given sector is 100*

	1981	1982	1983	1984	1985	1986	1987	1988	1989	1990
Rouble										
Energ.	3.8	3.2	3.8	3.9	4.2	4.7	4.3	3.6	3.2	2.1
Mach.	28.8	29.8	32.3	34.4	34.8	33.5	32.2	32.1	30.8	22.3
Chemic.	4.7	4.8	5.2	5.4	5.7	6.3	5.5	4.3	4.1	2.7
Light	11.5	12.1	11.4	11.6	11.9	11.7	10.5	9.5	9.2	5.3
Foods	7.1	7.5	6.5	6.1	6.1	7.2	6.1	6.1	6.2	2.6
Build.	3.6	2.7	2.4	2.8	3.0	4.1	4.6	4.5	3.6	2.2
Servi.	15.2	15.8	18.5	19.2	21.1	19.8	16.2	13.9	13.0	9.9
Dollar										
Energ.	13.3	11.2	12.8	14.8	12.7	11.9	13.4	18.7	23.7	25.4
Mach.	11.9	11.3	11.4	11.9	11.0	11.1	11.7	16.0	17.9	24.9
Chemic.	8.6	8.8	12.1	15.2	16.3	14.8	18.0	17.5	20.2	19.7
Light	9.1	9.1	11.0	11.3	10.9	11.8	13.8	15.9	17.0	18.7
Foods	19.5	19.8	17.2	20.4	22.0	15.0	11.9	18.7	16.3	12.9
Build.	4.1	5.7	5.6	7.5	5.3	5.0	4.8	7.7	8.4	10.4
Servi.	16.0	15.7	14.5	15.0	15.8	16.7	17.5	21.5	22.1	25.9
Domestic										
Energ.	83.0	85.6	83.4	81.3	83.1	83.4	82.4	77.7	73.1	72.4
Mach.	59.3	58.9	56.3	53.7	54.2	55.4	56.1	52.0	51.3	52.9
Chemic.	86.8	86.3	82.7	79.4	78.0	78.9	76.5	78.1	75.7	77.6
Light	79.4	78.8	77.6	77.0	77.3	76.5	75.7	74.6	73.8	76.0
Foods	73.3	72.7	76.3	73.5	71.9	77.8	82.1	75.2	77.5	84.6
Build.	92.3	91.6	92.0	89.7	91.8	90.9	90.6	87.8	88.0	87.3
Servi.	68.8	68.5	67.0	65.9	63.1	63.5	66.3	64.5	64.9	64.2

1988 (see table 9.16). The rouble export subsidy was more than 50% for firms in extraction until 1988, and was always higher than 20% for light industry. The subsidisation of rouble exports of food and agricultural products steadily increased; in 1990 it was 50%. The dollar export subsidy ratio decreased, and between 1988 and 1990 only Food processing had more than 10% subsidy compared to sales.

Profitability

Three groups of firms were distinguished according to the rate of return on their assets. The first class comprised those enterprises which either were loss makers or broke even in 1990; the remaining firms were divided into two equal-sized groups according to their rates of return on assets in 1990.

Table 9.15. *Profit rate of sales for firms, by sectors, in the sample, %,
1989–90*

	1981	1982	1983	1984	1985	1986	1987	1988	1989	1990
Rouble										
Energ.	3.4	5.1	0.7	0.8	3.8	4.5	6.5	−6.9	−135.0	−172.0
Mach.	11.5	13.6	14.2	14.4	14.9	13.6	10.1	4.5	−0.5	−12.3
Chemic.	−1.1	6.9	6.9	7.5	9.7	7.8	6.9	−5.7	−9.0	−7.7
Light	13.1	9.6	11.4	11.5	11.9	12.2	11.3	−11.5	−13.7	−35.4
Foods	2.1	−4.5	0.6	6.2	13.3	10.8	6.1	−2.0	6.2	1.1
Build.	17.7	9.8	9.0	7.5	−0.7	−0.0	5.5	−0.8	−11.5	−28.2
Servi.	13.2	13.1	10.3	6.7	10.2	6.9	5.0	3.7	5.2	0.5
Dollar										
Energ.	12.3	6.5	11.3	0.6	4.2	2.9	11.3	21.7	24.3	11.9
Mach.	7.5	5.8	9.1	4.5	6.2	5.1	12.0	7.7	10.3	2.1
Chemic.	11.7	10.7	9.0	12.9	16.6	−7.5	10.3	7.8	19.2	7.2
Light	17.8	16.7	11.3	6.5	8.6	4.5	7.6	1.1	3.5	−0.3
Foods	26.4	14.1	20.7	32.5	26.4	8.8	4.9	16.5	20.9	4.3
Build.	18.1	9.6	0.4	10.5	3.7	11.6	13.0	0.2	7.0	11.0
Servi.	15.7	15.7	12.6	16.6	15.9	15.8	16.0	11.1	13.1	15.3
Domestic										
Energ.	29.0	30.8	29.5	30.4	25.9	24.1	21.9	19.2	21.9	27.4
Mach.	14.1	13.6	15.0	14.5	14.8	15.8	14.7	10.3	13.0	7.9
Chemic.	5.8	5.5	5.4	6.9	8.4	11.7	13.4	12.6	12.7	12.0
Light	9.1	9.9	10.0	8.2	10.3	9.6	9.3	7.8	8.0	5.7
Foods	3.1	6.1	4.0	1.2	3.7	5.9	8.9	8.3	5.8	7.1
Build.	13.8	13.9	14.3	14.6	14.8	14.3	15.0	8.6	8.8	3.9
Servi.	12.4	12.3	11.0	8.4	7.3	10.1	10.4	8.6	8.0	4.4
Total										
Energ.	24.7	26.2	24.8	23.7	21.3	19.6	18.9	17.4	16.9	18.6
Mach.	12.5	12.7	14.1	13.2	13.9	13.8	12.9	8.1	8.8	2.5
Chemic.	5.9	6.1	6.0	7.9	9.8	8.5	12.4	10.6	13.4	10.2
Light	10.6	10.5	10.3	8.5	10.3	9.4	9.3	4.4	4.8	1.8
Foods	8.0	6.8	6.9	8.5	9.9	6.9	8.0	9.2	8.6	6.3
Build.	14.2	13.5	13.4	14.1	13.7	13.5	14.4	7.6	8.0	4.0
Servi.	13.1	13.0	11.1	9.3	9.4	10.5	10.5	8.4	8.7	6.6

The number of firms in the first group was somewhat lower than in the
other two.

The share of loss making firms in rouble exports rose to over 40% in 1990
from a constant 37% between 1981 and 1986, and their shares in dollar

Table 9.16. *Subsidy-to-sales ratios for firms, by sectors, in the sample,* %, *1981–90*

	1981	1982	1983	1984	1985	1986	1987	1988	1989	1990
Rouble										
Energ.	49.6	47.9	50.3	52.5	52.2	54.2	59.4	60.5	10.9	14.3
Mach.	−2.7	−0.4	3.4	4.9	4.4	1.0	2.8	−1.2	−10.9	−8.2
Chemic.	28.8	23.5	21.3	21.1	20.8	8.7	6.0	−1.0	−12.5	−13.2
Light	24.2	21.7	23.1	27.9	29.6	28.7	36.1	27.4	21.7	22.7
Foods	16.8	16.2	17.4	24.9	29.2	30.8	33.5	37.1	45.0	49.6
Build.	0.4	−15.5	−5.1	1.4	13.4	2.6	13.1	−3.4	−16.7	−11.6
Servi.	12.3	12.9	11.4	11.8	11.7	8.6	6.9	7.2	5.5	10.4
Dollar										
Energ.	11.0	11.0	11.7	2.3	10.9	11.8	12.3	3.2	0.0	0.0
Mach.	13.8	7.4	6.8	4.3	6.5	5.5	9.3	2.7	1.9	1.9
Chemic.	9.1	7.5	5.8	2.4	6.5	5.6	7.1	0.4	1.3	1.3
Light	17.0	13.4	7.9	5.2	8.9	7.9	11.1	3.8	2.6	1.4
Foods	3.7	3.3	7.1	3.4	4.4	15.3	26.0	18.5	11.2	13.9
Build.	10.1	5.3	3.3	1.6	6.8	5.0	6.0	0.6	2.7	4.7
Servi.	14.0	11.1	10.2	5.9	8.5	8.9	8.9	5.0	4.2	2.1
Domestic										
Energ.	−4.6	−3.6	−1.7	−0.6	1.8	2.9	0.5	1.2	1.1	1.1
Mach.	3.2	2.9	3.2	2.2	3.7	4.4	2.0	5.0	8.7	7.6
Chemic.	−1.4	−0.8	−0.3	−0.7	1.0	2.3	1.2	−32.1	−34.9	−37.1
Light	−3.1	−2.9	−2.5	−3.1	−1.3	−0.5	−1.8	1.0	1.9	2.3
Foods	−10.9	−11.9	−10.4	−10.2	−8.5	−6.7	−7.1	−8.0	−10.2	−13.6
Build.	0.7	0.9	1.4	1.0	1.1	1.0	0.9	1.8	3.0	2.8
Servi.	6.3	4.4	3.2	2.0	3.1	4.5	3.1	11.4	11.2	11.9
Total										
Energ.	1.7	1.4	4.0	4.0	7.1	8.8	7.8	6.6	1.2	1.2
Mach.	3.0	2.5	3.7	3.4	4.3	3.4	3.2	2.7	2.1	3.1
Chemic.	1.5	1.5	1.9	1.3	3.3	3.2	2.6	−23.4	−24.6	−26.7
Light	3.1	2.4	2.4	2.7	4.8	5.0	5.9	4.7	4.2	3.5
Foods	−5.3	−5.9	−4.7	−4.2	−2.2	1.1	1.8	2.2	−0.1	−5.8
Build.	1.1	0.8	1.4	1.1	1.8	1.3	1.8	1.5	2.3	2.8
Servi.	8.6	7.0	5.9	4.6	5.9	6.1	4.8	9.5	9.0	9.4

exports fell to 16% from a 23% peak level (see table 9.17). The loss makers are more exposed to export markets, especially to the rouble markets. Rouble exports were a more important factor in the total sales of loss making firms than of profitable ones, the difference being at least 10

Table 9.17. *Export shares for firms, by profitability, in the sample, %,*
1981–90

	1981	1982	1983	1984	1985	1986	1987	1988	1989	1990
Rouble										
loss	37.2	37.6	36.9	37.6	37.3	36.6	38.8	41.2	40.3	40.6
low	23.7	22.2	20.9	20.5	20.5	19.5	20.3	21.3	21.3	20.7
high	39.1	40.1	42.2	41.9	42.2	43.9	40.9	37.5	38.4	38.7
Total	100.0	100.0	100.0	100.0	100.0	100.0	100.0	100.0	100.0	100.0
Dollar										
loss	23.0	22.1	21.9	20.0	17.8	19.6	18.6	18.2	18.1	16.3
low	23.3	23.6	22.0	21.8	20.3	23.1	24.1	25.6	25.7	26.3
high	53.7	54.3	56.1	58.1	61.8	57.3	57.2	56.2	56.2	57.4
Total	100.0	100.0	100.0	100.0	100.0	100.0	100.0	100.0	100.0	100.0

Table 9.18. *Sales shares of firms, by profitability, in the sample, %,*
1981–90, total sales of firms in a given group is 100

	1981	1982	1983	1984	1985	1986	1987	1988	1989	1990
Rouble										
loss	20.2	20.7	22.1	23.9	24.7	23.7	22.9	22.2	21.0	16.4
low	9.8	9.7	10.1	10.5	10.8	10.1	9.2	8.6	8.3	5.5
high	9.2	9.5	11.0	11.1	11.8	12.9	10.8	8.4	7.9	4.7
Dollar										
loss	13.7	12.5	13.0	13.6	12.1	12.0	12.5	15.6	17.8	21.2
low	10.6	10.6	10.5	11.9	11.0	11.3	12.4	16.6	18.9	22.6
high	13.8	13.4	14.3	16.5	17.7	15.9	17.2	20.2	21.7	22.4
Domestic										
loss	66.1	66.8	64.9	62.5	63.1	64.3	64.6	62.1	61.2	62.4
low	79.6	79.7	79.4	77.7	78.2	78.6	78.4	74.7	72.7	71.9
high	77.0	77.1	74.7	72.4	70.5	71.1	72.0	71.4	70.4	72.9

percentage points. Quite interestingly, there was no difference in the dollar
export shares (see table 9.18).

Firms which were loss makers in 1990 were not always the worst ones; in
the first four years they had even higher profitability than the firms which
belong to the group of the low-profit firms (based on their results in 1990),
and in the next four years the difference between these two groups was rather
small (see table 9.19). The high-profit firms always had the highest profit

Table 9.19. *Profit rate of sales for firms, by profitability, in the sample, %, 1981–90*

	1981	1982	1983	1984	1985	1986	1987	1988	1989	1990
Rouble										
loss	15.6	18.3	18.6	15.7	17.2	14.9	11.1	7.0	1.3	−10.3
low	10.9	10.2	11.0	10.0	11.4	11.7	11.4	−1.7	−7.9	−19.1
high	4.6	4.9	3.4	4.0	7.2	4.9	3.1	−4.6	−16.2	−27.8
Dollar										
loss	15.8	14.4	17.7	14.7	19.3	17.2	17.9	13.7	14.0	7.7
low	7.7	4.2	0.3	−1.6	1.3	1.4	5.2	3.8	9.5	2.3
high	18.0	14.1	14.4	18.0	17.0	4.1	12.5	14.5	20.4	12.9
Domestic										
loss	12.8	12.5	10.9	7.9	4.8	6.4	6.2	3.8	5.3	−2.1
low	9.9	10.5	10.7	10.1	11.1	11.7	11.9	9.3	8.8	7.4
high	14.9	16.2	15.7	15.8	16.2	18.2	18.2	17.0	17.3	19.1
Total										
loss	13.7	13.9	13.5	10.7	9.7	9.7	8.9	6.0	6.0	−1.4
low	9.8	9.8	9.6	8.7	10.0	10.5	10.9	7.3	7.6	4.7
high	14.1	14.5	13.8	14.5	15.0	13.8	15.2	14.0	14.9	14.8

rate. Contrary to what could be expected from the previous paragraph, profit differences can explained by profit differences in domestic sales. The profitability of rouble exports was always the highest for the loss makers and the lowest for the high-profit firms. Moreover, the loss makers exported to the dollar markets at higher profitability than the low-profit firms.

Subsidies could not explain the profitability differences, indeed, the higher (lower) the profit, the lower (higher) the subsidy. This was mainly due to the subsidisation of domestic sales (see table 9.20). Export subsidies showed a totally different picture as the firms with higher profitability were given higher subsidies, but the difference was far more important in the rouble exports than in the dollar exports.

Econometric estimations

This section presents the results of an empirical econometric analysis aimed at identifying the explanatory factors of trade reorientation at the micro-level.

The first assumption made throughout the analysis is that there was no demand constraint on the dollar exports of Hungarian firms. This is of course a rather strict assumption, since there were, and still are, certain

Table 9.20. *Subsidy-to-sales ratios for firms, by profitability, in the sample, %, 1981–90*

	1981	1982	1983	1984	1985	1986	1987	1988	1989	1990
Rouble										
loss	−0.3	2.0	6.1	7.4	7.9	4.2	5.8	4.1	−5.2	−2.5
low	13.9	12.0	12.3	15.4	15.6	16.8	21.8	13.6	2.8	5.4
high	24.3	22.0	20.9	22.0	22.1	19.4	20.5	21.9	10.2	10.7
Dollar										
loss	13.0	9.8	10.6	4.0	9.5	11.4	12.0	6.0	1.7	0.8
low	13.8	10.3	9.1	4.2	8.7	8.5	11.0	3.4	2.7	2.1
high	9.6	7.9	7.6	3.7	6.6	8.2	10.3	5.0	3.1	2.2
Domestic										
loss	10.9	8.8	7.6	6.3	7.2	7.2	6.1	9.4	11.7	12.6
low	−0.3	−0.3	−0.4	−0.6	1.2	1.6	0.5	2.1	2.4	3.6
high	−5.5	−5.1	−3.6	−3.6	−1.9	0.1	−1.9	−12.8	−13.4	−16.0
Total										
loss	9.1	7.6	7.6	6.3	7.6	7.0	6.8	7.7	6.9	8.1
low	2.9	2.2	2.1	1.9	3.8	4.2	4.3	3.4	2.5	3.3
high	0.4	0.1	1.5	1.2	3.2	4.4	3.3	−4.9	−7.2	−9.9

products which have to face contingent regulations on entering EC markets, but there is no enterprise-level information available to deal with this matter.

It is also assumed that these firms are not irresponsive, inward-oriented, centrally commanded economic agents; a certain degree of cost-sensitiveness and market-orientedness is assumed to be already present in their reaction. That is the reason why a positive supply response to changes in subsidies, in prices, and in profitability is expected. The analysis does not intend to investigate the degree of profit-orientedness, or to test the eventual shift from wage-maximisation to profit-maximisation. Our assumption is confined to the supply responsiveness, which is assumed to be present and increasing. This type of analysis is possible, since in Hungary during the 1980s the possibility of influencing central regulation to gain advantageous discretionary treatment was significantly reduced.

It is widely known that exporting to rouble countries was advantageous in many respects: instantaneous payment was guaranteed by the Hungarian government; very loose delivery conditions; no marketing and servicing costs; positive economies of scale effect. The long-term cost of low technical and quality standards were offset by the short-term positive effects. Enterprises exerted constant pressure on the government to increase annual rouble export quotas as they always used up their full allowance. Either due to decreasing willingness, or to a constraint on raw material production capacity in the former Soviet Union, towards the end of the 1980s the Hungarian government had to adjust the export quotas to the expected value of imports, since no mechanism was available to convert the 'transferable' rouble trade surplus into hard currency or into hard products. The decreasing rouble export quotas set by the Hungarian government reduced demand at the enterprise level, so that rouble export demand was almost always equal to supply. In the short run falling demand may have effects on inventory accumulation of finished goods, on domestic sales or on dollar exports. In this analysis this latter will be quantified; the effect of changing domestic demand on dollar exports is not investigated.

Trade reorientation means a growing share of dollar trade at the expense of rouble trade. This can be represented by the annual change in the share of dollar exports in total sales, which is why, in our estimation, the dependent variable is the change in the share of dollar export volume in total sales volume. Our aim is to quantify its relationship with other variables. Trade reorientation may take place at different rates across countries or time periods. At this stage no information is available to assess the extent, the speed and the structure of the Hungarian trade reorientation. Economic common sense dictates that the intensity of trade reorientation might have changed during the 1980s (see Blahó, 1992).

Four groups of explanatory variables will be distinguished: subsidies, costs, prices and demand. Two types of demand variable were defined: the first is a proxy variable which tries to capture the effect of demand through the behaviour of the inventory of finished goods; the second type is simply rouble exports as described above. The expected effects of prices and subsidies are positive, those of cost and demand variables are negative, and the higher the inventory of finished goods and/or rouble export demand, the lower the dollar export supply.

It is supposed that trade reorientation may be influenced by additional factors, such as productivity level, capacity utilisation, the real wage, the technical level, and the level of inventories of intermediate inputs. The estimation method[7] used the information provided by these variables. It was tested to see whether parameters were stable over time and, if a parameter was unstable, then a different time period was chosen for the same variable.

The results

This chapter presents only the final specification. According to these results the change in share of dollar exports was significantly influenced by the change of its relative profitability, by the change of dollar export subsidy, by the change of relative dollar export price, and directly by the change of rouble export demand. According to the Wald test these parameters are jointly significantly different from zero. Neither the second-order serial correlation test, nor the Sargan test indicate misspecification.[8]

Variables[9]	Coefficient[10]	t-stat
Dependent		
$SALE		
Explanatory		
$SALE(–1)	0.271492	11.5
$SALE(–2)	– 0.106688	– 8.2
$SUB(89-90)	0.083081	3.0
$COST(84–88)	– 0.021105	– 22.8
$COST(-2)	– 0.006087	– 6.6
$PRICE(-1)	0.041086	2.2
RSALE(85)	0.043537	1.9
RSALE(86–87)	– 0.059583	– 3.2
RSALE(89)	– 0.051836	– 1.9

Test for second-order serial correlation: 0.416 [212]
Wald test of joint significance: 779.7 [9]
Sargan test: 84.0 [64]

$SALE	(dollar export sales/dollar export prices[11])/(total sales/total sales prices)
$SUB	dollar export subsidies/dollar export sales
$COST	(dollar export costs/dollar export sales)/(total costs/total sales)
$PRICE	dollar export price/total sales prices
RSALE	(rouble export sales/rouble export prices)/(total sales/total sales prices)

The specification includes two lagged values of the dependent variables. No higher orders of lags showed significant effect. The 2-digit figures in parentheses refer to the period in which the explanatory variable was taken into account. For the remaining years it was set to zero.

The subsidy had impact only in the last two years, as in earlier years a major part of the subsidies was a flat rate over the exchange rate. In that period the preferred economic policy was this type of export incentive rather than devaluation.[12] The subsidy variable was not significant either for the whole estimation period, or for the first period of time, that is, until 1987. It seems to contradict the macroeconometric estimations presented in Halpern and Székely (1992), but direct comparison may be misleading, since the dollar export subsidy was always higher for the irregular exporter firms than for the firms in the sample (see tables 9.3 and 9.8) and thus the dollar export subsidy of the irregular exporters might have been a significant explanatory variable even before the period concerned. These results show that the reduction of subsidies was accompanied by firm-specific differentiation.[13]

The equation has two cost variables, the first one effective between 1984 and 1988 only, and the two-year lagged variable effective for the whole estimation period. Several attempts were made to specify the cost effect in the trade reorientation period, but they were not successful. Significant cost adjustment took place during the period of slow trade reorientation, and when this process was accelerating, this cost adjustment disappeared. The estimated positive coefficients for 1989–90 were not significant in any specification. The available information was not sufficient to specify the causes of this disappearence of the cost adjustment during the intensified trade reorientation.

The rouble export demand significantly influenced the dollar exports in four years. In three of these four years the sign of the parameters conforms to expectation. In 1985 simultaneous trade increase took place, and no direct trade reorientation effect was quantified.

In every specification time dummies were added. They were always jointly significant explanatory variables; their parameter was rather high in 1990 and in 1988, showing that time-specific effects were also important and were not represented by other explanatory variables.

In the preceding part of the chapter the analysis was differentiated according to sectoral, profit and asset-size characteristics. Now these effects can be taken into account in the equation. Appropriate dummy variables were introduced to capture this effect. Only the services sector had a significantly positive parameter; no other sector, profit, nor asset-size groups obtained significant parameters. It means that either the specific effect does not take this form, or that the classification used is not able to capture it.

Summary and conclusion

The collapse of CMEA dramatically changed the foreign trade environment for the national economies of member states and for their individual firms. In the Hungarian case this trade reorientation had already begun earlier, and unambiguous results have been achieved. The responsiveness of firms to changing foreign market conditions has been improving. These improvements were, however, not enough to transform the whole economy from a modified centrally planned one to a market economy.

In 1990 the share of the domestic market in total sales increased, reversing the previous trend towards opening up the Hungarian economy. The rise in hard-currency exports could not counterbalance the withdrawal from CMEA markets. As a matter of fact, this fall in exports was mainly the consequence of a radical direct intervention by the government which introduced strict export licensing on rouble markets, because politically influenced economic regulators were not able to give satisfactory results. A drastic revaluation of the currency against the transferable rouble (the payments unit of CMEA) was out of the question; a radical change in payment conditions would have required tedious multilateral negotiations.

Overall economic performance showed the normal symptoms of a recession: rising inflation, unemployment, falling output and a growing budget deficit. The only areas where results outperformed the official forecast was dollar trade and the current account balance. This chapter has tried to reveal the role of the cost adjustment, the reaction of firms to changes in export subsidies and the demand-driven processes in the trade reorientation which proved to be smoother than expected. Our database did not make it possible to examine the effect of foreign prices at the level of individual firms or industries. Our analysis was unable to separate out the effect of the exchange rate, given that exchange rate devaluation had a uniform impact on firms; only the compound effect of foreign prices and exchange rate was shown. It is undeniable that, in 1987–9, dollar exports enjoyed a higher price rise than domestic and rouble export markets, but in 1990 the domestic market price increase was 26.6% while that of dollar exports was only 14.1%. This means that in 1990 other factors – cost, subsidy and demand – played a considerable role.

Export-oriented firms rapidly increased their share of dollar export sales, but it was not enough to compensate for the collapse of the rouble exports; the share of the domestic sales increased in 1990. Smaller firms were more exposed to the collapse of the CMEA since they depended heavily on rouble exports. The share of loss makers increased in rouble exports, but the loss suffered on domestic markets was blamed for this.

The regular exporters had higher profitability than the average, but this difference was diminishing as there were higher profits on domestic markets. Their average subsidy was generally lower than for the irregular exporters, so subsidy differences did not explain profit differences.

Econometric estimations showed the presence of cost adjustment in trade reorientation up to 1987. In the period of more intensive trade reorientation this cost adjustment was dissipated. During the last two years of the estimation period export subsidies played an active role, showing that the reduction of the subsidies does not necessarily mean that their effect will disappear. Relative dollar prices lagged by one year always turned out to be a significant explanatory variable of trade reorientation in the whole period. The direct impact of the reduction of rouble exports on dollar exports was important only in 1986–7 and 1989.

Notes

The research has benefited from financial support from the Hungarian research fund OTKA on Foreign Trade Strategy, KOPINT-DATORG and from the ACE 'Industrial Restructuring Trade Reorientation and East–West Integration' programme of the Economic Transformation in Eastern Europe project. Earlier results were published in Halpern (1991). The first version of this chapter has been presented at seminars in London, Cambridge and Prague organised by CEPR, DAE of the University of Cambridge, and by the Institute for Forecasting, respectively. Comments and criticisms of the participants are gratefully acknowledged, but any responsibility belongs to the author.

1 Dollars will be used to denote trade flows settled in convertible currencies carried on with Eastern or Western countries. The rouble trade covers the trade relations with CMEA countries paid in the so-called transferable rouble.

2 The link between the devaluation and the export subsidy has been analysed at the macro-level by Halpern (1989) and a theoretical and micro-analysis was given in Halpern (1991).

3 The dollar exports were US \$6.3bn in 1990 compared to US \$6.4bn in 1989 at current dollar prices according to the HNB *Report*. According to other sources (Ministry of Finance) dollar exports grew by 12% at constant domestic prices. The HNB's trade data are based on payments statistics which may be different from data obtained from customs statistics. Imported leased equipment, the inflow of foreign direct investment in kind and sub-contracting activities explain the difference.

4 Firms began to adapt to these rules by dropping the least profitable products from their export bundle, as the easiest way to increase their export profitability leading to a fall in export volume at the macro-level. The rules were supplemented with a constraint on export volume; a scale was introduced, which allowed 100% adjustment to changes in dollar export profitability above a certain export volume increase.

5 For the period 1985–90 in the computations it was assumed that the overheads were proportional to the direct costs in each sales direction. Our other assumption – constant ratio of overheads to sales – gave similar results.

6 Detailed insights about the trade reorientation for the whole corporate sector by branches for 1988–90 was given in Fölsz and Valentinyi (1991).

7 The estimation method is the generalised method of moments (GMM). The description is given in Arellano and Bond (1988), and detailed estimation results can be obtained from the author on request.

8 The description of the test statistics and specification procedure is given in Arellano and Bond (1988).

9 The variables were used in their first-difference form with the exception of those which were used only as instruments. It is supposed that the only-instrument variables impact the dependent variable by their level.

10 The magnitude of the coefficients cannot be compared with each other due to the linear specification. The most important descriptive statistics of the variables can be obtained from the author on request.

11 Prices always mean price indices, real variables are understood as variables at constant prices of the base year of price indices. The other variables are measured in national currency (HUF).

12 A detailed description of the exchange rate policy of the early 1980s can be found in Oblath (1988).

13 Another dollar export subsidy variable was also defined. The computations with the variable of dollar subsidy minus overall subsidy showed insignificant subsidy effect.

References

Arellano, M. and Bond, S., 1988. 'Dynamic panel data estimation using DPD – a guide for users', Institute for Fiscal Studies, 21

Blahó, A., 1992. 'Foreign trade and structural change in Hungary', 27 and appendix, mimeo

Fölsz, A. and Valentinyi, Á., 1991. 'Some characteristics of Hungarian export performance, 1988–90', Budapest 51, mimeo

Halpern, L., 1989. 'Effects of devaluation in a macroeconometric model for Hungary', *Acta Oeconomica*, 41, 293–312

1991. 'The effect of cost and subsidy on exports in the eighties', *Kulgazdaság* (Budapest), 35(7), 27–48 (in Hungarian)

1992. 'The effect of costs and subsidies on trade reorientation in Hungary, 1981–90', *Structural Change and Economic Dynamics*, 3(1)

Halpern, L. and Székely, I. P., 1992. 'Export supply and import demand in Hungary (An econometric analysis for 1968–1989)', *CEPR Discussion Paper*, 620, London: CEPR, 18

Oblath, G., 1988. 'Exchange rate policy in the reform package', *Acta Oeconomica*, 39(1–2), 81–93

OECD, 1991. *OECD Economic Surveys: Hungary 1991*, Paris: OECD, 204

10 Hardening of the budget constraint for Polish manufacturing enterprises, 1991–3

Marek Belka and Stefan Krajewski

Introduction

Macroeconomic policy has played, and is to some extent still playing, a dominant role in the process of economic transformation in Poland. Thanks to its consistency, inflation has been curtailed, convertibility of the Polish currency has been introduced and maintained, shortages eliminated and, most important, the whole philosophy of doing business has been changed. At the same time, several social and economic problems have appeared, some of which are linked to an insufficiently fast rate of adjustment at the microeconomic level. This concerns particularly the sector of state enterprises, whose behaviour may be described as 'non-capitalist', i.e. aimed at maximising the wage fund at the cost of development goals.[1] In fact, it is not difficult to quote spectacular examples of such behaviour by state firms.

One of the obvious prerequisites for setting in motion the process of deeper enterprise adjustment is a hard budget constraint. It can theoretically be instituted in a CPE, but only under conditions of market competition, open economy and convertibility of currency can a rigorous macroeconomic policy bring about a sustained tendency towards cost rationalisation, innovation and the market orientation of enterprises.

A key question for the Polish economy in 1994 is whether firms (particularly state-owned ones) are exposed to hard, or at least hardening, budget constraints. To put it differently, can a typical Polish firm count on any external source of 'soft' financing, or can it count only on itself? The answer to this question is crucial for evaluating the character of economic growth, recorded in 1993–4. If growing production results from, or is supported by, a changing production profile, higher quality of goods, new outlets, improved distribution, cost saving, including labour adjustment, investment, improved financial management, etc. then it acquires a more solid, self-sustained character. However, if it boils down to reproducing the

301

old, obsolete production patterns, financed by all sorts of hidden or open subsidies, then that growth is nothing more than a temporary statistical phenomenon, only making things worse in the longer run. A view sometimes expressed in Poland is that growing tax arrears and the so-called 'payment jams', resulting from the accumulating mutual claims and liabilities of enterprises and the allocative inefficiency of the still predominantly state-owned commercial banks, indicate that growing industrial output is at worst highly suspect, at best entirely due to the spontaneous expansion of the private sector.

It is not the purpose of this chapter to evaluate the situation in the state enterprise sector, although we have already signalled that widespread positive adjustments took place as early as mid-1992.[2] Here, we should like to take a closer look at the scale and nature of the phenomena that may dilute the consistent macroeconomic policy: tax arrears, interenterprise credit and 'soft' bank credit. We shall be concentrating on manufacturing industry, and thus can use not only the generally available macroeconomic statistical information provided by the Central Statistical Office (GUS) but also the firm-level data collected in our empirical research.

Banks and the hardening of the micro-budget constraint

In imposing financial discipline on firms, it is important that banks have an incentive to lend to the most efficient firms and to force the inefficient ones into liquidation. Through this process banks themselves will earn a return on their capital; productivity will be increased; the economy will be restructured; and exports will flow from sectors with an international competitive advantage.

Among the standard charges made against Polish commercial banks in the first two or three years of the transition were: (a) a tendency to extend credit 'automatically' to traditional customers – state firms,[3] and (b) a lack of capability to evaluate properly the viability of submitted projects and the financial standing of clients. More recently, however, banks stand accused of excessive caution, reluctance to take risks, formalism and red tape. The result of these two (contradictory) tendencies is, according to critics, the emergence of a significant portfolio of bad, uncollectable loans combined with inadequate credit for sound, viable firms – in a word, a serious allocative failure.

It is not our purpose here to inquire into the reasons for this situation, although we generally agree with the above criticisms: a major part of the increase in bank credit volume for enterprises is absorbed by the need to continue servicing old customers ('rolling-over' past credits, capitalisation of interest charges), leaving only what then remains for an active credit

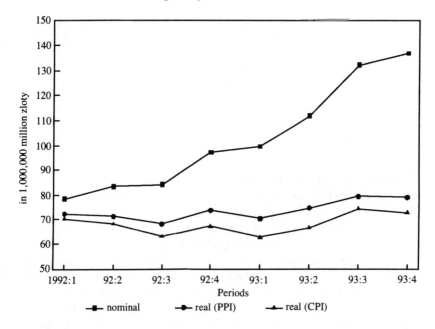

Figure 10.1 Bank credit, manufacturing industry, 1992–3

policy. Meanwhile, potentially attractive clients avoid taking credit, pointing to high real interest rates. The whole deadlock in bank credit for enterprises is well reflected in the interest rate differential of up to 20 percentage points between the rates for best and below-standard customers.

An interesting issue for us here is the impact of bank credit dynamics on the process of hardening of the micro-budget constraint.

In the first place, real bank credit for manufacturing industry (as well as for all industry and the whole enterprise sector) in 1992–3 has been fairly stable and generally low. Figure 10.1 shows that a temporary tendency to grow appeared between March and September 1993, only to be reversed later that year. Throughout the whole two-year period real bank credit grew by just a few percent, but industrial output and sales increased similarly. Nominal credit in relation to sales in current prices remained practically unchanged over the period 1991–3 (table 10.1) and fluctuated at 1–1.5 monthly sales, a level very low by international standards. Certainly, there is nothing that indicates a widespread soft financing of enterprises by banks.

Secondly, it seems likely that a qualitative change in bank behaviour from relative ease to great caution took place in approximately 1991/2. To

Table 10.1. *Ratio of bank credit (end of period) to nominal monthly sales (average for the quarter), Polish manufacturing industry, 1991–3*

Period	91:1	91:2	91:3	91:4	92:1	92:2	92:3	92:4	93:1	93:2	93:3	93:4
Bank credit-to-sales	0.94	1.16	1.12	1.23	1.32	1.25	1.18	1.17	1.22	1.21	1.48	1.34

Source: GUS data.

a certain extent this may be inferred from the macroeconomic data (table 10.1), as the bank credit-to-sales ratio was growing until the end of the first quarter of 1992, to fall later to an almost fixed level of 1.17–1.25. This is confirmed by both firm-level statistical data and by the opinions expressed by managers during an empirical study conducted at that time.

In a detailed study of 75 large SOEs from the manufacturing sector, covering the first two and a half years of transition up to mid-1992, comparisons were made between AAA (consistently profit making) and A (consistently loss making) firms to establish differences in various aspects of their behaviour.[4] The study shows that, after an initial moderation in early 1990, bank credit rose both for AAA and A enterprises, but much more for the latter group. Looking at it in nominal terms, in the 21 months from March 1990 to December 1991, loans to A firms rose by 214% compared to 92% for loans to AAA firms. This coincided with a rapid accumulation of finished goods inventories in A firms, indicating that working capital credit was indeed a factor softening their budget constraint. The period from December 1991 to June 1992 is notable. Working capital loans rose only slightly for AAA firms, but fell for A firms, suggesting that the commercialisation in late 1991 of 9 banks spun off from the National Bank of Poland and the appointment of Supervisory Boards, combined with the clearer view of privatisation, was having the desired effect. In sum, the data confirmed the initial laxity of bank credit. The big relative increase of loans to A firms did not support a higher level of activity, but was the result of banks rolling over interest payments as they fell due, and financing growing inventory stocks.

The opinions expressed by the managers in a 'qualitative' questionnaire accompanying the statistical analysis reinforce some of the above findings. Managers unanimously reported radically changed bank behaviour. As they described it, in 1990, banks acted like 'cashiers' eager to dole out money. By 1992 banks were behaving more like 'partners' with an equity stake in the company and had become extremely cautious. Based on a 0–5 point scale ranking, the AAA managers said that their firms experienced the same ease in getting loans over the period of three years under analysis (3.0, 2.8 and 3.2), while there was a sharp change for A firms in 1992 (3.2, 2.0 and 1.2). An improvement in the credit assessment practices of banks can also be inferred from the fact that of the 25 enterprises denied credit in 1991–2, 21 were As and only 4 were AAAs. The reason typically given was the general condition of the firm rather than the non-viability of the project for which the funds were sought, which may point to a continuing weakness in project evaluation.

Thirdly, however, there are reasons for maintaining that improper bank credit allocation patterns continue, with banks to a large extent financing loss making enterprises. In the study referred to above it was found that the role of working capital credit in financing the current activity of lossmaking firms (A firms) rose between March 1990 and June 1992 almost threefold, but for AAA firms it remained unchanged.[5]

Correlation of the bank credit-to-sales ratio, a measure of banks' involvement in company's financing, and their gross profitability was for the manufacturing sector in 1991–3 – as expected – very low and statistically insignificant. Moreover, for the whole three-year period and for 1991 and 1993 it was negative; lower profitability was connected with higher credit involvement.[6]

The above observations can be summarised as follows: real bank credit for enterprises remains under strict control in Poland; this is reflected not only in the general stance of macroeconomic policy but also in the banks' very cautious credit policy. Simultaneously, banks continue financing firms that (for many reasons) would not have a chance of getting credit were they not old customers of the banks. In many (maybe in most) of those 'inherited' cases, either credit volume does not change in nominal terms, or just the unpaid interest is being capitalised. So although there is no net cash inflow over time, the credit pipeline keeps embattled enterprises afloat. There are reasons to believe that big SOEs dominate in this group of companies, in fact crowding-out the existing credit capacities from the viable – both private and state – entities.

Interenterprise credit

There is a widespread view that interenterprise credit or, more precisely, accumulated overdue payables and receivables (known in Poland as 'payment jams') played, and are still playing, a significant role in substituting bank loans, thus diluting the effects of a restrictive macro-economic policy. Moreover, there has been a suspicion that loss making firms became net borrowers on this peculiar market, which boils down to

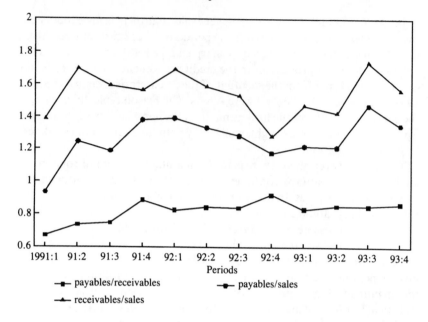

Figure 10.2   Interenterprise credit, manufacturing industry, 1991–3

better firms financing their unviable competitors. This amounts to another allocative failure.

A closer look at the data reveals a picture remote from the dramatic announcements of both banks and enterprises. The real value of accumulated accounts payable and accounts receivable is stable and low by international standards (figure 10.2).

Both firms' payables and receivables are at a level, respectively, of 1.2 and 1.5–1.6 of monthly sales and remained stable over the last years. Let us note that the volume of interindustry credit in relation to industry's sales is about the same as in Great Britain and much lower than in the Czech Republic. Moreover, the nominal value of this debt, as recorded in the official statistics (ca US$8.2 bn of payables and ca US$7.3 bn of receivables) comprise both regular and overdue accounts. In a survey of 200 manufacturing firms of different ownership status, 43–44% of such credit was classified as regular, which reduces the problem of payment arrears to a manageable level of less than one month's sales.[7]

Table 10.2 shows that firms of different ownership status display a different pattern as far as the structure of such credit is concerned. State firms (both traditional and commercialised) have a considerable number of

Table 10.2. *Structure of interenterprise debt (based on 200 manufacturing firms in late 1993), %*

Accounts payable

	Regular	1–3 months overdue	3–12 months overdue	Over 1 year overdue
SOEs	32.41	16.54	20.59	30.46
Commercialised				
SOEs	39.16	15.88	14.39	30.57
Privatised	79.90	12.04	6.15	1.91
Private	60.76	30.42	8.23	0.59
200	42.80	16.26	15.84	25.10

Accounts receivable

	Regular	1–3 months overdue	3–12 months overdue	Over 1 year overdue
SOEs	27.59	27.68	18.52	26.21
Commercialised				
SOEs	53.66	16.32	16.22	13.79
Privatised	61.08	19.68	9.51	9.73
Private	61.08	30.08	5.21	3.63
200	44.51	22.07	15.59	17.82

liabilities that are more than 3 months old, with the same occurring with receivables. In contrast, privatised and private firms have very little payment arrears in this category. This suggests that, although the overall scale of interenterprise debt is under control, a disproportionate part of it is probably concentrated in a minority of state firms, and a difficult situation is then projected on to the whole enterprise sector in Poland.

The next interesting issue is the dynamics of the ratio payables-to-receivables, which indicates 'who is financing whom' by means of interindustry credit. For the whole manufacturing industry this ratio grew from a low level throughout 1990 and early 1991 to reach a level of 0.8–0.9 in late 1991, where it still remains. This reflects the fact that, in the early phases of the transition, industry as a whole became a net creditor to commercial firms; this has partially changed since manufacturing industry's financial situation deteriorated in 1991. However, as the above ratio is

Table 10.3. *Ratio of net interenterprise lending to monthly sales, %
1990:3–1992:6*

	Mar 90	Sept 90	Mar 91	Sept 91	Mar 92	Jun 92
AAA	27.81	28.15	23.74	24.37	20.66	17.77
A	28.71	33.79	15.39	7.6	−3.73	−10.75

Note: Net interenterprise lending was calculated by aggregating accounts receivable minus accounts payable for firms of similar financial performance.
Source: Survey of 75 big manufacturing SOEs.

still under 1.0, manufacturing firms remain net lenders to the rest of the economy.

More significant would be to establish a link between the payables-to-receivables ratio and profitability. Aggregate data, both for manufacturing as a whole and individual branches, are not an appropriate basis for assessing this problem. Firm-level data could provide some information on whether interindustry credit serves to finance loss making firms, thus diluting their hard-budget constraint. More refined econometric analysis could also shed some light on whether such credit is a substitute for bank loans. Both issues seem to remain open and should be investigated on the basis of firm surveys rather than macroeconomic data.

At this moment we are able to quote only the rather outdated results from the survey of 75 large manufacturing SOEs mentioned previously. For the first $2\frac{1}{2}$ years of transition the following pattern could be observed: consistently profitable firms (AAA) remained net lenders, although at diminishing scale, whereas loss makers (A firms) became net borrowers (see table 10.3). This suggests that interindustry credit may have perversely influenced the situation of firms, helping loss makers to survive at the expense of their more profitable partners. It is doubtful, however, whether this trend continued later on, as the aggregate volume of such credit stabilised and firms reported more and more rigorous measures against unreliable customers. Just to illustrate the mood among the managers, 97 out of 200 who were interviewed in 1993 reported always demanding advance payments from new customers, 83 frequently demanding pre-payments even from old customers, suspending deliveries (166 cases), charging penalty interest (159 cases), using informal methods (165 cases) and more frequently resorting to legal measures (148 cases). All this leads us to conclude that it is now much harder for an average firm to obtain deliveries and not pay for them on time. It remains an open question what impact the wave of bank conciliatory procedures will have on the relations between firms involved as creditors and borrowers.

Table 10.4. *Ratio of tax arrears to taxes due, %, 1990–2*

	1990	1991	199
AAA	1.8	3.3	3.7
A	5.0	42.7	50.8

Source: Survey of 75 manufacturing SOEs – own computations.

Tax arrears

It is in the area of tax arrears that the least change is visible. Not only has the dividend criterion not been enforced (firms have found all sort of ways of persuading local tax chambers that deferments beyond the stipulated three months for triggering bankruptcy were justified), but any large-scale bankruptcy is not credible both for socio-political reasons and because of limited court capacity.

Aggregate tax arrears in December 1993 were estimated at 41.3 trillion zloty (without penalty interest), which was 44.9% more than at the end of 1992 in nominal terms and over 7% more in real terms. Almost 56% were overdue tax payments from previous years, and 60% of new arrears came from the unpaid 'popiwek'[8] obligations. To evaluate the above from the point of view of micro-budget constraints one needs more detailed information on the distribution of tax arrears among different types of enterprise (size, ownership status, profitability) and not only – what is usually available in GUS statistics – among types of unpaid taxes.

Firm-level data that we have collected in our empirical research broadly confirm the general concern expressed about this unresolved question. In the study of 75 large SOEs a clear picture of a widening gap in this respect between AAA and A firms emerges (table 10.4). One can say that loss making firms survived 1991 at the cost of the budget, with no clear prospect of how they could even partially repay the ensuing obligations. Notably, profit making firms recorded almost no overdue tax obligations.

In the more recent study of 200 firms, a striking difference in the pattern of tax arrears between state-owned, privatised and private firms was observed (table 10.5).

Interestingly, private firms have very few old tax arrears, which may suggest greater tax discipline on their part and higher efficiency of the exit mechanism for these firms. Privatised firms are almost 'clean', which reflects the fact that state companies in good economic condition are privatised first. State firms, particularly traditional SOEs, have large unpaid tax obligations both from the distant and more recent past. This

Table 10.5. *'Time structure' of tax arrears, %, 1993*

	Regular	1–3 months overdue	3–12 months overdue	Over 1 year overdue
SOEs	16.74	9.84	26.34	47.07
Commercialised SOEs	60.22	5.75	16.66	17.37
Privatised	89.81	1.01	6.87	2.31
Private	71.64	21.39	6.97	0.00
200	43.02	7.26	20.04	29.67

indicates that a number of state firms continued to accumulate tax arrears throughout the whole period of transition.

To sum up, relations with the state remain the main factor softening the budget constraint of Polish enterprises, particularly state-owned ones. One should remember however, that firms' behaviour in this respect is extremely diverse, which reflects their different financial situation, size and bargaining power.[9] Also, tax arrears do not represent any cash inflow to the enterprises in question, so their potential softening effect is smaller than that of new bank credit or interindustry credit.

Concluding remarks

A comprehensive analysis of the budget constraint on enterprises should include an in-depth discussion of the institutional and political factors. Our intention in this chapter is more modest. Using both macroeconomic statistics and firm-level data from empirical research based on surveys we wished to give a general picture of the problem, possibly suggesting topics for further investigation.

Our main conclusions are the following:

(i) Average manufacturing enterprises (including SOEs) operate now under conditions of significantly hardened budget constraints; an important change took place in 1991–2, when banks became much more cautious and firms themselves improved their management of claims and liabilities.

(ii) The issue of interenterprise debt seems to be overstated; the volume of interindustry credit is low and stable.

(iii) Banks ceased to be a source of easy credit, although they remain stuck with refinancing many of their traditional customers. A serious allocative failure thus results from the current state of Polish commercial banking.

(iv) Tax arrears are the main leak in the micro-budget constraint; unpaid taxes are not additional cash for firms, but they exert a perverse allocative efficiency effect on the economy, putting firms with greater bargaining power into a privileged position.

 (v) Both the financial situation and behaviour of state enterprises become more and more differentiated, with a majority adapting to the exigencies of the market economy and an important (highly visible and vocal) minority forming a 'political' or 'politicised' sector demanding all sorts of special treatment – outright subsidies, tariffs, tax concessions, sectoral industrial policy, etc.

Notes

This paper was presented at the conference 'Experience of Economic Transformation in Central Europe: Lessons for the Future' organised by the Polish Economic Association and PHARE in Warsaw, 14–16 April 1994.

1 An interesting theoretical analysis of the 'non-capitalist' behaviour of state firms can be found in: Józefiak (1993).

2 For the results of a survey of 75 big manufacturing SOEs see Pinto, Belka and Krajewski (1993), pp. 213–70.

3 Begg and Portes (1992) point to the fact that rational banks would not accelerate the bankruptcy of their clients, once they had inherited them. Let us observe also, that, at least in 1990, the financial results of enterprises looked healthy and it would have taken an expertise, absent in the banks at that time, to discover their transitory, inflationary nature.

4 See Pinto *et al.* 1993.

5 See Pinto *et al.* (1993), p. 230. The role of working capital credit in financing the current activity of a firm was measured by the ratio of credit volume at the end of a quarter to the average level of operating costs in that quarter.

6 Own computations on the basis of GUS data.

7 The survey covers 80 traditional SOEs, 40 commercialised state firms, 40 privatised enterprises and 40 private firms and is a part of a World Bank-sponsored comparative study of microeconomic adjustment in Poland, Hungary and the Czech republic, headed by I. J.Singh, Alan Gelb, Saul Estrin and Mark Schaffer.

8 'Popiwek' is a colloquial name for the tax on excessive wage growth in state enterprises.

9 One of main findings of a recent study of the Polish enterprise sector shows that about 10% of all companies (in terms of sales) accumulated about 90% of the

existing debts to banks, government and other enterprises. This group of enterprises, forming effectively a 'black hole' of the economy 'behave distinctly differently from the rest of the economy'; see Gomulka (1993).

References

Begg, D. and Portes, R., 1992. 'Enterprise debt and economic transformation: financial restucturing of the state sector in central and eastern Europe', *CEPR Discussion Paper*, 695, London

Gomulka, S., 1993. 'The financial situation of Polish enterprises 1992–1993 and its impact on monetary and fiscal policies', *Studies and Analyses*, 6, CASE Foundation, Warsaw

Józefiak, C., 1993. 'Rachunek mikroekonomiczny a decyzje przedsiebiorstw w okresie transformacji' (Microeconomic calculus and firms' decisions in the period of transformation), *Ekonomisata*, 4

Pinto, B., Belka, M. and Krajewski, S., 1993. 'Transforming state enterprises in Poland: evidence on adjustment by manufacturing firms', *Brooking Papers on Economic Activity* (Summer)

11 Industrial policy in the transition

Michael Landesmann and István Ábel

Introduction

Since the beginning of the dramatic recent wave of economic reforms in 1989, it has been difficult to hold a rational economic discussion about the specific role which industrial policy can play in the current context of the transformation in Eastern Europe. The notion of industrial policy was too highly charged with associations of past planning experiences in communist countries; hence it was seen as an anathema in any transition towards a Western-style market economy. In this atmosphere, people overlooked the fact that industrial policies form an integral part of the set of policy instruments used by Western economies and that, more recently, economic theory has developed rigorous foundations for such policies. They also featured prominently in the experiences of countries which had embarked upon successful catching-up processes.

The structure of this chapter is as follows: the second section develops the particular setting in which industrial policies have to be conducted in the current context of Eastern European transformation. The third section discusses the fundamental 'stock-flow' problem of the transition. The fourth section takes a critical look at the relationship between macroeconomic policy and industrial restructuring. The fifth section makes the case for, and discusses the methods of, industrial policy in the transition. The sixth section emphasises the role of industrial policy in making the state itself more sensitive towards the demands of a market economy. The seventh section analyses the budgetary dilemma of conducting an 'active' industrial policy in the present conditions of Eastern Europe and discusses policies *vis-à-vis* large-scale state enterprises. The eighth section emphasises the role of export orientation for an industrial strategy. The ninth section discusses particular areas of industrial policy, and the final section summarises some of the main points of the discussion.

The setting for industrial policies in the transition

While in the West the case for industrial policies is made on the basis of what the market cannot achieve, due to externalities, economies of scale, information problems, or capital market imperfections (Grossman, 1990; Pearce and Sutton, 1985; Jacquemin, 1984), in the present context of the transformation in Central and Eastern Europe (CEE) the theoretical argument regarding industrial policies has to be widened. We are here dealing with a situation in which resources have in the past been allocated according to the principles of a command economy and not a market economy. The legacy of such an allocation process is that resources are stuck in allocation patterns which are not the outcome of market allocation processes at all. Hence, the question which has to be addressed is whether, and with what time horizon, resource reallocation will take place in a period in which markets are only gradually emerging, and behaviour by both private and public actors is only gradually responding to such markets. The case for industrial policies in such a period of transition is consequently not simply one based on market failure, but one based on the non-existence of markets or the only rudimentary existence of markets and market responses. In such conditions, the vital question is not whether the state should or should not intervene, but rather what are the types of state intervention which can increase the response rate of agents (firms, households, workers) to a newly emerging market environment and equip them with 'capabilities' allowing them to respond more flexibly to market signals? The most relevant actual rigidities industrial policy must tackle arise from the particular barriers to entry and exit encountered in the period of transition.[1]

In addition, the CEE economies are experiencing cosmic changes in trade orientation and a collapse of traditional markets which even in established Western market economies would lead to large-scale redundancy of capacities. In such circumstances, it is questionable whether any type of industrial organisation could respond sufficiently quickly to facilitate the necessary reorganisation if left to market reallocation alone. Furthermore, this trap slows down the emergence of markets and affects market behaviour in a way which further delays the already slow process of building up entrepreneurial capabilities. While price liberalisation and temporary macroeconomic stability can be achieved fairly rapidly, the institutional and legal framework of a sound market environment takes time, and requires long-term commitment to gradual changes.

It is important to point out that the types of industrial policy advocated in this chapter have nothing to do with the system of centralised planning which characterised CEE economies in the past; rather, industrial policies are an integral part of policy making in Western economies.[2] There are also clear theoretical foundations within Western economics for the pursuit of industrial policies (see, e.g., Grossman, 1990) and, furthermore, industrial policies have been an integrated and central feature of most successful catching-up processes in a wide range of countries.[3] In fact, we shall argue that an important function of industrial policies in the current context is to ensure that the state–administrative machinery becomes sensitive towards operating in an evolving market environment and develops policies designed to assist the development of a competitive Western-type market economy. Industrial policy, being the branch of economic policy most closely involved with enterprise activity, is as such conducive to the development by the state of microeconomic insights and of policies which support such activity. Drawing both on the experiences of the Western market economies and on developments in the theoretical literature, we emphasise not only the longer-run strategic importance of well-designed incentives in a changing environment, but also the very short-run difficulties which firms necessarily face in adjusting to an environment where the problems are aggravated by the *lack of market institutions*, let alone by considerations of market failure.[4] With the state deserting the traditional areas of industrial policy before the markets are able to replace part of its functions, market failures are in danger of dominating the scene.

The fundamental 'stock-flow' problem in the transition

The author strongly shares the view that Eastern European economies have to undergo a dramatic process of structural adjustment, given that past resource allocation was determined by the resource allocation criteria of a command economy, which was also relatively autarkic in its trade relationships with Western trading partners. The dispute about the nature of structural adjustment, then, is not about whether it has to take place but, first, the time horizon over which it could be achieved and, secondly, the way in which it might happen. In other words, how much 'destruction' should occur over what time period, how could a particular timetable with respect to the reallocation of resources be achieved, and how could a process of the building up of new capacities, fully viable in a liberalised environment, be initiated and accelerated? The analysis of the timing of an appropriate process of structural adjustment involves a comprehension of the dramatic *'stock-flow' problem* which arises in all the transition economies. It differs radically from the one encountered in the processes of structural adjustment which periodically occur in market economies (and which Schumpeter referred to when he used the notion of 'creative destruction').

The stock-flow problem in the CEE economies in transition is constituted as follows: existing resources (the capacities installed, workers' skills, technologies adopted) are the result of past allocation patterns. Since the criteria for their allocation and use were not market criteria and, even if they had been, past price structures and the relative closure of those economies to world market competition would have ensured that the utilisation of a high proportion of these capacities would not be viable under a new regime in which:

- prices have been liberalised;
- trade liberalisation has taken place; and,
- there is some rigidity in the degree to which employees accept a fall in real wages.[5]

If strict market criteria were applied, a dramatic closure of plants and enterprises and large-scale dismissal of workers could be expected in a very short time. This is the 'stock' part of the problem. The 'flow' part arises from the fact that the building up of new capacities and skills and even the reallocation of existing capacities which could be made viable requires substantial investment flows. Such flows can be generated only gradually and the generation of such funds is handicapped by the condition of deep recession experienced until recently by all CEE economies. In any case, to replace the 'stocks' which were accumulated in the course of a whole generation requires a sufficiently long period of cumulative new investment flows, to be used both for building up new capacities and skills and transforming old ones. Such accumulation of new 'flows' is a gradual process, and thus the only option in order to maintain a (socially and politically) sustainable level of employment and level of supplies to support the living standards of the population is to keep 'stocks' in operation which would – if strict market criteria were applied – not be kept in operation.[6]

The question of utilisation of such capacities, for how long, and to what degree, has to be posed explicitly. First, the question of whether there is a case for such transitional utilisation has to be resolved. In the light of the above discussion of the stock-flow problem encountered by the economies in transition, it seems to us that such a case can, and has to be, made. Secondly, the question of what instruments are available to assure that such utilisation of capacities which are unviable in the longer run can be used effectively, and in such a way that they do not hinder but rather support a general process of restructuring and recovery, has to be decided.

We know that the utilisation of existing capacities is a function of a number of factors:

- the restrictiveness of macroeconomic policy and its effect on the level of domestic demand;
- the degree to which levels of exchange rates and wage rates protect or expose domestic producers to import competition;
- the degree to which price liberalisation reveals (given exchange rates and money wage rates) that certain capacities cannot produce products which can be sold profitably;
- subsidies in various forms.

The period of transition will therefore – by definition – have features which do not form part of the picture of a fully developed market economy:

(i) Enterprises which would not be viable under strict market rules, i.e. those making substantial losses, would continue to operate and the losses will be underwritten by banks or the government.
(ii) Certain linkages between enterprises or between enterprises and banks and public–administrative bodies will be maintained although, according to market criteria, they should be broken off.
(iii) A whole host of behaviourial characteristics of enterprise behaviour will change only gradually: such characteristics include employment–output flexibility; inventory behaviour, determinants of investment and scrapping of capital goods; the orientation of sales (and sales efforts) towards different markets, etc.

The sluggishness of enterprises and banks in conforming to strict market criteria is, in fact, an essential component in softening the impact of the fundamental stock-flow problem encountered in the transition: to repeat, if there were an immediate switch towards full compliance with strict market criteria, there would be an immediate and dramatic process of scrapping of existing capacities and large-scale redundancy of workers,[7] because the inherited structure of capacities and skills – after trade and price liberalisation and the maintenance of some 'floor' in real earnings – has become unviable. This is reinforced by an unfavourable macroeconomic climate in which government policies are predominantly oriented towards correcting external and internal imbalances by constraining the level of domestic demand.

Once it is recognised that the fundamental 'stock-flow' problem encountered in transition economies requires a particular time horizon over which the industrial restructuring process may proceed, it is important to design both macroeconomic and industrial policies in such a way that they are conducive to the aims of such a process. Industrial restructuring can be broken down into two important aspects, the *building up of new activities/capacities/skills* and the *restructuring of old ones*. Macroeconomic conditions influence both these two aspects of the restructuring process.

In general, the expansion of capacities depends upon the recovery of profitability, the availability of credit and the evolution of longer-term capabilities which enable one to produce a product that can sell. The current climate in most CEE economies, however, encourages a short-term outlook, often due to conditions external to the firm (see also Stiglitz and Weiss, 1981). Macroeconomic 'stabilisation' policies pursued by most transforming countries in the current period of transition contributed greatly to increasing the degree of uncertainty and, while narrowly oriented towards price and current account stability, led to dramatic destabilisation of output, investment and employment.

Macroeconomic policies boycotting industrial restructuring

It is clear both from measures of industrial competitiveness (Landesmann, 1991; Hughes and Hare, 1991) and from the experiences of Poland, Czechoslovakia, and Hungary since the implementation of the recent economic reform programmes, that developments on the *supply side* represent the Achilles' heel of the entire reform process. The fall in production levels in the manufacturing sector in all CEE economies was dramatic, as table 11.1 shows.[8] The weights to give to the various reasons for the lack of – or often negative – supply response in manufacturing are disputed by economists, but they include:

- the restrictive macroeconomic policy regime imposed by incoming governments;
- the series of external shocks to which these economies were exposed: (a) the impact of the shift to convertibility in trade relations and the impact of falling oil supplies from the USSR; (b) the collapse of trade links between the ex-CMEA countries;
- the longer-term difficulties of enterprises in adjusting to a radically new environment caused by the dismantling of the planning framework, the disruption in the sources of investment finance, a sudden influx of competing imports, and disruption in the coordination between interdependent companies.

The negative supply reaction is reflected in sharply increasing unemployment rates and increases in regional disparities. Economic policy reactions to high budget deficits in these countries not only contribute to a further increase in unemployment but also lead to a vicious circle which accelerates the deterioration in the budget and maintains stagflation in the economy. Monetary policy is restrictive and concentrates on keeping the balance of payments constraint. The thin capital markets are flooded by Treasury

Table 11.1. *Eastern Europe and the USSR, industrial output, gross fixed investment and unemployment, % change over the same period of preceding year, 1989–92*

	Industrial output				Gross fixed Investment			Unemployment
	1989	1990	1991	1992	1989	1990	1991	Dec 1991[b]
Bulgaria	2.2	−12.6	−23.3	−22.0	−10.1	−18.5	48.6	10.7
Czechoslovakia	0.8	−3.5	−21.2	−18.0	1.6	7.7	−32.3	6.6
Ex-GDR	2.3	−28.0	−50.0	—	0.9	−5.7	33.5	11.8
Hungary	−2.5	−4.5	−19.1	−13.1	5.1	−8.7	−11.0	8.3
Poland	−0.5	−24.2	−11.9	0.6	−2.4	−10.1	−4.4	11.5
Romania	−2.1	−19.0	−22.7	−23.5	−1.6	−38.3	−28.8	3.1
Yugoslavia	0.9	−10.3	−19.0	—	−1.5	−13.7	−23.5[a]	19.6
Eastern Europe	0.2	−15.2	−19.6	—	−1.5	−14.0	−23.5	
USSR	1.7	−1.2	−8.0[a]	—	4.7	−4.3	−7.0	0.8

[a] Goskonstat projection.
[b] From *UN Economic Survey of Europe* (1992, 1993).
Source: UN Economic Bulletin for Europe 43 (1991) Tables 1.3.2 and 1.3.3.

Bills crowding-out private securities and pushing up interest rates. Enterprises starved of capital and overburdened by high-interest bank financing are losing profits and a basis on which to restructure their operations. Increasing unemployment leads to additional increases in budgetary outlays already hard hit by higher financing charges and lower tax revenues.

The basic policy dilemma of stabilisation in the context of Eastern Europe seems to arise from its two rather contradictory objectives, i.e. how to reconcile the restrictive policies of conventional stabilisation which are believed to be needed to improve the trade balance and to lower the inflation rate, with stimulative or expansionary policies which will help the private sector grow at a sufficiently rapid pace to take over the task of growth. There is no unambiguous answer to this question either in stabilisation theory or in the recent stabilisation experiences of the developing countries (see Dornbusch, 1990; Taylor, 1988). Intellectual honesty demands that we recognise that the basic policy dilemma cannot easily be resolved. Neither group of economists – those who favour the type of stabilisation policies now operative in a number of Eastern European countries as well as those who oppose them – has adequate theoretical or empirical foundations to come to firm *a priori* conclusions about the effectiveness of these policies in bringing about the transition from stabilisation to sustainable economic growth. Economic reasoning can only caution us regarding why and how these policy propositions may fail under certain circumstances, and thus to point to new and/or different policies that may be needed.[9]

Current stabilisation programmes are built on the belief that trade liberalisation, real wage reductions and a general disentanglement of the state from the current tax and subsidy structures would lead to a recovery of private investment activity and eventually a thriving entre-preneurial economy. One central idea underlying apparently diverse policies such as expenditure switching towards the private sector, relative price shifts in favour of the tradable sector through devaluation, and labour market flexibility, is that these will also promote the profitability of private investment, which must be considered crucial for a successful process of transition. For instance, various tax concessions in favour of private business that might be encouraged by expenditure switching would increase post-tax profitability directly. Similarly, at constant labour productivity, lower real wages would increase the profit margin per unit of sale, while devaluation of the home currency would also tend to push up that margin of profit in domestic currency for domestic exporters.

The problem with the conventional stabilisation package – its insistence on government expenditure reduction as well as government expenditure switching, lower real wages through wage restraint, etc. – while intended mostly to increase the profit margins, is likely to decrease capacity utilisation and the volume of sales through its effect on the level of demand, so that the level of profits, as well as the expected rate of profit, may decline in the process. The result would be a worsening, not an improvement, in the climate for private investment. This points to the importance of maintaining a reasonably high degree of capacity utilisation in the course of the transition, if only for the sake of maintaining a favourable climate for private investment.

Against the above, an argument much deployed in the discussion concerning the transition in Eastern Europe is that a process of 'creative destruction' is an absolutely essential element in a successful transition towards a viable market economy. In such general terms, this can hardly be denied: Eastern European economies have to undergo a dramatic process of structural adjustment, given that past resource allocation was determined by the resource allocation criteria of a command economy which, in addition, was relatively autarkic in its trade relationships with Western trading partners. The dispute about the nature of structural adjustment is, to repeat, not over whether it has to take place, but, first, over its time horizon and, secondly, the way in which it can be achieved.

Methods of industrial policy for the transition

The severity of industrial restructuring currently taking place in Central and Eastern Europe makes industrial policy unavoidable; 'no policy' is not an option, but there is a choice between *reactive and active industrial policies*. We call those policies *reactive* which will be set in motion in response to the social and political pressures which will inescapably emerge as the painful process of structural adjustment affects social groups, regions and branches in different ways. As the restructuring process proceeds, the heavy burden imposed on the budget by such reactive policies could historically be observed in the drawn-out process of running down the shipbuilding industries in Western Europe (Carlsson, 1983; Strath, 1988). The reactive use of industrial policy funds is largely inefficient. If one defines restructuring as running down the old and building up the new, an *active* industrial policy emphasises the second component, which may greatly facilitate and ease the political and social pressures resulting from the first component as well.

The *targets* to be achieved through a transition towards a market economy are agreed by most economists, although the time horizon and the methods to be employed to achieve these targets are fiercely debated. Raising productive efficiency is a top priority. Improved utilisation of labour and other resources such as materials, fuels, machinery may be achieved by better management. To update the capital structure and close the technological and skill gap with Western European economies will, in most cases, be a protracted process, but this does not rule out the formulation of a policy aimed at producing competitive products for home and export markets by upgrading the quality of the production process and developing new design and marketing skills. For the medium and long run the aim must be to adopt a strategy of moving upstream in the spectrum of intra-industry trade which characterises trade amongst advanced Western economies.

The *time horizon* for achieving these targets might be quite far off. The experience of past catching-up processes in countries like Austria, Italy, Finland, and Spain which had already previously achieved a high level of development, suggests that it takes at least 15 to 20 years to move into the 20% band of the more advanced Western European economies. There is no particular reason to presume a shorter time than that for the Czech and Slovak Republics, Hungary and Poland. For the other Eastern European economies like Bulgaria, Romania, Russia, and ex-Yugoslavia (given recent developments) one should envisage a more protracted process of catching-up of anything between 20 and 30 years. The catching-up process will be characterised by the development of market and non-market institutions as well as a gradual adaptation of behaviour to the conditions of an open and competitive economy.

The *methods* to achieve these targets may vary from country to country and from time to time. Even the complete laissez-faire route cannot be ruled out. However, it is difficult to think of any historical precedent for a catching-up process achieved in this way. It is more likely, as many recent analyses of the catching-up processes over a wide range of economies indicate, that the process requires state involvement. The diversity of state involvement in such a process suggests careful consideration of all the circumstances when designing such a policy.[10]

Given the past orientation of industrial development patterns in Eastern Europe, there are strong reasons to believe that there will be strong linkage effects from public infrastructural investment and training policies (see also p. 328–31). Past industrial development has led to a dramatic underdevelopment of certain skills and activities (particularly managerial skills, marketing and product design). In such conditions, where the general level of skill of production workers is high but important complementary skills and activities are missing or in very short supply, one can expect strong effects from industrial policies if one is able to stimulate the supply of those complementary inputs.

Geroski and Jacquemin (1985) distinguish between two alternative kinds of industrial policies: one is the 'picking winners' approach, when governments try to anticipate changes and make decisions about the allocation of resources to be invested for future growth. The alternative is to provide an institutional framework in which private sector adjustment is facilitated (Geroski and Jacquemin, 1985, p. 177). As it is not important at this stage to create 'national champions' but to lift the general level of performance and provide a basic (human and material) infrastructure, the 'picking winners' strategy is not favoured. Foreseeing the success in such a risky and unstable situation is in any case beyond the talent of state–administrative bodies. Public policy in this case also should be to *lower the barriers to entry* for participation in market processes, and it has a major role to play in restructuring the existing state sector, given the stock-flow problem discussed on p. 315–18. Retraining programmes, support for modernising existing capacities through investment support and help in re-equipping with imported machinery better suited to world market production, and access to scarce managerial, marketing and advertising capacities are among the numerous possibilities to lower both exit and entry barriers.[11] The winners will emerge of their own accord and only then will the question be posed of whether they should be supported further. The latter will be the case only if there are further 'barriers to entry' to be overcome for success in international competition. As Cowling (1990) notes: 'the role of the state should be limited to the strategic oversight of development, rather than getting involved with the operational detail, and that strategic oversight is only essential in the case of a limited array of key industries, many sectors being left to market processes without strategic guidance. The role of the state has to be seen as catalytic, proactive rather than reactive' (Cowling, 1990, p. 178).

At present, the diversity of firm performance within the same industry is enormous. Kolanda and Kubista (1990) report that the spread of productivity performance across enterprises within the same industry can reach 1:60 as compared to an estimated spread in advanced Western economies of 1:6. They also cite that, across industries, the ratios of value added per worker in metallurgy and engineering, for example, are similar in Germany while in Czechoslovakia the value added per worker in engineering is only half that in metallurgy. Industrial policy in these countries should be oriented towards *lifting the average standard* and reducing the variances. Partly closures and partly restructuring will play a major role in achieving this goal.

Industrial policy as a means to changing state–administrative behaviour

Efficient state institutions need to be organised in the area of industrial policy as part of the transformation towards a Western-style market economy. State institutions have to learn how to use new instruments designed to interact with firms which are increasingly guided by markets. This learning process involves a shift towards the use of indirect policy instruments such as tax incentives, credit support, the infrastructural support of science and technology, training, and marketing, all issues intricately linked with the internal organisation and behaviour of the firm. While, in the past, enterprise performance was judged directly in relation to targets set by the government, the changes imply that both government policies and enterprises should be judged jointly by *performance on domestic and international markets*.

An important target for industrial policy in the process of transition to a market economy – apart from the potential benefit to the private sector itself – is to orientate the state–administrative machinery towards the goals of competing in national and international markets. Industrial policies can thus assist the infiltration of managerial objectives in an internationalised economy into the thinking of administrators and bureaucrats.

The evaluation and recommendation of appropriate policy instruments has to be distinguished from the particular institutions/bureaucracies which have been carrying out similar policies in the past: if the issue is bureaucracy, one should change the state institutions, but not throw away those instruments of industrial policy which have been successful in the West; the setting up of modern and efficient industrial policy institutions (preferably of a decentralised/regional type) is part of the process of becoming a modern Western-type market economy. Restructuring includes the restructuring of the state administrative machinery as well as public and private sector enterprises. The fact that the previous government machinery was not competent to achieve certain economic goals does not mean that after the changes both in the external and the internal environment this will still be the case. Indeed, a more express focus on raising the efficiency and skill of government agencies and improving knowledge about new policy instruments and their use in the new – national and international – market conditions is one of the most important – but currently neglected – aspects of systemic change. That is why it is crucial to counteract the current brain-drain of effective administrators and attempt to attract effective managers into the state sector in a period when the attraction of the private sector is great. One has to give comparable incentives to those in the private sector and introduce performance monitoring.

The budgetary predicament and the reorganisation of large state-owned enterprises

The budgetary consequences of an active industrial policy are significant and there will be a shift in public spending in the course of the transition.

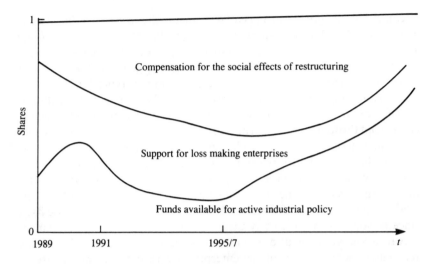

Figure 11.1 Composition of public spending on economic restructuring, 1989–1995/7

The public resources available for an active industrial policy will be squeezed by the basic dilemma of the restructuring process. Since the development of new firms, and change in the composition of industries, is a slow process, most public spending will go into a mix between continued support for loss making enterprises and dealing with the social effects of economic restructuring (unemployment, lower participation rates, regional support, etc.). The squeeze which these two components exert upon state spending is strongest in the period when the need for an active industrial policy is greatest (retraining, infrastructural investment, business start-up schemes, etc.) Efficient management of scarce public funds is thus vital over the transition period. This will be a difficult task, as the administrative bodies are themselves undergoing restructuring. The setting-up of new, technocratic bodies with a long-term brief and an assured guarantee that funds for particular purposes (retraining, R&D support) will be set aside from the annual budgetary bargaining process might be of some help in these circumstances. Figure 11.1 illustrates the dilemma of pressure on state resources caused by an active industrial policy, particularly in the period when it is most needed.

Figure 11.1 shows only the shares in public spending affected by the restructuring process. The absolute levels of funds available are strongly linked to the macroeconomic climate combined with the degree of foreign aid support. Infrastructural investment financed from external sources is obviously an important additional source.

One can learn a great deal that is of relevance to the newly emerging market economies (NEMs) of Eastern Europe from the *reorganisation of large state-owned companies* in Western Europe over the past 15 years. It is clear that the publicly owned sector in the West has emerged from the 1970s and 1980s with a managerial structure different from that typical in the 1960s. The streamlining of public sector companies and the commercial orientation of their operations was in most cases not achieved through a sudden regime change but through the gradual but sustained imposition of an 'increasingly hardening budget constraint'. The gradual but persistent nature of this process should be of great relevance to Eastern Europe at the present time.

By now, the discussion about reorganisation of SOEs before or after privatisation has become more pragmatic (see, e.g., Carlin and Mayer, 1992). It became clear that in many cases this question will not pose itself since nobody will want to buy these 'assets'. The danger that immanent privatisation would lead to 'plum-picking' and 'asset-stripping' is widely recognised, with the rest of the enterprise's operations being discarded. Brain-drain and asset-stripping can make existing SOEs even more rigid and less adaptable in responding to new market pressures. With privatisation fixed for a later date, company operations might be more comprehensively reorganised *ex ante*, as a result of which the value of the assets would increase. Furthermore, careful thought has to be given to raising the incentive for the existing management and workforce to initiate and participate in such reorganisation. The pay-off of such gradual procedures towards privatisation is that a larger proportion of activities could become viable.

Furthermore, the case for a measured pace in approaching the privatisation of 'strategic SOEs' (from an industrial or regional point of view) can also suggest the difficulty in judging long-term viability in a period of turbulence: What will happen to inherited firm debt? How will financial markets develop? Which managers/workers will stay? Which exchange rate/tariff regime will prevail? Which ownership arrangements? Which links to external markets including the former CMEA markets, etc.? Once the external environment of the firm has settled down, viability can be more easily judged. In the transitory period, companies might be seen as non-viable because of the uncertainty in the external environment (and also because of the loss of competent managers and skilled workers) and not necessarily because of internal performance indicators. That is why it is so important in the period of transition to find 'strategic groups' (managers, owners, even skilled workers) who identify with particular assets. This identification can be positive or negative: they might resist restructuring or they might advance the long-term development potential of the assets. Stabilisation of the external environment of the firm as well as an orderly and gradual transfer of asset ownership will increase the commitment of owners, managers and workers to exploit the long-term development potential of enterprises. In a chaotic and arbitrary process of privatisation, there is no guarantee that the new owners will build on the *long-term opportunities* of assets rather than exploiting short-run speculative gains. The actual circumstances will determine their behaviour.

The experience in Western Europe of some of the successful examples of reorganisation (and privatisation) of large SOEs over the 1980s shows that reorganisation is a drawn-out process, often requiring substantial resources over the transition (see, for example, the analysis of the gradual reorganisation of the Austrian State Holding Company in the 1980s as described in OECD country reports). For such reorganisation to be successful it is necessary to:

- set clear managerial targets;
- ensure that a clear timetable for financial viability is adhered to;
- develop clear guidelines as to the role and the extent of the public sector; and
- ensure (by setting up appropriate regulatory agencies and policies) that desired market organisational targets are achieved.

Export orientation as a means to recapturing the domestic market

The current situation in Central and Eastern Europe is, in one respect, similar to that in Japan after the Second World War, when it embarked upon an industrial policy. At that time Japan had a clear vision of which product markets to enter and which industries to develop: the example of the developed market economies determined the pattern. In a sense, the same is true now for Eastern European economies. The broad trends of market reorientation are known (see Collins and Rodrik, 1991; Hamilton and Winters, 1992); similarly, the basic direction in sectoral reallocation is clear (increase the role of tertiary activities, reduce the share of heavy industrial, heavy chemical, and metal producing industries); in addition, the likely trends in inter-industry and intra-industry specialisation of CEE economies are currently being researched (see e.g. Landesmann, 1992a; Rosati, 1992; Hamilton and Winters, 1992). The main unanswered question relates to the speed and the ability of the different CEE economies to develop their supply-side potential to achieve certain goals in overall trade performance and in detailed trade specialisation (see also Baldwin, 1992).

Export orientation is a clearly distinguishing characteristic of successful catching-up processes. Most of the successful catching-up economies made export performance a central target around which the overall process was organised. The relative failure of India to develop its competitive potential was a consequence of the domestic market orientation of its industry, induced by a very large and expanding domestic market. In the case of East and Central Europe the hard-currency shortage and the high burden of debt service makes it even more important that strong pressure on export performance should be exerted. There are a number of additional factors that make this case inevitable:

- the dramatic impact of the (almost complete) loss of traditional CMEA export markets;
- the strong pressure exerted by international organisations (such as the IMF) to achieve external balance, and also the countries' own desire to achieve association agreements and even membership of the EC as soon as possible;
- the high demand for imports both for consumption and as an important ingredient in the restructuring process itself.

A very important by-product of developing capabilities to produce commodities which can be exported is that it simultaneously generates capacities which can compete with imported goods. Export markets are characterised by demand structures which, on the whole, are more advanced than those found in home markets. Hence a sustained effort to improve export performance will also yield beneficial results in *recapturing the domestic markets* which have been flooded by imported consumer goods. A consistent attempt to upgrade standards is preferable to applying traditional instruments of protection.

However, the shift to an increasingly *liberalised trade* regime in countries like Finland was a gradual but sustained process over the post-war period, allowing sufficient time for producers to adjust, but setting a clear time limit, and applying consistent and credible pressure through well-designed trade and public sector policies. The transitional arrangements which Spain and Portugal negotiated as part of their membership deal with the EC is an example of such a gradual regime switch. The EC can play a role in providing credibility to such a strategy of sustained but gradual increase of pressure. Hence an intelligent use of exchange rate policies combined with more specific export-supporting schemes (see, e.g., Kolanda, 1991) are perfectly defensible and well-proven instruments to support a catching-up process.[12]

Areas of industrial policy

There are a number of areas in which industrial policy can play a useful role in the transition process:

- infrastructural investment;
- training;
- substantial reorganisation of R&D activity and of scientific institutions; setting up new R&D institutions, technology dissemination policies, R&D collaborations, etc.;
- support in setting up purposeful financing agencies, e.g., for small and medium-sized enterprises, venture capital, etc.;
- influencing the development of market structures:
    small and medium-sized business policies
    takeover and merger policies and control
    joint venture support
    incentives for foreign direct investment;
- restructuring of SOEs (see pp. 326–7);
- export promotion (see pp. 327–8).

Infrastructural investment must be seen as a very important aspect of industrial support. Transport and communications facilities are generally seen as an important bottleneck in the development of industrial activities in Eastern Europe. Major (1991, p. 76) mentions studies which estimate that the annual loss of GDP directly related to the poor level of telecommunications services amounts to 4–5% of GDP in Hungary. An additional 3–4% is accounted for by the backwardness of road transport and a further 2–3% loss comes from environmental damage.

Particular attention must be paid to *training and educational reform*. It is well known that Eastern Europe has engineering skills but many complementary skills are missing; the training and educational system has to be remodelled and redeveloped. This includes the current direction of much R&D activity and the workings of scientific institutions. A major overhaul of the educational system is currently under discussion in many CEEs but more interaction between the industrial reform process and the scientific, research and educational needs to support such a process would be beneficial (see, e.g., Nesporova, 1993). Skilled workforces are generally recognised as – possibly – the most important comparative advantage of a number of CEE economies (see CEPR, 1990, Hamilton and Winters, 1992). However, the lack of *complementary skills* (managerial, advertising, product design, marketing, etc.) seriously hampers the utilisation of this competitive potential. Training was also shown in most Western studies (see, e.g., Jackman and Rubin, 1992; Ryan *et al.*, 1992) to be the crucial variable counteracting the emergence of long-term unemployment and regional underdevelopment. Considerable experience has been accumulated in OECD economies as to which schemes are more or less effective in countering youth unemployment, long-term unemployment, and regional deindustrialisation. If used intelligently, such schemes can be an important component in removing resistance to industrial structural adjustment and the development of alternative economic activities.

Measures in support of *small and medium-sized businesses* are designed to help firms gain access to credit and create specifically targeted financial support units (see also below); to assist in access to and in the pooling of technology; to support training schemes and access to a skilled workforce; to organise contacts for imports of technology and for joint ventures; to pool R&D resources across firms (with state subsidies) and share training costs. These schemes will influence the direction in which small and medium-sized businesses will develop and in which activities they will be able to establish themselves (i.e. overcome initial barriers to entry).[13]

Directing the *emergence of financial markets and financial institutions* is also vital. The development of *capital markets* is a key element of enterprise development of CEE countries, as entry to a market often requires substantial amounts of capital. Emerging capital markets in East and Central Europe may give enterprises access to resources to develop new activities, build up complementary capabilities, enter new markets and help them overcome barriers to entry in export markets using new technologies. Svejnar remarks that '[t]he single most important hindrance to the outburst of new private activity is probably the limited availability of credit, which stems from the undeveloped financial sector, the limited collateral of the starting entrepreneurs and the high real interest rate that is a by-product of the stabilisation plans' (Svejnar, 1991, p. 131). He rightly notes: 'In this situation, there is strong economic justification for government to step in and provide credit insurance or other measures to stimulate bank lending to ... [the small- and medium-sized firm] sector' (1991, p. 133).

In all the transforming countries the *banking sector* has been modernised and a two-tier banking system is in place to facilitate the replacement of central planning by financial intermediation and so bring market forces into the allocation of resources.[14] However, banks which are overburdened by inherited bad loans and face the problems of under-capitalisation in a very risky business environment are reluctant to lend to new entrepreneurs with no reputation and limited collateral. The limited knowledge base of the new financial institutions and their bad asset position makes them very cautious in investing. They are not likely to be able to satisfy the growing needs for financing the transition. As Corbett and Mayer (1991) pointed out, the advantages of a German-type bank-based system for this region are clear. There are several consequences of a bank-based system as compared to a stock market-based system. The latter, which relies on dispersed shareholder ownership would not be able to solve the monitoring problem immanent in the control of enterprises. Allowing banks to hold equity and perform part of the control problem could facilitate restructuring.

Conclusion

We can now summarise the main points made in this chapter. First, the economic transformation currently taking place in Eastern Europe involves a major conversion of existing capacities, capabilities and organisational structures as well as the building up of new ones; such a process is, by definition, a time-consuming one. It will, on current estimates, take anything up to 20 or 30 years. Secondly, given that the existence of markets and of market-conforming behaviour is a necessary prerequisite for the effective functioning of a market economy, and that these conditions are only gradually emerging in CEE economies, the transition process cannot occur without a relatively *high degree of state involvement*. The experience of economic reform in Eastern Europe provides much evidence for such a view. Thirdly, it is in the nature of the evolution of market behaviour that in periods in which environmental parameters are constantly and dramatically changing, resources are less likely to be committed for the long term than the short term. Under such conditions, there is an important role for industrial policy to bring public resources to bear in areas which would be neglected by private agents, even in normal circumstances, let alone in the current circumstances of Eastern Europe. Infrastructural investment and training are two such areas which have been shown to be crucial for a catching-up process (see, e.g., Cohen, 1991). Fourthly, it was argued that the main impact of the state on the evolution of market structure will lie in the policies pursued with respect to the reorganisation of 'strategic' SOEs, on the one hand, and small and medium-sized enterprises on the other. In both these areas, policy makers in Eastern Europe should take a pragmatic look at the experiences in Western Europe over the past two decades in which policies of restructuring of state enterprises and the support of the small- and medium-sized enterprise sector have evolved. In the current context of Eastern Europe, the latter is intricately linked to the evolution of financial markets and financial organisations. Fifthly, a strong emphasis on export orientation has been the hallmark of successful catching-up of a great number of economies. Eastern Europe has some extraordinary potential comparative advantages (particularly in its human infrastructure) which could allow it to embark upon a successful upward movement in the international division of labour. Evidence from other successful economies indicates that industrial policy can be an important ingredient in tapping that potential.

Notes

1 See Geroski and Jacquemin (1985) for a discussion of such barriers in the circumstances of Western Europe.
2 For a survey of the range of policies falling under this rubric, see the yearly reports by the OECD on *Industrial Policy in OECD Countries*.
3 See Okimoto (1989), Dore (1986), Magaziner and Hont (1980) on Japan; Amsden, (1989), Chang (1991), Paik *et al.*, (1988), Luedde-Neurath, (1986) on Korea; Gustafson, (1986), Lindbeck, (1990), Lindgren (1990) on Sweden; Pekkarinen (1988) on Finland, etc.
4 We endorse Svejnar's observations (1991, p. 132) about the inactivity of governments in eliminating major obstacles on the road towards a market economy: 'the inability of governments to create a complete and consistent legal framework to guide economic activity; inadequate emphasis on the creation of competitive market institutions, infrastructure and supporting practices in the areas of financial services, real estate, domestic trade, transportation, and telecommunications; the slow creation of accounting, auditing and other information systems; and the lack of strong market-oriented managerial and worker incentives in state enterprises'.
5 This is not to ignore the fact that substantial falls in real wages have taken place in all CEE economies; the argument here relies only on the existence of some 'floor' in the level of real earnings acceptable to the working population.
6 An indication of the enormity of the flows required to sustain living standards and initiate new industrial growth, in the presence of a dramatic process of scrapping and demanning, can be obtained from the figures of transfers from western to eastern Germany, which in 1991 amounted to about 60% of eastern Germany's GDP. Of course, the ex-GDR represents an extreme case, both with respect to the degree of exposure of the industrial structure to Western competition at an extremely unfavourable exchange rate and with respect to the expectation of the population of achieving living standards comparable to the West in a short span of time.
7 Such a process of large-scale scrapping could, of course, be observed in the ex-GDR, where production levels in manufacturing are now about 30–40% of the 1989 levels. In the specific context of eastern Germany, monetary unification and the ensuing *de facto* revaluation of the currency followed by strong wage pressures were the main reason for the speed of large-scale underutilisation and redundancy. In the other CEE economies exchange rates were originally devalued; nevertheless, there as well the losses in production levels were dramatic and, consequently, the levels of underutilisation of capacity very high (see table 11.1, p.319).
8 It is well known that the emergence of private enterprise activity has not, so far, been fully ascertained statistically. Nonetheless, given the very low starting base of private activity in that sector, the overall decline would not be seriously affected by the incomplete coverage of private sector activity. The picture is quite different in tertiary activities, where the private sector has been growing very rapidly.

9 The argument in this and the next two paragraphs is based on Bhaduri (1992).

10 Geroski (1989) emphasises that the 'application of industrial policy is largely directed at realising microeconomic goals (like growth in industry exports, or stimulating the rate of product or process innovation) rather than macro-economic goals (like full employment or zero inflation). Of course, systematic and repeated application of successful micro-based supply-side policies will, sooner or later, ease major macroeconomic constraints' (p. 21); 'the complexity of industrial policy programmes often arises from the need to reconcile the various conflicting effects that different types of policy create, and, occasionally, to reconcile conflicting policy targets' (p. 22); 'The major policy dilemmas arise from the fact that the instruments typically used have multiple effects, that policy must often be selectively applied and custom-designed. In practice, all of this means that industrial policies must be carefully crafted ... That the job is difficult does not, of course, mean that it cannot or should not be done' (pp. 23–4).

11 Jacquemin defines industrial policy measures as 'tools used to affect the speed of the process of resource allocation among and within industrial sectors'. Later he expands: 'Manpower policies can also reduce the costs of adjustment, hence increasing the speed of allocating human resources. Similarly, economic growth-oriented, science and technological policies can be a useful complement to private R&D programmes when externalities, information failures, and risk aversion could lead to a socially insufficient flow of resources. There is also a case for subsidising R&D in high technology industries affected by large fixed costs: governmental intervention could enable a domestic firm to be among the "happy few" constituting an international oligopoly in the field' (Jacquemin, 1984, p.1).

12 See e.g. the very different use of exchange rate policies in the post-war development of Austria and Finland (Landesmann, 1992b).

13 'The success of the transformation hinges on a rapid expansion of the *small- and medium-sized* firm sector that can ensure output growth, generate new employment, provide a tax base, and generally augment the flexibility and dynamism of these economies' (Svejnar, 1991, p.133).

14 An evaluation of the achievements and the problems is given in Murphy and Sabov (1991), who compare the financial structure of the Hungarian banking sector with the German one.

References

Amsden, A., 1989. *Asia's Next Giant*, New York: Oxford University Press

Baldwin, R., 1992. 'An Eastern enlargement of EFTA: why the East Europeans should join and the EFTAns should want them', *CEPR Occasional Paper*, 10 London: CEPR

Bhaduri, A., 1992. 'Conventional stabilisation and the East European transition', in Sandor Richter (ed.), *The Transition from Command to Market Economies,*

The Vienna Institute for Comparative Economic Studies, Yearbook IV, San Francisco and London: Westview Press

Bicanic, I. and Skrel, M., 1991. 'The service sector in East European economies: what role can it play in future development?', *Communist Economies and Economic Transformation*, 3(2)

Calvo, G. A. and Frankel, J. A., 1991. 'Credit markets, credibility and economic transformation', *Journal of Economic Perspectives*, 5(4)

Carlin, W. and Mayer, C., 1992. 'Restructuring enterprises in Eastern Europe', University College London, *Discussion Paper*, 92–15

Carlsson, B., 1983. 'Industrial subsidies in Sweden: macro-economic effects and an international comparison', *Journal of Industrial Economics*, 32, 1–29

CEPR, 1990. 'Monitoring European integration: the impact of Eastern Europe', *CEPR Annual Report*, London: CEPR

Chang, H.-J., 1991. *The Political Economy of Industrial Policy*, unpublished Ph.D., Faculty of Economics and Politics, University of Cambridge.

Cohen, D., 1991. 'The solvency of Eastern Europe', *European Economy*, special issue no. 2

Collins, S. M. and Rodrik, D.,1991. *Eastern Europe and the Soviet Union in the World Economy*, Washington DC: Institute for International Economics

Corbett, J. and Mayer, C., 1991. 'Financial reform in Eastern Europe: progress with the wrong model', *Oxford Review of Economic Policy*, 7(4)

Cowling, K., 1990. 'A new industrial strategy: preparing Europe for the turn of the century', *International Journal of Industrial Organisation*, 8, 165–183

Dore, R., 1986. 'Industrial policy and how the Japanese do it', *Catalyst*, 2, 45–58

Dornbush, R., 1990. *From Stabilisation to Growth*, NBER Working Paper, 3302, Cambridge, MA: NBER

Ford, R. and Suyker, W., 1990. 'Industrial subsidies in the OECD economies', *OECD Economic Statistics*, no. 15 (Autumn), 37–81

Geroski, P. A., 1989. 'European industrial policy and industrial policy in Europe', *Oxford Review of Economic Policy*, 5(2), 20–36

Geroski, P. A. and Jacquemin, A., 1985. 'Corporate competitiveness in Europe', *Economic Policy*, 1 (November) 1985, 170–218

Grossman, G. M., 1990. 'Promoting new industrial activities: a survey of recent arguments and evidence', *OECD Economic Studies*, 87–125

Gustafson, C., 1986. *The Small Giant: Sweden Enters the Industrial Era*, Ohio: Ohio University Press

Hamilton, C. and Winters, A., 1992. 'Opening up international trade with Eastern Europe', *Economic Policy*, no. 14, April 1992

Hughes, G. and Hare, P. G., 1991. 'Competitiveness and industrial restructuring in Czechoslovakia, Hungary and Poland', *European Economy*, Special Edition, 2, 83–110

Jackman, R. and Rubin, M., 1992. 'Training the Unemployed', paper prepared for the meeting on Vocational Education and Training held at the Centre for Economic Performance, London School of Economics (February)

Jacquemin, A., 1984. 'Introduction: which policy for industry?', in A. Jacquemin (ed.), *European Industry: Public Policy and Corporate Strategy*, Oxford: Clarendon

Klacek J. *et al.*, 1991. *Economic Reform in Czechoslovakia*, Institute of Economics of the Czechoslovak Academy of Sciences, Prague

Kolanda, M., 1991. 'The strategy for joining the international division of labour', in *Prognostic Reflections of the Transition Problems towards Democracy and Market Economy*, Forecasting Institute of the Czechoslovak Academy of Sciences, Prague

Kolanda, M. and Kubista, V., 1991. 'Costs, performances and behaviour of Czechoslovak manufacturing enterprises on world markets in the 1980s', Prague, Institute for Forecasting of the Czechoslovak Academy of Sciences, internal document

Landesmann, M., 1991. 'Industrial restructuring and the reorientation of trade in Czechoslovakia', *European Economy* (June)

1992a. 'Industrial restructuring and East–West trade integration', *Department of Applied Economics Working Paper*, No. 9213, University of Cambridge

1992b. 'Industrial policies and social corporatism', in J. Pekkarinen, M. Pohjola, and R. Rowthorn (eds.), *Lessons from Corporatist Experiments*, Oxford: Oxford University Press

Lindbeck A., 1990. 'The Swedish Experience', Paper presented at the OECD Conference on the Transition to Market Economies in Central and Eastern Europe, Paris

Lindgren, A., 1990. 'Long-term contracts in financial markets: bank–industry connections in Sweden. Illustrated by the operation of the Stockholm's Enskilda Bank', in M. Aoki, B. Gustafson and O. Williamson (eds.), *The Firm as a Nexus of Treaties*, London: Sage

Luedde-Neurath, R., 1986. *Import Controls and Export-Oriented Development: A Reassessment of the South Korean Case*, London: Westview Press

Magaziner, I. and Hont, T., 1980. *Japanese Industrial Policy*, Policy Studies Institute, London

Major I., 1991. 'Private and public infrastructure in Eastern Europe', *Oxford Review of Economic Policy*, 7(4), 76–92

Murell, P. and Olson, M., 1991. 'The evolution of centrally planned economies, *Journal of Comparative Economics*, 15(2), 239–65

Murphy, A. and Sabov, Z., 1991. 'Financial institution structures in a developing two-tier banking system: an empirical perspective from Eastern Europe', *Journal of Banking and Finance*, Vol. 15, 1131–42

Nesperova, A., 1993. 'Preconditions of the Industrial Restructuring in the Skill, Professional and Age Structure of the Labour Force in the Czech Republic', paper presented on the ACE Workshop on 'Industrial Restructuring, Trade Reorientation and East-West European Integration', WIIW, Vienna (27–29 March)

OECD various years. *Industrial Policy in OECD Countries, Annual Review*, Paris: OECD

Okimoto, D., 1989. *Between MITI and the Market: Japanese Industrial Policy for*

High Technology, Stanford: Stanford University Press

Paik, N. K., Chang, S. I. and Lee, D. H., 1988. *Industrial Organisation Policies of Korea*, Korea Institute for Economics and Technology (KIET), Seoul

Pearce, J. and Sutton, J., 1985. *Protection and Industrial Policy in Europe*, London: Routledge & Kegan Paul

Pekkarinen, J., 1988. *Keynesianism and the Scandinavian Models of Economic Policy*, WIDER Working Papers, 35, Helsinki

Rosati, D., 1992. 'Problems of post-CMEA trade and payments; in J. Flemming and J. Rollo (eds.), *Trade, Payments and Adjustment in Central and Eastern Europe*, Royal Institute of International Affairs, London

Rosenstein-Rodan, P. N., 1943. 'Problems of industrialisation in Eastern and South-Eastern Europe', *Economic Journal*, 53, 202–211

Ryan, P., Garonna, P. and Edwards, R, C., 1992. *The Problem of Youth, The Regulation of Youth Employment and Training in Advanced Economies*, London: Macmillan

Rybczynski, T., 1991. 'The sequencing of reform', *Oxford Review of Economic Policy*, 7(4)

Schaffer, M., 1991. 'A note on the Polish state-owned enterprise sector in 1990', London School of Economics, mimeo

Sharp, M., 1987. 'Europe: collaboration in the high technology sectors', *Oxford Review of Economic Policy*, 3, 52–65

Shaw, R. and Shaw, S., 1983. 'Excess capacity and rationalisation in the West European synthetic fibres industry', *Journal of Industrial Economics*, 32, 149–166

Stiglitz, J. E. and Weiss, A., 1981. 'Credit rationing in markets with imperfect information', *American Economic Review*, 71, 393–410

Strath, B., 1988, *The Politics of Deindustrialisation*, London: Croom Helm

Svejnar, J., 1991. 'Microeconomic issues in the transition to a market economy', *Journal of Economic Perspectives*, 5(4), 123–138

Taylor, L., 1988 *Varieties of Stabilisation Experience*, Oxford: Clarendon Press

Tronkakis, L. and Strauss, R., 1988. 'Crisis and adjustment in European steel: beyond laisser-faire', *Journal of Common Market Policies*, 23, 207–228.

12 Financial intermediation and industrial restructuring in Central and Eastern Europe

István Ábel and István Székely

Introduction

A relatively fast and substantial restructuring of the economies of Central and Eastern Europe (CEE) is necessary for a successful economic transformation and sustained growth in the longer run. It requires the restructuring of existing enterprises, the reallocation of capital to more profitable activities and enterprises, increased investments, and an economic environment within which successful private enterprises can expand their activities at a much faster pace than before. A necessary element of such an environment is a well-functioning and efficient financial system which can both collect savings and channel them to the most efficient uses, and provide high-quality, low-cost financial services for producers and financial investors. The availability of the latter to the newly emerging private sector consisting mainly of small and medium-sized producers is a vital prerequisite for a smooth and robust economic development. Financial institutions, in particular commercial banks, also have a central role in the restructuring of (formerly) state-owned enterprises (SOEs) and in imposing proper corporate governance on large (already or not yet privatised) enterprises.

This chapter investigates the possible roles that banks and other financial institutions can play in the process of industrial restructuring and also the impact of the problems financial systems in CEE face on this process.

The second section focuses on corporate finance during economic transformation. It investigates the reasons for the lack of and high costs of long-term investment finance. On the supply side, financial investors are reluctant to hold long-term assets due to the high level of uncertainty inherent in the process of economic transformation. On the demand side, the typically large budget deficits,[1] reflecting the high social costs of economic transformation (e.g. unemployment) and the equally high costs of dealing with the legacies of central planning (such as bad loans), mop up

337

most of the available long-term finance, crowding-out private business. The very limited access to private international capital markets is an additional reason for the scarcity of long-term finance. Regarding the commercial banks, their fairly limited capacity to assume risk and the newly introduced Western-style prudential regulations are the most important factors explaining why they tend to opt for rather conservative lending policies. Regarding the newly emerging private sector, the lack of proper track record and collateral are further factors making banking finance a difficult to obtain source of long-term finance.

The third section is devoted to the role banks can play in imposing proper corporate governance on (former) SOEs and in enforcing and facilitating the restructuring of these enterprises. The fourth section focuses on the issue of 'bad loans'. The low and fast deteriorating quality of loan portfolios of banks is a natural consequence of economic transformation. Previously made long-term (investment) loans reflected the priorities of central planners and the strength of the different industrial and agrarian lobbies, rather than any sort of economic rationale. As previous chapters have shown, the simultaneous collapse of this system in CEE countries and the consequent collapse of trade among CEE countries changed the environment surrounding enterprises drastically. The different ways in which governments in CEE try to cope with bad loans have different consequences on the capital allocation mechanism. The section investigates the damaging repercussions of bad loans on capital allocation and industrial restructuring and the impact of the bad-loan schemes implemented so far.

Finally, the fifth section focuses on the degree of competition in the financial system. Competition has a direct and strong impact on allocative efficiency and on the quality and costs of capital and financial services for industry which is an important factor of international competitiveness. Though currently, the international competitiveness of CEE economies is based on low wage costs, this advantage can well be offset by high costs of capital, and by the lack of access to proper financial services and export credits.

Financing industrial restructuring in Central and Eastern Europe

Economic transformation inevitably leads to corporatisation and a sudden and sizeable decrease in the extent to which the state is involved in the allocation of financial resources (see, e.g., Ábel and Bonin, 1994a): corporate finance then becomes an important issue. Therefore, when one thinks about industrial restructuring, trade reorientation and export-led growth, it is important to pay attention to how new investments, one of the most important elements and prerequisites of restructuring, are (can be) financed at the enterprise level. In what follows, we shall investigate four main sources of corporate finance: banking (intermediated) finance, direct (bond and equity) finance, foreign direct finance, and retained earnings.

Bank (intermediated) finance for investment

During economic transformation, long-term (investment) bank finance has been (and will be) available for industrial firms to a rather limited extent, for several reasons. First, because of the limited supply of long-term loanable funds. Private financial investors are and in the foreseeable future will most likely be rather reluctant to hold long-term financial assets in large amounts, even in those countries where stabilisation polices have been relatively successful and private saving has increased (see, e.g., Ábel and Székely, 1993; Wyczański, 1993). Moreover, commercial banks have fairly limited capacities to carry out maturity conversion (converting shorter-term deposits into longer-term loans) due to the newly introduced Western-type prudential regulations. Furthermore, banks have little experience with and knowledge of commercial lending (credit appraisal, monitoring), especially at massive scales and in granting longer-term loans (Golden, 1994; Wyczański, 1994).

Regarding the actual development so far, as a result of these factors, the share of long-term loans in new loans and the average maturity of bank loans decreased rapidly, while the share of short-term assets in banks' asset portfolios increased immensely (see, e.g., Ábel and Székely, 1994; Kokoszczyński, 1994). In general, with very few exceptions, the share of long-term financial instruments declined radically. Interbank deposits also became very short term (see, e.g., Dobrinsky, 1994; Kokoszczyński, 1994), long-term refinance credit from the Central bank diminished (see, e.g., Ábel and Székely, 1994), and bonds other than government ones practically disappeared. Thus banks with weak deposit base, in particular among households, had practically no access to long-term loanable funds.

Second, enterprises (will) have to compete with the government for long-term funds. Massive budget deficits characterising economic transformation and costly rescue operations carried out by governments (such as the bad-loan schemes discussed below) create a strong demand for long-term funds on the part of the government.

While this is true in general for CEE countries, the extent to which these factors are present are different across countries and over time. Table 12.1 gives the figures for some of the CEE countries for the period 1990–3. It shows that in countries where macroeconomic stabilisation was relatively successful, such as the Czech Republic (formerly Czechoslovakia), Hun-

Table 12.1. *Supply and demand of loanable funds, %, 1990–3*

		1990	1991	1992	1993
Bulgaria	personal saving[a]	1.4	10.8	23.0	15.9
	budget deficit[b]	4.9	3.4	6.0	11.5
	CPI inflation[c]	23.8	338.5	91.3	74.0
Czecho-	personal saving[a]	−0.1	5.9	5.3	
slovakia[d]	budget deficit[b]	−0.1	2.0	1.6	
	CPI inflation[c]	9.9	57.9	10.8	20.8
Hungary	personal saving[a]	3.9	10.5	9.1	
	budget deficit[b]	−0.9	4.6	7.2	6.0[e]
	CPI inflation[c]	28.9	35.0	23.0	22.5
Poland	personal saving[a]	11.0	5.0	6.7	
	budget deficit[b]	−3.5	6.2	7.2	
	CPI inflation[c]	584.7	70.3	43.0	35.0

Notes:
[a]Personal net financial saving as percentage of GDP; for Bulgaria, changes in household deposits with banks (end of the year over end of previous year).
[b]Consolidated budget deficit expressed as share of GDP.
[c]Annual rate of CPI inflation.
[d]Czechoslovakia until 1992, the Czech Republic afterwards
[e]Provisional estimate
Sources: Figures for personal net financial saving and consolidated budget deficit for Czechoslovakia, Hungary and Poland are from Dittus (1993). CPI inflations are from national sources. Figures for saving and budget deficit for Bulgaria are from personal communication.

gary, and Poland (after 1991), private saving increased significantly (as a share of both disposable income and of GDP, the latter being shown in table 12.1). However, even in (former) Czechoslovakia, which is a very special case in this respect, a part of private saving was mopped up by the budget deficit. In Poland after 1990, the current budget deficit exceeded private saving, while in Hungary the positive gap between private saving and current budget deficit narrowed rapidly.[2]

But the current budget deficit does not fully reflect the finance requirement of the government. Since table 12.1 suggests that the extent of the government's borrowing requirement was perhaps the largest in Hungary, in table 12.2 we further investigate this issue for Hungary. As the figures in table 12.2 suggest, the share of government borrowing (credit) in total domestic borrowing (credit) steadily increased during the economic transformation, from 43.6% in December 1990 to 57.3% in June 1993. This increase was much higher than current budget deficit figures for the same period would suggest. The two very substantial upward jumps in June 1991 and March 1993 shown in table 12.2 are due to two loan consolidation schemes. The first one was related to the scheme that dealt with the concessional housing loans (for more details see Székely, 1994), while the second one was related to the scheme that dealt with a part of bad corporate loans (the latter will be discussed in more detail on pp. 347–51 below). The nature of the borrowing requirement related to such schemes may be different from the one related to current budget deficits, but from the viewpoint of enterprises, the bottom lines in both cases are the same, namely that the number of competing needs for available finance, in particular long-term finance, increases significantly.

As table 12.2 also shows, due to the rapid decline in the share of household credit, enterprises could for a while increase the size of their slice of the shrinking pie of total domestic credit. However, their share started to decrease rapidly after September 1992. Ironically, this happened exactly when the whole pie, that is domestic credit, started to increase rapidly in real terms, reflecting the loosening of monetary policy in Hungary. The story of investment credit is even more characteristic of economic transformation. As table 12.2 shows, with the exception of one quarter, the share of investment credit in total domestic credit declined gradually during the period under investigation from 8.5% at the end of 1990 to 5.2% in June 1993. In real terms, the stock of investment credit declined dramatically during the same period (by 45.4%). That is, in spite of the increase in household saving and decrease in household borrowing, enterprises had practically no access to banking finance for investment purposes.

The decline of investment credit is one of the most important aspects of economic restructuring (see also chapter 10 in this volume). This is a very complex issue that can be understood only when one investigates a large number of factors. Dittus (1993) finds the conservative lending policies of commercial banks as the major factor explaining this development and, at the same, time rejects the crowding-out hypothesis. The introduction of new Western-type prudential regulations has undoubtedly contributed to the decline of lending to enterprises, especially in the longer run. Sudden trade reorientation and a radical liberalisation (of goods and financial markets, including imports though mainly that of goods) – leading to fast and substantial changes of relative prices, including that of capital (that is, interest rates) – have indeed increased the risk attached to corporate lending. A sizeable part of large SOEs, the core of the traditional clientele of large state-owned commercial banks (SOCBs), abruptly lost their

Table 12.2. *Allocation of domestic credit in Hungary, 1984–93*

	Total real DC[a],[b] (1989=100)	Net credit to government		Enterprise credit[g]				Household credit[g]	
		% of DC	change as % of change in DC[f]	% of DC	change as % of change in DC[f]	IC[c] as % of DC	real[a] IC (1990=100)	% of DC	change as % of change in DC[f]
1989		47.9		31.9		8.7		20.2	
1990	100.0	43.6	5.5	37.1	84.2	8.5	100.0	19.2	9.6
1991:1		44.7		38.6		8.7		16.4	
1991:2		48.7[d]		39.5		8.4		11.2	
1991:3		48.8		40.2		8.2		10.7	
1991:4	87.8	47.4	98.8[h]	41.5	103.1[h]	7.8	80.9	11.0	−102.5[h]
1992:1	83.6	48.7	−16.8[i]	41.0	68.1[i]	7.8	76.6	10.2	49.3[i]
1992:2	83.7	49.8	71.7	40.5	60.7	7.4	73.4	9.5	−22.1
1992:3	82.8	50.3	75.6	40.5	40.5	7.4	72.0	9.1	−11.5
1992:4	85.8	51.9	94.9	37.9	2.4	6.7	68.0	10.3	3.6
1993:1	85.6	55.9[e]	176.0[e]	34.4	−65.7[e]	5.8	58.8	9.5	−10.4
1993:2	88.7	57.3	98.1	33.3	−6.3	5.2	54.6	9.1	6.9

Notes:
[a] Deflated by PPI.
[b] DC stands for domestic credit.
[c] IC stands for investment credit (credit with maturity over one year).
[d] Includes the impact of the mortgage loan scheme.
[e] Includes the impact of the 1992 loan consolidation scheme (bad corporate loans).
[f] Changes in total domestic credit (DC) also include changes in credit to non-bank financial institutions. Therefore percentages in this table do not necessarily add up to 100. This component was rather volatile, though its absolute value was very small throughout the whole period.
[g] Credit to small enterprises are included in enterprise credit.
[h] Changes in stocks are calculated for the whole year (December 1991 over December 1990).
[i] The change in the total (nominal) stock of domestic credit (DC) for this quarter was negative (HUF −35.7 bn).
Source: Authors' own calculation based on data from the NBH *Monthly Report* and *Annual Report* (consolidates balance sheets of the banking sector, various issues).

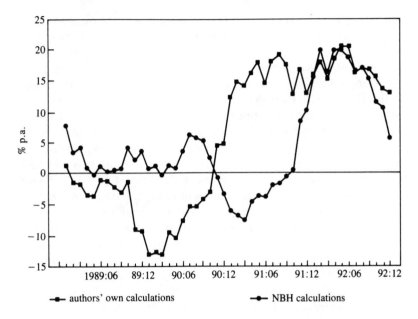

Figure 12.1 Real long-term lending rates in Hungary, 1989–92

Notes: Average lending rates on bank loans to enterprises with maturity over one year. Real rates are calculated by using PPI inflation rates for the 12-month period ending in the month of observation (NBH's real rates) or beginning in the month of observation (author's own calculations).

Sources: Rates calculated by NBH are from NBH (1992), p. 153; rates calculated by the authors are based on nominal interest rates and PPI inflation rates given in NBH (1992) and (1993).

foreign and domestic markets. This change undermined their creditworthiness and capacity to borrow under market conditions. Under such conditions, a prudent bank management would (or should) indeed radically reduce lending to these firms. On the other hand, the newly emerging private sector, consisting mainly of small and medium-size firms, though hungry for bank loans, in particular for investment loans, cannot take the place of the ailing SOEs, because it has hardly any proper track record and has very little to offer as collateral. This explanation has undoubtedly pointed to one of the important determining factors in the decline.

Another frequently mentioned explanation, especially by bankers, is that demand of enterprises for credit has declined dramatically. This is again undoubtedly an important element of the situation. Real borrowing (lending) rates for enterprises increased enormously during the same period. As figure 12.1 shows, real (ex post) lending rates[3] on investment loans increased from −3.1% in 1989 to 16.8% in 1992.[4] It is extremely difficult to believe that any sound business can support such high real rates. That is, at these prices enterprises with a reasonably hard budget constraint and a strong interest in maximising the market value of the firm would undoubtedly decrease their demand for bank finance substantially.

But this is the point where one starts seriously to question the outright rejection of the crowding-out hypothesis. If enterprise demand for bank finance was low and declining why did prices (interest rates) remain high, or in fact increase rapidly? The only reasonable explanation is the high demand by the government. Government securities, that is a virtually risk-free form of investment, offered rates of yield for banks comparable if not higher (at least for certain periods) than corporate loans. In our interpretation of the facts, the crowding-out of corporate borrowers from credit markets by the government was thus indeed an important factor explaining the dramatic decline in investment finance. Though owing to limitations of space we analyse this process in some detail only for Hungary, where this problem is perhaps the most acute, available evidence suggests that crowding-out is a very important factor in general, Czechoslovakia (the Czech Republic after 1992) being the only notable exception.

Direct (non-intermediated) finance for investment

Bond and equity finance will perhaps be even more scarce than long-term bank finance. With high and fluctuating rates of inflation characterising CEE economies (with very few exceptions, see table 12.1), long-term fixed rate (bond) finance is just too risky for both parties. The lack of institutional investors with long planning horizons and wholesale financial markets (Király, 1993; Székely, 1994) makes this situation even more severe. For small investors, the costs of monitoring enterprises and gathering a reasonably good understanding of future macroeconomic development are just too high. The collapse of the Hungarian bond market in 1988, when inflation started to accelerate and government guarantees on new corporate bonds were terminated, was a clear example of the problems involved (see Székely, 1990).

Equity finance faces the same problems. Without Western-type accounting and a proper track record, it is just too risky for private investors to hold equity directly. On the other hand, for the same reason, the supply of tradable shares is also rather limited (Járai, 1993). The underdeveloped financial system is a further stumbling block, because in the absence of industry analysts and finance houses keeping track of industries' performance, it is very expensive to gather information on specific firms or industries. Hedging is also very difficult, that is, portfolios are bound to be far from optimal. Though stock exchanges in the Central European transition countries, in particular in Poland, are hot places right now recording unprecedented increases in stock exchange indices (see, e.g., Kokoszczyński, 1994) and providing excellent investment opportunities for foreign and domestic portfolio investors, the amounts of fresh capital they have generated for enterprises in these countries have so far been negligible. Most of this boom is related to underpriced shares floated in the course of privatisation, rather than to new issues: this boom, at least so far, has generated very little extra (investment) finance for the enterprises whose shares are traded in these stock exchanges.

Foreign direct investment (FDI) is thus a very important source of finance, especially for larger projects. Besides finance, it is also expected to bring in know-how, expertise and access to distribution networks in the West (market access). The problem is that FDI into the whole region is very limited and, in addition, it is highly concentrated in very few countries where the legal and financial infrastructure is relatively well developed (Gray et al., 1992; Sárközy, 1993), and which enjoy relative economic and social stability (former Czechoslovakia, now the Czech Republic, and Hungary). Even these countries face a fierce competition with other very dynamic countries or regions (such as Portugal and Spain, Mexico, South East Asia, China, and Vietnam). Much of the FDI at present is absorbed by the process of privatisation, that is by the purchase of existing capacities. It is hoped that this will generate future investment, but the extent is still rather uncertain.

Domestic direct investment (private placement), though not fully recorded by official statistics, is perhaps the most dynamic source for finance, in spite of the fact that this source has been very much neglected. The advantage of this form, as is the case with any other direct investment, is that moral hazard is less of a problem. However, this process is almost exclusively confined to small private ventures, at least in the first couple of years of economic restructuring. The lack of collateral and track record, as well as that of competition and experience in the financial sector makes it very difficult for these firms to rely on banking finance. New firms created by this process will therefore go through the natural life-cycle of firms mainly relying on retained earnings and direct investment, like many by now large and famous firms in Western Europe after the war. The successful ones will increasingly be able to attract direct equity (including equity holdings by foreign investors and bonds) and banking finance, but this process is bound to be slow, and no solution for large existing SOEs in dire need of restructuring.

The most important source of finance for large SOEs during economic transformation will thus be retained earnings (see McKinnon, 1991). Though retained earnings is the major source for corporate finance in market economies as well (Stiglitz, 1992), in CEE countries this will have a rather different impact on the pattern of industrial restructuring. Owing to the lack of other sources of finance and any sort of state assistance in the process (industrial policy or some other less comprehensive schemes) the former (or existing) SOEs which most need restructuring will simply have neither access to the necessary external finance nor the necessary internal funds to do so. While FDI, as pointed out earlier, can be a way out for a handful of the large SOEs (for firms like Skoda, or TUNSGRAM), the vast majority are just too risky a venture for foreign investors. Unemployment, especially regionally, may turn out to be a reason for governments to keep some of these enterprises alive in the short to medium term. However, without a major restructuring they have very little, if any, hope for survival.

Corporate governance, industrial restructuring and financial institutions

What one can observe as industrial restructuring at the macro- or mezo- (industry) level can take distinctively different forms at the micro- (enterprise) level. One of these forms, perhaps the one that has attracted the most attention by academics, is the restructuring of existing SOEs. While there is a wide agreement that the lack of proper corporate governance is the major factor explaining why the process of restructuring (former) SOEs is (will be) so painfully slow (see, e.g., Dittus, 1993; Mayhew and Seabright, 1992; Phelps et al., 1993; Wijnbergen, 1994), views regarding the question of which of the possible ways to impose a tight corporate governance on large (privatised, or not yet privatised) SOEs are the most efficient and fastest or, put differently, who should be the 'agent of change' (Wijnbergen, 1994), are rather diverse. As Wijnbergen (1994) points out, 'governments throughout Eastern Europe have been singularly unsuccessful in dealing with large loss-making SOEs'. For the very same reason, governments were also unsuccessful in privatising these enterprises through outright sale: privatisation which is thought to be the ultimate solution for the corporate governance problem is hardly a solution for the vast majority of large (loss making, or low-profit making) SOEs.

As in many other instances, the exception is Czechoslovakia (now only the Czech Republic) where policy makers embarked upon a wholesale voucher privatisation of a large number of SOEs in a very early stage, though by construction not choosing from notoriously loss making SOEs. In the Czech case, the main question is whether the investment funds created in the course of voucher privatisation will be successful in imposing tight corporate governance on the privatised enterprises. The other peculiar aspect of the Czech voucher scheme is that the enterprises involved in the scheme were not made subject to any serious bankruptcy regulation prior to privatisation. That is, their real financial situations – together with those of the commercial banks also involved in the voucher scheme – might have been left unrevealed. By now, policy makers in Hungary and Poland are also hastily implementing similar schemes to involve small investors in large numbers, but the major difference is that in these countries, with few exceptions, the firms to be involved are chosen among those that were not attractive for large (foreign) investors through most conventional forms of privatisation.

Many researchers find the commercial banks are the ones best positioned to impose the needed corporate governance on (large) SOEs (Ábel and Bonin, 1994b; Hrnčíř, 1994; Wijnbergen, 1994). The main argument is that banks possess the necessary insider information about the enterprises through their previous credit links. But the problem is that these commercial banks themselves lack the necessary corporate governance due to the sheer fact that they themselves are (again with the exception of the Czech banks) state-owned and loss making. Moreover, they are overburdened with bad loans partly inherited from central planning, partly made by themselves due to the lack of proper internal organisation, corporate governance, and credit appraisal procedures (Golden, 1994; Montias, 1994; Wyczański, 1994). Moreover, as we shall see in more detail on pp. 351–5, the privatisation of large SOCBs, which still dominate the banking system, is a very slow process. If that is so, why should these state-owned so far rather poorly performing banks all of a sudden be able and motivated efficiently to deal with the ailing SOEs? Not surprisingly, some other researchers are rather sceptical as to the capacity and willingness of large, loss making SOCBs to perform this function (Phelps *et al.*, 1993; Montias, 1994).

The conclusion we can draw in this regard is that even if some of the commercial banks were willing and able to act as 'agent of change', the overall impact of this will be rather limited and delayed.

Bad loans and industrial restructuring

What is known as the *bad-loans*[5] *problem* in the literature (Begg and Portes, 1992; Marrese, 1992; Várhegyi, 1993) is in fact a mixture of problems of rather different natures, though with a common origin. The CPEs of CEE were characterised by highly centralised capital allocation mechanisms, coupled with an almost perfect isolation from competitive world markets. Since the price system, as compared to the prevailing prices on competitive world markets, was highly distorted, due to its rigidity, it was not able to establish prices under which a capital allocation system based on expected future profitability could have properly functioned.[6] The necessary corrections had thus to be made by using an enormously complicated system of taxes, subsidies and exchange rates (multiple exchange rates) lacking any sort of transparency (Newbery, 1990) and finance was allocated directly by the centre. This system rooted out any competitive (market) pressure on firms and made the allocation of production and investment resources rather arbitrary.

When the socio-economic systems of CEE countries collapsed, the quality of the accumulated real and financial assets, not surprisingly, deteriorated rapidly. Economic transformation brought about a large number of changes in the economic environment industrial (and other) enterprises faced. The liberalisation of prices, domestic[7] and foreign trade resulted in fast changing relative prices (including the price of labour and foreign exchange). Moreover, the almost inevitable massive budget deficits resulted in high and fluctuating rates of inflation, creating erratic price expectations (including the price of foreign exchange and labour). With a fast changing and rather uncertain economic environment and high nominal interest rates, it is not at all surprising that the quality of loan portfolios, irrespective of who held them,[8] deteriorated rapidly.

In fact, even in a relatively strong and stable market economy, such as the Finnish one, one of the elements listed above, namely the loss of the Soviet market, was enough to produce a large proportion of bad loans in the asset portfolios of commercial banks and create a severe crisis in the financial system (see, e.g., Bordes, 1993; Currie, 1993; Hukkinen and Rautava, 1992; Nyberg and Vihriälä, 1993). Though in principle, with an optimal coordination among the former CPEs, this process could have been kept under some control, and thus could have been more gradual and consequently less painful, it is rather unlikely that countries which spectacularly failed in devising coordination to build up something would have been able to do so when dismantling it, even if the political conditions had permitted it and the political will had been there.

Bad loans were difficult to identify because of the lack of proper accounting standards and bankruptcy regulations (see, e.g., Mizsei, 1994). Moreover, banks may have very strong incentives to either overestimate or underestimate the precise amounts of bad loans in their portfolios, depending on which way is more favourable for them given the conditions of the prevailing bad-loan scheme. Thus, it was, and in many countries still is, difficult to estimate the amount of bad loans at any given point in time. Nonetheless, the widely known estimates suggest that at least about 20–30% of loans in the portfolios of the commercial banks may turn out to be bad (problem) loans (see, e.g., Dittus, 1993). Moreover, these loans are highly concentrated mainly in the portfolios of large SOCBs (or their own 'hospital banks').

The literature suggested several different ways to deal with bad loans.[9] Begg and Portes (1992) suggested removing these loans from the portfolios of commercial banks and replacing them at face value with government bonds providing the banks with adequate yield to become (and remain) profitable. The advantage of this scheme is that it lifts the pressure on commercial banks to build up huge amounts of provisions against bad loans financed from wide interest rate spreads. The problem with this scheme is that it ignores the insider information banks possess about the enterprises involved, and thus gives no incentive to the banks to reveal the information they have on the liquidation values or the viability (future financial situations) of the enterprises involved. Székely (1994) suggests a scheme in which loans would be sold in a special type of auctioning process. During this process the sale of the loans would be subsidised in order to bridge the gap between what the banks originally holding the loan could afford to lose on a loan (as compared to the face value) and what the purchaser could afford to pay for it (given its expectation about the actual value of the loan contract). The advantage of this scheme is that it gives some incentive to banks to reveal the information they have on individual loan contracts and enterprises. The disadvantage is that it takes a much longer time than the Begg–Portes scheme and relies on agents and information that may simply not exist in many CEE countries. Gurgenidze (1993), while still opting for a market-based solution, points to the problems involved in trying to market non-standardised individual loan contracts and to the fact that this is very rarely done even in developed market economies. Instead, he suggests a scheme that is based on the securitisation of the bad loans involved. The problem of this solution is that it relies on even more sophisticated instruments that do not exist in any of the CEE countries. Ábel and Bonin (1994b) questions the feasibility of a market-based solution and the merits of a wholesale transfer of bad loans to a government-run 'hospital bank' at face value. They suggest a system of incentive contracts for 'lead' banks that would give strong incentive to the commercial banks to work out the acquired bad loans and collect as much as possible. Finally, Várhegyi (1994) argues in favour of a recapitalisation of the commercial banks involved.

Naturally, the decision on how to deal with sub-standard loans will have profound impact on the interest margins of commercial banks (Begg and Portes, 1992; Dittus, 1993) and, through this, on lending rates. However, as pointed out earlier (pp. 338–46), crowding-out was at least as important as interest rate spreads charged by commercial banks in producing high lending rates, thus even the most generous solutions will take away only part of the pressure on interest rate spreads. Moreover, if the costs of cleaning up of the loan portfolios of banks is assumed by the state budget and not financed by borrowing from capital markets, it results in either a budget deficit monetised by the Central bank, or an increase in the tax burden (on successful firms and individuals). In the former case, as pointed out earlier, the impact on portfolio (re)allocation is immediate and unfavourable (a shift towards more liquid short-term assets) again pushing up lending rates. In the latter case, retained earnings are further taxed, reducing the available finance successful enterprises have for new investments.

CEE countries have so far implemented several bad-loan schemes aimed at cleaning up the loan portfolios of commercial banks including certain elements of the solutions mentioned above. However, the results are, at least so far, disappointing (see, e.g., Dobrinsky, 1994; Hrnčíř, 1994; Várhegyi, 1994). This apparent lack of success was mainly due to the fact that the (so far) implemented schemes did too little, too late. The solutions were partial and the amounts involved were inadequate. On the other hand, they paid very little attention to the problem of whether the financial institutions involved ('hospital' agency or commercial banks) were able to assume the task of working out the bad loans (see, e.g., Kruse, 1994), and whether the proper incentives had been created for them to do so.

The Hungarian case is rather instructive in this regard. The (too) tough bankruptcy regulation (see, e.g., Mizsei, 1994) made the extent of bad loans, and the real financial situation of SOEs, painfully visible. However, commercial banks, with one exception, made very little effort to impose tight corporate governance and reorganise these firms. They were much more successful in lobbying, together with the SOEs involved, for wholesale rescue operations by the government. As a result, several bad-loan schemes were implemented. The 1992 bad-loan scheme proved that a government-run 'hospital' agency (formally a properly incorporated and licensed bank) can do little with the acquired loans, giving an obvious, though rather expensive, support to the argument put forward by those who argued against creating such agencies in CEE (see, e.g., Ábel and Bonin, 1994b; Székely, 1994; Várhegyi, 1993). The outcome of this scheme also cast some doubt on the merits of the scheme suggested by Begg and Portes (1992), at least in the Hungarian case.[10] The only thing the Hungarian 'hospital' agency did was to contract back the management of the acquired loans to the commercial banks where they originally were. This move brought very little success in recovering the loans.

In the 1993 scheme, Hungarian policy makers thus decided not to remove the loans from the portfolios of the commercial banks, but rather to recapitalise the banks themselves. Moreover, the government-run 'hospital' agency started to prepare for the selling-off of the previously acquired loans[11] most likely back either to the borrowers themselves or to the banks from which they came in the first place. The irony of this scheme is that it 'levelled the playing field for banks', that is, it gave vast amounts to those banks that have done very little if anything at all to cope with the bad loans and the enterprises involved, and almost nothing to the ones that made serious efforts and were relatively successful in this regard. This is a typical case of *'ex post'* recapitalisation, with an unsurprising outcome. The major problem is that it can (and will) seriously undermine the credibility of the government and can (and will) take away any incentive for the banks to try to collect these loans or take equity stakes in the enterprises involved.

Though the recently implemented Polish scheme may deliver more promising results (see, e.g., Wijnbergen, 1994), the time that has elapsed since its launching in April 1994 is too short to allow us to draw any firm conclusion in this regard.

The competitiveness of the financial system: market structures, privatisation and foreign participation

The industry most in need of restructuring was (and still is) the financial services industry (Bonin and Székely, 1994; Brainard, 1991; Calvo and Fenkel, 1991; Kemme and Rudka, 1992; Long and Sagari, 1991). With the exception of Hungary, and to some extent Poland,[12] CEE economies started off with basically a monobank system.[13] That is, it is not the case that a relatively well developed financial sector will contribute to, let alone initiate and supervise, industrial restructuring, but rather that these two processes will take place in parallel, interacting with each other. As was already touched upon above, the collapse of many of the large SOEs brought many of the large directly and indirectly state-owned banks to the verge of a collapse because of the massive provisioning requirement due to sub-standard loans (Várhegyi, 1993) and also because of their inability to attract more dynamic private firms as clients and to enter relatively dynamic financial markets (Ábel and Székely, 1994).

While in each CEE country there was a spectacular increase in the number of banks and some consequent increase in the degree of competition, the extent of the latter remained limited. The markets for banking products are still highly concentrated and dominated by the large SOCBs.[14] While this general finding is true for each CEE country, the differences in the extent to which markets are uncompetitive, concentrated and dominated by large SOCBs are significant, being much lower in the lead countries (Hungary being the leader in this respect) and higher in the late reformers (such as Bulgaria, after the bank consolidation,[15] and Romania). Moreover, there is a wide variation in the extent of the problem across different markets. With very few exceptions, the lower the risk involved (the more short-term the product and the smaller the amount of up-front investment needed to enter that specific market) the lower the degree of concentration (and consequently the more competitive the market).

Thus, in certain groups of fee-based services (related to forex transactions), in (foreign) trade finance for good clients, derivative products related to forex transactions, and in general at the upper ends of markets (that is, in the areas pointed out below when investigating the strategies of foreign banks), the markets are much more competitive. On the other hand, in retail banking, long-term (investment) loans, and in general at the lower ends of markets, there is very little competition, market structures are highly concentrated and pricing is seriously distorted.[16]

A characteristic example of the differences across markets for banking products is given in the analysis for Hungary by Ábel and Székely (1994). Between 1987 and 1991, the market share of the large SOCBs as measured by the balance sheet total declined from 58.2% in 1987 to 42.4% in 1991. The same pairs of figures for the corporate deposit market were 84% and 54.9%, for the corporate loan market 91.6% and 62.9%, while for the market for discounting of bills of exchange 90.3% and 20.3%. Regarding long-term investment loans, the share of SOCBs in 1991 was around 74%, much higher than for corporate loans in general. Though the new banks (including the newly created SOCBs) did enter the retail market, consumer and housing loans, as well as retail deposit markets remained much more concentrated, dominated by the National Savings Bank.[17]

The lack of adequate degree of competition is also shown by the wide interest rate spreads mentioned above.[18] More precisely, the indication of the lack of competition is not so much (not necessarily) the fact that spreads are wide in general, but that (new) banks that were free from bad loans, forcing large SOCBs to finance their heavy provisioning needs from wide spreads, gradually started to follow the pricing policies of the large SOCBs by charging similar spreads (see, Ábel and Székely, 1994; Dobrinsky, 1994).

Privatisation of SOCBs, in particular the large ones, has been very slow, much slower than expected and also significantly slower than in other sectors of the economy. The main form of the expansion of the private sector was through new entries and relatively fast growth of new banks (see, e.g., Ábel and Székely, 1994; Dobrinsky, 1994; Daianu, 1994; Hrnčíř, 1994; Wyczański, 1993). While this process was a very important factor in increasing competition and decreasing market concentration, it also meant that the expansion of the private sector in the financial system was less than sufficient.

With the exception of the Czech Republic (formerly Czechoslovakia) where the generally adopted wholesale privatisation involved the large SOCBs as well, governments decided to separate the privatisation of SOCBs from that of SOEs, and deal with the banks on a case-by-case basis. With the exception of early sell-off of few relatively small SOCBs, this resulted in major delays in the privatisation of SOCBs.[19]

Regarding the actually privatised SOCBs, it is important to pay attention to the outcome of the process. Though the Czech voucher privatisation led to the sell-off of a major part of the equity shares of the large SOCBs (the Consolidation Bank, which is the Czech 'hospital bank', remaining the only fully state-owned bank), the state retained a substantial equity stake in the large former SOCBs (on the average some 42%). It remains to be seen whether any of the investment funds will be able to impose the much-needed tight corporate governance on these banks and attract foreign strategic partners. These two elements are thought to be vital to the eventual success of these banks.

In Poland, the two privatisation deals completed so far raise very similar concerns. While the participation of EBRD is indeed important in attracting (future) foreign strategic partners, in itself it will probably do very little to improve the efficiency of a bank. The example of Wielkopolski Bank Kredytowy, which was publicly offered in the first half of 1993, clearly attests to this suspicion (see, e.g., Kokoszczyński, 1994). The case of Bank Śląski, which was privatised in 1994, is much more exciting and promising, since this is the first case when a relatively large SOCB was privatised with the participation of strategic investors with much-needed expertise, know-how and access to foreign capital markets. The success or failure of this bank will have a strong bearing on the process of bank privatisation in the whole region.

As in other industries, foreign participation is thought to be an important factor in increasing competition in the financial services industry. In the lead countries of CEE, foreign participation became significant in the financial system, in particular in banking.[20] But even in the lead countries, the nature of the business strategies of foreign and joint venture banks turned out to be quite different from what policy makers expected at the beginning of economic transformation. Foreign banks, in particular major international banks with the much desired capital strength, international network, access to international financial markets, and expertise and know-how have showed, at least so far, very moderate interest in exactly those areas where they are most desperately needed. Thus, the interest in buying into large SOCBs or moving into the least competitive (and most costly or risky) segments (such as retail banking or servicing small enterprises) has been, to put it mildly, moderate.

On the other hand, in those segments where foreign banks have huge comparative advantages (such as foreign payment services and related primary and derivative products) and where the risk is limited, the capital and staff requirement to efficiently and prudently pursue business is relatively small, and there is no need for a large branch network, foreign and joint venture banks captured significant market shares. Put differently, they concentrated their business activities in areas where the profit–risk ratio is the highest and where activities can be expanded (and contracted) rapidly. Moreover, in each segment where they have significant market share they concentrate on the upper end of the market, that is, they cream off the market and take only the best clients. Thus, in handling corporate accounts and financing corporate units, they attract the foreign and joint venture firms by offering Western standards of services.

While some researchers (see, e.g., Várhegyi, 1994) and policy makers appear to be somewhat irritated by this attitude of foreign and joint venture banks, from the viewpoint of economic theory it is a very rational approach and not that much different from the experiences of some Western countries (see, e.g., Savela and Herrala, 1992 for the Finnish experience). Moreover, it gives a good indication of what business strategy a relatively small bank with proper corporate governance and, consequently, a strong interest in increasing its market value as an enterprise, tends to have in an environment such as the present one in CEE.

Financial markets in CEE are highly volatile and risky for several reasons related to the very nature of economic restructuring. The macroeconomic environment is rather unstable by Western standards, even in the most successful countries. Due to the rapid changes in relative prices, the sudden trade reorientation, and the consequent massive changes in the market values of enterprise assets, the real financial situations of firms, as well as their economic viability in the future, are extremely difficult to judge. This is made more difficult by the massive and continuous changes in corporate law and other legislation (including such very important areas as accounting and tax regulations). Moreover, regulations regarding financial institutions are new, in many cases yet untested in courts, and rapidly changing, and supervisory agencies are inexperienced. On the other hand, domestic banks and financial institutions are very inexperienced and ill-equipped to provide certain services and make markets for sophisticated products (such as options or commercial papers). They also lack the necessary infrastructure to meet Western standards in very traditional banking services for foreign and joint venture firms that require this (and are able to pay for it). It is therefore natural for these banks to concentrate their activities and resources on these markets and clients.

With the exception of interbank deposit markets, and some competitive refinance schemes in the lead countries, wholesale financial markets are virtually non-existent and the financial system is hardly more than the banking system (Hrnčíř, 1994; Király, 1993; Kokoszczyński, 1994; Székely, 1994; Wyczański, 1993). There is hardly any external source of competitive pressure on banks (see also what was said above about direct finance on pp. 344–6). As a consequence, the costs of capital and financial services are high, much higher than the ones competing producers in Western Europe face, the quality of services is low, and the necessary products to share or hedge risk are not available. Exporters cannot offer export credits. Export credits are an important tool in market penetration, and the lack of them is a major stumbling block in the process of revitalising intra-regional trade in CEE.

Future reforms of the financial system, hopefully resulting in higher degrees of competitiveness, more able banks taking part in financing and conducting industrial restructuring, lower costs of capital and financial services, will undoubtedly be important factors in the process of economic transformation, in particular in industrial restructuring, but this will again be a slow and gradual process, where competitive financial firms themselves have to grow up. This is again a factor which supports our general finding that industrial restructuring is more likely to be based on newly emerging and gradually developing and growing enterprises than on the existing large SOEs. These producers will no doubt need proper access to high-quality and low-cost financial services and low-cost capital if they are to be competitive in international markets. This gradual process will to a large degree depend on how successful the reform of the financial system in CEE economies is.

Conclusion

The chapter investigated the role of the financial system in economic transformation, in particular in industrial restructuring, and the likely impact of a more competitive financial system, in particular a more competitive and efficient credit allocation system, on the pattern of industrial restructuring in the short to medium run.

The analysis presented suggests two main conclusions. First, if commercial financing becomes the dominating (or even only) source of external investment finance for enterprises then, with very few exceptions, large SOEs will have very little, if any, chance to find the necessary internal or external financial sources to embark upon restructuring and new investment projects. On the other hand, emerging new private enterprises, with a few exceptions, will need considerable time before they can rely on banking finance on any large scale.

Second, financial institutions will need a considerable time, even in the lead countries, before they will be able to assume the roles that financial institutions, in particular commercial banks, play in developed market economies. In particular, large SOCBs themselves will have to go through a substantial restructuring and, eventually, privatisation before they will be able to act as the 'agent of change' and impose financial discipline and tight corporate governance over (large, loss making) SOEs. The degree of competition, though gradually increasing, and the share of the private sector, though again gradually increasing, are just too low at the moment to support a rapid change in this respect.

However, without restructuring and massive new investments, large and inefficient SOEs are bound to suffer and eventually to disappear altogether. If large SOEs are not able to restructure their production, the 'constructive phase' of industrial restructuring, that is, the process of building up of new, competitive, and export-oriented industrial production capacities will mainly be confined to newly emerging private firms. These firms will however need considerable time to get strong enough to be able to use capital-intensive production technologies. Put differently, the product structures of industrial production and exports will in most part concentrate on products which do not require heavy up-front investments. The process is going to be a slow and gradual *reindustrialisation*, based on natural comparative advantages and limited by the capacity of enterprises to assume risk and penetrate markets. Unemployment is then going to be a long-term rather than a short- or medium-term problem.

CEE economies will probably therefore need a long time until they reach the sort of industrial and export structures their potential would suggest (see chapter 3). Market concentration (Newbery and Kattuman, 1992) will consequently be less of a problem, once the large SOEs lose their market power.

The goal of the chapter was to argue neither for, nor against, industrial policy or any other less comprehensive form of state assistance to industrial restructuring. The only aim was to point out the likely direction towards which commercial finance with gradually strengthening financial systems, without a substantial involvement of the state, will inevitably push this process. The privatisation of industrial firms and banks will make this impact even more imminent and pronounced.

Notes

The views expressed here are the authors' and do not necessarily reflect those that may be held by Budapest Bank and the United Nations Secretariat respectively.

1 The Czech Republic (formerly Czechoslovakia) is the only notable exception throughout the whole period. In 1993, Poland also showed a surprisingly low (significantly lower than expected) level of budget deficit (see table 12.1). This example shows that strong economic growth can solve this issue even in countries where other factors tend to produce a high level of budget deficit.

2 The figures in table 12.1 are expressed as percentages of GDP, but since the denominator is the same for saving and budget deficit, this statement remains valid.

3 These real interest rates were calculated on the basis of monthly (weighted average) nominal interest rates on loans with maturity over one year deflated by the (*ex-post*) rate of PPI inflation for one year ahead. Given that the average maturity was not much longer than one year, this assumes a perfect foresight on the part of lenders and borrowers. Given the very high level of real rates and the sizeable month-to-month fluctuation in this series, one is inclined to question the rationality of price expectations. The NBH calculates real rates (see NBH, 1992, p. 153) by deflating nominal rates by the PPI index for the year preceding the observation period. This implicitly implies naive price expectations. As we have very limited understanding of price expectations in transition economies, it is very difficult to decide which one is the correct way of calculating the real rate expected by lenders and borrowers. For comparison, in figure 12.1 both series are shown.

4 Average values for the year as a whole, based on monthly figures shown in figure 12.1 (authors' own calculations). Dittus (1993) reports real lending rates for Czechoslovakia (Czech Republic) and Poland, as well, though figures are average rates for all types of loan, not only longer-term (over one year) loans. Nonetheless, the actual figures for Czechoslovakia are significantly lower, but the tendency is rather similar. For Poland, figures are quite similar to those for Hungary. The Czech figures seem to support our views in that lower budget deficit and public borrowing requirement put less strain on (real) borrowing rates for enterprises.

5 The term 'bad loan' will refer to all kinds of problem loans throughout this section. This is admittedly not a fully precise way of referring to problem loans, but this term is widely used in the literature with such a meaning. Moreover, CEE countries have no uniform classification of problem loans or even the same terms for (the different kinds of) problem loans.

6 'Properly' in the sense that it would have led to an allocation of capital in line with planners' intentions.

7 The liberalisation of foreign trade got much more emphasis in the literature than that of domestic trade, though the latter is perhaps more important in imposing real competitive pressure on domestic producers. One of the main characteristics of CPEs was the almost perfect monopolisation of wholesale trade and a large degree of centralisation of retail trade. If one forgets about this and carries out the liberalisation (privatisation) of foreign trade, as was done in many countries in the first phase of reform, the outcome is anything but a competitive system (reflected by distorted pricing behaviour).

8 This refers to the debate whether it was wise to transfer the investment portfolio of the previous monobank to the newly created commercial banks. We would like to point out here the simple fact that though this issue is important technically and has some influence on the extent and precise dynamics of the process, the origin of the problem is independent of this choice.

9 Due to the focus of our chapter, we do not attempt to give a complete overview of the existing proposals. We concentrate only on those that have some relevance to our discussion. For a more detailed discussion of the existing proposals, see Dittus (1993).

10 Hrnčíř (1994) reports on some success of the Consolidation Bank (the Czech 'hospital' agency) to collect impressive proportions of the bad loans in its portfolio in certain cases.

11 That is, the eventual outcome will be what Székely (1994) suggested. The major difference is however that between the two steps (acquiring the loans and selling them) the best part of a year will have elapsed. During this period the market values of the loans involved will most likely have decreased to a considerable extent, resulting in unnecessary loss to the budget.

12 Hungary started to implement financial reforms in 1984 and established a Western-style two-tier banking system in 1987 (see, e.g., Bácskai, 1989). Though, as a result of these reforms, Hungary had a more sophisticated financial system than other CEE countries, the first phase of reforms had very little impact on the behaviour of the financial services industry (Székely, 1990; Blejer and Sagari, 1991). Poland started financial reforms in 1988 and introduced a two-tier banking system in 1989. However, the impact of these reforms was even less significant than that of the Hungarian ones (see Wyczański, 1993). For a general survey on the starting positions of the other CEE countries in this regard, see Kemme and Rudka (1992).

13 For a description of the monobank system which characterised CPEs see Podolski (1973) and Zwass (1979). For a general overview on the reform of the financial system in CEE see Bonin and Székely (1994) and Kemme (1994).

14 In the case of the Czech Republic, by the large commercial banks that were privatised via the voucher privatisation. These banks, while the majority stakes of their equity shares were floated, remained under the heavy influence of the National Property Fund, which retained 40–45% of the equity shares, while the floated stakes are not necessarily held in one hand.

15 Bulgaria is a very special case in this respect, because in the course of the initial break-up of the monobank system a large number of very small SOCBs were created. Nonetheless, at the local level, this created very little competition, but rather weak banks. This was later realised by policy makers and a bank consolidation scheme was launched. The eventual outcome of this process will determine future market structures. For more details, see Dobrinsky (1994).

16 For detailed information on market structures in Bulgaria see Dobrinsky (1994), in the Czech Republic Hrnčíř (1994), in Hungary Ábel and Székely (1994), in Poland Wyczański (1993), in Romania Daianu (1994), and in general in CEE Dittus (1993).

17 The other end of the spectrum is probably occupied by Romania where, as reported by Daianu (1994), the four biggest SOCBs accounted for 94% of total credits in 1991 and for 80 per cent in June 1993. Concurrently, the State Saving Bank (CEC) accounted for 95% of sight deposits and 40% of term deposits by individuals in June 1993.

18 It is again difficult to define and measure precisely interest rate spread, because both the liability and assets structures of banks in CEE are sometimes rather different from those of banks in developed market economies. Sometimes the shares of refinance credit (from the central bank) with very special (non-market) rates, as well as special loans to (mainly) enterprises with again special (non-market) rates might be rather significant. Thus, comparing simply deposit rates to (market) loan rates might be rather misleading. To avoid this, Ábel and Székely (1994) use spreads calculated on the basis of average rates over assets and liabilities. Such figures may however not always be available for other countries. Nonetheless, the typical figures for CEE countries have recently been in the range of 8-15 percentage points and with a tendency to increase. The Czech Republic (formerly Czechoslovakia) occupies probably the low end (rising from 2.8 in the first quarter of 1990 to 6.7 in the last quarter of 1992 in Czechoslovakia, to 7.8 percentage points in June 1993 in the Czech Republic), even if adjustment is made for inflation (see Hrnčíř, 1994). Among the countries for which data are available, the widest nominal spreads were reported for Bulgaria, around 26 percentage points (see Dobrinsky, 1994). For Hungary and Poland, figures are in the range of 10–20 percentage points (nominal) (see, e.g., Dittus, 1993; Ábel and Székely, 1994).

19 For more details on privatisation of SOCBs in CEE, see Ábel and Bonin (1994b); Daianu (1994), Kokoszczyński (1994), Mortimer (1994) and Wyczański (1993).

20 In the Czech Republic in (June) 1993 there were 19 banks with foreign participation and 6 branches of foreign banks (out of 50 banks in total), in Hungary in 1992, 13 banks with foreign participation (out of 38), and in Poland in 1992 11 banks with foreign participation (out of 94). In the other countries, foreign participation is very moderate (see Dobrinsky, 1994; Daianu, 1994).

References

Ábel, I. and Bonin, J. P., 1994a. 'State desertion and credit market failure in the Hungarian transition', *Acta Oeconomica*, forthcoming

1994b. 'Financial sector reform in the economies in transition: on the way to privatising commercial banks', in J. P. Bonin and I. P. Székely (eds.), *The Development and Reform of Financial Systems in Central and Eastern Europe*, London: Edward Elgar, forthcoming

Ábel, I. and Székely, I. P., 1993. 'Changing structure of household portfolios in emerging market economies: the case of Hungary, 1970-1989', in I. P. Székely and D. M. G. Newbery (eds.), *Hungary: An Economy in Transition*, Cambridge: Cambridge University Press, 163–80

1994. 'Market structures and competition in the Hungarian banking system', in J. Bonin and I. P. Székely (eds.), *The Development and Reform of Financial Systems in Central and Eastern Europe*, London: Edward Elgar, forthcoming

Bácskai, T., 1989. 'The reorganisation of the banking system in Hungary', in C. Kessides, T. King, M. Nuti and C. Sokil (eds.), *Financial Reform in Socialist Economies*, Washington, D.C: World Bank

Begg, D. and Portes, R., 1992. 'Enterprise debt and economic transformation: financial restructuring in the state sector in Central and Eastern Europe', *CEPR Discussion Paper Series*, 695, London: CEPR

Blejer, M. I. and Sagari, S. B., 1991. 'Hungary: financial sector reform in a socialist economy', Working Paper WPS 595, Washington, DC: World Bank

Bonin, J. P. and Székely, I. P., 1994. *The Development and Reform of Financial Systems in Central and Eastern Europe*, London: Edward Elgar, forthcoming

Bordes, C., 1993. 'The Finnish economy: the boom, the debt, the crisis and the prospects', in *Three Assessments of Finland's Economic Crisis and Economic Policy*, Series C:9, Bank of Finland, Helsinki

Brainard, L., 1991. 'Strategies for economic transformation in Central and Eastern Europe: the role of financial market reform', in H. Blommenstein and M. Marrese (eds.), *Transformation of Planned Economies: Property Rights Reform and Macroeconomic Stability*, Paris: OECD

Calvo, G. A. and Fenkel, J. A., 1991. 'Obstacles to transforming centrally-planned economies: the role of the capital markets', Working Papers Series 3776, Cambridge, MA: NBER

Currie, D., 1993. 'The Finnish economic crisis: analysis and prescription', in *Three Assessments of Finland's Economic Crisis and Economic Policy*, Series C:9, Bank of Finland, Helsinki

Daianu, D., 1994. 'Banks in Romania today', paper presented at the conference on 'Banking Reform in the FSU and Eastern Europe: Lessons from Central Europe', Budapest (14–15 January)

Dittus, P., 1993. 'Corporate governance in Eastern Europe: the role of banks', Bank for International Settlement, Basle, mimeo

Dobrinsky, R., 1994. 'Reform of the financial system in Bulgaria', in J. Bonin and I. P. Székely (eds.), *The Development and Reform of Financial Systems in Central and Eastern Europe*, London: Edward Elgar, forthcoming

Golden, R. A., 1994. 'Discussion of Chapter 5', in J. Bonin and I. P. Székely (eds.), *The Development and Reform of Financial Systems in Central and Eastern Europe*, London: Edward Elgar, forthcoming

Gray, C. W., Hanson, R. and Heller, M., 1992. 'Legal reform for Hungary's private sector', *Working Papers*, WPS 983, The World Bank, Washington, DC

Gurgenidze, L., 1993. 'Securitisation of non-performing loans in transitional economies', Institute for EastWest Studies, New York (December), mimeo

Hrnčíř, M., 1994. 'Reform of the banking sector in the Czech Republic', in J. Bonin and I. P. Székely (eds.), *The Development and Reform of Financial Systems in Central and Eastern Europe*, London: Edward Elgar, forthcoming

Hukkinen, J. and Rautava, J., 1992. 'Russia's economic reform and trade between

Finland and Russia', *Bank of Finland Bulletin*, 4

Járai, Zs., 1993. 'Ten per cent already sold, privatisation in Hungary', in I. P. Székely and D. M. G. Newbery (eds.), *Hungary: An Economy in Transition*, Cambridge: Cambridge University Press, pp. 77-83

Kemme, D. M., 1994. *The Reform of the System of Money, Banking and Credit in Central Europe*, New York: Institute for EastWest Studies, forthcoming

Kemme, D. and Rudka, A. (eds.), 1992. *Monetary and Banking Reform in Postcommunist Economies*, New York: Westview Press

Király, J., 1993. 'A short run money market model of Hungary', in I. P. Székely and D. M. G. Newbery (eds.), *Hungary: An Economy in Transition*, Cambridge: Cambridge University Press, pp. 137-148

Kokoszczyński, R., 1994. 'Money and capital market reforms in Poland', in J. Bonin and I. P. Székely (eds.), *The Development and Reform of Financial Systems in Central and Eastern Europe*, London: Edward Elgar, forthcoming

Kruse, D., 1994. 'Discussion of Part One', in J. Bonin and I. P. Székely (eds.), *The Development and Reform of Financial Systems in Central and Eastern Europe*, London: Edward Elgar, forthcoming

Long, M. and Sagari, S., 1991. 'Financial reforms in socialist economies in transition', *PRE Working Paper*, 711, The World Bank, Washington, DC

Marrese, M., 1992. 'Solving the bad-debt problem of Central and Eastern European banks: an overview', Evanston, IL, Northwestern University, mimeo

Mayhew, K. and Seabright, P., 1992. 'Incentives and the management of enterprises in economic transition: Capital markets are not enough', *Oxford Review of Economic Policy*, 8, 26–34

McKinnon, R. I., 1991. *The Order of Economic Liberalisation*, Baltimore: Johns Hopkins University Press

Mizsei, K., 1994. 'Bankruptcy and banking reform in the transition economies of Central and Eastern Europe', in J. Bonin and I. P. Székely (eds.), *The Development and Reform of Financial Systems in Central and Eastern Europe*, London: Edward Elgar, forthcoming

Montias, J. M., 1994. 'Financial and fiscal aspects of system change in Eastern Europe', in J. Bonin and I. P. Székely (eds.), *The Development and Reform of Financial Systems in Central and Eastern Europe*, London: Edward Elgar, forthcoming

Mortimer, K., 1994. 'Banking privatisation policy in Poland and Czechoslovakia', paper presented at the conference on 'Banking Reform in the FSU and Eastern Europe: Lessons from Central Europe', Budapest (14–15 January)

NBH, 1992. *Annual Report 1992*, National Bank of Hungary, Budapest

NBH, 1993. *Havi Jelentés 1993/7* (Monthly Report), National Bank of Hungary, Budapest

Newbery, D. M., 1990. 'Tax reform, trade liberalisation and industrial restructuring', *European Economy* 43, 67–95

Newbery, D. M. and Kattuman, P., 1992. 'Market concentration and competition in Eastern Europe', *World Economy*, 515–534

Nyberg, P. and Vihriälä, V., 1993. 'The Finnish banking crisis and its handling', Discussion Papers, 8, Bank of Finland, Helsinki

Phelps, E. S., Frydman, R., Rapaczynski, A. and Shleifer, A., 1993. 'Needed mechanism of corporate governance and finance in Eastern Europe', Working Paper, 1, London: EBRD

Podolski, T. M., 1973. *Socialist Banking and Monetary Control*, Cambridge: Cambridge University Press

Sárközy, T., 1993. 'Legal framework for the Hungarian transition 1989–1991', in I. P. Székely and D. M. G. Newbery (eds.), *Hungary: An Economy in Transition*, Cambridge: Cambridge University Press, pp. 239–248

Savela, J. and Herrala, R., 1992. 'Foreign-owned banks in Finland', *Bank of Finland Bulletin* 66(4), 8–12

Stiglitz, J. E., 1992. 'Interest rate puzzles, competitive theory, and capital constraints', invited paper presented at the tenth World Congress of the International Economic Association, Moscow (August)

Székely, I. P., 1990. 'The reform of the Hungarian financial system', *European Economy*, 43 (March) 107–23

1994. 'Economic transformation and the reform of the financial system in Central and Eastern Europe', in A. Agabegyan, and E. Bogomolov, (eds.), *Economics in a Changing World*, vol. 1, Macmillan, (forthcoming)

Várhegyi, É., 1993. 'Key elements of the reform of the Hungarian banking system: privatisation and portfolio cleaning', *CEPR Discussion Paper Series*, 826, London: CEPR

1994. 'The "second" reform of the Hungarian banking system', in J. P. Bonin and I. P. Székely (eds.), *The Development and Reform of Financial Systems in Central and Eastern Europe*, London: Edward Elgar, forthcoming

Wijnbergen, S. van, 1994. 'On the role of banks in enterprise restructuring: The Polish example', *Discussion Paper Series*, 898, London: CEPR

Wyczański, P., 1993. 'Polish banking system 1990–1992', Economic and Social Policy Series No. 32, Friedrich Ebert Stiftung, Warsaw

1994. 'Discussion of Chapter 5', in J. Bonin and I. P. Székely (eds.), *The Development and Reform of Financial Systems in Central and Eastern Europe*, London: Edward Elgar, forthcoming

Zwass, A., 1979. *Money, Banking and Credit in the Soviet Union and Eastern Europe*, New York: M. E. Sharpe

Index

363

DATE DUE